FREE INDEED

BY
GLORIA BLOWERS

First printing: August 2007

ISBN-13: 978-0-9796289-0-0
ISBN-10: 0-9796289-0-3

Copyright © 2007 by MGB Publishing. All rights reserved. No part of this book may be reproduced without permission of the publisher except in case of brief quotations in articles and reviews.

All Scripture taken from NASB (New American Standard Version) except where designated otherwise.

All names in the personal examples and anecdotal material have been changed to protect the privacy of those involved.

This book is a discipleship Bible Study and is not meant to be a professional medical manual. One's own personal health and the decisions regarding how it is managed is each person's responsibility. The author and publisher accept no responsibility for any decisions made that may affect one's health.

Note: Poetic expressions of the NASB are written in narrow columns in original text. This format has been modified to utilize the full length of the line in this study book.

Cover Design - Janell Robertson, Farewell Communications
Interior Layout - Judy Lewis

<u>Rivers of Joy Bible Study Series</u>:

Free Indeed is Book One of a 3-Part Series. Projected release for Book Two, *Oaks of Righteousness*, is January 2008. Book Three, *That Your Joy May Be Full*, is scheduled for publication August 2008.

MGB Publishing
58 Misty Creek Cove
Sautee Nacoochee, GA 30571

This book is lovingly dedicated to the following:

Dennis, Roberta, Paul, Mark, Gita, Jaydeep, Kavita, Kelly, Chris, Randy, Lori, Joy, Daelen, Don, Ilania, Janna, Petru, Slavko, Maida, Joy, Richard, Xuan, Bridgette, Carrol, Loretta, Kim, Tomas, Inger, Caroline, Linda, Roland, Lena, Alex, Christina, Lief, Lars, Matts, Tom, Lisbeth, Robert, Rebecca, Fikrita, Nancy. I love you more than you can imagine and pray for you daily. You will always have a very special place in my heart. God bless you!

Acknowledgments and Special Thanks

As is so frequently the case, there is not enough time or space to adequately acknowledge all who have contributed significantly to the making of this book. I am deeply grateful for every word of encouragement via a phone call, e-mail, personal visit, note with "just the right words," or beautiful hand-made card, and for every prayer that has gone up on my behalf throughout this project. May the Lord bless each one of you in every rich and rewarding way—*pressed down, shaken together, running over into your laps (Luke 6:38)*. I must pause briefly, however, to mention specifically just a few without whom this book would never have come to fruition.

To my dear husband, Mel, who encouraged me and prayed without ceasing (1 Thess. 5:17) for the successful completion of this book each step of the challenging, oft trial-beset journey. Thank you first of all for loving God with all your heart and for building our home upon the secure principles of God's precious Word. Your godly leadership and Christlike example of humility, love and joy in serving the Lord were a continual source of inspiration. Thank you for sacrificing untold "together" time while I worked on the book through long days, short nights, and years of writes and rewrites. Thanks for all the glasses of cool refreshing water and the soothing back and neck massages; for making and collating hundreds of copies of the various "editions" through the years. Thanks, my soul-mate and my hero, for being the "best husband in the whole world"!

To Lynn Haynes whose continual and consistent encouragement enabled me so often to "push past the fear" in getting the study into print. Heartfelt thanks also to Fio Weaver, Nancy Wright, Lois and Mark Brown and Pastor Bob Williamson for their excellent editing skills and theological counsel.

Huge thanks to Janell Robertson for outstanding work on cover and book project coordination—and to Judy Lewis for her excellent work on the interior layout. You both are amazing.

To Ms. Blanche, Ms. Polly, and Ms. Evelyn, my faithful prayer partners who prayed me through many humanly impossible "Red Sea" situations. Special thanks to Ms. Blanche who was always "there" for me, wiping away the tears, when the trials and discouragements were *humanly* overwhelming. Her words of encouragement and comforting prayers kept me going so often!

To Carol, Brandi, Stacy, Lynn, Fio, Ellen, Phyllis and all the other women through the years who so faithfully completed every lesson and attended the weekly Bible study sessions. It was truly a joy to dig into the Word of God with you. The Lord bless you for your diligence!

To Mom and Dad Upham, Mom and Dad Blowers, Uncle Bill and Aunt Lois, Ms. Dora Mae, Ms. Linnie, and Ms. Ethel for your never failing love and beautiful example of steadfast faith in serving God which inspired me so often. Thanks also to Billy and Terri, Kenny and Kathy, Denny and Kathy, Helen and John, Larry and Jan, Ray and Nancy and Jeff, for your love and supporting prayers.

To Dana, Geta, Arlene, Ruth, Vivian, Charles and Sudheer, dear friends and "soul mates", who share the daily challenges of "the affliction." Your courage and perseverance are a never-ending source of hope and strength, enabling me to *press on*.

Table of Contents

Foreword 9
Abbreviations of Bible Translations and Books of the Bible 10
Bible Study Instructions 11

Chapter 1 13
   Day 1: My Personal Testimony 14
   Day 2: Introduction to Book One – Free Indeed 26
       A Word from Mel 29
   Day 3: From My Heart: The Making of This Bible Study 32
   Day 4: Building a Strong House of Indestructible Faith 39
   Day 5: In the Beginning…GOD! – Part 1 44
   Day 6: In the Beginning…GOD! – Part 2 51

Chapter 2 55
   Day 1: The Authority, Inerrancy, Immutability and Sufficiency of the Word of God – Part 1 56
   Day 2: The Authority, Inerrancy, Immutability and Sufficiency of the Word of God – Part 2 62
   Day 3: The Awesome Creation of the Universe 69
   Day 4: In the Image of God 75
   Day 5: The Revolt of Satan 82

Chapter 3 85
   Day 1: The Tragic Fall of Man – Part 1 86
   Day 2: The Tragic Fall of Man – Part 2 93
   Day 3: Without the Shedding of Blood… 101
   Day 4: Behold the Lamb of God 107
   Day 5: You Must be Born Again 114

Chapter 4 121
   Day 1: The Sabotaging of Salvation 122
   Day 2: Examine Yourself — Proofs of Salvation – Part 1 129
   Day 3: Examine Yourself — Proofs of Salvation – Part 2 134
   Day 4: Progressive Sanctification 139
   Day 5: I'm Not OK, You're Not OK 145

Chapter 5 151
- Day 1: Priorities: The Quintessential Priority of Knowing God 152
- Day 2: God's Inexorable Gift of Free Will 159
- Day 3: Man's Wisdom vs. God's Wisdom 165
- Day 4: The Psychologization of Sin 171
- Day 5: Beware! The Deceptiveness of Sin 176

Chapter 6 183
- Day 1: Thy Kingdom Come 184
- Day 2: The Problem of Self-Esteem 190
- Day 3: God's Solution to the Self-Esteem Problem 196
- Day 4: The Very, Very Serious Sin of Idolatry 203
- Day 5: The Person and Ministry of the Holy Spirit: Part 1 210

Chapter 7 219
- Day 1: The Person and Ministry of the Holy Spirit: Part 2 220
- Day 2: The Person and Ministry of the Holy Spirit: Part 3 226
- Day 3: The Unpardonable Sin…Beware! Take Heed! Grave Danger Ahead 233
- Day 4: The Very Real Pain and Problem of…FEAR 239
- Day 5: Come, Let Us Go Up to the Mountain of the Lord 248
- Day 6: Closing Thoughts and a Preview of Things to Come 255

Appendix 261
- Update on Personal Testimony 262
- Psychology: A Biblical Analysis 264
- Resources 267

Foreword

Knowing God and becoming conformed to the image of His Son is the ultimate goal of our faith in Jesus as our Savior, accomplished through His Grace. Growing into the image of Jesus is a freedom and joy increasing process as intimacy in a trusting, obedient relationship with God is developed. God uses each person's life circumstances to fulfill His purposes and to develop the character of Christ.

In this book series, God uses Gloria, and her life circumstances, to "come alongside" you as a friend and encourager in this process. As you read the graphic descriptions of her pilgrimage, you will experience a deep assurance of God's goodness and overcoming Grace. Gloria shares valuable lessons that will help you draw closer to God and experience His abiding presence in your life. You will also gain a greater awareness of the depth and power of God's Word in giving strength, assurance and the counsel needed to be victorious in every day living.

This book is not about a woman who just wants to tell about her difficult, pain-filled life. Rather, it is a book about God's triumphant love, mercy and grace in the life of one who has placed her total trust in Him and in the unfailing promises of His Word. Whether you are experiencing the normal challenges of life in a fallen world or a more difficult, intense physical, spiritual, or mental warfare, you will relate to what Gloria shares as you see yourself in similar situations that she experienced. You will hear words of comfort and hope. You will be encouraged. You will receive solid, practical biblical solutions to life's most challenging problems and God will show you the path to true freedom and joy in Him.

    Darrel L. Anderson, TH.D
    Positions Held: Pastor, First Baptist Church, Minneapolis MN
    VP/Field Director, National Association of Evangelicals
    Executive Director, Romanian Missionary Society
    Currently Pastoring in DesMoines, Iowa.

Abbreviations of Bible Translations and Books of the Bible

Please note the following abbreviations of Bible Translations and the books of the Bible used in this study:

cf. – Indicates comparative references; references making similar point.

sel. – designates "selected" portions of text listed.

Bible Translations

NASB – New American Standard Bible
KJV – King James Version
NKJV – New King James Version Bible

NIV – New International Version
TLB – The Living Bible (A Paraphrase)

Books of the Bible

Old Testament

Genesis – Gen.
Exodus – Ex.
Leviticus – Lev.
Numbers – Num.
Deuteronomy – Deut.
Joshua – Josh.
Judges – Judges
Ruth – Ruth
1 and 2 Samuel
    1 and 2 Sam.
1 and 2 Kings
    1 and 2 Kings

1st and 2nd Chronicles
    1st and 2nd Chron.
Ezra – Ezra
Nehemiah – Neh.
Esther – Esther
Job – Job
Psalms – Ps.
Proverbs – Prov.
Ecclesiastes – Eccles.
Song of Solomon – Song of Sol.
Isaiah – Is.
Jeremiah – Jer.
Ezekiel – Ezek.

Daniel – Dan.
Hosea – Hosea
Joel – Joel
Amos – Amos
Obadiah – Ob.
Jonah – Jonah
Micah – Micah
Nahum – Nah.
Habakkuk – Hab.
Zephaniah – Zeph.
Haggai – Hag.
Zechariah – Zech.
Malachi – Mal.

New Testament

Matthew – Matt.
Mark – Mark.
Luke – Luke
John – John
Acts – Acts
Romans – Rom.
1 and 2 Corinthians
    1 and 2 Cor.
Galatians – Gal.

Ephesians – Eph.
Philipians – Phil.
Colossians – Col.
1 and 2 Thessalonians
    1 and 2 Thess.
1 and 2 Timothy
    1 and 2 Tim.
Titus – Titus
Philemon – Philemon

Hebrews – Heb.
James – James
1 and 2 Peter
    1 and 2 Pet.
1, 2 and 3 John
    1, 2 and 3 John
Jude – Jude
Revelation – Rev.

Bible Study Instructions

Welcome to Book One, *Free Indeed* of the Bible Study series, <u>Rivers of Joy</u>. Your love for God and your desire to grow in His *wisdom, knowledge, and grace (2 Peter 3:18)* are a special encouragement to me. But, far more importantly, it is pleasing to God, who bids us all to *hunger and thirst after righteousness* and *to seek first His kingdom*, promising that in so doing, we will be *satisfied* and *our deepest needs met (Matthew 5:6, 6:33)*. Jesus commended Mary for choosing *the one thing needful*—to *sit at His feet, listen* and *learn from Him (Luke 10:42)*. Because she had chosen this most important pursuit, Jesus promised that she would experience a special security and joy that could never be taken from her. It is the same promise for you and me and all who will sit at Jesus' feet, listen, learn, and *take God at His Word (Deut. 32:46,47)*.

My prayer as you begin this new study is summed up well by the words of Paul: *I pray that…your heart may be enlightened, so that you may know what is the hope of His calling, what are the riches of the glory of His inheritance…and what is the surpassing greatness of His power toward us who believe (Eph. 1:18-19)*.

How to Use This Study

This is an interactive study of the Word of God. Devotional material discussing the foundational spiritual truth of the day is followed by a Bible Study Supplement with applicable Scripture that will help you apply the principles taught in the study material. This is, by far, the most important part and it is crucial to complete the questions to gain the lasting benefits intended.

Whenever a Bible verse is given with a small (a) or (b), i.e., Isaiah 31a or Isaiah 31b, it is referring to the first part of the verse (a) or the last part of the verse (b).

<u>Please Note</u>: The theme of this book is John 8:31,32,36: *If you continue in my Word…you will know the Truth and the Truth shall make you free. If the Son, therefore, shall make you free, you shall be **free indeed**.* The Bible defines "truth" as *the sum of God's Word (Ps. 119:160, cf. John 17:17)*. Therefore, it is crucial to know the "truth" and to obey the "truth" if we are to realize the full blessings of freedom that Jesus came to give us (John 10:10; Rom. 8:1,2; Gal. 5:1, etc.). To help us recognize and pay attention to this, the word **"truth"** is capitalized whenever it refers directly to Jesus or to biblical Truth found in God's Word. Also, in keeping with the theme of this series, <u>Rivers of Joy</u>, the word "joy" is capitalized where appropriate.

Abbreviations for translations and books of the Bible are given on the page preceding these instructions—page 10. <u>Please note these</u>.

If possible, please use the NASB or NIV translation for this study. The Bible Study supplement was designed around these versions and the questions will be clearer if either the NASB or NIV is used. Please do not use a paraphrase for this study. Doing so may lead to confusion in understanding and answering the questions.

The study is designed for five days each week (except for week one and week seven, which have six days to accommodate introductory and closing material). This will leave one day to review what you have learned or to "catch up." The other day is for worshiping God in your local assembly.

There will be two verses given for memorization (hiding in your heart - Ps. 119:11) each week. Please ask God to help you to be faithful in memorizing at least one of these verses, and if, possible, try to memorize both of them. As you do, you will be amazed at how often God uses these Scriptures to encourage, strengthen, and guide you. Also, there will be a Bible verse(s) listed at the top of each day's meditation. Please read these carefully. They are the *focus verses* for the day and will set your mind on the biblical Truth that will be studied that day.

Before you begin each day's study, it is very important to start with a word of prayer. Sit for a moment in quietness before the Lord. Ask the Holy Spirit to remove any distracting thoughts so that you may be able to give your attention fully to the study of God's Word. Also ask God, through His Holy Spirit, to give you true biblical clarity in your understanding and to always guard your heart from deception or inaccurate interpretation. There are several prayers in Scripture that are excellent in asking God to do this: *Open my eyes that I may behold, wonderful things from Thy Word (Psalm 119:18). May the words of my mouth and the meditations of my heart be acceptable to You, O Lord, my Rock and my Redeemer (Psalm 19:14). Search me, O God and know my heart; try me and know my anxious thoughts; And see if there be any hurtful way in me and lead me in the everlasting way (Psalm 139:23, 24).*

May God richly bless you as you embark on this adventure of *learning* and *growing in the wisdom, knowledge, grace, and freedom of our Lord Jesus Christ (2 Peter 3:18; John 8:36).*

Chapter 1

> Memory Bible Verse: *Then Jesus said to those who believed: If you continue in my Word, then are you my disciples indeed and you shall know the Truth and the Truth shall make you free . . . if the Son, therefore, shall make you free, you shall be **free indeed** (John 8:31,32,36).*
>
> Bonus memory verse: *He sent His Word and healed them (Ps. 107:20).*

Day 1

Bible Study Instructions

My Personal Testimony

*Please see note below

Day 2

Introduction to Book One – Free Indeed

A Word From Mel

Day 3

From My Heart: The Making of This Bible Study

Day 4

Building a Strong House of Indestructible Faith

Laying the Foundation

Day 5

In the Beginning . . . God! – Part 1

Day 6

In the Beginning…God! – Part 2

***NOTE:**

Please begin today by reading: "My Personal Testimony."

There is no Bible Study Supplement for Day 1 because of all the introductory material.

We will begin this on Day 2.

Chapter 1 — Day 1
My Personal Testimony

> *Then Jesus said to those who believed, "If you continue in My Word, then are you My disciples indeed. And you shall know the Truth, and the Truth shall make you free… If the Son, therefore, shall make you free, you shall be **free indeed** (John 8:31,32,36).*

The following is my personal testimony. I pray that as you read it you will be reminded of the greatness of our heavenly Father's love, mercy, and faithfulness in your life just as He demonstrated these again and again in mine, long before I *knew* Him.—Gloria Blowers

Broken Pieces

I stared at the image in the mirror. I did not recognize the stranger before me. The face was drawn, contorted into a frightening countenance reflecting the intensity of the destructive battle going on inside. A loud voice within screamed: "*Hopeless, hopeless, hopeless!*" Suddenly, fisted hands began beating mercilessly upon my stomach: "*Destroy! Destroy!!*" I doubled over, collapsing into a heap of agonizing pain and…helpless hopelessness.

It was a scary experience. Just one of many in the fourteen-year battle with the various eating disorders—first bulimia, then anorexia, and finally, compulsive eating—that threatened to destroy my marriage, my life, and my eternal destiny. I couldn't understand what was happening. I had always prided myself on being intelligent, assertive, strong-willed, able to handle whatever came my way—not just successfully, but commendably. But on this day, reality struck me in the face as clearly as the image that stood before me. I could finally see that all the outward success was in itself a huge mockery serving as a cloak of deceit over what was happening inside. I was not the happy, together, stable person I projected to others. I was, in reality, a powerless prisoner, held captive by a host of life-dominating obsessions and addictions. And I was too proud to admit it to anyone. So began the tormenting, endless charade of the dual life. I became, as it were, two people: on the outside—intelligent, high achiever, successful. But inwardly, I was a miserable, tormented failure, incessantly plagued by uncontrollable compulsions, mental and emotional turmoil—and *fear*.

I've struggled for a long time with just how much of my story I should share. There's so much that I would prefer not to talk about, for to do so means embarrassing humiliation. And it is certainly *not* politically correct to talk about such things. We are all supposed to be happy, together, paradigms of success who can handle anything life throws at us confidently and with a smile on our face. To admit anything less is social suicide. But the Bible says we are to *speak the truth in love (Eph. 4:15)* even if it hurts or is momentarily embarrassing, because only the Truth—God's Truth—sets people *free*, ourselves and others (John 8:31,32,36). So I am going to take that risk of ridicule and rejection. I am going to be painfully honest, and as I do, it is my fervent prayer that all who read this testimony will be encouraged by the greatness of God's love, mercy and grace. I pray also that many who are discouraged—who have endured too much pain for too long—will find hope and a renewed strength to press on to the true freedom and joy that Jesus came to bring us all *(John 8:31,32,36; 15:11)*.

I grew up on a small farm near Junction City, Kansas. I was the second of four children: two brothers and a sister. Life was hard on the farm and beset with difficulties and losses. On two separate occasions, in a matter of a few terrifying moments, tornadoes ravaged our farm, destroying not only our barns, animals, and my mom's pretty flowers and white picket fence, but also years of hard work, hopes, dreams—and my parents' financial stability. Still in the process of building back from these, a third tornado struck, adding to the heartaches and financial pressures. (Looking back on all this today, I am totally amazed at my mom and dad's courage and perseverance. I can never remember them grumbling or complaining or losing heart in any way. They just kept working hard, rebuilding, and doing the best they could. This memory would later serve as a stabilizing influence in my most difficult trials).

My earliest recollections of life were characterized by loneliness, fear of rejection, and mental and emotional turmoil. Even at an early age, I sensed I was different from other kids. I felt things deeper. When others hurt, I hurt. I cried a lot. Sometimes I would lock myself in my room and just cry and cry until I had such a pulsating headache I couldn't see straight. At other times, the relentless turmoil manifested itself in the form of grand mal seizures.

Because the inner pain was so great, I longed for comfort and affirmation. Neither of my parents were by nature outwardly affectionate, so I soon *perceived* great deprivation in this area. I know now that my parents *were* expressing their love in the best way they could through their hard work and doing all they could to keep our family together and as stable as possible, given all the humanly overwhelming difficulties and losses. But I was too absorbed in my own pain and problems—the never-ending mental and emotional torment, accompanied almost continually by physical pain—to see beyond this. Basically, I was a sad, mentally and emotionally oppressed, lonely child.

I mistakenly interpreted my mother and father's lack of affection as rejection. This introduced at a very early age, an obsessive preoccupation with earning approval and acceptance through achievement. This drivenness for achievement invaded every area of life. In my schoolwork, my best was not good enough. It had to be straight A's! Sports soon joined academics in my quest for affirmation. As early as junior high, I was a captain and leading scorer on school and community soccer and softball teams. I was also a record setting track competitor. One year, at a regional tournament, I swept the girls' track competition, taking first place in all the major running events and setting a new record. But in my sports endeavors, as in my academics, I could not participate for the sheer joy of competing. I had to win or I deemed myself a worthless failure. The destructive seeds of self-imposed perfectionism had already taken root.

In high school, my pursuit of approval and significance through academic achievement continued. I was determined to acquire as much of the world's knowledge as I possibly could. Every night, I brought home a stack of books. I quickly changed clothes, did my chores, then barricaded myself in my room and studied until my brain hurt.

The hard work paid off with a number of academic awards and scholarships.

My successes in academics and sports contributed to the popularity I also longingly craved. I was an officer in several extracurricular clubs as well as secretary of my senior class. But each and every brief moment of acknowledgment faded ever so quickly into a preoccupation with the next needed quest for recognition. Like a dark cloud over a Fourth of July parade, the fear of future failure in achieving the needed praise and approval, dampened every joy of the moment.

With a number of scholarships to support my academic ambitions, I enrolled in St. John's College, Winfield, KS. After earning my A.A. degree, graduating magna cum laude, I continued my education at the prestigious, academically acclaimed River Forest University, River Forest, (Chicago) Illinois. My college experience followed a similar pattern as high school. As a consistent high honor student, cheerleader, accomplished athlete, and officer in various collegiate clubs, my social and academic life flourished, giving all the external markings of success. Yet, the peace and contentment for which my turmoiled heart yearned continued to elude me. Big was never big enough. Perfect wasn't perfect enough. Enough was never enough! The accusations of futile insignificance beat mercilessly upon me night and day. "More…more…more!" the cruel taskmaster within screamed with relentless painful lashings.

During my childhood, teen years, and early adult life, I was hospitalized a number of times for mental and emotional-related problems.

"Religion" played a significant part in my early years. Mom and Dad were very active in a formal, liturgical church. They faithfully took us to Sunday school and church every week and read to us from the denominational devotional literature every night at bedtime. I was taught that I was "saved" (going to heaven) at the time of my baptism as a baby through a statement of faith made by my sponsors. This was "confirmed" by correctly answering questions from the Catechism and reciting designated Bible verses at the time of my confirmation in the eighth grade. But there was never any discussion about the *new birth* or what it meant to have a *personal* relationship with God through faith in Jesus so I did not understand what this really meant and I certainly did not have one. With no personal commitment to God or to His Word, after leaving home for college, I began to drift away from my religious moorings. In time, I abandoned them all together.

My attention to academics led to another magna cum laude graduation from River Forest and an exciting offer to become the Director of Guidance and Psychology at a prominent private academy in Denver, Colorado. I pursued graduate studies at Kansas State University in the summer, then moved to Colorado to begin my new job in the fall. I enjoyed the students, counseling, and teaching Senior Psychology. But something was still missing. Finally, after a year of yet more restless mental turmoil, I decided that academics had been my life too long! I needed to expand my horizons. So I left my teaching career to seek something *bigger*—more exciting and challenging.

The field of aeronautics and space exploration was at that time a relatively new, exciting career field with virtually limitless possibilities. I decided that was the place to be. I joined the ranks of Martin Marietta Aerospace Corporation, pursued specialized training in aeronautical engineering, then helped pioneer the role of women in this previously male-dominated field. Within one year I had climbed the corporate ladder to hold the position of release department head for all Martin Marietta's contractual drawings. Soon, I was winning awards and enjoying social contacts with the astronauts and upper management. Life was good! At age twenty-four, I had acquired all the trappings that the world claimed would satisfy that deep longing for love, acceptance, and fulfillment. Yet, the inner turmoil persisted. There was still something missing. As I wrestled to subdue the growing agitation, another siren call beckoned me away. It was the call to world travel. I wrestled long and hard with giving up my successful, highly regarded career. Yet the call persisted, tempting and cajoling day and night until I could resist it no more. I gave my notice, put my belongings in storage, and set out on my new adventure to travel the world. Surely I would find it—the peace, the contentment—somewhere…out there!

My plane touched down in Stockholm, Sweden. My cousin was waiting and drove me to Orebro where I stayed with my mother's <u>very</u> kind, hospitable relatives, Maj-Britt and Yngve Larsson. They ever so lovingly took me into their family and treated me like one of their own for over three months! I shall never forget their unselfish, daily deeds of kindness, and will be forever grateful to them and their family! But, again, the yearning to move on compelled me to pack my bags. I hitchhiked and traveled by train, crisscrossing the European continent for a year picking up exciting jobs along the way: working in a beautiful après ski lodge in the heart of the majestic Austrian Alps, and tutoring a wealthy European entrepreneur's children in France where I lived in a luxurious French provincial mansion with a lavishly landscaped courtyard, fountains, and lavender gardens. This gracious couple even offered the use of their spacious condo in Cavelaire on the beautiful French Riviera near Cannes. I spent two months in this romantic paradise during the exciting Mimosa Festival and world-famous Monte Carlo Road Race.

Even all this—the lavish accommodations and Eden-like surroundings—could not quiet the discontent that yet stirred within. I longed for more independence, my own place, and a stable, well-paying income that would enable me to continue in the flagrant, luxurious lifestyle to which I had become accustomed. By this time, I spoke four languages, which landed me another exciting job: a top security position with the Drug Enforcement Administration, International Division, Frankfurt, Germany. I traveled extensively throughout Europe and Asia on business and pleasure-related trips. My dating life flourished. I was wined and dined in some of the most elegant restaurants on the European continent. Yet, even then, the inner turmoil and mental harassment refused to be quieted. There was never any real, lasting peace or contentment. It was just one outward masquerade after another. How long could I keep this up?

But then, finally, the most wonderful thing in all the world happened. It was, I was sure, the missing piece to the proverbial happiness/contentment puzzle. Into my life walked the man of my fondest, most romantic dreams—tall, *very* handsome, promising career. His 6'5" stature, dark hair, piercing brown eyes, and warm, congenial smile would melt any woman's heart. He was a captain (pilot) in the US Air Force, with the prestigious 7th Special Ops Squadron—the Fulton Recovery/James Bond-type rescue guys who worked with the Green Berets and Navy Seals. Captain Blowers was also very intelligent, kind, and courteous. He brought me beautiful flowers and took me to fine restaurants, on picnics in the countryside, and on weekend excursions exploring castles and touring walled cities. Then one night in the quaint, romantic Tzigone Cave Restaurant in Brussels, Belgium, his eyes glistening in the soft candlelight, he pulled from beneath the table a small black velvet box. As I opened it, a large beautifully cut, perfectly hued diamond, surrounded by nearly a dozen smaller diamonds, sparkled like stars on a clear summer night. The long-awaited question followed: "Will you . . . ?" "Yes!"

Surely, this was what I had been searching for all my life: Someone special with whom I could live and learn and laugh and share my dreams and aspirations. Like a schoolgirl anticipating her first prom, I excitedly began to make preparations for the upcoming wedding which included a trip to London and the John Lewis Bridal Salon for purchase of my wedding gown. There were showers and going-away parties as we prepared to return to the United States for the wedding and Mel's transfer to Hurlburt Air Force Base, Fort Walton Beach, Florida. Back home in Kansas and Pennsylvania (where Mel was from), there were more showers and open houses to wish us well. I was easily caught up in the momentary excitement, keeping the inner turmoil at bay.

The wedding was an idyllic sunset ceremony at Vesper Point, Rock Springs Ranch, overlooking the tranquil rolling countryside. The breathtaking purple and crimson sky with splashes of gold provided the perfect backdrop to the wedding service. Afterward, at the reception, an elaborate multi-tiered cake surrounding a sparkling fountain (made by my dear and very talented Aunt Lois) served as an elegant centerpiece to the festivities. Everything was—outwardly—*perfect*.

Then it was off to Hawaii and our luxurious honeymoon condo on Waikiki Beach. But a pulsating migraine and the return of the disquieting agitation deep inside greatly dampened the celebration.

We returned to Fort Walton Beach where we began our married life together. I loved our first cozy apartment not far from the base. I wanted so much to be a good wife and make my husband happy and proud. Three months into our marriage something wonderful—and frightening—happened. I got sick! I went to the doctor, where I received the news. I was pregnant! There came with the news a dichotomy of intense emotion: ecstatic joy mingled with a paralyzing fear. As a little girl I loved to play with dolls and dreamed of the day when I would be a mother and have a real baby to hold and care for. Now that dream was about to come true. Yet, doubt and *fear* flooded my mind. I was not ready to be a mom.

As I struggled to prepare for my new role, just two short months into the pregnancy, tragedy struck for which I was not prepared. I had a spontaneous miscarriage. Rather than feeling a sense of relief as I thought I would (when I wished so often that I were not pregnant), I was devastated! I realized then that I really did want this baby more than any of the other dreams and ambitions of the past. It was as if a part of me died with the baby that day. A dark, overpowering depression set in, along with that all-too-familiar agitation in my heart. Try as I might to convince myself that I still had Mel and together we possessed all for which I had ever dreamed—and so much more—I could not quiet the inner turmoil or overcome the awful depression.

One day, in an attempt to break through the ever-thickening clouds, Mel called from work and asked me to join him for dinner at the officer's club. As we enjoyed our favorite meal, chateaubriand for two, in the lovely, candlelit dining room overlooking the beautiful Okaloosa Bay, he told me about a graduate program in counseling that was about to begin on base. I'd been longing to return to school and complete my master's, so this news was very exciting. The next day I enrolled in the program.

I threw myself into my studies and completed my master's in Clinical/Agency Counseling with a perfect 4.0. Soon after graduation, I was hired as director of Okaloosa county CETA (Comprehensive Employment and Training Act), a state-administered, vocational-training program. In a short time, I had developed a model program for the state of Florida. More awards, featured front-page newspapers articles and other recognitions followed, fueling the insatiable flames of discontent once more. I could not understand what was happening. The more I achieved, the less content—and more depressed—I became. Would this relentless, oppressive cycle ever end?

When Mel's service obligation was over, I terminated my job with CETA, and we moved to Kansas City where he flew for the Air Force Reserves, and I tried desperately to cope with the deepening depression. I enjoyed cooking and had attended culinary arts classes in Cordon, France while living there, so in an attempt to keep my mind occupied and alleviate the pain of the internal agony, I started a culinary arts/cooking school. Then I got pregnant again. A paralyzing fear gripped me once more. How could I bring a baby into this state of chronic depression and relentless mental turmoil? I was unfit as a wife. I could never make it as a mom. Moms are strong and happy and love their kids and find unending joy in caring for and nurturing them. I couldn't even care for myself and Mel. I was miserable and I would make my child miserable. What kind of a life would that be?

The paralyzing fear and all the questions and uncertainties were soon complicated by a very serious flu-like illness. I ran a high fever and was continually nauseous with extreme vertigo for several weeks. After a number of visits to the doctor, he, in a very concerned voice let me know that what was happening had nothing to do with any normal morning sickness but that something very serious was going on. He suspected a life-threatening uterine infection. After several more weeks of trying unsuccessfully to treat the infection, he told me that the baby was probably dead or severely damaged because of the high fever and other complications I'd had for so long. He advised a therapeutic abortion. Depressed or not, I was *not* ready for that! I must have time to think about it and discuss it with my husband. For two long, painful, nearly sleepless weeks, I wrestled with the decision to follow the doctor's advice or to carry the baby full-term. When I became so exhausted from the emotional battle that I began to have blackouts, the doctor insisted that I have the abortion.

Mel, fearing he would lose me if something were not done soon, agreed. In desperation for relief, I gave in and signed the papers. In a few hours, I was being prepped for the surgery. To this day I can not find words to adequately describe this horrid experience—the pain, the guilt, the depression that settled in, darker than anything I had experienced previously. (Just a side note here. Anyone who says that an abortion does not affect the life of the mother is believing a very tragic and destructive lie. It affects her very much, for the rest of her life: the nightmarish pain/recovery of the procedure itself haunts for years, the inevitable consequence of never being able to hold her precious baby, of never experiencing the love that he/she would have brought, or seeing him/her fulfill the plan God had for his/her life, brings painful tears often!) For weeks after the procedure, I could not sleep adding further to the mental and emotional torment.

A few months later, by the grace of God alone, Mel was hired by Delta. (At that time there were over a thousand applications for every commercial airline pilot position). A flicker of hope was rekindled. Maybe now, at last, things would get better and peace would come. We moved to Atlanta—the exciting, emerging city of culture, entertainment and endless job possibilities. Again, by God's merciful provision (even though I did not know Him and certainly did not pray for His guidance and help), I very quickly landed yet another exciting position with the IBM corporation. As a systems support specialist, I enjoyed an exceptionally successful career, quickly winning the coveted Sales Support Rep of the Year plus numerous other awards and national recognitions. What more could I possibly want! I had a wonderful husband, a beautiful home, a successful career, and even unlimited flying privileges! We took advantage of this and made frequent trips: Sightseeing in Seattle, Cancun (Mexico), San Juan (Puerto Rico); Broadway shows in New York; ski trips to Colorado and the Alps of Switzerland; a bed and breakfast tour of Ireland…and dozens more. Once we flew to San Francisco (from Atlanta) for dinner! Wine became a regular part of our meals and any other time in between when we felt like kicking back and relaxing. It seemed to numb the emptiness. There were spas, exotic weekend excursions, luxury cruises, and every other pleasurable indulgence my heart desired in an attempt to overcome the relentless mental unrest and empty void inside. But it just didn't work. The turmoil and discontent churned ceaselessly within, no matter the momentary outward pleasure.

In fact, the more we made and the more we acquired, the greater became the emotional upheavals.

There were times the mental torment became so bad, I would beat myself mercilessly with fisted hands or bite my arm until the blood came, in a convoluted attempt to bring relief to the hellish pain of the internal embattlement. At this point, there were several suicide attempts. It was obvious that I could no longer handle what was going on alone. I needed help. So I turned to psychotherapy—along with its accompanying liberal use of psychotropic drugs—as my last hope to end the relentless internal war. Now, I added to alcohol and all the other pleasures and distractions, uppers to get me up, downers to calm me down, and tranquilizers to help me sleep.

I spent two years undergoing extensive psychotherapy. I was labeled at one time or another along the rocky road of treatment: epileptic, mentally and emotionally unstable, clinically depressed, bipolar (manic-depressive), obsessive/compulsive, codependent, neurotic, psychotic, schizophrenic. I had every symptom listed in the DSM (Diagnostic and Statistical Manual of Mental Disorders) for all these disorders.

Even though the more socially acceptable labels—such as clinical depression or bipolar—offered a comforting excuse when needed in my public life for a short while, pride would not allow me to live with such labels for long, for I considered them terribly demeaning and reserved for the real "crazies". So I began a campaign of deception that rivaled the best of Broadway productions. On the outside, I was all smiles and exuded a life-is-great attitude. I had become a master at deceit, pretending to be what I was not: happy, content.

Though incredibly effective on the outside, the deception could not fool nor ameliorate the conflict and torment within. So I turned to a former "god" for relief—food. Only this time the devastating control it had over me was far more intense than ever before. And thus began the most hellish mental and emotional battle ever! I had so often thought in the previous years that the only good thing about my life was that I had certainly reached the bottom of the pit, so the next move would have to be up. Little did I know that all the pain and problems endured thus far would soon pale in comparison to the horror I was about to enter: a horror that lasted nearly fourteen long, truly indescribably miserable, life-threatening years! First it was bulimia, then anorexia, and finally, compulsive eating with its typical endless binge/starve cycle. Unless you have been in the grips of a life-dominating obsessive compulsion such as this, you cannot even begin to imagine the totality of such misery! Life ceases to be, and you exist in a pseudo world of pretend and make-believe, because if anyone knew how bound and helplessly enslaved to the compulsion you were, they would either walk as far away as they could or else they would do all in their power to get you committed, because happy, healthy, together people don't act like that! And they are right. They don't!

I certainly wasn't happy, healthy, or together. My latest "god," food, like all the others—education, sports, success, pleasure—could not deliver on its promise to satisfy, though I worshipped faithfully at its altar day after endless day. In fact, food became my life. I did not *eat to live* as healthy, happy, together people do. I *lived to eat*. Food was the first thought on my mind when I awoke in the morning and the last thought before I went to sleep—*if* I fell asleep at all, as chronic insomnia robbed me of more and more of that. My life—more accurately, my intensely miserable *existence*—consisted of but two dismal choices from which I was forced to choose daily and throughout the oft long, sleepless nights of nocturnal cravings. I could choose to eat what I wanted, which always resulted in an uncontrollable binge and the physical misery—the bloated stomach and agonizing emotional guilt that accompanied it—or I could starve myself and remain even more miserable in my self-imposed deprivation and hunger. There was absolutely no choice in between. I was incapable of sitting down to a normal, nutritious meal, enjoying it, and then leaving the table satisfied. I was never satisfied—whether I ate enough for twelve people or only enough to keep a starving sparrow alive. The self-inflicted beatings and bitings intensified, as did the suicide attempts.

Yet, convolutedly, I was, at the same time (using my degrees as professional qualification), heavily involved in therapeutic counseling, counseling other people how to solve their problems throughout those fourteen years!

I knew (human knowledge) all the physiological and psychological reasons why I was doing what I was doing, and what I needed to do to change it. Yet, I was absolutely and utterly powerless to do it, and I was passing on to others this same head knowledge of powerless, empty solutions.

After more soul-searching, I concluded that there was only one thing that I had not yet done that I had always wanted to do, and that was to have my own business. After all, I was a hard worker and I'd done so much for all those *other* people; now I wanted to do something for *me* and be personally rewarded accordingly.

Just four years into my rapidly climbing, successful career with IBM, I gave my resignation notice. We moved to the quaint Alpine village resort town of Helen in the beautiful North Georgia mountains, where I designed and operated a riverside restaurant, Cafe International. The restaurant flourished and, during Octoberfest and Fall Leaf Season, it was one of the most popular gathering places in town. People waited in line almost continually to get a seat on the picturesque covered deck overlooking the Chattahoochee River. The Atlanta Journal/Constitution even featured the restaurant as the cover story in its weekend leisure magazine. Surely, I could rest now in this latest success.

At this point, Mel was flying as Second Officer on the L-1011 with Delta. We built a lovely new home. It is hard to imagine that there would be any room for discontent or inner turmoil with all that we had going for us! But there was. I can vividly remember stopping at the bank's night deposit box night after endless night and hearing the hollow, clanging sound of the bulging money bag making its way to the bottom of the chute. And as it did, I could hear the question of a popular song echoing through the deepest chambers of my own hollow, empty heart: "Is that all there is, my friend?"

It was never a matter of not wanting to change. I wanted to change more than life itself, for I knew that if I did not change—soon—there would be no future, for there would be no life. My destructive eating habits had begun to take a heavy toll on my health. I began to develop serious problems:

relentless strep throat, swelling and intense pain in muscles and joints, nausea, vertigo, fever, stomach and intestinal problems. Endless visits to doctors and specialist added to the list of labels ascribed to my condition: CFIDS (Chronic Fatigue Immune Dysfunction Syndrome), Fibromyalgia, Lupus, and a few other strange names of rare diseases I cannot even remember now. The endless series of antibiotics and other drug therapies destroyed what little was left of my already weakened, overstressed immune system. Recurring infections added to the out-of-control downward spiral toward total destruction. Death seemed imminent, and at this point, welcomed, because of the chronic insomnia that accompanied all the other problems. There was never any break from the pain day after day, night after endless night. A dark impenetrable sense of *helpless hopelessness* permeated every futile attempt to find relief. Truly, there are no words to adequately describe the relentless, torturous, hellishness of it! As so often before, suicide seemed to be the only way out. And I am sure, but for the grace of God, at that point, I would have carried it out! But a pervasive and powerful *fear* (that I now know was the mercy of God!) kept me from completing a number of well-laid plans. I did not know God. Yet I knew there was a God and there was life after death—*He has planted eternity in their hearts (Eccles. 3:11).* There was a heaven and there was a hell, which was exactly where I was headed! And I'd experienced enough *hell on earth* to know I did not want to go there forever!

My marriage was as rocky as my physical, mental, and spiritual condition. Totally obsessed for so many years with *my* needs, *my* wants, *my* quests for fulfillment, *my* compulsions, and now, *my* pain, I totally neglected my responsibilities as a wife and helpmate for my husband. Consequently, one cold, blustery February morning, the inevitable happened. Mel, who had received little more than the crumbs of my time and attention, while at the same time enduring my emotionally bizarre, unstable, self-centered mania for all those years, had taken all he could take! He had his own masculine needs that were not being met. Slamming his fist upon the breakfast bar, he said without a hint of mercy in his eyes: "Your restaurant, or me! No compromises!" He turned and walked away. He was going on a three-day trip. I had three days to decide my immediate marital status and my forever-after destiny.

I went to work in a daze. The threat of the inevitable destruction of my world hung over me like a guillotine about to drop. How could I give up my restaurant, which had become my identity in my deluded quest for significance? On the other hand, I knew my husband was the best thing that had ever happened to me. He had brought a sense of stability to my life, a buffer to the unmitigating pain and confusion. I knew he was inextricably linked to any hope for future security, stability—peace. I was at the proverbial crossroads in life where I was forced to choose one direction or the other. Yet, I wanted and I needed *both*.

When I got to work, the pressure of the no-win situation became overwhelming. I was nauseas and faint. Suddenly, the distressing vertigo sent me to the floor. My manager ran quickly for a cold cloth, which she pressed against my pallid brow as she issued her own instructions: "Go home and get some rest!"

Having no recollection of how I actually got there, I pulled up in front of our house, staggered to the front door, and with shaky hand fumbled for the keyhole. I stumbled through the bedroom door, tripping on an object in my path to the bed. (To this day, neither my husband nor I have any recollection of leaving the yellow suitcase there, but there is not a doubt regarding the fact that it was mysteriously, strategically located directly in my path, for it was the instrument God used to start the life-altering series of events about to transpire). Tripping on the suitcase, I fell flat on my face. As my tense, pain-wracked body slammed against the hard floor, the pent-up anger, the hurt, the confusion, the long years of endless strivings, the growing awareness of the vanity in the self-deception flooded through me from deep within like torrents over a broken dam. Angrily, I jumped to my feet, grabbed the yellow suitcase and whirled around the room—round and round and round—then recklessly let it go. Leaning against the wall in the path of the projectile was a beautiful, two-hundred-year-old antique stained glass window, imported from a judge's chamber in Ireland, which we had purchased for the bedroom in our new home. The suitcase crashed through the center of the glass, shattering it into a myriad of jagged pieces. I fell on the floor, shaking and weeping uncontrollably. Finally, I lifted my head peering at the broken glass. "Oh, God," I cried, "That's my life! Broken pieces. Nothing but *broken pieces*. That's all it's ever been—broken pieces! If you think it's worth putting back together, you are going to have to do it this time, because I can't. I can't do it any longer. I quit! Help me, God. Please, God. *Save me, Jesus…*"

I shall never forget that moment as long as I live. God heard my prayer, and He answered so compassionately, so quietly, I cannot yet fully describe it. Every cruel, demanding voice inside was stilled. There was a calm and there was a peace, a deep, tranquil peace I'd never before experienced, a *peace that passed all human understanding (Phil. 4:7)*. After sitting totally absorbed in the sweet, restful, serenity of the peace for several minutes, I suddenly had a compelling desire to read the Word of God. "I must find God's Word, and I must read it! I must learn about God and what life is really all about. I must find out who God created me to be, *His* plans for my life and how to have real, lasting love, joy, peace, and purpose."

As I began to obey the prompting to go to God's Word, the sweet quietness was broken. The familiar accusing voice that had controlled my life all those years reared its ugly head in determined defiance: "Stupid idea! Stupid! Stupid! Stupid! The Bible is no more than an ancient archaic book that weak, ignorant Christians read and hang on to for a crutch because they aren't smart enough—like you—to figure life out on their own." For so many years, I had believed that lie and was thoroughly convinced in my own mind that this *ancient manuscript* could not possibly teach me anything I did not already know. Yet, somehow, the quiet prompting would not go away. At one point, I seriously considered the temptation to forget it. Fear and trembling came upon me at that thought, however, as something inside seemed to warn me that this very well could be the last time I would be able to hear the quiet voice, the gentle prompting.

I ran upstairs, pulled down boxes from the attic, searching until I found the green-covered, paperback Bible I had picked up somewhere in my desperate search for peace. As I began to read, my eyes stared in unbelief. The words were so plain, so understandable, so personal!

"Woe to My rebellious children", says the Lord; "you ask advice from everyone but me, and decide to do what you want to do without consulting Me…adding sin to sin. For without consulting me you have gone down to Egypt to find aid and have put your trust in Pharaoh for his protection. But in trusting Pharaoh, you will be disappointed, humiliated and disgraced, for he cannot deliver on his promises to save you!" (Is. 30:1-3 TLB)

In these few sentences, I saw my life clearly. Egypt was the world and all the places to which I ran to find the peace, joy, and happiness for which my troubled heart longed. Pharaoh was my knowledge, my achievements, my accumulated material goods—and later, food—that had become my *gods* to which I ran for comfort, for satisfaction, for deliverance. And there were so many carefully executed plans along the way. How often I asked for advice from unbelievers—others just as lost and far from God as I. Not once had I ever stopped to read God's Word, talk to Him, or ask Him what *His* plans for my life might be. With every new self-directed plan, I only widened the gap between my heavenly Father and me—*adding sin to sin*. I continued…

Therefore, the safety of Pharaoh will be your shame, and the shelter…of Egypt, your humiliation. Through a land of distress and anguish you travail…(You) carry your riches…and your treasure…to a people who cannot profit;…And you felt secure in your wickedness and said, 'No one sees me'…Your wisdom and your knowledge…deluded you. For you have said in your heart, 'I am, and there is no one besides me.' But evil will come on you; and disaster will fall on you for which you cannot atone. You are wearied with your many counsels;…(you) cannot deliver (yourself) from the power of the flame;...There is no one to save you (Is. 30:3-5; 47:10-15).

The broken pieces were coming together.

They weary themselves committing iniquity. "Your dwelling is in the midst of deceit; through deceit you refuse to know Me," declares the Lord. "Your ways and your deeds have brought these things to you. How bitter! How it has touched your heart!" (Jer. 9:5b,6, 4:18)

Hear, O earth: behold, I am bringing disaster on this people, the fruit of their plans, because they have not listened to My Words. As for my law, they have rejected it also. (Jer. 6:19)

Every man is stupid, devoid of knowledge;... In their discipline of delusion, (they) worship worthless idols...idols (that) are deceitful; there is no breath in them; they are worthless, a work of mockery. Who would not fear Thee, O King of the nations? Indeed it is Thy due. For among all the wise men of the nations, and in all their kingdoms, there is none like Thee (Jer. 10:14,15,7,8).

I am the Lord your God, who teaches you to profit, who leads you in the way you should go. If only you had paid attention to My commandments! Then your well-being would have been like a river, and your righteousness like the waves of the sea (Is. 48:17).

How I would set you among My sons, and give you a pleasant land, the most beautiful inheritance of the nations. And I said, You shall call Me...Father, and not turn away from following Me... For thus the Lord God, the Holy One of Israel, has said, In repentance and rest you shall be saved, in quietness and trust is your strength...But you were not willing (Jer. 3:19; Is. 30:15).

The words continued, offering hope.

For Thou, O Lord, art our Father, our Redeemer from of old... He said surely, they are My people, Sons...so he became their Savior...Come now, let us reason together, though your sins be as scarlet, they shall be white as snow. If you consent and obey, you will eat the best of the land; but if you refuse and rebel, you will be devoured by the sword. Truly the mouth of the Lord has spoken (Is. 63:16, 64:8,9, 1:18-20).

Having totally neglected the Word of God for so long, my weak, hungry soul was famished. I could not get enough of its life-giving nourishment! I read and read through the night until 4:00 A.M. when exhaustion overtook me. I slept for about an hour, then got up and eagerly began to read again. *For God so loved the world that He sent His only begotten Son, that whosoever believeth in Him might not perish but have everlasting life...Repent...and believe in the Lord Jesus Christ. (John 3:16 KJV; Acts 2:38, 16:31).* So right there, in my kitchen, on March 1, 1983, I *believed.* I confessed and repented of my sins of pride and rebellion, of rejecting God and stubbornly going my own way all those years. I thanked Jesus for dying on the cross for my sins and for making a way back to God and peace with Him. I asked Jesus to forgive me, to come into my heart, and to help me live for Him and fulfill God's purposes for my life. And He did come into my heart that very moment to be my own personal Lord and Savior. It was so simple and so *real.* I know it was real because in that moment that I made this simple, genuine, confession of faith, God gave me the *seal of His Holy Spirit, (Eph. 1:14)*—that *blessed assurance* that says: "I know that I <u>know</u> that I <u>know</u> that I have been born again by the Spirit of the living God. I am His redeemed, blood-bought child and have *eternal life* with Him...forever." (John 11:25,26). I have never doubted that for one second since that time, not once! This assurance of the Holy Spirit's presence became an unending source of stability, strength, and security.

Finally, I realized that salvation was not joining a church, memorizing Bible passages, or even baptism and partaking in the sacraments. It was a *personal relationship with God through Jesus* (through faith in what He accomplished for us on the cross). It was a precious mutual, living, interactive, *relationship.*

I had fallen into the trap so very common: mistakenly assuming that "religion" and "salvation" were one and the same. But now I could see the nearly fatal delusion in this assumption. *Religion* is man's attempt to get to God, or, as is even more common, to *be his own God (Gen. 3:5; Is. 14:13). Salvation* is

God's grace reaching down to lost man, offering forgiveness, unconditional love, and acceptance through the redemptive work of Jesus on the cross. I had been very religious at times, looking to an institution—i.e., a church with its religious traditions (infant baptism, confirmation, church membership)—to somehow save me. But it didn't, and it couldn't. That's why my life remained so empty and full of turmoil. When I got my eyes off myself, off of religious traditions and off of other people—most of whom were just as lost and living under the same delusions as I—and onto God as revealed in His Word, the pieces of my fractured, broken life began to fit together. At last the real missing piece to the puzzle of inner peace and contentment had been found—a loving, forgiven, *relationship* with God. Into my life flowed for the first time, unconditional love and acceptance and the assurance of a glorious sure and secure future. Finally, I knew who I really was, why I was here, and where I was going! I could, for the first time truly *enjoy the present moment* and *smile at the future (1 Tim. 6:17; Prov. 31:25)*.

Then Jesus said to those who believed: If you continue in My Word then are you my disciples indeed and you shall know the Truth, and the Truth shall make you free. If the Son, therefore, shall make you free, you shall be free indeed" (John 8:31,32,36). I believed that promise; and I continued in God's Word every day from that beautiful beginning until now, and I continue still. God, through the wisdom and Truth found in His Word, has already set me free from so much. He liberated me from the awful torment of bulimia, anorexia, and compulsive eating, along with all sorts of other destructive habits that kept me bound in a world of oppressive sin and guilt. How can I ever thank Him enough for bringing me from a weak, unstable, drug-dependent mental and emotional basket case who spent as much time in the sick bed as out of it, to one who is **completely drug free, and has not spent one single day in bed for sickness in more than seventeen years!** To me, this is nothing short of a very real miracle. To God be the glory!

The Bible says: *If any man be in Christ, he is a new creature, old things pass away, behold all things become new" (2 Cor. 5:17)*. My life is a dramatic, living testimony of this profound truth. God has overcome the destructive power of all the former labels: manic-depressive, bipolar, neurotic, psychotic, etc., and has given me new names: *Redeemed, Born Again, Saved by Grace, Child of God, Joint Heir of Heaven, The King's Daughter - Glorious Within, Bride of Christ (Ps. 45; Is. 60; John 3:3; Eph. 1:1–14, etc.)*.

There is much more I wish I had time to tell you about the way God put back together our nearly destroyed marriage, giving us a beautiful relationship and a wonderful home permeated with His love, joy, and peace; or the many other ways He has worked in my life to bring yet more freedom and joy-producing purpose. But that would take many more pages and much too much of your precious time. You've already been so very patient. Thank you so much for that!

However, before I close, I must take just a moment to share something far more important than anything I've said to this point. For thirty-five years of my life, I cannot remember one person coming to me personally to share the gospel and tell me (biblically) how I could receive forgiveness of my sins and eternal life with God in Heaven when I die, or how I could understand God's plan for my life presently and why this was so important. As mentioned earlier, my parents faithfully took us to church every Sunday and I even attended a parochial school, so I heard a lot of Bible stories and sermons on good moral living. But there was never any instruction concerning a *personal relationship with Jesus* that comes only with the new birth (genuine repentance and personal faith in Jesus' redemptive work on the cross) and the necessity of this for *eternal life (John 3:3–16; Rom. 10:9,10*, etc.). I am truly *deeply* grateful for all that my parents did in their loving and sincere desire to raise us children right. They were diligently following what they had been taught, as did their their parents before them. And I am sure that seeds were planted that played a significant role in my salvation (Is. 55:11). But I also know now that the faith of a parent, diligent, strict adherence to religious tradition and practice—including infant baptism with the confessions of a "sponsor" or "godparent" on one's behalf, and partaking of the sacraments—or even being *good* (doing "good works"), will not get one person into Heaven. The Word of God could not be clearer: *Truly, truly, I say to you, unless one is born again, he cannot see the kingdom of God...My people parish for lack of knowledge (John 3:3; Hosea 4:6).* This *lack of knowledge* nearly cost me, not only my present life, but also eternal separation from God. I was perishing because I did not understand what the Bible says about salvation, the new birth, God's plan for my life, and many other things.

> *"Lies and not Truth prevail in the land" declares the Lord...From the prophet even to the priest, everyone practices deceit. And they heal the brokenness of My people superficially, saying, 'Peace, peace,' But there is no peace" (Jer. 9:3; 8:10-11).*

I lived in that dreadful, terrible condition all those long painful years of deceptive mental and emotional instability, superficial healing, self-manufactured (false) peace. It was God's Word that broke through the darkness of the deception and illumined the way back to God in whom I found real, lasting healing and the filling up of all those empty places in my heart for love, acceptance, purpose.

Jesus said: *I am the Way, the Truth, and the Life; no one comes to the Father* [to Heaven] *except through Me (John 14:6).* People have tried for centuries to ignore or argue against this basic foundational truth to their own hurt and eventual eternal damnation. But argue as they will, ignore as they choose, it will never alter the reality of this truth nor the consequence of its rejection. I cannot help but think often of how very close I came to this point, because the Bible also clearly teaches that there comes a time when God will close the door of salvation to those who continue to reject His Son...*trampling underfoot His precious blood and the suffering He endured for our redemption...and there will never again be an opportunity to turn back, to repent (Heb. 6:4–6, 10:26–29).* This is a very sobering fact that yet sends me to my knees in overwhelming gratitude to God for His *patience and longsuffering (Ex. 34:6)* towards me. It is also the reason I cannot help but share the wonderful good news with others before it might be too late for them.

And that is what this Bible study is all about. It is not only about true salvation—forgiveness of sins and eternal life with God in Heaven one day—it is also about *freedom* and *joy* and *showers of blessings* along the way.

> *And I will make a covenant of peace with them and eliminate harmful beasts from the land, so that they may live securely...And I will cause showers to come down...they will be showers of blessing (Ezek. 34:25-26).*

> *These things I have written that My joy may be in you and your joy may be full (John 15:11).*

> *If you continue in My Word, then are you My disciples indeed. And you shall know the Truth, and the Truth shall make you free...If the Son, therefore, shall set you free, you shall be...free indeed (John 8:31,32,36).*

Chapter 1 — Day 2
Introduction to Book One — Free Indeed

> *Then Jesus said to those who believed: If you continue in my Word, then are you my disciples indeed and you shall know the Truth and the Truth shall make you free…if the Son, therefore, shall make you free, you shall be **free indeed** (John 8:31,32,36).*

What a beautiful promise Jesus has given us in John 8 (above), the theme of this book.

Let me share with you why this promise is so precious to me. As you read yesterday in my testimony, when I first became a Christian, I was in abject life-threatening bondage to bulimia and compulsive eating. Food was my "god" to whom I ran—for comfort, for solace, for reward, for pleasure. It was delightfully delicious and pacifyingly pleasurable—*for the moment (Heb. 11:25)*. It brought immediate gratification to my fleshly cravings…and multitudinous other inner *hungers*. It soothed my frustrations, ameliorated my pain and served as a pleasurable momentary escape from the relentless troubles and tribulations. But the outcome was always the same—painful bloating, oppressive guilt, shame, bondage. I always hated myself after every repulsive out-of-control orgy—feeling very much like a wild dog in a garbage dump. I felt weak, cheap, fat, and ugly. I knew that what I was doing was wrong and disgusting. Yet, I was powerless to do anything about it. Every new resolve, every promise to myself that "this would be the *last time*" ended in agonizing failure and a deeper entrenchment in the pit of despair—a sense of helpless hopelessness. How desperately I wanted to stop the vicious cycle: sin, shame, guilt, more sin, deeper shame, greater guilt…more sin, more guilt.

…for by what a man is overcome, by this he is enslaved (2 Peter 2:19).

I was a slave to sin. It ruled over me like a tyrannical slave master. I vacillated between discouragement and depression. Life as I knew God intended it—with meaning and purpose, blessing and peace, victory over sin and its awful consequences—was so far removed from the reality of my daily experience, I could no longer even dream of it. A pervasive gloomy sense of futility and doom settled into every fiber of my being and refused to be dispelled—no matter how hard I tried to overcome it. Consequently, joy—real, lasting JOY—had long ceased to be for me. I could no longer even embrace a realistic hope of ever experiencing that kind of inner peace and pleasure, (contentment) again. Oh, I pretended to have it when I was out in public—putting on the proverbial "smiley face," *appearing* happy and cheerful to prove to others that I was OK, in control. But that, too, was a huge—and very painful—lie.

Deep inside, more than anything else in all the world, I longed to be free of this sin and the awful grip it had on me so that I could serve God with a whole and undivided heart. I knew that this terrible habit (sin!) was an affront to the precious name of Jesus whose representative I now was. And I knew that I was not honoring or glorifying God in this area of my life. As a redeemed child of God, habitual sin had no place in my life. It had to go.

Added to this conflict were the endless debilitating, hellish bouts with the bipolar. As if controlled by some overpowering force within, I would be flying as high as a kite one moment, (when engaged in a pleasurable, joy-producing experience, or a momentary reprieve from the pain) only to be hurled down to the lowest pit of hell the next—a state in which all seemed black, futile, hopeless. And I was frighteningly beginning to recognize that the "highs" were never as "high" as they once were and occurred with far less frequency, while the "lows" plunged me into an even deeper abyss with each new episode extending for weeks or months at a time with not a moment of relief. The proverbial *bottom of the pit* to which I sank each time seemed only to get lower and darker so that any hope that things would ever change was dismally fading away. How often a voice within argued temptingly: "What a fool you are to continue fighting this thing. Quit dreaming that it will ever get any better and accept the medical diagnosis and treatment. You are bipolar. You were born bipolar. You will always be bipolar. Bipolar is an *incurable disease* and nothing you can do will ever change that! Bipolar people are *supposed* to be depressed, so just accept this reality, apply for disability, and settle into a life of *coping* with the aid of relaxation techniques, psychotropic drugs and pain medication." (Even though I knew from years of experience using every coping technique and drug available for the treatment of bipolar, that the relief from the pain was temporary at best and dangerous at worst, with the drugs dulling the acuity of the mind to think and deal with problems clearly and rationally while increasing the instability of the emotions as a result of the unpredictability of the medications along with the almost endless drug-related side effects).

Thankfully, the Spirit of God gave wisdom and strength and would not allow me to give in to these temptations—strong as they were! Having read and studied the Bible for a number of years by this time, I was aware that there was not one example given throughout the Word of God of joyless, chronic depression being a God-honoring, Christ-exalting way of life. Was God so weak and so powerless that He could not lift one of *His children* from the grips of so awful an existence? I knew well the answer to that:

> *Behold, I am the Lord, the God of all flesh; is anything too difficult for Me?...With God all things are possible...I am the Lord, your healer...in all these things we overwhelmingly conquer (Jer. 32:27, Gen. 18:14, Matt. 19:26, Ex. 15:26, Rom. 8:37).*

Because I *knew* this, guilt was added to shame. Something had to be done if I were to continue naming the Name of Jesus and professing to be His called-out, redeemed, *set-free* child.

With this desire burning in my heart, my husband and I attended a spiritual growth/marriage enrichment seminar. The leader gave a glowing introduction telling of all that we would learn and be able to *take away* from the seminar to make our personal lives and our marriages "richer, fuller, more rewarding." He then quoted *John 8:31,32,36:*

> *So Jesus was saying to those Jews who believed… "If you continue in My Word, then you are truly disciples of Mine; and you will know the Truth, and the Truth will make you free"… if* **the Son**, *therefore, shall make you free, you will be **free indeed** (John 8:31,32,36).*

I can remember so vividly how those words, which were meant to evoke encouragement and hope, hit deep in my soul like a splash of icy water on a cold wintry day. Rather than comfort and encourage, they stirred within me a very unsettling sense of doubt, fear, futility, even a little anger as I painfully recognized that I had known many experiences in my life, but never, not once, had true inner freedom been a part of any of them. There was always *something more* that needed to be fixed, overcome, abandoned. I was yet very much like a shackled prisoner, held captive by my own sinful compulsions, unstable emotions, and restless discontent. And this internal embattlement was complicated even more by chronic physical pain—relentless, oft intense, excruciating. That promise might *work* for others. But it didn't work for me. Even at this point, after I had been a Christian for several years and was faithfully, diligently studying the

Bible, going to church and Sunday school every week and prayer meetings on Wednesday evenings, I was not free, and I certainly was not *free indeed*. So either God was a liar, I was a helpless, hopeless mental case…**or** this promise was true—*even for me*!

Something happened to me that day. The words of Jesus in John 8 would not leave me. There was planted a seed of hope deep within my heart. I knew that *God was not a liar (Titus 1:2)*. And I also knew that He did not create me to be a helpless, hopeless emotional basket case:

> *For I know the plans that I have for you, declares the Lord, plans for welfare and not for calamity to give you a future and a hope…But in all these things we overwhelmingly conquer through Him who loved us and gave Himself up for us…I can do all things through Christ who strengthens me…for as many as are the promises of God, in Him, (Jesus) they are yes and amen to the glory of God (Jer. 29:11, Rom. 8:37, Phil. 4:13, 1 Cor. 1:20).*

Jesus promised freedom—mental, emotional, spiritual—to all who would *continue in His Word (John 8:31,32,36; Is. 61:1,2)*. Therefore, this promise *was* for me and for everyone who would *take God at His Word (Deut. 32:46,47)*. So the next morning in my quiet time, I bowed my head: *Lord, I believe; help Thou mine unbelief (Mark 9:24, KJV)*. I then asked God to help me to remain faithful, *continuing* in my pursuit of the Truths of His Word (*knowing* them, *obeying* them) until I entered that blessed promised land of soul liberation and true contentment—not just so I could be "free" to enjoy life and have more fun, but so that I could be free to truly *know, love, serve and glorify God with all my heart, soul, mind, and strength*, and, in that Christ-exalting freedom, to help others do the same (John 17:3,4; Matt. 22:37; 2 Cor. 5:20). With heart brimming with hope, I opened my Bible and took my first step onto God's glorious path of *freedom, peace and JOY in the Holy Spirit (John 8:31,32; Rom. 14:17)*.

(Please read "A Word from Mel," then complete the Bible Study Supplement for today.)

A Word from Mel

It is with joy and anticipation for what I believe God wants to do through it, that I affirm the writing of this Bible Study. It was only at my encouragement that Gloria pushed past many fears regarding her ability to take on such a project, as well as deep concerns over her "place" as a woman to write a book such as this. She has a strong desire to obey God in all things. Gloria clearly recognizes her role as my wife and helpmate and that God has placed her under my authority. She has sought my counsel and approval on every chapter. I know that she would never have pursued writing any book without total support and affirmation from me as her spiritual head. That I wish to give here.

I personally know of Gloria's desire to be totally committed to God and to His Word, walking in obedience to the Holy Spirit as He leads her daily. She is also committed to our marriage and to supporting me in building our home upon the principles of God's Word in which the love, compassion and forgiveness of Jesus permeates all. She *rises also while it is still night (Prov. 31:15)* in order to spend uninterrupted time in God's Word and prayer, then proceeds to give herself daily to the fulfillment of God's will for her life. As a diligent student of God's Word for more than twenty years, Gloria not only *knows* God's Word thoroughly, she seeks daily to *live* it, by depending upon God and His Grace, and looking to the Holy Spirit for guidance and strength. Though she would be the first to confess that she is far from perfect in doing this, I know her deepest desire is to walk always in *a manner worthy of the Lord (Eph. 4:1)*. I know of few others who so fervently and faithfully *press on*, persevering daily—come what may—towards this *upward, holy calling (Phil. 3:14)*.

As I think of Gloria, I think often of Paul's words: *Holding fast to the Word of God…even if I am being poured out as a drink offering upon the sacrifice and service of your faith, I rejoice and share my joy with you all (Phil. 2:17)*. She *pours her life* into praying for, loving and serving others and finds her greatest joy in so doing, and in sharing the joy of knowing Jesus with others.

God, according to His perfect providence, has taken Gloria through many incredibly difficult trials. I have watched her weather these oft *humanly* impossible situations with her strong faith and never-wavering desire to bring honor and glory to God through obedience to His Word—no matter the depth of difficulty or pain. Through these experiences, God has purified and strengthened her faith and equipped her to communicate to others His life-giving Truths. For Gloria **not** to share this godly wisdom would be tantamount to hoarding these treasures *(Matt. 25:14–30)*.

So it is with wholehearted affirmation that I put my hand of blessing upon this book and I join Gloria in praying earnestly that God will use it to strengthen, encourage, and bless all who join her in diligently reading, studying and applying the unfailing truths of God's Word. To God be the glory in and through and for all that is accomplished. It is ALL because of Him *(John 3:16)*.

In His matchless love,

Mel Blowers

Bible Study Supplement

Chapter One – Day Two — Introduction To Book One

1. Read John 8:31,32,36.

    a. What does God promise for all who will continue (hold to, abide) *in His Word?* (vs. 32)

    b. Do you believe that God will keep His Word?

    c. What do you think God means by continuing (holding to, abiding) *in His Word?*

2. Read Matt. 4:23,24.

    a. How many kinds of diseases did Jesus heal? (vs. 23)

    b. Name specifically just a few of the diseases Jesus healed. (vs. 24)

    c. Do you think Jesus still does this?

3. Read Heb. 13:8.

    a. Regarding Jesus' character and power, how is it compared to "yesterday" and "tomorrow"?

4. Read Titus 1:1,2.

    a. Can God lie? (vs. 2)

For far too long, most of us have been listening to many lies about God—His nature, His love, His redeeming power. We have thus been laboring under the heavy yoke of another "master" that God never intended us to serve. It is from this kind of bondage that Jesus wants to set us free and bring us to that glorious place of true *freedom, peace and joy in the Holy Spirit* (Rom. 15:13).

5. As you begin this study, take a few moments to think about your own life. Where are you in your spiritual journey? Are there still areas in which you are not yet *free?* Are there *burdens and bondages* that keep you shackled—impeding your progress and the fulfilling of God's good purposes for your life? Are you bound by an addiction, compulsion or other life-dominating habit that keeps you from *running with endurance the race set before you? (Heb. 12:1)*. Is there anything that continually haunts and harasses you and robs you of the liberty and joy of a Spirit-filled, victorious life?

    a. What are these areas? (Ask God to help you to be completely honest and specific).

    b. What is your hope regarding these in relationship to this Bible Study?

    c. Do you believe that it is possible for God to bring this *hope* into reality?

    d. Are you willing to make a commitment to God that with His help you will be faithful in your reading and studying of God's Word and in the completion of your daily assignments?

I pray that your heart is as full of joyful anticipation as mine as we begin this exciting journey into *freedom, peace and joy in the Holy Spirit…from glory to glory* (John 8:36, Rom. 14:17, 2 Cor. 3:18).

God's richest blessings as you *continue in His Word*, walking daily in its light, and experiencing more and more the warmth and radiance of all God's promises *in Christ (2 Cor. 1:20)*.

> *…for the walk of the righteous is like the light of dawn that grows brighter and brighter until the full day! (Prov. 4:18)*.

Write out a Bible verse that had special meaning to you today.

Based upon what you have learned today, write a prayer to God expressing the desires of your heart in applying these Truths to your life.

Chapter 1 — Day 3
From My Heart: The Making of This Bible Study

And they came to the other side of the sea, into the country of the Gerasenes. And when He had come out of the boat, immediately a man with an unclean spirit met Him, and he had his dwelling among the tombs. And constantly night and day, among the tombs and in the mountains, he was crying out and gashing himself with stones (Mark 5:1–5).

Soul Pain

Each of the following paragraphs describe an encounter with various people that God brought across my path over the past several years. There was an immediate bond in every situation for I could relate to what they were experiencing. God used these people to bring comfort and encouragement to my own heart and to show me that I was not alone in my personal battle against the strange, oft confusing *affliction*. There will always be a very special place in my heart for each of these precious people.

My husband and I sat at the dining room table with our new friends. They had graciously invited us to dinner and an evening of fellowship. The father of the family had a sweet smile and a kind, gentle spirit. But, we would learn as the evening progressed that behind the calm, outward appearance was a man who had known pain—real, unmitigating, soul-wrenching pain—for most of his life.

The phone rang. I could hear the sound of human wailing in the background. A concerned and troubled mother was distraught: "I don't know what to do with her. She is incoherent, screaming, and beating on herself! Her mouth is quivering, and she is shaking all over. Her eyes are glazed in a piercing angry glare. What can I do? Please help me!"

She knelt beside the bed in our guesthouse room on the campus of New Theological College in northern India where we were ministering. She said: "I came tonight to tell you the truth about me—about my life. It is embarrassing and shameful for me to tell it. But you are my 'parents' now. You need to know…" She then began to tell my husband and me the story of a life that had known the pain of total rejection, emotional upheavals, and a mental breakdown which drove her to attempt to take her life a number of times.

Sometimes Cindy doesn't tell me about her pain, but I find out a few hours later when her face and hands, even her hair turns a beet red. Then I know she's suffered one of the hellish episodes of excruciating pain. Few people understand. Too many Christians point to either "sin in her life" or "lack of faith." It's just not that simple.

An e-mail from one of our spiritual children shared this plea: "Thank you for your prayers. I desperately need them at this time. The oppression has been nearly unbearable…the enemy is still accusing me of many mistakes and I cannot seem to do anything right—even now. Everything is pressing down on me—continuously, relentlessly—to the point that I am not able to sleep. So the pain remains—through the day, through the night…I pray for you that you would be strengthened and encouraged in this spiritual warfare we all experience for different reasons. Now I understand it and hope that the Lord will help us both to make it through."

The very same day we received a similar e-mail from a dear friend in India: "I don't remember ever being 'well.' Even as a child, I suffered much pain…I had depression. When I was in engineering school, the pain was so great—so overwhelming, so confusing, I could not deal with it. I had to take pills and I slept a lot—it was the only way I could cope. When I found a job after that, I experienced more strange problems. I was taken to a doctor who diagnosed schizophrenia and prescribed antidepressants and tranquilizers. So I took them and got hooked on them. It destroyed my brain, my morale, my social life…I was like a wounded mad street dog wandering…and the drugs…they did not help. The side effects were sometimes worse than the mental torment. They only added to it, making it worse. I used to collapse with changing mental illness signs. In the summer it was very difficult with restlessness. Winter it was the opposite. Twenty-four hours in bed not able to do daily chores. It happened very badly this winter…I go through terrible emptiness and void that nothing interests me… Please forgive me for not writing long letter. I think it has to do with weariness of the mind. I was under evil Hindu influence as a child…Maybe that is the reason for the problems."

A few months later, I sat with this man's wife on a visit to India. I felt her pain as she described what the past twenty years of living with this man had been like. As I listened, I became convinced that her pain was no less severe than that of her husband's.

An excerpt from my own journal as I was seeking God to make sense of *the affliction*:

I don't know when it started for me: the inner turmoil, the confusion…the unmitigating pain. Since I can remember, life was hard for me. Even as a child I vividly recall feeling different from other kids. I felt things more deeply. When other kids hurt, I hurt. And I seemed to have a drive inside me—to do more, bigger, better—that could not be quieted.

The longer I live, the more acutely I become aware that there are many kinds of pain with which we must deal in life: physical pain, mental pain, emotional pain, spiritual pain. External pain, internal pain. But pain is pain. It hurts, regardless of its nature or specific cause.

The most common kind of pain of course is physical pain that comes from injury, infection, or a myriad of other temporary (non-terminal) dysfunctions of the body. That kind of pain is accepted by all as normal, a part of life. Everyone has it at times; everyone accepts it, and with time, every one gets through it.

There is the pain of sorrow at the loss of a loved one or other significant loss, failure, or disappointment. That, too, is considered normal and acceptable.

But there is another kind of pain that people don't like to talk about and certainly would never accept as *normal*. It is a pain that is much harder to diagnose and *heal*. But it is pain—very real and oft very intense—all the same. It is pain that emanates far deeper than what is visible, testable, or even explainable. It involves the deepest recesses of our human nature, the *pseuche,* or *soul* (mind, emotions, and will); that part of us that is not accessible through standard physical means, yet controls so much of who we are and how we respond to life. *Doctors can't heal a hurting, pain-wracked soul, and pills will never cure it.*

In most cases, people who suffer the unmitigating (yet very real) pain of a tormented soul are diagnosed with all sorts of physical and psychological labels—sicknesses and syndromes— to give a greater acceptability to the suffering. According to published reports a number of years ago by NORD (National Organization for Rare Diseases), there were more than *five thousand* rare diseases for which there was no known cause or cure. With a plethora of new diseases being *discovered* and added frequently to diagnostic medical journals, we can safely assume this number has grown by hundreds since that time. And with each new label comes the bad news that the illness is *incurable*, oft leading the one afflicted into further mental and emotional debilitation and a greater sense of inner despair.

But no one wants to talk about this kind of *sickness*—sickness that we cannot, with all our sophisticated advancements in medical science, *control* or *cure*. It involves very real physical symptoms to be sure. Job's boils were real! Yet, there was not one thing that any doctor or any medicine—no matter how sophisticated it may have been—could have done to *cure* those boils *(Job 2:7)*. Excruciating backaches are real, blinding, sick migraine headaches are real, deep arthritic joint and muscle pain is real, grueling chronic nausea and vertigo are real. But in many—if not most—cases of chronic pain that refuses to go away, there is a *soul* issue involved that has to do with things like our relationship with God, sin and the rebellious, depraved nature of our fallen heart, our level of faith, trust and obedience, or *vicious, merciless direct attacks from Satan, unclean spirits,* and *demonic influences*—topics that are taboo within our "politically correct" man-centered, modern-medicine/science-is-"god" culture. As a matter of fact, it is almost guaranteed social suicide for anyone to even broach these subjects. And, even though our society prides itself on being tolerant—loving and accepting of all—no matter their physical/mental condition, there is a very real and very ugly stigma associated with anyone who manifests mental or emotional (pseuche/soul-related) problems. They are often misunderstood, scorned and looked down upon by family and friends, and, sadly, far too often, medicated by health care professionals into a drug-induced stupor of passivity to help them cope and to keep them quiet. It is a recipe for disaster. The weaker ones often capitulate and become prescription drug addicts—debilitated *invalids,* as a result of the overuse of drugs, with all their further endless crippling side effects. Engaged in a continual battle to *find relief* (going from doctor to doctor, adjusting medications and trying desperately to deal with the never-ending side effects of the drugs), they, so often, withdraw from society. Devoid of genuine support and encouragement, and weakened by the complications with the drugs, they become unable to deal with their problems effectively, adding to their oppression and feelings of hopelessness.

The stronger, more determined ones become what our society terms *type-A* personalities; those who travel at breakneck speed through life, always busy, always achieving, always moving up the ladder of success in a vain attempt to *prove their worth* and gain the recognition their turmoiled soul demands, but never finding real peace, true contentment, or lasting satisfaction. I understand. I lived there for thirty-five long, torturous years!

I have a dear friend in Germany who sent an e-mail just the other day. I had asked about my cousin, John, who suffers from *type-A personality disorder*. In her e-mail she said: "I talk to John every week on the phone. He is, as always…always in a hurry. But nobody knows why."

With the ever-escalating pressure placed on all of us for recognition and the approval of others, type-A's would rather die than admit that they have even a hint of mental or emotional (soul) problems.

Another reason for the lack of understanding regarding pain related to the soul is because there truly is no way to describe the depth of this kind of pain. It is too deep, too pervasive, too overwhelming. Its demonic, tormenting intensity defies description with mere human words. Attempts to do so are looked upon with scornful judgment as exaggeration or a beg for pity. But the descriptions are not exaggerated. They are very real and very accurate to the degree that they can be verbalized. Truly, no one can understand the magnitude or the debilitating power of such pain, except those who have lived there. And even they find it impossible to articulate, even to others who themselves have lived there. So this sense of isolation—no one *really* understands—only adds to the confusion and intensity of the pain.

For many the battle has gone on too long; they are battle-weary and devoid of energy or the will to fight on. It just isn't worth it any longer. "Why try?" they conclude. "Nothing ever changes—no matter the time and effort invested." So they sink into an ever-deeper state of perceived hopelessness. This unmitigating oppression is most often diagnosed as chronic clinical depression, manic depression, or bipolar. Sadly, in so many cases, the progression does not stop there but slides even further into suicidal depression, for death appears to be the only way of escape from the relentless hellish internal torment.

When I was in this state, as is the case with many others, in my mind, I could identify irrational thoughts or feelings. I knew what I was doing wrong and what I needed to do to fix it. But the power to apply this knowledge to bring about the needed change could not be found. I, like so many others, tried everything that came down the pike that promised *deliverance…healing*: doctors and specialists of every kind, psychotherapy, drugs, clinics specializing in *this kind* of *affliction*, self-help books, endless retreats and seminars. But the healing did not come; deliverance never actualized; the pain remained. And my experience is not unique. We live in a world with a lot of really hurting, soul-tormented people.

In my case, as with a myriad of others, loved ones could see the effects of the pain, and they wanted to help. They tried. But their most sincere efforts brought no real help or lasting relief, so they began to feel a sense of failure and confusion as well. And the pain of the afflicted is inflicted upon another.

God alone knows how vast this throng of people of perpetual pain has become. It is impossible to count them because, as mentioned, most have been diagnosed with some kind of "acceptable" disease. And they are being treated with all sorts of drugs and other psychological therapies: Drugs that don't work and therapies that don't give lasting healing, only momentary relief as coping techniques, are applied. But coping is a dead-end street that gives no hope of real or lasting healing—a sentence that is all the more depressing!

I often thought, when I was in the most excruciating, prolonged times of suicidal depression, surely this must be what hell is like. Constant torment and pain with no way out and never a shred of relief.

The hardest part for me so often was the sense of isolation that is an inevitable part of the endless embattlement. It's a lonely place because you can't talk about it. To do so would mean ridicule (overt and covert), rejection, and loss of any respectful influence in the lives of others. It still is.

But that doesn't matter to me anymore. It doesn't matter what all those really together, politically correct people (who have no idea what this kind of pain is all about) think. What matters is what God thinks. And what matters is that God, in His infinite love, reached down and did what no doctor, no specialist, no drug could ever do. He touched this sin-sick soul of mine with His forgiveness, love, and healing compassion. Through the glorious miracle of salvation (the new birth) and the Truths of His Word, He gave me a n*ew life (2 Cor. 5:17)* in which there was an immediate assurance of God's love, acceptance and eternal life with Him in Heaven along with an ever increasing sense of purpose, peace, and a blessed hope that refused to be extinguished. I owe a huge debt of gratitude to my Heavenly Father, one which I know I will never be able to adequately repay in the limited days I have upon this earth. But I have dedicated my life to doing what I can with as many as I can for as long as God grants me the breath to do so.

Since I began to do this, God has brought across my path literally hundreds of men and women who suffer from the same inner embattlement, people for whom there has been no relief, no lasting healing, or deliverance; people for whom even the dim flicker of hope has been extinguished. I've shared my testimony and the precious Truths from God's Word with countless numbers of these, and I've seen the great mercy and love of God rekindle that flame and bring new life and victory time and time again.

But so many more have never experienced this kind of healing that only God can give. They haven't experienced it because no one has ever told them about it. Or maybe the pain was so great when they were told, they could not believe it because the history of past failures had totally obliterated any reason to hope again. So, in fear of yet another failure, they withdrew and attempted to fight it alone, growing weaker and weaker until the chronic pain became a chronic disability, resulting in becoming all the more shackled to the overpowering internal torment. For others, they have nearly killed themselves running all the harder to prove their ability to overcome! For precious souls in either camp, life becomes a relentless, tumultuous battle of inner turmoil, mental torment, and excruciating pain that refuses to go away, no matter how many pills they take, surgeries they have, seminars they attend, or therapists they see. The pain remains.

These are not crazy people. Quite the contrary. Most of the people thus tormented are extremely gifted. But because their pain is so great, even their gifts have been shackled and kept from the full expression God desires. In reality we all experience *soul pain* in one form or another. It's the universal reality of living in a fallen world. But for some, the magnitude of this kind of suffering is disproportionately more severe. I have a huge heart for all so afflicted. And God has an even bigger heart.

> *Blessed be the God of our Lord Jesus Christ, the Father of mercies and the God of all comfort; who comforts us in all our afflictions so that we may be able to comfort those who are in any affliction with the comfort with which we ourselves are comforted by God (2 Cor. 1:3,4).*

That is why I am sharing my testimony. That is why I am writing this study, a project that has been more than twenty years in the making. It hasn't been an easy undertaking. The associated conflicts, trials, and spiritual warfare (the enemy fighting against God's plans) have been great every step of the way. So many times I was tempted to abandon it all together. But I could not do that. God in His infinite mercy and grace had done so much for me. His blessed Holy Spirit had taught me so much that had brought stability and peace to my tormented soul. Now He was asking me to *comfort others in their affliction with the same comfort with which (I) had been comforted by God (2 Cor. 1:3,4)*. How could I do otherwise? With a heart filled with gratitude to God and a deep love for my precious brothers and sisters, I so often fell on my knees and sought His divine guidance and enablement that this project might be completed, and be a blessing and encouragement to many precious hurting souls. I continue to pray this.

How often the Words of Jesus resonate in my mind:

> *If you continue in My Word, then are you my disciples indeed and you shall know the Truth and the Truth shall set you free…If the Son, therefore, shall set you free, you shall be free indeed… then Jesus entered the synagogue and stood up to read…The Spirit of the Lord is upon me, for He has anointed me to bring good news to the afflicted…to bind up the brokenhearted, to proclaim liberty to captives and freedom to prisoners…to comfort all who mourn, giving them a garland instead of ashes, the oil of gladness instead of mourning, the mantle of praise instead of a spirit of fainting…they will be called oaks of righteousness, the planting of the Lord, that He may be glorified (John 8:31,32,36; Luke 4:16–19; Is. 61:1–3).*

Yes, Jesus came to give all mental and emotional—soul-tormented—people *liberation, unconditional love, unspeakable joy, and that precious, priceless peace that passeth all human understanding* so that in that liberated love, joy, and peace, they can begin to minister His same life-giving Truths to others *(Is. 61:1; Jer. 31:3; 1 Pet. 1:8; Phil. 4:7; 2 Cor. 5:18–20).*

It is my heartfelt prayer that God, in His infinite mercy and love, through the power of His Word, will minister healing grace to every precious soul who goes through this study with an open, searching, receptive heart. Jesus died and rose again to secure for us not only forgiveness of sins and eternal life but also the power to live a joyful, Spirit-filled, victorious life here on earth— including victory over *afflictions of the soul*—depression, addiction, compulsions, drivenness, discontent, and every other form of oppressive internal bondage *(Col. 1:27–2:3; Eph. 1:17–21; Rom. 8:27; Ps. 40:1–3; Ps. 46:1–5; Matt. 19:26; Gen.18:14a, etc.).* May God help us all to be diligent students, to *learn and grow* in His precious, *life-giving Truths*; to *take Him at His Word* (obedience) that we might become *trophies of His Grace, oaks of righteousness, the planting of the Lord…a vast army, strong, equipped, and pressing on for the advancement of the Kingdom God and the JOY of all (Deut. 32:46,47; Is. 61:3; 2 Tim. 2:21; Is. 25:3; 2 Tim. 3:16,17; Phil. 3:12; Matt. 28:19,20).*

Bible Study Supplement

Chapter 1 — Day 3 — From My Heart: The Making of This Bible Study

1. Read Ps. 69:13–20, 29,32,33.

    a. To whom does the psalmist turn in his time of distress and suffering? (vs. 13)

    b. Upon what is he counting? (three things—it could be four, depending upon your version of the Bible and how you list them) (vs. 13b,16,29b).

    c. What words of encouragement does he give? (vs. 32)

    d. Why can he offer this encouragement? (vs. 33)

2. Read Is. 41:8–10, 20.

    a. What promising words does God give to all His children? (vs. 9b,10)

    b. Why is He going to do this? (vs. 20)

Psalm 107 is a beautiful story of the faithfulness of God in delivering His rebellious children from manifold troubles. I still read it often to remind me of God's mercy, longsuffering and compassion. We'll just look at a few verses today.

3. Read Ps. 107:10–20.

    a. Why were the people imprisoned in their own misery and chains? (vs. 11,17a)

    b. What did the Lord do when they cried out to Him? (vs. 13,14)

    c. How did the Lord <u>heal</u> them? (vs. 20a)

Be sure, God still uses His Word to minister wisdom, grace and healing. That is why He lovingly urges us to come to Him daily, to sit at His feet, to listen, learn, be strengthened and empowered by the Truths of His precious, powerful infallible Word (Prov. 8:33,34; Lk. 10:43).

In the Old Testament, we read about a city called Gilead. This was a very special city established by God as a strong, fortified refuge where people who were being pursued by their enemies or those who were distressed in body, soul, mind or spirit could flee for safety and protection. Within this city were found springs of *healing balm—the balm of Gilead.*

Gilead is symbolic of God. The springs of healing balm reflect God's Word that has the power to heal the pain inflicted by the inevitable trials and tribulations of life in a sinful, fallen world. God wants to be our *Gilead*. He wants to be our refuge, our place of peace and protection where we can "run to" and find rest and comfort. His Word soothes and heals hurting wounds. I wonder where we would be if we accepted God's invitation to run to Gilead, the refuge of His presence, mercy and grace, instead of to food, to the mall, a movie, a plethora of drugs, or yet another "specialist." God is the source of all lasting healing and joy. Let's be wise and accept His invitation to *run to* and dwell in the land of Gilead, in the peace and security of His presence, protection, and guidance, applying freely the soothing balm of His Word—knowing it, obeying it—for our healing and comfort.

Write out a Bible verse that had special meaning to you today.

Based upon what you have learned today, write a prayer to God expressing the desires of your heart in applying these Truths to your life.

Chapter 1 — Day 4
Building a Strong House of Indestructible Faith
Laying the Foundation

> *Therefore, everyone who hears these words of Mine, and acts upon them may be compared to a wise man, who **built his house upon the rock**. And the rain descended and the floods came, and the winds blew and burst against it; and yet it did not fall; for it had been **founded upon the rock** (Matt. 7:24,25).*

And when He saw the multitudes, He went up on the mountain…And He began to teach them… Blessed are those who hunger and thirst for righteousness, for they shall be satisfied. Blessed are the pure in heart, for they shall see God (Matt. 5:6,8).

Therefore, everyone who hears these words of Mine, and acts upon them may be compared to a wise man who built his house upon the rock. And the rain descended, and the floods came, and the winds blew and burst against that house, and yet it did not fall, for it had been founded upon the rock. And everyone who hears these words of Mine, and does not act upon them, will be like a foolish man, who built his house upon the sand. And the rain descended, and the floods came and the winds blew and burst against that house; and it fell, and great was its fall (Matt. 7:13) .

As you read in "From My Heart," this study has been more than twenty years in the making. There are many reasons for this. Primarily, it was because I needed to *study to show (myself) approved, handling accurately the Word of Truth (2 Tim. 2:15)*. There was so much I did not know; so much I needed to study and apply to my life. I did not want to bring shame to the Name of God by misrepresenting His precious Word. Nor did I want to be like the Pharisees of whom Jesus said: *This people draw near with their words, and honor Me with their lips, but their hearts are far from Me (Matt. 15:8)…Woe to you, scribes and Pharisees, hypocrites! For you are like whitewashed tombs which on the outside appear beautiful, but inside they are full of uncleanness" (Matt. 23:27 KJV/NASB)*. I needed time for God to purify my heart by the *washing of His Word* and *renewing of my mind (Eph. 5:26; Rom. 12:2)*, so that I might be as clean on the inside as the words I proclaimed on the outside *(2 Tim. 2:21)*.

Secondly, I came to salvation later in life, at the age of thirty-five. By this time many strongholds of worldly thinking and demonic deceptions were well entrenched. This carnal mindset continually influenced my interpretation of situations, resulting in unbiblical responses and habits, and with them, repetitive failures. Being fully aware of the grave responsibility God ascribes to one who aspires to *teach others (James 3:1)*, I knew that personal sinful desires and motivations had to be exposed by the Word of God, repented of, and cast out. It would be hypocritical to teach others what I, myself, was not, by the grace of God, practicing *(Eph. 4:1,2; 2 Tim. 2:21)*.

The third reason follows the principle of *Luke 14:28–30:*

For which one of you, when he wants to build a tower, does not first sit down and calculate the cost, to see if he has enough to complete it? Otherwise, when he has laid a foundation, and is not able to finish, all who observe it begin to ridicule him, saying, "This man began to build and was not able to finish" (Luke 14:28–30).

We live in an age big on words and promises but infinitely small on "delivering"—standing behind the words, fulfilling the promises. There is a plethora of instructional, inspirational seminars and self-help books by the myriad that offer everything from dynamic nutrition and fitness programs that promise to reverse the aging process and give us strong, pain-free, healthy bodies, to having a blissful, conflict-and-trial-free marriage, to instant deliverance from compulsive and addictive behaviors, to "name it and claim it" financial prosperity, to losing weight on the ice cream and cookies diet! Experts and self-proclaimed authorities abound, wooing the public with their alluring propaganda but, sadly, delivering little, to the hurt of many. I did not want to contribute to this pain. But even more crucial was the fact that as a professing Christian and disciple of Jesus, it was not merely *my* name and reputation that was at stake, it was God's Holy Name (Ezek. 36:20,21) that was put on the line. It was His Word and promises that I was representing. To bring reproach to His precious Name through a life of duplicity—claiming to have faith and to being led by the Holy Spirit, yet living according to fleshly lusts, dependence on self and consequently repeated failure, would be the epitome of hypocrisy with its inevitable result—becoming a *stumbling block* for many *(Matt. 18:8)*. It grieved my heart to even think about being a part of that.

Therefore, in earnest prayer and led by the Holy Spirit, I set my heart to build my own house of faith according to the Word of God that I knew (because *God* said so - *Matt. 7:25)* would stand strong in times of trials and difficulties so that others might *see and believe (Psalm 40:3)*. With God's help, hard ground was broken up, debris removed, and foundational stones carefully and securely anchored into the solid rock of Jesus: His life, teachings, death, and resurrection. In time, fortified walls were raised up and rooms within were built that have withstood many a ravaging gale. Finally, after fourteen years of working diligently building and fortifying this *house of faith*, God spoke to my heart: "It is time…"; time to step out, and in the same *faith* that built the house, write a study that would share with others what God, through His precious Word had taught me. These, then, would be able to build their own houses of faith that would stand firm and strong through the storms of life…and they, in turn, would begin to teach yet others.

There was, however, a *seven-year* delay after God gave the word to proceed, to actually beginning a serious writing of the study, stretching the preparation/waiting period to more than twenty years. That delay was due to the reason given in yesterday's meditation: *soul pain.* I was agonizingly aware of the cruel, destructive stigma associated with exposing weaknesses—especially those society quickly judges as being of a mental or emotional nature. The fear of rejection and ridicule—the social suicide—was far greater than my fledgling faith could endure at that point. I had invested too much in perfecting my successful, achievement-oriented image. To let down my guard and expose the real condition of my soul—unstable, in torment, driven, discontent—for all those years would undoubtedly result in yet more pain associated with the loss of admiration and popularity. I did not yet then recognize a sinful need for the *approval of men (Gal. 1:10)*. That was, undoubtedly, the greatest barrier in keeping me from stepping out in faith to answer God's call. But, all praise to God, through the conviction of the Holy Spirit and the strength found in His Word to overcome the fear, that sin was exposed, confessed, and forgiveness and repentance was sought and received. My heart is filled with praise to God for His *amazing grace* in *setting this captive free (Is. 61:1)*, and keeping me daily in the freedom of forgiveness, as I share His love and redeeming grace with others.

It was during these last seven years of waiting and preparation that I was able to really understand what Jesus meant when He spoke of the necessity of building our *house of faith* upon the *solid rock* of the *pure and unadulterated teaching* of the Word of God. Some of these foundational Truths that are paramount if we are to build strong, invincible houses are:

Who is God? – His true nature and character.
Why did God create the universe…man…me?
What does it mean that I have been created *in the image of* God?
How does this affect my everyday life?
God's sovereign rule over the universe...man.
The necessity of a personal relationship with God.
The problem of sin and separation from God.
The total depravity of the human heart apart from salvation and the redemptive work of Jesus.
Jesus! Who He *really* is and what He has done for us.
The necessity of the *new birth*.
What is "saving faith"?
What is progressive sanctification and why is it so crucial?
Who is Satan – his true nature, character, purposes and plans
The person and ministry of the Holy Spirit
The essential role of faith and grace in the salvation/sanctification process.
The very real existence of a literal Heaven and Hell and that we all will spend eternity in one place or the other.

I could now recognize that my original understanding of these crucial foundational doctrines was greatly tainted by false teachings and a lazy neglect of a serious study of God's Word. That was why my vulnerable *house of faith*, with all its weak, self-construed plans and aspirations had, on more than one occasion, come crashing down…and *great was the fall (Matt. 7:27)*.

However, having at last established a firm, indestructible foundation anchored in the Truths of God's Word, I can confidently tell you, that those who *listen intently*, and, by the power of the Holy Spirit, *carefully obey (James 1:25)* the promises and Truths that God gives us in His infallible Word, will remain strong and steadfast in secure houses of His love, mercy, and grace—come what may!

Because the Bible is an inexhaustible source of life-giving Truths, we will barely scratch the surface of its *rich fields (Matthew 13:44)* in this study. It is, however, my fervent prayer that the discovery, or rediscovery, of some of the most precious gems of godly wisdom found in this study will but whet the appetite for a lifetime of *seeking, finding*, and joyously *living out* yet more and more *priceless treasures (Matt. 7:7; John 13:17; Matt. 13:44–46; Prov. 24:3,4)*.

To help us get started in this glorious pursuit, the study has been divided into three parts. Part One involves laying a firm foundation for our house of faith, for without this, we will be building upon sand and we can *be sure* that the house we construct will never stand in times of great deception and distresses of every kind as we are currently experiencing in these *wicked, end-time days (2 Thess. 2:9–12; 2 Tim. 3:1–5)*. This is, therefore, the most crucial part of our construction project. As we take the time to diligently establish a strong, firm foundation, the rest of the building project will be successful *(Matt. 7:25)*. In Part Two we will construct secure walls of yet more stabilizing, protective Truths and begin the joyous task of filling the rooms *with precious and pleasant riches (Prov. 24:4)*. Then, when our *strong house of indestructible faith* is complete we can move about within its walls with *confidence, freedom and JOY*, never fearing the *descending rains of adversity* or the threatening *winds of opposition and trials (Heb. 10:35–39; John 8:36; Rom. 14:17; Matt. 7:24,25)*.

*Therefore everyone who hears these words of Mine, and acts upon them, may be compared to a wise man, who built his house upon the rock. And the rain descended, and the floods came, and the winds blew, and burst against that house; and yet it did not fall, for it had been **founded upon the rock** (Matt. 7:24–26).*

Bible Study Supplement

Chapter 1 – Day 4 — Building a Strong House of Indestructible Faith

1. Read Matt. 5:6,8.

    a. Who is truly blessed? (vs. 6)

How long has it been since you really hungered and thirsted after righteousness? May God help us to develop a true heartfelt yearning for godly wisdom and holiness.

    b. Who else is blessed? (vs. 8)

As God looks on your heart today, what does He see? Is it truly pure—cleansed by the washing of His Word and purified by the blood of Jesus (through true repentance)? God wants to do this mighty work in all of us, so that we might experience true soul liberation and in that freedom, an abundant life of purpose, meaning, and fruitfulness... *that our JOY might be full*...and God's kingdom advanced (John 8:31,32,36; John 10:10b; John 15:11; Ps. 40:3; Matthew 28:19,20). If you have not yet come to the place where you have a personal relationship with God, and do not in reality even understand what this is all about, do not fear or be ashamed. We've all stood in that place and it is only by the Grace of God that any of us are members of God's family. And that same Grace is offered freely to you. God loves you so much (John 3:16) and He longs to have a relationship with you. In the next several days, we will be looking at how you can accept God's invitation to join His eternal family.

2. Read Psalm 119:1–5, 9–11.

    a. Who is blessed? (vs. 1,2) (four characteristics—note especially 2b)

    b. For what does the psalmist long? (vs. 5)

    c. How can a young man keep his way pure? (vs. 9b)

    d. What does the psalmist set his heart to do? (vs. 10a)

    e. What does he ask God to do for him? (vs. 10b)

    f. What has the psalmist hidden in his heart? (vs. 11a)

    g. Why? (vs. 11b)

3. Read Matthew 7:24–29.

    a. What kind of man is wise? (does two things) (vs. 24a)

    b. Why was this man's house so strong? (vs. 24b)

Note: Jesus is very clear here that it isn't enough just to hear God's Word. We must act on it (obey it), to be wise and strong.

    c. What do you think Jesus meant by building the house upon the *rock*? What is the *rock*?

d. What happened to this man's house when the rain descended, the floods came, and the winds burst against it? (vs. 25) Why? (vs. 25b)

Note: The solid rock to which Jesus is referring is the inerrant, infallible Word of God. A foundational teaching throughout the Word of God is the message of God's Holiness and man's sinfulness that separates him from God and how God sent Jesus to bridge this gap. Jesus paid the penalty for man's sin (death—Jesus died on the cross for our sins) so that man can now enjoy a loving, forgiven, intimate relationship with God filled with His blessings and JOY. (More about this in upcoming lessons).

e. How does Jesus describe the man who does not act on (obey) God's Word? (vs. 26)

f. What happened to this man's house when the rains descended? (vs. 27)

g. Describe the fall. (vs. 27b)

Think about the last time you faced the howling winds, rising floods, and beating rain of adversity. What happened to your house of faith? Did it remain firm, strong, and secure, or did it come falling down with a great crash? God wants us all to live in fortified, warm, and secure houses of faith that will stand firm and indestructible in the midst of even the most vicious attacks against it.

h. How did Jesus teach? (vs. 29)

i. Do you believe Jesus still has the authority to fulfill every promise He makes?

Write out a Bible verse that had special meaning to you today.

Based upon what you have learned today, write a prayer to God expressing the desires of your heart in applying these Truths to your life.

Chapter 1 — Day 5
In the Beginning...GOD! — Part 1

The heavens declare the glory of God, and their expanse is declaring the work of His hands (Ps. 19:1).

Hear, O Israel! The Lord is God, the Lord is One! I am the LORD, *and there is no other; Apart from me there is no God (Ps. 19:1; Deut. 6:4; Is. 45:5).*

Foundational Truth # 1: In the beginning...GOD!

There is a God who created the great expanse of the heavens and the earth and everything and everyone in it, and this God, the only one, true God, still sovereignly reigns and rules over His Creation, directing the activities of all that happens in it (Gen. 1:1; Col. 1:17).

The proud, stubborn, and rebellious may continue to be *arrogant, obstinate, and disobedient (Is. 30:9–11; Jer. 16:9-13)*, scoffers may scoff *(2 Pet. 3:3,4)*, the *naive and lazy* may bury their heads *(Prov. 1:22)*, idolaters may *run to their idols (Jer. 11:9-13, 18:15; Is. 57:13)*, philosophers and wise men may *philosophize and debate (1 Cor. 1:18-25)*, and the evolutionists may shout their ludicrous, contradictory theories from the highest mountain *(Ps 2:1,2; Prov. 1:7)*, but none of that will change the very basic, fundamental Truth: There is a God who created this universe and everything and everyone in it. This same sovereign Creator God also has an eternal plan for the universe and everyone in it; and this plan—God's plan—*will not be thwarted (Col. 1:16,17; Rev. 4:8-11; Is. 45:5-7)*. God's plan is a good and loving plan *(Jer. 29:11-14)*. God created us to be a part of this beautiful plan and He wrote a book to tell us how we can do this. That book is called the Bible and it tells us all that we need to know to experience daily the fullness of God's love and peace. When we read this book and obey this book, our lives will have meaning and purpose and value and...our *joy will be complete (Jer. 29:11–14; John 15:11)*.

But, there is an enemy to God's wonderful plan. His name is Satan. And he has a plan as well. His plan is to keep us from God and from knowing and obeying His loving will. The devil's plan is wicked and brings evil and destruction into every person's life who follows it. Many people don't understand about these two plans. They have never heard the true story of the creation of the world, of Satan's rebellion against God, and later, through his temptation, man's prideful rebellion as well. They have not heard what happened as a result of this terrible history-altering revolt—the introduction of sin into the world along with its awful consequences—separation from God...*death*. But most sadly, they've never had anyone tell them that God, being so unfathomably loving, had already made a plan for His rebellious, wayward sons and daughters to come back and to enter into relationship with Him again, a forever relationship in which His love, grace and JOY would only grow in their hearts, *from glory to glory (2 Cor. 3:18)*.

Since so many people have never heard the real Truth of God's love, they get all confused about the evil and suffering in the world. They mistakenly blame God for causing the suffering, which is a huge lie and keeps many from coming to know His redeeming love, provision, and protection. One of the main purposes of this study is to expose that lie—and many other lies—that Satan has foisted upon so many by various means of deception, so that precious souls will begin to understand the *height and depth and breadth of God's love (Eph. 3:18),* and through this understanding will gladly, with deep gratitude, choose for themselves to enter into, and live daily in the beauty, security and joy of an intimate, loving relationship with their Creator Father. We'll talk more about all these things in later chapters, but for today we just want to lay the first solid, anchoring stone into the foundation of our indestructible *house of faith* that we are building:

In the beginning, God!

We need to settle once and for all the unarguable, irrefutable fact:

God, the Creator and sovereign ruler of the universe, does not have to prove Himself.
He's already done that!

The heavens declare the glory of God and their expanse is declaring the work of His hands; day to day pours forth His speech (Ps. 19:1,2).

The immensity and perfect order of our universe—along with thousands of *other infallible proofs within it (Acts 1:3)*—have proven through the ages the existence and sovereign rule of God.

Consider for just a moment the vastness of the universe with its incalculable galaxies of stars and planets beyond our own immense solar system!

The expanse of creation is staggering. Have you ever reflected on the size of the universe?

A ray of light travels *186,000 miles a second*, so a beam of light from here will reach the moon in a second and a half. Imagine traveling that fast! You could reach Mercury in four and a half minutes, Jupiter in thirty-five minutes. If you decided to go farther, you could reach Saturn in about an hour, but it would take four years and four months to make it to the nearest star. Traveling just to the edge of our galaxy, the Milky Way, would take you about 100,000 years! If you could count the stars as you travel, they would number about 100 billion in the Milky Way alone. If you wanted to explore other galaxies, you would have billions to choose from. The size of our universe is understandably incomprehensible. If you refuse to recognize a Creator, it's difficult to explain how this marvelous, intricate, immeasurable universe came into being (MacArthur, John, *First Love*, (Victor Books, Wheaton, IL, 1995, pg. 22, emphasis, mine).

I learned of another mind-boggling statistic that illustrates the vastness of the universe and God's indisputable role in not only creating it but in keeping it in perfect order day by awesome day when watching a video entitled: "The Young Age of the Earth" by Dr. Kent Hovind. He said that our solar system, the Milky Way, contains more than 100,000,000,000 (one hundred billion!) stars, and the Milky Way is but one very small "page" of God's huge catalogue of the heavens. There are literally more than a billion other galaxies, most of which are many times larger than our galaxy! Dr. Hovind said that if the stars (nearly all of which are hundreds of times larger than our sun, which is hundreds of times larger than our earth) were evenly divided among every inhabitant of the earth today, every man, woman and child would have more than two trillion stars!...And *God knows them all by name! (Is. 40:26).*

God has further proven Himself in the complex, perfect design of countless other entities within His vast creation. Paul Bartz of Creation Moments has written eight volumes of books on the unique design of plants and animals that totally defy evolutionary explanation. It is scientifically absurd to attempt to explain these unique creatures—of which there are thousands—apart from intelligent design by a Creator. As I was studying for this lesson, I read about hundreds of these amazing creatures. I could not put the books down because the information was so fascinating and the evidence so irrefutably supportive of God's incredible, far-beyond-human-capability design. It is interesting to note that in recent years, some of the most renowned, most highly respected within the scientific community today—the majority of whom are non-Christians!—are standing up and rejecting the theory of evolution, confessing that it is scientifically impossible to explain all the uniqueness in plant, animal, and human life without "intelligent design."

I found it nearly impossible to select just a few examples to give as illustrations here. There were so many truly awe-inspiring in design and function—plants, animals, birds, fish—that clearly and unarguably defy every evolutionary theory ever espoused. (Please see the appendix, "Resources," for more information on how to get these wonderful books from Creation Moments Ministries. You will be amazed and reminded once again of the incredible greatness and irrefutable ingenuity of our Creator God!)

One such creature (that defies evolutionary explanation) is the large-eyed rove beetle. Like many other insects, this beetle can walk on water…Should you see the large eyed rove beetle you will notice that he glides gracefully across the water, stops, turns, and starts up again without moving any part of his body! How does this work?

The rove-beetle has special glands that produce a chemical that changes the surface tension of the water—something like detergent. When the surface tension of the water near his back feet is different from the surface tension of the water near his front feet the beetle is pulled forward. Such unique method of movement requires a sophisticated interdependent functioning of both hydrodynamics and chemistry that defies mindless, unintelligent evolutionary processes (Bartz, Paul A, Letting God Create Your Day, Volume 2, ColorSong Productions, Inc. St. Paul, MN 55112, pg. 188).

Another of God's endless masterful creations is the European Water Spider. (God must have smiled when He created this one!) This amazing little creature swims up to the top of the water, does a somersault to catch a bubble of air which he holds over his tummy where his breathing holes are and swims to the bottom of the lake, weaving a silken screen as he goes. Then he drops the bubble into the screen, goes to the top and gets another bubble of air, drops it inside the screen. He keeps getting bubbles of air until he builds a big bubble of air in the water. Then he goes in and *lives there!* (Piper, John, "God's Pleasure in Creation," Teaching Tape Series, <u>The Pleasures of God</u>, Desiring God Ministries, Minneapolis, MN).

My personal favorite of God's endless examples of divinely creative ingenuity is the process of metamorphosis—a process which also baffles the most learned of scientists. An ugly gray larva (caterpillar) builds a cocoon (chrysalis) around itself. Its body then completely disintegrates into a thick, pulp-like liquid. Days or weeks later an adult insect emerges—one that is dramatically different, and, as in the case of a butterfly, gloriously beautiful. (Eighty percent of all insects pass through this metamorphosis process.) Food, habitat, and behavior of the larva differ drastically from the adult, once again defying every possible explanation based upon the debunked theory of evolution (Brown, Walt, PH.D, <u>In the Beginning</u>, Center for Scientific Creation, Phoenix, AZ 85016, pg. 15,16,64,65).

And there are literally thousands of other complex, uniquely designed animals, birds, and flora that possess similar evolution defying characteristics, such as the Venus flytrap, the incredible plant that snatches its lunch by closing around it instantly through astonishingly rapid cell growth; a sophisticated Bombardier beetle whose defensive system of protection would rival even the most sophisticated military strategy; and the incredible aerodynamic abilities of the tiny hummingbird (I love this one!)… and so many more! I hope you will consider getting a couple of the inexpensive paperback books from

Creation Moments. You will be blessed to be reminded of the incredible genius of our awesome Creator God.

Before I close, I want to mention just one more mind-boggling example within God's amazing creation that never ceases to cause me to stand in praiseworthy awe every time I gaze upon one. It is the beautiful, yet oft inexplicable, waterfall. Have you ever wondered how a mammoth waterfall on or near the top of a mountain can heave thousands of gallons of water per minute over its vast rocky face hour after hour, day after day, and never run dry? What is the source of that vast supply of water? It would be one thing if the waterfall were in a basin fed by dozens of tributaries, but from where does a mountaintop waterfall draw? Every time I see one of these, I cannot help but lift my eyes to heaven in thanksgiving for God's love and majesty in creating and maintaining such beauty. I also cannot help but think of *Job 38* in which God talks about the *secret storehouses of the water and snow (Job 38:22,28,34,37).*

These *infallible proofs* in themselves would be more than enough to prove God's existence, His intelligent design of the Universe and His sovereign rulership over it. But there's yet one more that pushes one step beyond the arguments of even the most stubborn skeptic—it is His masterpiece of creation, His crowning glory—the human body and mind created…*in His Image*. We'll take a look at this tomorrow, but for today, let's ask God to "open our eyes" as we go through our day today—and the night ahead of us—that we might see the beauty of His creation and His keeping power all around us…

Lift up your eyes on high and see who has created these stars; The One who leads forth their host by number, He calls them all by name; because of the greatness of His might and the strength of His power, not one of them is missing…When I consider your heavens, the work of your fingers, the moon and the stars, which you have set in place, what is man that you are mindful of him…that you care for him…O Lord, our Lord, how majestic is your Name in all the earth…I will praise you, O Lord, with all my heart; I will tell of all your wonders…The heavens (and earth and all they contain!) declare the glory of God, and their expanse confirms the work of His hands, day to day pours forth speech! (Is. 40:26; Ps. 8:3; Ps. 19:1,2, 8:3).

Bible Study Supplement

Chapter 1 – Day 5 — In the Beginning…God! – Part 1

I love the Book of Job. There is so much in this book! I hope you will take time after this study is over to read through it. You will be comforted, encouraged, amazed, and your faith will be strengthened. We only have time today to look at one key chapter in the Book of Job that reveals much of the beauty and awesome sovereignty of God through His Creation - Job 38.

Before we begin to look into this chapter, however, let's take a moment to consider the background behind it. It is as if God had already foreseen (which, of course, He had) the day when the devil would deceive and blind the eyes of many to even the obvious Truths He had so majestically displayed before them through His creation. Just prior to this chapter, there had been a good deal of dialogue between Job and his three friends—much like the *dialogue* between people today discussing evolution. They had all been trying to *explain* God—His nature and character according to how they perceived Him in their prideful, fallen state—rather than according to His true holy nature as revealed in His Word. This was a very serious mistake. It is like a fly understanding and *explaining* astrophysics…or the complexity of man. It is not possible. And so it is with God: *As far as the heavens are from the earth so are My (God's) thoughts from your thoughts and My ways from your ways…oh, the depth of the riches both of the wisdom and knowledge of God! How unsearchable are His judgments and unfathomable His ways! For who has known the mind of the Lord, or who became His counselor?...for from Him and through Him and to Him are all things. To Him be the glory* (Is. 55:9; Rom. 11:33,34,36).

It is the same mistake that we often make even today. God can't be explained apart from the revelations He has given us in His Word. All other explanations will be tainted by a proud, selfish, sinful nature, ours and that of the ones to whom we are trying to make our explanation. So to set the record straight about who He is and His supremacy over all His creation, God begins to ask Job some questions. They are the same questions God would ask any skeptic today if he would take the time to sit down before Him and listen as He speaks. To make His point, God uses sarcasm to show the prideful vanity and foolishness of assuming a position equal to God. He confronts this kind of haughty vanity a number of times, i.e., verse 21: *You know, for you were born then, and the number of your days is great.* Obviously, Job and his friends weren't born then (when God created the world), yet they had made a number of statements that put them on a level with God or even one step above, as if they actually knew how to handle things better than God. We still do this today to our own hurt, don't we? It's an easy trap into which to fall. We need to take God's loving warning about the dangers of this—assuming a position (wisdom, understanding) equal to God. It's a formula for disaster because we are sinful and our thoughts and assumptions are skewed by our own pride and selfishness and by sin's deceptions so that we often come to very wrong and hurtful conclusions. So we need to come daily to God and seek His wisdom and guidance because He knows and understands everything about every person, just as He has understood…*from the beginning.*

Just prior to this conversation, Job had requested an audience with God. *Oh that I might plead with God as a man with his neighbor!* (Job 16:20). God granted him that request. And God gives us that same opportunity each and every time we go to Him in prayer or open His Word and listen as He speaks to us. Let's imagine for a few moments that it is us to whom God has granted the request to sit before Him in His presence, and let Him speak to our hearts.

1. Read Job 38.

Answer the following questions as if you were sitting before God as He talks to you (just as you, in reality, are now doing).

Note: You don't have to look up or reread these verses, just answer the questions.

a. Where were you when I laid the foundations of the earth? (vs. 4)

b. Who set the measurements of the earth? (vs. 5)

c. Who stretched the equator all around it? (vs. 5)

I will give the text here so you can answer this next question because it is a beautiful picture of how we should respond each day we awaken and behold the awesome wonder and beauty of God's creation:

...the morning stars sang together, and all the sons of God (angels) shouted for joy (Job 38:7)

d. How did the "morning stars" and the "angels" respond to God's glorious creation of the universe? (vs. 7)

e. Who enclosed the sea into its place? (vs. 8)

f. Have you ever in your life commanded the morning or caused the dawn to awaken the day? (vs. 12)

g. Have you entered into the springs of the sea? (vs. 16)

h. Have you understood the expanse of the earth? (vs. 18)

i. Have you entered the storehouses of the snow…or hail? (vs. 22)

j. Who has created the path of the thunderbolt? (vs. 25)

k. (I love this one!) Has the rain a father? (vs. 28)

l. Or who has begotten the drops of dew? (vs. 28b)

m. Can you lead forth a constellation . . . and guide the Bear with her satellites? (vs. 32)

The Bear referred to here is one or both of the two constellations in the Northern Hemisphere, the Great Bear and the Little Bear.

n. Can you lift your voice to the clouds so that water may cover you? (vs. 34)

o. Can you send forth lightning…or tip the water jars of the heavens, when the dust hardens into a mass and the clods stick together? (vs. 35,37,38)

p. Who has put wisdom in the innermost being or given understanding to the mind? (vs. 36)

q. What thoughts come to your mind as you answer these questions?

2. Read Psalm 19:1,2.

   a. What is telling of the glory of God? (vs. 1)

   b. What do various aspects of God's creation do day and night? (vs. 2)

God is talking to us day and night through His creation: the exquisite intricacy of a delicate flower; the cheerful chirping of a chickadee or melodic refrain of a meadowlark; a gentle breeze; the peaceful sound of a cascading brook; a glorious sunset; a star-studded night. If only we would open our eyes and ears to see and to listen. God is "speaking" to us through it all, reminding us continually of His love, His beauty, His provision, His care!

3. Read Psalm 103:19 (Please use NASB below to answer the question).

   The Lord has established His throne in the heavens and His sovereignty rules over all (Ps. 103:19).

   a. What has God established, and what rules over all?

4. Read Deut. 6:4.

   a. How many Gods are there?

5. Read Is. 45:5–7.

   a. Again, how many "Gods" are there? (vs. 5)

   b. What does God do for us? (vs. 5b)

   c. Why? (vs. 6)

Write out a Bible verse that had special meaning to you today.

Based upon what you have learned today, write a prayer to God expressing the desires of your heart in applying these Truths to your life.

NOTE: You're doing great! You have just one more day in this first week. Hang in there. Tomorrow's lesson is very special. You'll be blessed as we take a look at God's crowning glory in His creation.

Chapter 1 — Day 6
In the Beginning...GOD! — Part 2

> *I am the Lord, and there is no other; apart from Me there is no God. I will strengthen you, though you have not acknowledged Me, so that from the rising of the sun to the place of its setting, men may know there is none besides me. I am the Lord, and there is no other (Is. 45:5, NIV, NASB).*
>
> *The fool has said in his heart, "There is no God" (Ps. 14:1).*

I had a very dear, wise friend that I visited on Tuesdays for seven years, from the time he was eighty-seven until he was in his mid 90s, at which time the Lord in a most gracious and glorious way, took him home. I wish I had time to tell you that amazing story…but that will have to wait until another time. I loved to sit at John's feet on these visits and hear him tell of "days gone by." I especially enjoyed his stories of his "growin' up" days without running water or indoor plumbing, and plowing with a mule. John was born in 1898. He personally knew people who fought in the Civil War! And he loved to tell me of his adventures far from home as a young serviceman of seventeen marching across France with heavy gear and few rations during *WW I!* One of my favorite stories, however, was about his early years with his bride, Lillian. "She was a fine lassie, a good Christian woman, mind you." She would get up early in the morning—around 4 o'clock—to study her Bible. Then she'd fix John a southern country breakfast of bacon and eggs and melt-in-your-mouth homemade buttermilk biscuits generously doused with red-eye gravy. She'd fill a skin of spring water to send along with him to help quench his thirst as he worked in the fields. He would plow all morning from 7 o'clock on, working behind his Bessie-mule as the rays of the hot Georgia sun grew more and more intense until dinner time—right at twelve noon. He knew that dinner was ready when Lil would stand on the porch and wave her white hanky. What a sight that was. He'd finish plowing to the near end of the field, hitch ol' Bessie, and walk briskly to the farmhouse where he knew that Lillian would have a good dinner of turnip greens, black-eyed peas, Irish potatoes (or other fresh veggies from the garden), and a pone of cornbread. Ah, she was a fine cook! And there were so many other wonderful stories.

But there was something else John did that I will never forget, and every time I think of John today, I still see this picture in my mind so clearly. It's summertime and we are sitting on the porch of his weathered country home overlooking the beautiful, picturesque Nacoochee Valley below. John gets up from the well-worn wooden porch swing, walks down the stone steps to one of his flourishing flower beds. I follow him and watch as he bends over, picks a colorful flower, holds it up against the backdrop of a brilliant summer blue sky, as he gazes with awe and says: "Just look at that, would you? Now that's a masterpiece. How can anyone look at the intricate design of a beautiful flower like this and say, 'There is no God'? Why, he'd be a fool to say such a thing." And John was right.

The fool has said in his heart, there is no God. The workers of wickedness have no knowledge… They are corrupt, and have committed abominable things (Psalm 53:1,4).

There's just one more *infallible proof (Acts 1:3)* of God's existence and His sovereign divine creation of the universe and of man who occupies it, that we must consider. It is the greatest *proof* of all: the human body and mind.

For Thou didst form my inward parts. Thou didst weave me in my mother's womb. I will give thanks to Thee, for I am fearfully and wonderfully made (Ps. 139:13,14).

There are more than 30 trillion cells that make up every human body. Inside each cell is a nucleus. There is an incredible plethora of activity going on in this nucleus at every second of the day and night. Within each nucleus of a cell are 23 pairs of chromosomes. These form the genetic code that makes every individual unique—color of hair, height, complexion, etc. They also, through input from the brain, tell every cell how to act in various situations from birth to death. There is so much information stored in each cell that if you could write it down, it would equal 4,000 volumes of written material—**per cell.** So how much is 4,000 volumes? It is 20 billion bits of information which is 3 billion letters. At 6 letters per word that is 500,000,000 words. Taking an average of 300 words per page that would equal 2,000,000 pages. Considering 500 pages per book, that would equal 4,000 volumes. You could fill the Grand Canyon several times with the information contained in the cells of one human body. And all of that is working together at any one moment. We are, indeed, fearfully and wonderfully made!

A few summers ago, 50 mathematicians, biologists, and physicists came together at the Wistar Institute in Philadelphia and for the entire summer scientifically studied the theory of evolution. Spokesman, Dr. Eden from MIT, (Massachusetts Institute of Technology), wrote the following conclusion: "Based on our understanding of the laws of chemistry, physics and what we know about randomness, we see no way that the complexity of life could come about (through evolutionary processes) (Heitzig, Skip, "The Rise and Fall of Man" tape series, Connection Communications, San Juan Capistrano, CA 92693).

Think for just a moment about what God has allowed us to accomplish with the use of the computer, and satellite communications! Sports fans can watch the Super Bowl while waiting in the airport in Singapore. In the time it takes to blink your eye, the computer can access any subject in the entire Encyclopedia Britannica, scan a worldwide telephone directory, or send an e-mail from a computer in Georgia to a remote village in Africa. It can also store the information found in dozens of "Encyclopedia Britannicas" on a memory chip the size of a baby's thumbnail!

Who has put wisdom in the innermost being, or has given understanding to the mind? (Job. 38:36).

It is, undeniably, GOD who formed man's mind…*in His Image (Gen. 1:26)* – Not just so that he could create computers and satellites and other such amazing phenomena, but He gave him an intelligent, communicative mind primarily for the glorious purpose of having a living, interactive *relationship* with *Him*. We'll talk more about this in the chapter, "*In the Image of God,*" but for today, it is important to recognize these fundamental Truths that relate to our uniqueness as complex, intelligent beings, created *by God*.

Long before I became a Christian, I *knew* that there was a God.

He has planted eternity in their hearts (Eccles. 3:11).

Even though I was very proud, stubborn, and rebellious by nature and fought continually against thoughts of heaven and hell and everything else that might have to do with *God*, I never could extricate my mind completely from the haunting awareness of them (God, heaven, hell). There were days—many days—I realized fully exactly what John was saying: to deny the existence of God was truly *foolish*. I knew that this beautiful world that surrounded me every day and every night did not just happen by chance or evolve from some primordial soup. But there was a huge *lie* that I had believed through all the years of *making it on my own*. It was that age-old lie from Satan that said that if I acknowledged the existence of God I would have to be accountable to Him and He would take away all my fun. (I was so blind I could not even see that the very things I perceived as *fun* were the very things that were destroying my life, and robbing me of real, deep, lasting joy). So, in fear, pride and determination to maintain *control*, I garnered even more determination to rebel against even this kindness of God in making Himself known to me in my conscience. I refused to listen to those deep wooings from God *(Job 36:16)*, to return to Him, to enter into relationship with Him.

Under the power of satanic deception, I convinced myself that if I denied the existence of God long enough, my conscience would be stilled and "God" would cease to be. He would, as it were, become no more than a figment of the uninformed, the uneducated's overactive imagination, the poor man's crutch. What I didn't understand at that time is the horrific reality that God will let this happen. He will *give us over* to a seared conscience and a life of separation from Him and from His precious love if we rebel long enough.

For even though they knew God, they did not honor Him as God, or give thanks, but they became futile in their speculations, and their foolish heart was darkened. Professing to be wise, they became fools, and exchanged the glory of the incorruptible God for an image in the form of corruptible man (whoever he wanted God to be—intellect, education, money, popularity, pleasure…all various forms of the god of "self"). Therefore God gave them over to the impurity of the lusts of their hearts. For they exchanged the Truth of God for a lie and worshiped and served the creature rather than the Creator, who is blessed forever. For this reason God gave them over to their own degrading passions (Rom. 1:21–26).

For if we go on sinning willfully after receiving the knowledge of the Truth, there no longer remains (a way to repentance), but a certain terrifying expectation of judgment, and the fury of a fire which will consume the adversaries. Anyone who has set aside the law of Moses (Thou shalt not kill) dies without mercy on the testimony of two or three witnesses. How much severer punishment do you think he will deserve who has trampled under foot the Son of God, and has regarded as unclean the blood (of Jesus shed for our redemption), and has insulted the Spirit of grace?... For in the case of those who have once been enlightened and have tasted of the heavenly gift and the good Word of God, and then have fallen away, it is impossible to renew them again to repentance, since they crucify to themselves the Son of God, and put Him to open shame (Heb. 10:26–29, 6:4–6 sel.).

How often I yet lift my eyes to Heaven and say, with tears of overwhelming gratitude, "Thank You, God, for Your loving mercy and grace that extended beyond my rebellion!"

Bible Study Supplement

Chapter 1 – Day 6 — In the Beginning ... GOD! – Part 2

1. Read Ps. 139:13,14.

    a. How did you come into being? (vs. 13)

    c. How are you made? (vs. 14)

2. Read Is. 42:5–8.

    a. Who is God? (vs. 5a,8a) (Another name for God)

    b. What does this Name mean to you?

Note: The name, Lord, is the translation of the Hebrew word, YHWH (Yaweh), and means Master, eternal Ruler. We see it first used when God called Moses to deliver His people from bondage under the cruel hand of the Egyptians. Moses asked God who he should tell the people had sent him? God said to tell them that Yaweh, "I am who I am" (sometimes used in its shortened form, "I am") had sent him and that He, the eternal Ruler, Master would deliver them. Yaweh (Lord) expressed God's character as the dependable and faithful God. It is the Name by which God desired to be called because it acknowledges God's supreme, loving rulership that gladly warrants our trust and obedience. Adonai is another word for "Lord."

    b. What has God done? (vs. 5)

3. Read Is. 40:18–26.

    a. What does God invite us to do? (vs. 26a)

    b. What is God able to do concerning those vast galaxies of stars? (vs. 26b)

4. Read Psalm 104:24–34.

    a. How has God created all that He has made? (vs. 24)

    b. What should be my response to all that God has done and continues to do? (vs. 33,34b)

Write out a Bible verse that had special meaning to you today.

Based upon what you have learned today, write a prayer to God expressing the desires of your heart in applying these Truths to your life.

Chapter 2

Memory Verse: *Jesus answered, Man does not live by bread alone, but by every Word that proceeds out of the mouth of God (Matt. 4:4).*

Bonus Memory Verse: *Thy testimonies are wonderful; Therefore, my soul observes them. The unfolding of Thy Words gives light. It gives understanding to the simple (Ps. 119:129,130).*

Day 1
The Authority, Inerrancy, Immutability, and Sufficiency of the Word of God—Part 1

Day 2
The Authority, Inerrancy, Immutability and Sufficiency of the Word of God—Part 2

Day 3
The Awesome Creation of the Universe

Day 4
In the Image of God

An Introduction to My Purpose and Reason to Be

Day 5
The Revolt of Satan

The Assault on God's Perfect Kingdom of Love, Joy and Holiness

(The Beginning of "The Long War Against God")

Chapter 2 — Day 1
The Authority, Inerrancy, Immutability and Sufficiency of the Word of God—Part 1

> *Take to your heart all the words with which I am warning you today, which you shall command your sons to observe carefully; For it is not an idle word for you; indeed it is your life. And by this word you shall prolong your days in the land, which you are about to cross the Jordan to possess (Deut. 32:46,47).*

Foundational Truth # 2

The Bible is the final, authoritative, inerrant, immutable and sufficient Word of God. It is the plumb line against which all "Truth" must be established and judged. (Immutable means steadfastly secure, not subject to change, unalterable.)

A popular saying among Christians a few years ago was "God said it, I believe it, and that settles it for me." But that is a biblically erroneous statement. It should be: "God said it—that settles it!" Whether I choose to *believe it* or not, I can be sure that every *thus saith the Lord*—and every word in between—from Genesis to Revelation, is true, and it will happen just as God says. In other words, God is who He says He is and He will do what He says He will do. *For as many as are the promises of God, in Christ they are Yes and Amen! (2 Cor. 1:20).* I find that incalculably reassuring in an age of ever-increasing instability and uncertainty.

As many have rightly said, the Bible is God's love book to His children. In it, God reveals Himself to us—His nature, His character, His love for us. He tells us how we can enter into and enjoy a secure, loving, protective relationship with Him along with the very best of all His good plans for us both presently and in the glorious world yet to be (Rev. 21,22). He also tells us the wonderful good news of all that He has in store for those who believe and obey His Word as well as the bad news of what will happen if we ignore or rebel against it.

The most frequently asked question through the ages has always been: "Why am I here? What is my purpose in life?" People ask this question because they know that they were created for a purpose. God lovingly planted that seed in their hearts as a way to draw them into a relationship with Himself, so that He could protectively nurture and care for them as He leads them in the fulfillment of all His good plans for them.

> *He has set eternity in their hearts…For I know the plans I have for you," declares the Lord, "plans for welfare and not for calamity to give you a future and a hope. Then you will call upon Me and come and pray to Me, and I will listen to you. And you will seek Me and find Me, when you search for Me with all your heart" (Eccles. 3:11,14; Jer. 29:11–13).*

The wise ones, therefore, with joy and deep gratitude, enter into a relationship with God and set their hearts on knowing and fulfilling His good purposes, because they realize that if they don't, they will be most miserable—and make a lot of others around them miserable as well!

The way of the transgressor is hard…It is hard to kick against the goad (God's will/purpose for one's life) (Prov. 13:15b; Acts 9:5).

They also realize that the greatest joys in all of life will only be found in an ongoing, growing relationship with God as His good purposes are fulfilled:

These things I have spoken to you, that My joy may be in you and your joy may be full (John 15:11).

Whether we recognize it or not, there are only two concepts that drive us in all that we do: our concept of God and our concept of our purpose and reason to be. The answer to these two questions—who is God and what is my purpose and reason to be—will be at the heart of every man and every woman's thoughts, motivations, actions, and eternal destiny.

There is only one place we can go to discover the answer to these fundamental questions concerning who God is, and His purposes for our lives: the authoritative, inerrant, immutable Word of God.

We can choose to embrace this Truth and cherish the Word of God—reading it, studying it, obeying it—or we can reject it. But be sure, if we choose the latter, our lives will be superficial and barren of real, lasting peace and contentment—even though we may, with the help of Satan, do a masterful job of deceiving ourselves into believing that "all is well" and we are satisfied and content. It is a lie—a sad, pitiful lie.

Because you say, I am rich and have become wealthy, and have need of nothing, and you do not know that you are wretched and miserable and poor and blind (Rev. 3:17).

When we who have had free access to the Word of God stand before God one day, there will be no excuse for not knowing Him or fulfilling His will because God has made Himself and His will for our lives perfectly clear in His Word. No wonder Jesus told us: *Seek ye first the Kingdom of God and His righteousness, and all these things (for which your heart longs—fulfillment, meaning, purpose, peace, joy, etc.) will be added to you (Matt. 6:33).*

Sadly, few read and study God's Word diligently so that they can begin to truly know God and to enter into the only relationship that will ever be able to fulfill their deepest God-created needs and longings. Just as the French philosopher, Blaise Pascal, said centuries ago: "There is a God-shaped vacuum in all of us that only God can fill." It is that part of us that has been created in the image of God to have fellowship with Him and to reflect His nature and glory. Refusing to acknowledge this or trying to create our own image—characterized by selfish, worldly aspirations and desires—will only leave us in a most miserable state, just as you have seen in the lives of countless others and probably by now have experienced personally in your own life as well.

You, too, have done evil, even more than your forefathers; for behold, you are each one walking according to the stubbornness of his own evil heart, without listening to Me (Jer. 16:12).

These words yet ring often in my heart, reminding me of my previous condition, and of the tendency even now in my fallen state to desire to walk *according to the stubbornness of my own evil heart, without listening to God*. It is also a sad but accurate picture of many in God's family today who think that going to church once a week is all they need in order to *listen to God* and develop a loving, growing relationship with Him. Can you imagine trying to have an intimate, fulfilling marriage if you only spent one hour a week with your spouse? How can you possibly come to know and understand the heart of your spouse if you never spend time with him/her. It won't work. And neither can we develop an intimate, and fulfilling relationship with God by spending only one hour with Him a week (or less, if we are sporadic in our worship). And it is impossible to *know God* and to *love God* apart from His communication to us in His Word.

We also need to be in God's Word consistently—daily—in order to keep our minds alert and discerning—able to cut through Satan's crafty lies and deceptions that appear so innocent and enticing but lead only to agonizing disappointment and destruction *(Prov. 14:12; John 10:10a)*. It breaks my heart when I see people stubbornly resist setting aside time to be in God's Word every day, because without the Word of God we are powerless to stand against the enemy, being without *sword or shield (Eph. 6:10–17)*. Whoever walks out into the day without a fresh renewing of their minds through the reading and study of God's Word will be unprotected and vulnerable to the enemy's deceptions and temptations and the wounds inflicted will often be painful and deep. And the even sadder part is that the consequences of our own willful rebellion (sin) affects those around us, causing yet more hurt and suffering. Guilt-driven outbursts of anger and impatience nearly always follow sinful acts—it is the nature of guilt to produce this kind of fruit. Therefore, it is my fervent prayer that if nothing else is accomplished through this study that every person who participates will realize how desperately we all need the Truths of God's Word refreshing and renewing our hearts and minds daily, and will begin to set aside a consistent time for study and prayer fellowship with God. After all, at the heart of God's plan for our lives is a living, loving, growing, relationship with Him. It is impossible to develop such a relationship without spending time getting to know God through *the one thing needful* - His precious Word (Luke 10:42).

We would be wise also to remind ourselves daily that there is a consequence for all who discount, ignore, and defame the One and only true God, by refusing to come to Him and seek to know and to fulfill His good purposes for their lives.

> *Be not deceived; God is not mocked. For whatever a man sows, this he will also reap. For the one who sows to his own flesh shall from the flesh reap corruption…We have sown the wind. We are reaping the whirlwind. The standing grain has no heads; it yields no grain (Gal. 6:7; Hosea 8:7).*

Let's take a few moments today to *look intently (James 1:25)* into the Word of God, to confirm in our hearts once again its authority, inerrancy, immutability, sufficiency…and necessity.

*Take to your heart all the words with which I am warning you today…***For it is not an idle word for you; indeed it is your life.** *And by this Word you shall prolong your days in the land, which you are about to (enter)…to possess (Deut. 32:46,47).*

As with God, the Bible does not have to *prove itself*…

It was established and *settled* long before any of us arrived on the planet!

Forever, O Lord, Thy Word is settled in Heaven. Thy faithfulness continues throughout all generations. Thou didst establish the earth, and it stands (Ps. 119:89,90).

Bible Study Supplement

Chapter 2 — Day 1 — The Authority, Inerrancy, Immutability and Sufficiency of the Word of God—Part 1

1. Read 2 Tim. 3:16,17.

Note: The word translated as "inspired" in some translations comes from the Greek, *theos* (God) and *pneo* (to breath) and actually means "God-breathed." (The NIV translates it correctly).

    a. How much of the Bible is inspired/God-breathed? (vs. 16)

    b. For what is the Word of God profitable? (4 things - vs. 16)

    c. What does it do for the diligent student (one who not only hears but obeys it)? (vs. 17)

Do you see the vital role the Word of God plays in equipping us to do the job to which God has called us? In fact, it is impossible to be adequately equipped without it. That is why we need the Word of God each day in our lives to keep us on God's path and to give us wisdom and discernment in all the complexities of life.

2. Read Ps. 119:89–93.

    a. How does the psalmist describe God's Word and His faithfulness? (vs. 89,90a)

    b. What did God do that confirms this? (vs. 90b)

    c. What would have happened to the psalmist if God's Word hadn't been his delight? (vs. 92)

    d. What have God's precepts done for him? (vs. 93b)

3. Read Ps. 119:97–105.

    a. What does the psalmist love, and what is this to him all day, every day? (vs. 97)

    b. What do God's commandments make the psalmist? (three things - vs. 98–100)

    c. From what has the psalmist restrained his feet? (vs. 101a)

    d. What has he not done? (vs. 102a)

    e. Who has taught him? (vs. 102b)

    f. How are God's words to him? (vs. 103)

    g. What do God's words provide as he walks through life? (vs. 105)

4. Read Ps. 119:111,112.

    a. What are the testimonies of God to the psalmist? (vs. 111b)

b. What has he inclined his heart to do? For how long? (vs. 112)

5. Read Ps. 119:129,130.

    a. How does he view (think of) God's testimonies? (vs. 129)

    b. What does the unfolding of God's Word do? (two things - vs. 130)

6. Read Ps. 119:160 - Please use NASB translation below to answer the question that follows.

    The sum of Thy Word is Truth, and every one of Thy righteous ordinances is everlasting (Ps. 119:160).

    a. What is Truth? (vs. 160a)

7. Read Ps. 119:165.

    a. What happens to those who love God's law? (two things - vs. 165)

8. Read Matthew 4:4.

    a. What does man need to truly live?

9. Read Deut. 32:46,47.

    a. What are we to take to our hearts? (vs. 46)

    b. Why is this so important? (vs. 47)

10. Read Psalm 1.

    a. Who is blessed? The man who does <u>not</u>… (three things - vs. 1)

Note: We learn here the importance of choosing our friends wisely. We should be careful not to seek important counsel from those who are not walking closely to God. We will be blessed and make our way secure if we heed this good biblical instruction.

    b. In what does the psalmist find his greatest delight and upon what does he meditate day and night? (vs. 2)

    c. What will he be like? (vs. 3a)

Note: In this verse (vs. 3), we are told that the man who loves and meditates upon God's Word will be like a strong tree that is firmly planted by a stream (God's Word) from which it continually draws nourishment to remain strong and healthy.

    d. What will characterize this strong, healthy tree? (three things - vs. 3)

    e. What are the wicked like? (vs. 4)

    f. What will happen to the wicked? (vs. 6b)

Note: Whenever the word *wicked* is used in the Bible, it is rarely referring to murderers, thieves, or other vile criminals. It most often is used to refer to anyone who is not in a right, loving obedient relationship with God, but is, instead, walking *according to his own stubborn heart without listening to and following God (Jer. 16:12)*. In other words, it is anyone who is out of the will of God because of outward or inward rebellion against Him. We can be in rebellion inwardly as well as outwardly by exercising an unsubmissive, unyielded (demanding/controlling) spirit or by nursing an ungrateful, unthankful, unforgiving, bitter attitude. This kind of internal rebellion (attitudinal) against God is a sin and grieves the Holy Spirit who instructs us in God's Word to be *thankful in all things* (1 Thess. 5:18), to *rejoice always*, and to *offer sacrifices of praise from the rising of the sun to its setting* (Heb. 13:15; Ps. 113:3). God gives us these good instructions because He knows that if we don't meditate on God's Word, filling our hearts continually with the hope and joy of its promises, we will focus upon ourselves and our insatiable fleshly lusts and desires. We will, as a result, be discontent and lacking that real, deep, unshakable peace and joy. Please take note of this so that you will have a correct biblical understanding of "wicked" when you come across it in future Bible readings.

Write out a Bible verse that had special meaning to you today.

Based upon what you have learned today, write a prayer to God expressing the desires of your heart in applying these Truths to your life.

Chapter 2 — Day 2
The Authority, Inerrancy, Immutability and Sufficiency of the Word of God—Part 2

> *But know this first of all, that no prophecy of Scripture is a matter of one's own interpretation, for no prophecy was ever made by an act of human will, but men moved by the Holy Spirit spoke from God (2 Pet. 1:20,21).*
>
> *Remember the former things long past, for I am God, and there is no other; I am God, and there is no one like Me, declaring the end from the beginning, and from ancient times things which have not been done, saying, My purpose will be established (Is. 46:9,10).*

Three Irrefutable Facts about God's Word, the Bible

Having been a diligent student of the Word of God for many years, I can say with total honesty that there is not one shred of doubt in my mind concerning the authority, inerrancy, immutability, and sufficiency of Scripture. In fact, I believe this so strongly that I would give my life before I would deny God, the author of the Bible, or His precious Word that He has given us. Why? Why would I, like thousands before me, literally *stake my life* on the authority and inerrancy of the Word of God? There are many reasons for that. We won't have time to examine all of them today, but let's consider just three that in themselves prove that the Bible is exactly what it claims to be: The Infallible Word of God.

1. **The Continuity and Antiquity of the Bible** – The Bible is unique from all other books that have ever been written in that it contains 66 books written by 40 authors over a period of 1500 years on 3 different continents and in 3 distinct languages. People who never met together, never talked, and were totally separated from each other by time, space, occupation, language, all write with complete unity. Without question, it would have been impossible for mere, fallible, mortal man to have accomplished such an undertaking. Only God, Himself, who was present throughout those 1500 years, could have accomplished this kind of transcendent symmetry as He omnisciently *breathed* the Words through His chosen vessels (2 Tim. 3:16; 2 Pet. 1:21).

   The original manuscripts of the Bible are by far the oldest, most consistent, historically verified writings in existence. No other book of its size and detail comes even close to the age of the earliest manuscripts of the Bible, as authenticated by scientific dating methods and corroborating historic documentation. The discovery of the Dead Sea Scrolls in the Qumran Caves on the northwestern edge of the Dead Sea in 1947 further validates the authenticity of the Word of God. Only divine protection and direction in locating these manuscripts, some of which date one thousand years earlier than any previous manuscripts, account for this preservation/discovery.

The fact that the Bible has survived thousands of years of history, including endless wars, collapses of entire civilizations, rebellions, godless men who tried to destroy it, persecutions, martyrdom, the Dark Ages, and dozens of other destructive obstacles, further proves its God-breathed origin and divine protection/preservation. There is no other book that even remotely compares to the antiquity, consistency (in the hundreds of manuscripts found), and historical authenticity of the Bible. And just the fact that it is *still*, by far, the most read book in the world, proves that there is a loving Heavenly Father who desires to communicate with His children and has preserved His Word through which He does this faithfully from generation to generation.

As I was preparing this meditation, I could not help but think of one of my very special historical treasures. It is an old Swedish Bible that is nearly two hundred years old. But the cover is worn, the pages are frayed, and parts of it are already illegible. To think that this precious keepsake is only two hundred years old and that some of the original Hebrew manuscripts of the Bible are more than two thousand years old and still perfectly legible and historically consistent and accurate…well, it would take, as my wise friend John said so often, a genuine fool to attempt to explain this apart from divine intervention.

2. **Prophecy** – God says in His Word: *Remember this, and be assured;…Recall it to mind, you transgressors. Remember the former things long past, For I am God, and there is no other; I am God, and there is no one like Me;* **Declaring the end from the beginning**, *and from ancient times things which have not been done, saying, 'My purpose will be established, and I will accomplish all My good pleasure. I have planned it, surely I will do it.' Listen to Me, you stubborn-minded, who are far from righteousness. I bring near My righteousness, it is not far off" (Is. 46:8–10,12,13).*

    No other "god" through the ages could ever make and keep such a claim—to be able to *declare the end from the beginning:* that is, from the very beginning of time, tell of all the major events that would transpire down through the ages until the very end of time, as God has done to this point with 100% accuracy! Those who have attempted to replicate this kind of prophetic ability, even during very brief windows in time, have consistently been proven false in the fulfillment of their prognostications. God's prophecies have never failed. Not once! And we can be sure they never will. The first time I read the entire Bible through I stood in total awe again and again at the hundreds of prophecies that were fulfilled to the minutest detail: prophecies that would have been impossible to feign, having been written hundreds, and in some cases thousands of years before their fulfillment. These prophecies have been further substantiated—the times of both the prophecy and its fulfillment—by closely examined and dated historical records.

    The Bible contains more than *two thousand prophecies,* each and every one of which has been fulfilled *exactly* as God said it would happen—except for the very few remaining that await fulfillment in the final days just before and at the time of Jesus' return. When God says, *thus saith the Lord,* you can be sure that *and it was so* will inevitably follow. I never once doubted one word of God's Word after that first read-through-the-Bible experience. And every subsequent year that I have read it from Genesis to Revelation that assurance has been reinforced all the more. I have not found one promise or one significant statement of fact (Truth) refutable. God is Who He says He is; He has always done what He said He would do and He will continue to be true to every promise He has made both for the present and the future. We can count on that!

3. **Changed lives!** Though the above two reasons alone would have been more than enough to thoroughly convince any rational-thinking individual to recognize the authority and inerrancy of God's Word, the power that it holds to change lives is irrefutable. You just can't argue against a radically changed

life. It is living, on-going proof of the power of the Spirit of God working through the Word of God as it is read, believed, and obeyed. I know what God's Word has done (and continues to do) in my life. And history is replete with examples of that same power working in the lives of others through the generations and continues in countless numbers of lives today. Its power to totally change a life—from one of chaos and destruction, to one of order, confidence, purpose, and peace—is irrefutable evidence of its divine origin and power. (For nearly 3,000 documented testimonies of such *irrefutable evidences* of changed lives, see Appendix, Resources, "Unshackled").

No wonder the Word of God warns that only *fools despise wisdom* (the wisdom of God's Word) *(Prov. 1:7)*. One would have to have a totally depraved mind to examine all the evidence and then conclude that the Bible is anything less than the inspired, inerrant, infallible, *God-breathed* Word of God *(2 Tim. 3:16,17; 2 Pet. 1:21)*.

> *For the Word of God is living and active and sharper than any two-edged sword...able to judge the thoughts and intentions (motivations) of the heart...moreover by (it) Thy servant is warned; in keeping (it) there is great reward. (Heb. 4:12; Ps. 19:11)*

The Word of God remains as *living and active* today as the days in which it was written. It still has the power to change, encourage and strengthen lives. How often this precious truth was proven in my own life. When I was going through the darkest times of pain and confusion associated with the mysterious affliction that sapped every ounce of energy and kept my body wracked in pain, threatening to destroy my hope that things would ever change—or that I would even survive—it was God's Word alone that kept my heart encouraged and gave me the strength to *press on*. I can remember so vividly countless days when I was so weak and so sick that I could not get out of bed or hold my head up. But as I prayed and trusted God to help me, God gave me the strength to get up, go to my quiet time corner where I would prop my head in my own cupped hands resting on the table for support, and I would read God's Word through blurry eyes. Every day—*every day*—God would speak life-giving promises to me through His Word—promises that gave encouragement and strength—*living, empowering strength*:

> *There is a river whose streams make glad the (children) of God…God is in the midst of her, she will not be moved; God will help her when morning dawns…How precious is Thy lovingkindness, O God…the children of men take refuge in the shadow of Thy wings. They drink their fill of the abundance of Thy house; and Thou dost give them to drink of the river of Thy delights. For with Thee is the fountain of life (Ps. 46:4,5; Ps. 36:7–9).*

> *Now on the last day of the feast, Jesus stood and cried out, "He who believes in Me, as the Scripture (says), From his innermost being shall flow rivers of living water" (John 7:37,38).*

The *living waters* of God's love, mercy and grace, began to flow into every depleted cell reviving my languishing body and soul. My spirit would be renewed—refreshed—to not just make it through another day, but to be productive and accomplish God's good purposes in it (Ps. 119:153–159; Heb. 4:12). I went to bed with a sweet sense of God's presence and cherished affirmation: *Well done, good and faithful servant (Matt. 25:23)*. And I can say with <u>total certainty</u>, that had I not remained faithful to reading and studying God's Word, receiving from it daily the assurance of God's love and presence, wisdom, guidance, hope and encouragement, this book would never have been written, nor would I even "be here" to tell its story. I would, instead, be: 1) dead (suicide), 2) totally disabled or 3) a non-productive, mental and emotional prescription drug zombie by this point. There is not a shred of doubt in my mind about this! Not one! God's Word is not only *living and active*, it is *powerful*, imparting *life-giving wisdom and strength*.

Before closing today's meditation, I just want to say a few words concerning the sufficiency of Scripture. Sadly, just as the Bible warned would happen *in the last days, many deceivers* (false teachers) have *crept in unnoticed* as *savage wolves, leading My people astray (2 Pet. 2:1–12; Acts 20:29–32; 1 John 4:1–6; 2 John 1:7–9, sel.).* God warns us and bids our vigilance concerning these *wolves in sheep's clothing (Matt. 7:15),* so that we are not seduced by their enticing temptations to abandon or doubt the Word of God. Under the influence and deception of Satan, these false teachers (some of whom are actually well-meaning, born-again believers who have been blinded by the incredible power of Satan through the false teaching of respected, powerful leaders in the Christian community) have stirred the hearts of many so that there is a great battle waging against the *sufficiency* of Scripture. Many modern day "biblical scholars" say that they affirm the accuracy and the authority of Scripture but quickly cast doubt upon its *sufficiency* for guiding us in our complex 21st Century lives. They claim that we need the additional "revelation" of humanistic (man-centered rather than God-centered) psychology, psychotherapy, and any of a number of other rebellious modern man's intellectual enlightenments. They thus raise doubt in the minds of many who do not know Scripture nor its thorough, divinely powerful *sufficiency:*

> *…Seeing that His divine power has granted to us* **everything** *pertaining to life and godliness, through the true knowledge of Him who called us by His own glory and excellence (2 Pet. 1:3).*

God says here that He has given us *everything* we need pertaining to life and godliness. Therefore, we can confidently put our trust in the sufficiency of Scripture for <u>all</u> matters of life. God knew about all of our problems, concerns, needs when He wrote the Bible and He has given us instructions on all of these things. That means there is nothing that I will ever experience in this life concerning which the Word of God does not speak and give direction. Nothing! I find that Truth incalculably reassuring.

May God help us all to love and cherish His Word for what it is: God's eternal, *living and active* (life-giving) wisdom, power and unfailing promises to us. It is through God's Word that He fellowships with us and guides us in all His good plans daily, blessing our lives and filling them with *precious and pleasant riches (Prov. 24:3,4).*

> *Thy testimonies are wonderful; therefore my soul observes them. The unfolding of Thy words gives light; it gives understanding to the simple. (Ps. 119:129,130)*

Bible Study Supplement

Chapter 2 — Day 2 — The Authority, Inerrancy, Immutability and Sufficiency of the Word of God—Part 2

1. Read 2 Pet. 1:19-21.

    a. What do we do well to "pay attention to"? (vs. 19)

Note: In the early days of God's revelation of Himself to man, He called prophets through whom He spoke to the people. Later, God spoke to us directly through Jesus (Heb. 1:1,2). Today, He continues to speak to us through His Word and through His Holy Spirit who is present in the Word instructing and guiding us, comforting and strengthening us. (John 14:16,17; 16:7–15).

    b. What does God say that we are to know, understand? (vs. 20)

    c. Whose words were actually "spoken" through the prophets? (vs. 21)

2. Read Is. 46:8-10.

    a. What has God done that distinguishes Him from all other "gods"? (vs. 10a)

3. Read Ps. 19:7–11 (Please use text below to answer the questions):

    7. The law of the Lord is perfect, reviving the soul; The statutes of the Lord are sure, making wise the simple.

    8. The precepts of the Lord are right, giving joy to the heart; the commands of the Lord are radiant, giving light to the eyes.

    9. The fear of the Lord is pure, enduring forever.

    10. They are more precious than gold, than much pure gold; they are sweeter than honey, than honey from the comb.

    11. By them is your servant warned; in keeping them there is great reward (Ps. 19:7–11, NIV).

Fill in the blanks and answer the questions:

    a. (vs. 7a) *The law of the Lord is* _____. What does it do for the soul?

    b. (vs. 7b) *The statues of the Lord are* _____. What do they do?

    c. (vs. 8a) *The precepts (teachings) of the Lord are* _____. What do they do?

    d. (vs. 8b) The commands of the Lord are _____. What do they do?

    e. Together, how valuable are all these things? (vs. 10a)

    f. How *sweet* are they? (vs. 10b)

    g. What do they do for the servant who reads and studies them? (vs. 11a)

i. What do they do for the servant who *keeps (obeys)* them? (vs. 11b)

4. Read Heb. 4:12.

    a. List three major characteristics of the Word of God.

    b. What is it able to judge/discern?

5. Read Is. 40:8.

    a. How long will the Word of God stand?

6. Read 2 Pet. 1:2,3.

    a. What has God given/granted us? (vs. 3)

Please note this verse—**2 Pet. 1:3**—carefully. It is a pivotal text confirming the sufficiency of God's Word. God is saying to us here that He has given us everything we need to make wise, life-giving decisions and to live righteous, godly lives through His divine power (the Holy Spirit) working in and through the Truths of His Word (the true knowledge of Him). I find this promise wonderfully reassuring and encouraging.

We have talked about three "irrefutable facts" that establish the inerrancy and authority of God's Word: (1) the antiquity and continuity of the original manuscripts, (2) prophecy, and (3) the power of the Word of God to change lives. I want to close today's study by focusing for just a few moments upon the second proof—Prophecy. I believe this is important because it is such a powerful testimony of the supreme, eternal, omniscient rule of God.

As mentioned in the meditation, there are more than two thousand specific, detailed prophecies in the Bible. In preparation for this study I did quite an in-depth study of prophetic Scriptures. I was continually awed regarding the minute detail in which God gave and fulfilled every prophecy. I wish we could do a short study here on several of these, but there just won't be time for that today. In lieu of that, let me give a brief overview of one of my favorite prophetic events. It involved the "handwriting on the wall." Here's how it went:

Because of their vile immorality, blatant idolatry and repeated rejection of God, God had allowed the southern Kingdom of Judah to be invaded by the Babylonians under wicked King Nebuchadnezzar, who defeated them and carried them away into exile where they were treated with oppressive cruelty. In agony, they cried out to God. And God, in His compassionate mercy, just as He had done so many times before, heard and answered their cry. He raised up *His servant, Cyrus, the Mede* (Is. 44:28; 45:1–6), (who, by the way, was a pagan idolater), to deliver His rebellious, wayward children from captivity.

One night, as was his frequent custom Belshazzar, the current ruling king of Babylon, was giving a bacchanalia (wild, drunken party). He brought out *the gold and silver vessels* which *Nebuchadnezzar his father had taken from the temple in Jerusalem (Dan. 5:2)*, and he and his concubines were defiling them by drinking out of them and getting drunk. It was during this profane orgy that the mysterious hand appeared and began writing on the wall: *Mene, Mene, Tekel Upharsin*. When none of the king's "wise men" could interpret the meaning of the strange script, the Hebrew captive, Daniel, who now served in the king's court, was summoned. After *praying to his God for wisdom*, Daniel gave the meaning of the dream to King Belshazzar: *God has numbered your kingdom and put an end to it…your kingdom has been divided and given over to the Medes and Persians* (Because of the King's continual rejection of God, blatant blasphemies, idolatry, and leading God's precious people astray to worship foreign gods). Under the direction of God, Himself, (Is. 44:28; 45:1–6), Cyrus was at that very moment marching up to the impregnable city of Babylon with its 187 feet thick walls and towers that extended to a height of three hundred feet, enclosing an area of 196 square miles. In one short night, Cyrus, fulfilling to the minutest detail a number of prophecies made by God through His prophet Isaiah years earlier, invaded this invincible city, overcame the king, and destroyed the iron-fisted rule of the Babylonians. Amazing story! But it doesn't end there. Cyrus (Persian name for Darius) became the King of the new Persian Empire. Through a series of events only God could have orchestrated, He brought into King Darius's life the prophet Daniel who shared his faith and the true knowledge of God with Darius. Darius respected Daniel and he listened. His heart began to soften. Then after Daniel's miraculous deliverance from the jaws of the lions, King Darius recognized that Daniel's God was indeed the one and only true God. He then joined Daniel in worshipping God, making this bold declaration: *I, (King Darius) make a decree that in all the dominion of my kingdom men are to fear and tremble before the God of Daniel; For He is the living God and enduring forever, and His kingdom is one which will not be destroyed, and His dominion will be forever. He delivers and rescues and performs signs and wonders in heaven and on earth (Dan. 5:1–6:27).*

Every time I read this story I am reminded of the magnitude of the length and breadth and height and depth of the love of God in reaching out to rebellious lost sinners to draw them to Himself.

And there are hundreds of other similar prophetic accounts that are equally as fascinating as this one, giving yet further evidence of God's matchless sovereign rule and His never failing love, protection and faithfulness to *His children* from generation to generation.

Write out a Bible verse that had special meaning to you today.

Based upon what you have learned today, write a prayer to God expressing the desires of your heart in applying these Truths to your life.

Chapter 2 — Day 3
The Awesome Creation of the Universe

> *In the beginning, God created the heavens and the earth…and God saw all that He had made, and behold, it was very good (Gen. 1:1,31).*

Foundational Truth # 3

In six literal 24-hour days, God created the great expanse of the heavens and the earth. And all was *very good* and functioned in perfect order, magnificent beauty, radiantly expressing God's glory and joy.

Since the Bible is the inspired, authoritative, inerrant, immutable Word of God, we need to go back to its beginning to answer the fundamental questions: Who is God? Why did He create the world…me? What is the purpose for my life?…and many other very important questions. This will be our focus for today and the rest of this week.

Many of us have both read and heard the creation story so many times that we no longer stand in awe of the grand and glorious magnitude of what God did in this incredible event. Today we are going to ask God, through His Holy Spirit, to help us lay aside all familiarity and take a fresh new look.

Let's pause for a moment now as we do this:

Dear Holy Spirit, we ask you to please illumine the eyes of our understanding that we might be able to comprehend with deeper, clearer awareness, the awesome magnitude of what *really* happened during those seven miraculous days in which God's creative powers were released into one of the most amazing expressions of beauty and love the world would ever know. Fill us now with inspired, divine wisdom and enlightenment. In Jesus Name, Amen.

Bible Study Supplement

Chapter 2 — Day 3 — The Awesome Creation of the Universe

In preparation for this Bible study I read the first three chapters of Genesis a number of times. I could not get over the vastness of revelation and wisdom! In fact, *every other book* in the Bible that follows relates in some way to Genesis 1–3. Without a thorough understanding of what transpired in these chapters, it is impossible to fully understand the nature of God, His plan for planet Earth, and for each of us who will ever walk the face of it.

Just a word before we begin. Since the material that we will be covering today is bursting with wisdom, I have included a number of "notes" along the way to stimulate a more thorough consideration of various spiritual insights. There will be a lot of extra Bible verses given in these notes. You do not need to take time to look up these verses (found in the supplemental notes *beneath* the questions) now, as we will be covering most of them in detail in later chapters. I only wanted to list them in context here to show the interrelatedness of the Word of God—from Genesis to Revelation.

Note: The word "Genesis" means origin or the coming into being of something; Genesis is, therefore, the book of origins or the book of beginnings.

1. Read Genesis 1:1,2.

    a. What did God create *in the beginning*? (vs. 1)

    b. Was the earth here before God? (vs. 1, see also Rev. 4:11)

    c. Was God here before the earth? (Same references as above.)

    d. Who else was here before the creation of the world? (John 1:1–3)

Note: The Greek word translated "Word" here is *logos* and means: "a statement of God." Throughout the Old Testament, its Hebrew counterpart "dabar" is used to indicate God's direct instruction to His people through His chosen prophets (spokesmen for God). It is the very same word that is used to refer to Jesus Himself, who is the incarnate, *living Word* (John 1:1-18), a personification of the written Word of God. Jesus is "God's statement" in human form. It is as if, for that brief span in history, the Word (Jesus) literally stepped out of the pages of the written Word of God to *live and dwell among us* in bodily form (John 1:14), in order not just to teach us God's Word, but to show us through His example, how to live it. Jesus was, therefore, the embodiment of the Word of God in human form, the *incarnate, living Word* (John 1:1-18). This same Jesus was not only present with the Father on that glorious day of the creation of the universe but was actively involved in it (Col. 1:17).

    e. Besides God the Father and God the Son, who else was present *in the beginning*? (vs. 2b)

Note: So here, in the very first two verses of the Bible (and verified by John 1:1 and Rev. 4:11), we see the Triune Godhead present, involved together in the second most dramatic, most miraculous event in all of history, the creation of the world and of mankind. (The most dramatic event would come a few millennia later when this same Godhead—God the Father, Son, and Holy Spirit—would join together in the most glorious expression of love of all time, the eternal redemption of mankind.)

    f. What did the earth look like in the beginning, before God brought order to it? (vs. 2)

g. What are our lives like before God? (Before we enter into a personal relationship with Him.)

Note: It is interesting to note the similarity between our lives and the condition of the world before God entered into its disorderly (confused), dark, void. We will be studying in greater detail in a subsequent chapter the seriousness of not dealing with this condition (Eph. 2:1; Rom. 5:6-8,12-14). It is gravely serious because, as mentioned in last week's study, the Bible clearly teaches that it is possible, through demonic deception and hardness of heart (the result of rejecting God over and over) to *sear the conscience.* A seared conscience is a *dead* conscience. It is no longer able to function as God designed it to function—initially, to help us recognize our need for God and to draw us to Him and later to help us avoid sin and its awful consequences. In this state we are no longer able to even *recognize* the true condition of our lives—dark, void, and hopelessly estranged from God. We need to be very careful to not allow our consciences to become that hard and unresponsive to the things of God. It is a very, very dangerous condition (Heb. 6:4–6; Heb. 10:26).

2. Read Gen. 1:3–5.

   a. What did God create on the first day? (vs. 3–5)

Note: In John 8:12, Jesus said, *I am the Light of the World. Whoever follows me will not walk in darkness but will have the Light of Life.* Just as God created the light on the first day, so we must have the light of Jesus in our hearts to pierce the darkness of sin and to light the way to God and to all the good plans He has for us (John 8:12, 14:6).

3. Read Gen. 1:6–8.

   a. What did God create on the second day? (vs. 6,8)

Note: Remember God's conversation with Job? God asked him: *"Have you entered the storehouses of the snow…the hail…Can you tip the water jars of the heavens when the dust hardens into a mass and the clods stick together?…Can you lift your voice to the clouds so that an abundance of water may cover you?" (Job 38:37,34)*

Having been raised on a farm, I can testify to the awful devastation of drought and to the power of God's mercy when a band of hurting, desperate farmers gather and pray for rain, then to witness with my own eyes thunderclouds gather as God *tips the jars of Heaven* to bring rain to replenish the earth.

4. Read Gen. 1:9–13.

   a. What did God create on the third day? (vs. 9–11)

Do you see God's creative order here? God was preparing a natural habitat—a home and food—for the birds and animals He would soon create.

5. Read Gen. 1:14–19.

   a. What did God create on the fourth day? (vs. 16)

Remember that incredible universe that we read about last week, the billions of stars and galaxies? God "spoke" them all into existence on the fourth day!

Note: The Sun is 12,000 degrees Fahrenheit! It is 93 million miles from earth. If it were any closer we would burn up. If further, we would freeze. That's how precise was God's creation and placement of the Sun.

I love the beautiful, God-exalting symbolism here. The "Sun" represents God the Father who is ever present with us, giving light and direction to our lives *(Ex. 40:36–38; Num. 12:5; Psalm 119:105, etc.)*. The blinding brightness and intense heat of the Sun also illustrates God's Holiness. Just as we cannot look on the Sun directly—it is too powerful and too penetrating—so it is with God. His transcendent Holiness (Glory) far exceeds our human understanding or capabilities to endure. *No man can look on Me and live (Ex. 33:20)*. The purifying fires of God's Holiness would consume the sin in us, and us with it! That is how awesome and how consuming His transcendent Holiness is. But we can look upon that transcendent Glory in the pages of God's Word in which He reveals Himself: His nature, His will, His plans and purposes. And we can also behold a perfect reflection of God in Jesus, who is the *radiance of God's glory and the exact representation of His nature (Heb. 1:3)*.

The Moon, therefore, is representative of Jesus. The Moon, in reality, has no light of its own. It is strategically located in space at just the right position to reflect the rays of the Sun, and that is exactly what Jesus does. Jesus came to this earth to show us the Father: to reflect the very nature and attributes of God Himself—His love, His compassion, His Holiness. *If you had known Me, you would have known My Father also; from now on you know Him and have seen Him… I and the Father are one—He is in Me and I in Him* (John 14:7,10; 10:30,38).

The Moon, like the Sun, gives light and direction. Like the *pillar of fire by night* for the children of Israel (Ex. 13:21,22; Num. 9:15–20), so Jesus gives light to the darkest night when trials and tribulations, intense suffering, and tribulation assail us (Daniel 3:5; 1 Peter 4:12). He is the one who is ever present with us when we go through those inevitable dark and difficult times (Is:43:2). Jesus Himself said, *I am the Light of the World…I will never leave you nor forsake you" (John 8:12; Heb. 13:5)*. The light of Jesus' love shines the brightest in the darkest night bringing comfort and assurance. *Let not your heart be troubled. Trust in God, trust also in Me (John 14:1)*.

The *stars of the sky* represent the Holy Spirit, for in them is beauty and points of reference, signs to guide us. What did God use to guide the wise men to Jesus? And so God's Holy Spirit is present in the world, ever shining a light to God. First, He brings conviction of our sins, drawing us to Jesus. And if we respond to His invitation, repent of our sins and come to God, He then comes into our hearts to guide, and empower us to know and do the will of God. Stars also display the awesome majesty and Glory of God to fill our lives with wonder, beauty, and joy.

I love the description in Ex. 13: *The Lord was going before them in a pillar of cloud by day to lead them on the way, and a pillar of fire by night to give them light, that they might travel by day and by night. He did not take away the cloud by day, nor the pillar of fire by night from before the people (Ex. 13:21,22)*.

Together these glorious bodies of light give continual illumination and the assurance of God's presence so that we who look to the One who created them may never again *walk in darkness but shall have the Light of Life* (Micah 7:8–9b; Ps. 139:12; John 8:12; 1 John 1:7). It is my sincere prayer that God will indelibly impress upon each of our hearts the exquisite beauty and glory of His awesome Creation so that we will never again look upon a breathtaking sunrise or sunset, feel the penetrating rays of the noon-day sun, experience the warmth and romance of a full-moon-lit night, or gaze upon a star-studded sky in the same way again. I pray that in each new encounter with any of these—and the rest of God's glorious creation—we will recognize them for what they really are—resplendent expressions of God's love, beauty and awesome, magnificent glory!

Note: Just a caveat about the beautiful symbolism found in the sun, the moon and the stars. God clearly warns in His Word against worshiping the *creature rather than the Creator (Rom. 1:23–25)*. We are to worship only Him, the Creator. "New Age" and many other modern cults worship the sun, the moon and the stars in the place of God. That is a terrible sin and we should never engage in that kind of idolatrous pagan worship.

6. Read Gen. 1:20–23.

   a. . What did God create on the fifth day? (vs. 20,21)

To me, the resplendent beauty found in the *birds of the air* and the *fish of the sea* are the "exclamation point" of God's creative genius and Glory. A careful study of these endless masterpieces of exquisite beauty and abilities confirms beyond any shadow of doubt the existence of a divine, far-beyond-human-intelligence-or-understanding Designer/Creator—God!

7. Read Gen. 1:24,25.

   a. What did God create on the sixth day? (vs. 24,25)

Note: On this day, God created the animals who would serve man and beautify His world through their varied, ingenious character and color: the sweet, endearing nature of a young spotted fawn with her mother, the zany design of the African zebra, the antics of the chimpanzee, the companionship of dogs and cats, the quickness of a gazelle, the strength of the horse and oxen, and the unique design and purposeful function of a thousand other animals. What a God! What a world of perfect beauty and order He created for man's enjoyment!

8. Read Gen. 1:26–28.

   a. What else did God create on the sixth day?

Finally, it was time for the crowning glory of God's creation: The very *likeness of Himself*—man and woman (Gen. 1:26). With these He would fellowship and commune and lavish upon them His boundless love, provision, and joy (Is. 43:4a; Zeph. 3:17; Is. 42:1; Ps. 17:8, etc.). We'll talk more about this beautiful expression of God's love tomorrow.

9. Read Gen. 2:1-4.

   a. What did God do on the seventh day? (vs. 2,3)

Note: Be assured that God did not do this because *God* needed to rest. God created this special day because He loved us and He knew that *we* needed a day to rest, renew, and refresh our depleted bodies and spirits. He also created this special day so that we could come apart from our work and troubles and enjoy intimate oneness and fellowship with Him. It is such a beautiful picture of the tender, compassionate heart of God.

A Closing Insight

There is just one more principle that is important for us to note before leaving this beautiful account of *in the beginning*. There was clearly a pattern that seemed a bit odd as I read through the story of God's masterful genius in the creation of the world? Did you notice it?

> *And there was evening and there was morning, one day…and there was evening and there was morning, a second day…and there was evening and there was morning, a third day (Gen. 1:5,8,13, etc.)*

God's day always began in the *evening*. Already here, *in the beginning*, we are introduced to the important principle of vision, planning, and accountability that is taught throughout the Word of God.

Where there is no vision, the people are unrestrained (no direction or purpose) (Prov. 29:18).

Prepare your work . . . then afterwards, build your house (Prov. 24:27).

May my prayer be counted as incense before Thee; the lifting up of my hands as the evening offering (Ps. 141:2).

In the Old Testament, the evening was seen as a time of special communion with God. We see this pattern already in the very first book.

And they heard the sound of the Lord God walking in the garden in the cool of the day (Gen. 3:8).

In that exquisite paradise, Adam and Eve met with God at the close of every day to commune and to fellowship. What a precious time this must have been!

Later in the Old Testament, after the fall, we see that these twilight hours were used as the time for the *evening sacrifice,* a time to stop the work of the day, to come to God, to offer up fragrant sacrifices and prayers in worship and thanksgiving for His care through the day. It was a time to reflect on the goodness and mercy of God.

Jesus continued this same special time of fellowship with His disciples in the New Testament. Jesus often met with His disciples at "eventide."

And when it was evening, He came with the twelve…and reclined at the table (Mark 14:17).

In both the Old and the New Testament the Sabbath began *in the evening,* at sundown. It was a time to stop working and to prepare hearts for worship and fellowship with God.

I believe that God wants us to come to Him each evening in a similar manner. He wants us to spend a few moments reflecting on our day and how we did with what God entrusted to us for the fulfilling of His good purposes and plans and then to thank Him for His help in the successes, to ask His forgiveness and mercy for the failures, and to praise Him for His unconditional love and faithfulness throughout. And then I think He wants us to spend a few more moments seeking His good plans for the next day's activities and taking a moment to write these down. This has been very beneficial for me, because I find that when I go to bed with some "prayed-over plans" for the next day, I sleep better and get up with a sense of focus and anticipation. I have a plan and a purpose to fulfill—God's plan and purpose.

I can personally testify to the special joy participating in the *evening sacrifices* brings. For many years now, regardless of what may have transpired in the preceding hours, my husband and I have always ended each day with family devotions—together with God—reading His Word and praying together. It is still one of my favorite times of the day!

It is good to follow God's example in the creation of our days: *"And the evening and the morning were one day (Gen. 1:5,8,13,19,23,31).*

Write out a Bible verse that had special meaning to you today.

Based upon what you have learned today, write a prayer to God expressing the desires of your heart in applying these Truths to your life.

Chapter 2 — Day 4
In the Image of God

An Introduction to My Purpose and Reason to Be

> *Then God said, "Let Us make man in Our image, according to Our likeness...that they might **know** (Me), the only true God (Gen. 1:26, John 17:3).*
>
> *For the sake of My holy name, I will save you from all your uncleanness...so you will be My people and I will be your God (Ezek. 36:22,29,28).*
>
> *Bring My sons from afar, and My daughters from the ends of the earth, everyone who is called by My name, and whom I have created for My glory, whom I have formed, even whom I have made (Is. 43:6,7).*

Foundational Truth # 4

We have been created by God, in the Image of God, that we might enjoy a personal relationship with God through which we bring glory to God. It is God's desire that we all enter into a forgiven, loving, growing relationship with Him—through faith in Jesus and what He accomplished for us on the cross—and in this relationship, fulfill His good purposes for our lives day by day. As we do this, we begin to experience that blessed life God intends for all of us—a life of *purpose, peace and joy in the Holy Spirit (Eph. 2:10; Rom. 14:17).*

Today's study is one of the most crucial in this entire series. If we miss what God is saying to us here, we will miss the very purpose for which we were created and whatever we do, wherever we go, whatever we achieve, will be superficial at best and lead to eternal separation from God at worst. God created us to live in a loving, protective relationship with Him. As we commune with Him—through His Word and prayer—He guides us in all His good plans. In fulfilling these, He is glorified, we are satisfied, and joy flows in never-ending streams (John 7:38; Ps. 46:4).

Through demonic deception and my own pride and stubborn rebellion, I nearly missed this wonderful Truth! I spent 35 long, turmoiled "seeking but never finding" years in a most determined effort to pursue my own goals and aspirations on my own, totally independent of God. My heart became hardened and my conscience seared by habitual rejection of God. Pride blinded my eyes to the point that I was not even able to recognize my own *wretched, miserable state (Rev. 3:17).* But, by God's marvelous grace, there was yet an ember of life left in my dying conscience and through that tiny ember (Is. 42:3) God enabled me to experience the pangs of emptiness ever more acutely until I realized that something profoundly important was missing. That *something* was a personal relationship with Him. On that blessed life-altering day that I accepted Jesus' invitation (Rev. 3:20) to take care of that—to enter into that relationship—the restless, empty heart was filled with the warmth of God's love, forgiveness, and total acceptance. It was wonderful! And it was just the beginning of the joys that were yet to be realized as the relationship grew and God began to teach me through His precious Word all that He had in mind when He created me *in His image*.

We'll deal specifically with *how* we complete God's good purposes for our lives in chapter four when we study sanctification. For today, let us focus our attention upon the central theme of our created purpose: to know God and to bring honor and glory to God as we live daily in a loving, trusting, obedient relationship with Him.

> *For as the waistband clings to the waist of a man, so I made (my people) to cling to Me, that they might be for Me a people for renown, for praise and for glory (Jer. 13:11).*

> *He chose us…to adoption as sons, through Jesus Christ to Himself, according to the kind intention of His will. In Him we have redemption…the forgiveness of our trespasses, according to the riches of His grace which He lavished upon us…that we who were the first to hope in Christ should be to the praise of His glory (Eph. 1:4,5,7,12).*

St. Augustine expressed it well: "Thou hast made us for Thyself, O God and our hearts are restless until they find their rest in Thee." God created us with an innate need to love and be loved *by Him*, then out of the overflow of this love, share His love with others. He created us to be people who function *in relationship*. Tragically, through deception, selfishness and rebellion, or fear and unbelief many no longer have any clue of this, or of all the other good plans God has for us. Until we enter into a relationship with God and become actively involved with Him in the pursuit of fulfilling His ordained purposes for our lives, and helping others to do the same, we will experience a void that nothing else will ever be able to fill—nothing…ever!

So what about *God's image*. What exactly is the *image of God?*

The image of God is a reflection of the very nature and character of God. At the heart of this *image* is the *human soul* which is comprised of a *volitional mind, emotions,* and *will*. It is this unique *image* that sets us apart from all the rest of God's creation and enables us to commune and fellowship with God.

There are many aspects of God's nature and character. We could easily devote an entire study to this topic. Because time will not permit that here, we will look at just two "core" qualities that are interwoven into all other aspects of God's divine nature according to which we also were created for the purpose of reflecting and bringing glory to God. We lay another foundational stone:

Foundational Truth # 5

God is perfect love and transcendent holiness.

God is love (1 John 4:8). God is the essence and perfection of love. In God, love is perfect and love is complete. And that's the way it has always been in the Godhead. God the Father, God the Son and God the Holy Spirit, perfect and complete in their love for one another. It was out of the abundance of the overflow of God's perfect love, along with His intimate relational nature—that He chose to create a beautiful Universe and to place within it, to rule over it, a man and a woman who would *bear His image*, and reflect…*His glory!*

There is an aspect of love that must be discussed briefly here—and developed in more detail later—and that is that love must always have at its core the freedom to *choose*. Without this choice, there could be no true love, only coercion. In our relationship with God, we would be nothing more than automatons, performing the constricted duty demanded by an autocratic dictator. How thankful we should be that

God created us with the capacity to *choose* so that our relationship with Him is based on mutual love and fellowship built upon the freedom of *choice*—not coercion.

It is important to note here that the Word of God also clearly teaches the sovereignty of God—that today God rules over all. So how can man have *free will* and God still be *sovereign*? We don't have time to adequately study the human dilemma of this biblical mystery here today—the sovereignty of God in relation to the free will of man. We will look into this important topic in more detail later. For now, we need simply to recognize the freedom of choice God gives us as a gift of His grace.

One of the saddest realties of living in a fallen world is the incredible deception that pervades the world regarding the nature and attributes of God. Because of false teaching—or no teaching—for far too many, their concept of God is grossly distorted and vastly removed from a correct biblical view. These distorted images keep many from coming to God and entering into a personal relationship with Him. For example, one popular false teaching today diminishes God into a universal *force* that operates in the world through the *mind power* of people who are able to manipulate and control the *force*. What a sad and pitiful heresy. To many others, their perception of the "God of the Bible" is that of a mean, cruel tyrant who sits in heaven angrily waiting for someone to "mess up" so He can rain down severe and painful judgment upon them. This equally heretical view is the total fallacious opposite of the Truth (John 3:16!). Yet others have seared their conscience to the point that God does not exist at all. In their deluded state they claim to be their own "god" and "controller of their destiny." I think this is the saddest of all because of the degree of demonic deception and the impenetrable hardness of heart that develops as a result. I know how powerful this delusion can be, having lived in such a state for many years. I am only now beginning to recognize the true miracle of the mercy and grace of God that rescued me from it—a state that is so often, eternally fatal. There is rarely a day that goes by that I do not yet lift my hands to heaven in deep, oft tearful gratitude…and pray for those who may yet be there.

Who then is God? What is He *really* like? How has He revealed Himself in His Word?

The Lord, the Lord God, compassionate and gracious, slow to anger, and abounding in lovingkindness and Truth; who keeps lovingkindness for thousands, who forgives iniquity, transgression and sin (Ex. 34:6,7).

Thou art good and doest good; the Lord God is a sun and a shield; the Lord gives grace and glory; No good thing does He withhold from those who walk uprightly. O Lord of hosts, how blessed is the man who trusts in Thee! (Ps. 119:68, Ps. 84:11,12).

Do not be afraid, O Zion; Do not let your hands fall limp. The Lord your God is in your midst; He is mighty to save. He will exult over you with joy, He will quiet you with His love, He will rejoice over you with shouts of joy (Zeph. 3:16,17, NASB/NIV).

Surely God is good to Israel, to those who are pure in heart (Ps. 73:1).

God's love is manifest in His gracious compassion and perfect eternal *goodness*.

Another aspect of God's Divine nature is holiness.

Holy, Holy, Holy is the Lord God of hosts (Is. 6:3).

Holy: sacred; set apart; characterized by *transcendent* perfection and commanding adoration and reverence; spiritually pure; evoking or meriting veneration or awe; being awesome; *beyond human comprehension*. (A compilation of definitions taken from Nelson's Illustrated Bible Dictionary, 1968, Thomas Nelson Publishers, New York, p. 485; The Revell Bible Dictionary, 1990, Wynwood Press, New York, p. 489–90; Webster's Seventh New Collegiate Dictionary, 1965, G.&C. Merriam Co. Springfield, Massachusetts, p 397).

God is holy. At the heart of holiness is transcendency—set apart, separate from. God is transcendent. He is separate, set apart from His creation. He is transcendently pure, righteous, just, loving, flawless in perfection. We have been created *in His image*—to *reflect* His holiness, His glory. We will never be transcendent like God. But we are to reflect His glory through the new nature God gives us when we become His children (II Cor. 5:17). And we are called to be *set apart* from the rest of the world. We'll talk about this later when we study the new birth and regeneration. But for now we must recognize this radiant, glorious quality of God's nature—His transcendent, majestic, pure, flawless holiness. In all of the Word of God, there is not another aspect of God's nature that is emphasized in repetitive trilogy in both the Old and the New Testament:

Holy, Holy, Holy is the Lord of Hosts, the Lord God, Almighty, who was and is and is to come…worthy art Thou, O Lord our God to receive glory and honor and power (Rev. 4:8,11).

Please note that transcendent holiness manifests itself as the *glory of God*. We'll discuss this awesome attribute—holiness—in greater detail in a later chapter, but for today, just take a moment to ponder this aspect of the image of God that we were created to reflect! (1 Pet. 1:15).

And so it was that God, in the overflow of His love and joy, created a glorious, awe-inspiring Universe—the height and breadth of which we have not yet even begun to tap or comprehend. And even this was but a veiled reflection of His glory for surely: *the earth and the heavens and the highest heavens cannot contain the glory of God (Deut 10:14; Ps. 113:4–6; Rom. 11:33; 1 Tim. 6:15,16).* Then God, in His relational, inexpressible love, created a man and a woman—the very *image of Himself*—to fellowship with Him and to both *reflect and share the beauty and joy of His transcendent love and holiness (1 Cor. 10:31; Heb. 12:10).*

How blessed are the people who are so situated; How blessed are the people whose God is the Lord; He will fulfill the desire of those who fear Him; He will hear their cry and save them; For the Lord takes pleasure in His people; He will beautify the afflicted ones with salvation; they will go out with JOY and be lead forth in peace (Ps. 144:15, 145:19; Ps. 149:4; Is. 55:12).

Bible Study Supplement

Chapter 2 – Day 4 — In the Image of God

1. Read Gen. 1:26,27.

    a. What did God say? (vs. 26a)

Please note here that God said, *Let Us make man in Our image.* God—Father, Son, and Holy Spirit—in complete unity created man and woman. And this they did in their very own *image* in order that there might be intimate fellowship between the Creator and His most prized creation.

    b. In whose image did He create "male and female"? (vs. 27)

Note the distinction given already here *in the beginning* between the sexes: *male and female, created He them.* We are not the same, gender neutral, or "equal" in our bodily make-up or chemistry. God created us sexually unique to fulfill His perfect purposes in the perfect roles to which He has assigned us. We should rejoice in our God-created uniqueness and use it to enjoy beautiful harmony, love and fellowship with our mates—and others—just as God designed.

In Genesis 2 we are introduced to a technique of communication that God uses often in His Word when He wants to make an important point. He takes the same subject and repeats it a second (and sometimes a third or even fourth) time, usually in greater detail, or from a different perspective, to make sure that the point He is making is clearly understood. So, chapter two is, in reality, a repeat of critical points in chapter one. As you read and study the Word of God, be careful to always give extra attention when this means of communication is used, emphasizing a point through repetition.

2. Read Gen. 2:7.

    a. Who made man?

    b. How?

    c. How did man become a *living soul?*

Note: The *breath of God* is used throughout the Bible to refer to "life." The Bible says that God's Word is *God-breathed* (2 Tim. 3:16). That is why it is *living and active and sharper than any two-edged sword and able to judge the thoughts and intentions of the heart (Heb. 4:12).* (Because the *life of God* is living and active in it and through it) It is this *breath (life of God)* that we take into our soul every time we open, read, and meditate upon His Word. And it is in the strength and wisdom of this God-empowered life that we are able to know God and His great love for us and to fulfill His wonderful plan for our lives.

3. Read Gen. 2:18-25.

    a. For the first time since God began creating the world, He said: "It is not good." What was not good? (vs. 18)

    b. How did God solve this problem? (vs. 21–22)

    c. What role would this woman play in her relationship with her husband? (vs. 18b)

What a beautiful picture of God's love for relationship and completeness in this unity.

4. Read Ps. 139:13,14.

   a. What did God do? (for the psalmist and for you and me!) (vs. 13)

   b. Why did the psalmist praise (give thanks to) God? (vs. 14a)

5. Read Jer. 1:4,5.

   a. Who knew Jeremiah before He *formed him* in his mother's womb? (vs. 5)

   b. What else did God do before Jeremiah was born? (vs. 5)

You can be sure that the same God who knew Jeremiah long before he was knit together in his mother's womb also knew you and knitted every part of you together for His very special "set apart" (consecrated) purposes.

6. Read Ps. 103:8,11,13.

   a. List four characteristics of God. (vs. 8)

   b. How does God relate to us (vs. 13a)

   c. To whom does God relate in this manner? (vs. 13b)

7. Read Rev. 4:8,11.

   a. What did the four special angels surrounding God's Throne never stop saying? (vs. 8b)

   b. Of what is God worthy (vs. 11a)…why? (vs. 11b)

Two of the most beautiful passages in Scripture that tell of the love of God and the reason He created the glorious heavens and earth, man and woman, are found in Deut. 10 and Is. 43.

8. Read Deut. 10:14-17, 20,21.

   a. To whom do the heavens, the earth, and all that is in them belong? (vs. 14)

   b. What has God done for our fathers (and for us), their descendants? (vs. 15)

   c. Who is "the Lord your God"? (vs. 17)

   d. What should be our response in knowing this? (vs. 20,21a)

9. Read Is. 43:6b,7.

   a. Why did God create us? (vs. 7)

Note! – As we continue to study God's Word, we will discover why God creating us in His image and for His glory was the most loving thing He could have done, for indeed, it enables us to share in His divine nature, glory and JOY! (Heb. 12:10, 1 Pet. 1:8).

Love, Relationship, Joy – These were at the heart of all that God had in mind when He created the world, Adam and Eve, you, me. How incomprehensibly loving that God created us *in His image* that we might enter into a personal, intimate relationship with Him! Imagine with me what that must have looked like on that glorious 6th day in the paradise called Eden.

There He was, God, the Creator and sustainer of the vast Universe He had just completed, surrounded by the magnificent grandeur of His Creation—the stately majestic mountains, plush green, serene, flower-strewn valleys, colorful winged fowl of the air that flew gracefully above, and the elaborate iridescent beauty of the sea life in the ocean waters below—this great and awesome Creator God on that glorious day, knelt down and carefully, meticulously, with undivided attention, began to shape that cold, lifeless clay into the *very likeness of Himself*, the one with whom He would fellowship and commune in boundless love and endless joy…

Then God bent over and *breathed into his nostrils the breath of life, and man became a living soul (Gen. 2:7)*. And every time an egg and a sperm come together, that same God has already shaped that tiny soul *into His image* and breathed into him/her the breath of life!

> *Worthy art Thou, our Lord and our God, to receive glory and honor and power; for Thou didst create all things, and for Thy pleasure, they are and were created (Rev. 4:11, NASB, KJV)*

Write out a Bible verse that had special meaning to you today.

Based upon what you have learned today, write a prayer to God expressing the desires of your heart in applying these Truths to your life.

Chapter 2 — Day 5
The Revolt of Satan

The Assault on God's Perfect Kingdom of Love, Joy and Holiness
(The beginning of "The Long War Against God")

> *Then Lucifer (Satan) said in his heart, "I will raise myself above the stars of God; I will ascend above the heights of the clouds; I will make myself like the Most High" (Is. 14:12–14).*

Foundational Truth # 6

Obsessed with selfishness and pride, Satan chose to rebel against the loving reign of God and in so doing introduced into God's perfect Kingdom, sin and evil and the awful consequences they brought—separation from God, guilt, death.

We live in a world of two kingdoms in conflict. There is an enemy who has raised himself up against the loving sovereign rule of God. His goal is the destruction of the Kingdom of God. The world is currently in conflict because of this war: the *kingdom of Satan* against the *Kingdom of God*. The kingdom of Satan is a kingdom of darkness, wickedness and evil. The Kingdom of God is a kingdom of light, love and goodness. We, man and woman, are the focus of the conflict—the prize that will inhabit and fill the triumphant kingdom, or forever be separated from it.

Genesis 3 is one of the most crucial texts in Scripture. It records the details of the eternally consequential results of Satan's heinous scheme to usurp the power and position of God—the tragic fall of man (sin!), the corrupting of the perfect, holy image of God in man, separation from God...death. And this initial fall was only the beginning of Satan's diabolical war against God and against all who would choose to follow Him. It is imperative to our spiritual well-being that we examine this text carefully and prayerfully, for this scene, this diabolical scheme, is being played out over and over again in our own personal lives, in the lives of those we love, and in the lives of every man, woman, and child who will ever walk the face of this earth. How quickly, and with tragically little thought, we have read over this pivotal chapter far too long. We have not heeded the warnings that God lovingly gives us, so we continue to do what Adam and Eve did: *believe the lies of Satan over the Truth of God (John 8:44,31,32,36)*…and great has been the *fall*.

But God does not want us to be like this any longer *(Eph. 4:14)*. He doesn't want us to be *ignorant of Satan's schemes (2 Cor. 2:11)*. He wants us to be wise and confident, armed and prepared. So let's ask God to give us an alert mind and a courageous heart that we might be good soldiers who stand strong and victorious in these daily *kingdoms-in-conflict* battles.

Now the serpent (Satan) was more crafty than any beast of the field which the Lord God had made (Gen. 3:1).

Who is this serpent and from where did he come?

Here is another example of how we need the *sum of God's Word (Ps. 119:160)* to answer this question. The Bible tells us that Satan was originally created by God as an angel to rule with Him in the heavens (Is. 14:12–14; Ezek. 28:2–13). In fact, it tells us that he was the highest ranking angel in God's vast angelic realm (Ezekiel 28:14). He served at the right hand of God, dispensing and overseeing God's commands that maintained perfect beauty and order in the universe. And so it was. Everything was perfect and perfectly beautiful…until…

(Lucifer) said in his heart, "I will ascend to Heaven… above the heights of the clouds; I will make myself like the Most High (Isaiah 14:12–14).

In a totally unconscionable display of selfishness, pride and rebellion, Lucifer chose, through the free will God had given him, to rebel against his loving Creator. His diabolical scheme was to *raise (his) throne above the stars of God*—to dethrone God and become the ruler of the universe. With premeditated malice he began his wicked campaign to usurp the power, authority and position of God. *I will make myself like the Most High (Is. 14:12–14).*

And so began the long war against God, the battle between God (perfect, holy, unconditional love, order, and good) and Lucifer (selfishness, pride, murderous rebellion—evil), and the war continues. When Satan (Lucifer) rose up in prideful rebellion against God, he severed the beautiful relationship he had with God, and he introduced evil and chaos into God's perfect order. Therefore, God had no choice but to expel him from Heaven (Rev. 12:9; Is. 14:12). Good and evil (sin) could not live together because God is holy, and His holiness could not then, cannot now, and never will be capable of tolerating wickedness and evil and the pain and sorrow it causes. That is the very heart and nature of divine, holy love. There would be none of that (wickedness, evil, hurt and pain) in God's home, Heaven. And, praise God, there never will be!

So Lucifer was cast out of Heaven, down to earth (Rev. 12:9; Luke 10:18). On the day that Lucifer was cast out of Heaven, he began his diabolical plan to destroy God's perfect world of love, peace and order. To do this, he knew that he would have to destroy the one whom God created to fellowship with Him and to rule and reign over it—man. So Lucifer sought immediately to scheme against God's most precious *created-in-His-image* prodigy, for he knew that as man fell, so would fall the entire planet, and in its fallenness would yearn for a return to order and peace. And Lucifer would be there for the yearning soul. He would *make himself like the Most High (Is. 14:14).* Deceiving the world, he would lie and tempt and cajole all who were searching. He would become their "god" (under the guise of "self rule" by man) and the deception would be so great that none under his power would recognize their captivity—until it would be *too late* to turn back.

Little did man recognize that by listening to the lies and rebelling against God, he was entering into relationship with the one whose only goal was his temporal and eternal destruction. It was a mercilessly wicked scheme.

That is why Genesis 3 is one of the most important chapters in the Bible, for it records the details of the tragic results of Satan's heinous scheme: *The fall of man who **chose to believe the lies of Satan over the Truth of God** (Gen. 3:1–6).*

Bible Study Supplement
Chapter 2 — Day 5 — The Revolt of Satan

In Isaiah 14 and Ezekiel 28 we have the account of Satan's rebellion.

1. Read Is. 14:12–14.

    a. What did Satan say in his heart? (vs. 13,14b)

2. Read John 8:42–47.

    a. What is Satan's nature? (vs. 44) (List two major qualities.)

Please note that "lying" means to deceive. God warns us over and over of the deceptive power of Satan. Only the Word of God can cut through this kind of satanic deception in the spiritual realm—in our minds, hearts, wills, emotions.

    b. What do people who belong to God do? (vs. 47)

    c. Who do those who do not belong to God follow…and what do they want to do? (vs. 44a)

3. Read John 10:10a.

    a. What is Satan's chief and only purpose?

4. Read 1 Peter 5:8,9.

    a. What is Satan doing now? (vs. 8)

    b. How are we to be knowing this? (vs. 8a)

    c. What are two other names for Satan? (vs. 8) (Please fill in the blanks below).

    Your _____, the _____, *prowls about…seeking someone to devour.*

    d. What are we to do when Satan attacks—(tries to devour us)? (vs. 9a)

5. How has God spoken to your heart today through these clear warnings about the diabolical evil and deception of Satan?

Write out a Bible verse that had special meaning to you today.

Based upon what you have learned today, write a prayer to God expressing the desires of your heart in applying these Truths to your life.

Chapter 3

Memory Bible Verse: *The wages of sin is death, but the gift of God is eternal life in Christ Jesus our Lord (Rom. 6:23).*

Bonus Blessing Verse: *Truly, truly I say to you, unless one is born again, he cannot see the kingdom of God (John 3:3).*

Day 1

The Tragic Fall of Man – Part 1

(The Image of God Corrupted)

Day 2

The Tragic Fall of Man – Part 2

(Guilt, the Curse)

Day 3

Without the Shedding of Blood…

An Introduction to the Sacrificial System of Redemption

Day 4

Behold the Lamb of God

God's Unspeakable Gift of Salvation in Christ

Day 5

You Must be Born Again

Chapter 3 — Day 1
The Tragic Fall of Man — Part 1
(The Image of God Corrupted)

> *...and the Lord God commanded the man, saying, "From any tree of the garden you may eat freely; but from the tree of the knowledge of good and evil you shall not eat, for in the day that you eat from it you shall surely die"...and when the woman saw that the fruit was good for food, pleasing to the eye and desirable for gaining wisdom, she took some and ate it. She also gave to her husband and he ate it (Gen. 2:16,17, 3:6).*
>
> *Your sin has made a separation between you and your God (Is. 59:2).*
>
> *The wages of sin is death...and so sin entered the world and death by sin (Rom. 6:23, 5:12).*

Today we begin the most difficult week in this series as we face the unpleasant realities of the introduction of sin into the world and the awful consequences it caused...and continues to cause. But it is crucial to our spiritual well-being that we face this enemy with courage and the wisdom of God's Word that we may consistently overcome sin's deadly deception, power and control.

Foundational Truth #6

Sin is anything that rejects, rebels against or violates the perfect love and holiness of God. God created the universe to operate in holy love and righteousness. He created man and woman *in His image* to share the joy of such a kingdom. Sin corrupted God's beautiful plan and it destroyed the perfect holy image of God in man and woman. Sin also separated man from God because God is holy and holy and unholy cannot fellowship (dwell) together. Sin continues to separate man from God and brings death every time it is chosen: *The wages of sin is death (Rom. 6:23).*

God is Holy, and He created a perfect, holy world, which operated in complete harmony under His loving rulership. To maintain this perfect order, there was only one *law* given at the beginning and that was the very clear instruction that Adam and Eve were not to eat from the tree of the knowledge of good and evil. Up to this point, Adam and Eve had no experience of evil because all that God created was good and perfect. God wanted to protect them from the terrible, painful consequences of evil (sin)—separation from Him...death.

It is hard to imagine that Adam and Eve would ever disobey God, for they had everything they could possibly want or need in God's beautiful, perfect paradise. They even had God Himself as their friend and companion with whom they fellowshipped freely (Gen. 3:8). What more could they possibly desire?

Yet their hearts turned quickly away from loyalty and obedience to God's loving protection at the first temptation for *self-rule*—to exalt themselves over God. We can only conclude that such is the nature of an untested, undisciplined, uncommitted-to-God-alone *free will*. It is not able to perceive the value of God's deep and perfect love or the awful consequences of rejecting it.

We were introduced yesterday to the primary tool that Satan used (and continues to use) to destroy man's relationship with God: deception. Let's take a closer look at exactly how this weapon was employed in that first encounter between God's perfect love and Satan's rebellious, diabolical evil.

> *Now the serpent (Lucifer/Satan) was very crafty (deceptive, wicked)…and he said to the woman, "Indeed, has God said, You shall not eat from any tree of the garden?" And the woman said to the serpent, "From the fruit of the trees of the garden we may eat; but from the fruit of the tree which is in the middle of the garden, God has said, You shall not eat from it or touch it, lest you die." And the serpent said to the woman, "You surely shall not die! For God knows that in the day you eat from it your eyes will be opened, and you will be like God" (Gen. 3:1,4,5).*

Satan is a master *liar, deceiver and destroyer! (John 8:44, 10:10)*. Therefore, we can be sure that everything Satan says is a lie from the pit of hell with one goal in mind: to *rob, kill, and destroy (John 10:10)*. May God help us never to forget that. As a diabolical deceiver (employing supernatural deceptive powers), Satan knows exactly what to say to cause us to doubt God's perfect love and His sovereign protective rule. He also knows exactly what to say to appeal to that part of a proud, undisciplined will that is ever desiring to be *like God*: in control. Through his well-planned seductive lies and demonic deception, Satan captured the hearts and minds of Adam and Eve and deceived them into believing that God was withholding something good from them and that they knew better than God what was best for them. Therefore, they, not God should be in control of their lives.

But this was a total distortion of reality, because God *created us* to be dependent people—*in relationship with* and *dependent upon Him (Col. 1:17)*. In such a trusting father/son, father/daughter dependency, we enjoy the fullness of His love, fellowship and protection. He, Himself fills our souls and satisfies our deepest longings (Ps. 63:1–5). Whenever we try to fill that part of our soul created in the *image of God* reserved only for God (to occupy and fill) with "anyone" or "anything" apart from Him—food, drugs, alcohol, materialism, pleasure, a career, education, intellectual achievement, the "love" and attention of another human (usually leading to illicit sexual involvement), the applause of man (human recognition),, etc.—you can be sure that disillusionment and disappointment will be our haunting companion. None of these counterfeits will ever satisfy that God-created need for a loving, intimate relationship with *Him*.

Do you see the tragic twisting of Truth (the deception) in Satan's temptation to Eve? *You surely shall not die! For God knows that in the day you eat from it…your eyes will be opened, and you will be like God (Gen. 3:4,5).*

Satan always makes evil (disobedience and rebellion against God) appear as good! How good it *appears* to be *in control*, to answer to no one. But think of the consequences of such a situation. If man were *in control*, how many "gods" would there be? We would have as many "gods" as there are men and women. The result? Continual conflict, chaos, and destruction as each "god" vied for his own "sovereign rule." Exactly what it was like when Israel abandoned God in the days of the judges. *Everyone was doing what was right in his own eyes (Judges 17:6)*. And precisely what it is like today, with precious little respect or reverence for God or His Word—His good rules that insure order, keep us safe, and show us how to live in love and peace with God, with ourselves and with one another.

God created man both a physical and spiritual being. He created man from the dust of the earth (physical), then breathed into him the breath of life (spiritual). When God first created Adam and Eve, their physical body and spiritual soul were in complete harmony because they were holy, and in this perfect, sinless state they were "at one" with God and each other. But when Adam and Eve sinned, their *spirits*, that life-giving spiritual part of them that was created in the perfect holiness of God for the purpose of fellowshipping with Him, died. Their spirits were immediately separated from God and thus from the breath/life of God. This is because God is holy, and holy and unholy (sin) cannot dwell or fellowship together (Is. 59:2). So this was the first, immediate death. It is what the Bible calls spiritual death, or separation from God (Eph. 2:5; Is. 59:2).

Separation from God always results in the loss of the basic sustaining and enriching spiritual qualities that are at the heart of *life*—love, joy, peace, value, purpose, contentment—because God is the author, provider, and sustainer of all these good, *life-giving* gifts. Yes, we can develop counterfeit emotions of love, joy and peace, etc. (Satan is great at counterfeiting). But these counterfeits will eventually let us down because there is no *life* in them. They are built out of spiritual deadness. It is impossible to experience real life out of deadness. That's why whenever we try to find the fulfillment of these emotional needs apart from God, it will be but a superficial and temporal counterfeit experience producing painful disappointment, disillusionment, and discontent.

Another devastating result of spiritual death and separation from God is the tormenting pangs of guilt, because we are living in violation of our primary purpose: to have a personal, loving, satisfying, glorifying relationship with God.

> *...therefore, sin entered the world and death through sin, and so death spread to all men, because all sinned (Rom. 5:12).*

When Adam and Eve chose to sin, the perfect holy image of God in which they had been created was fatally flawed. They now possessed a *sin nature*—an innate *desire* to sin and rebel against God—that dominated their "will," causing corruption and distortion to the holy image of God. This *sin nature* is also referred to in the Bible as *indwelt*, or *indwelling sin*: that fallen condition in which sin is present—dwells—in every human being that is conceived. This *sin nature* has been passed on to every person in every generation since Adam and Eve. You have it. I have it. Our children have it. All of mankind has inherited this unholy *sin nature*. But before we condemn Adam and Eve for blowing it, the Bible also clearly teaches that every one of us would have made the same choice that Adam and Eve made had we been there under the same circumstances at that moment when the temptation to sin was given (Rom. 5:12). This is proven every day by the sinful choices we yet continue to make, even though we still have a choice—to trust and obey God or to rebel against Him, sin. And sin still brings its inevitable consequences—separation from God...death.

Adam and Eve's rebellion—sin!—also brought physical death as well: *and Adam died (Gen. 5:5)*.

How tragic that Adam and Eve *chose* to disobey God. How could they do this after God so lovingly and so clearly told them what the awful consequences would be? They did it for the very same reasons that we so often *choose* to believe the lies of Satan over the Truth of God: pride and unbelief.

Adam and Eve obviously did not *believe* God when He said: *In the day you eat of it, you shall surely die.* Instead, they *chose* to defy God's loving instruction and to believe Satan: *You surely shall not die! You will be like God (pride!).*

Equally as tragic is the fact that millions of people today still willingly choose to believe this root lie of Satan: "You can be *like God*—in control. You can be your own god." And so they continue in a life of prideful rebellion against, and thus, separation from, God. The result of this stubborn rebellion is always the same: spiritual death or deadness. And, even more tragic is the fact that continuing to believe this lie will lead eventually to eternal separation from God—hell.

The consequences of sin and the spiritual death it always produces can never be stressed enough. Spiritual death—separation from God—always results in *death* to all that God produces in us when we are in fellowship with Him: true and lasting blessing and joy, spiritual health and wholeness, fulfilling meaning and purpose, etc. (Gal. 5:16–25).

I can hardly imagine the untold pangs of guilt and remorse that Adam and Eve suffered as a result of their own dreadful choice. To have had that firsthand experience of life with God in that precious oneness and holy perfection of an intimate and mutually loving relationship with God in a beautiful, perfect environment—and then to lose it in a second, all over a rebellious lust for *self-rule* and a moment's pleasure. May we heed well the warning!

...and so sin entered the world, and death by sin (Rom. 5:12).

Bible Study Supplement

Chapter 3 – Day 1 — The Tragic Fall of Man — Part 1

(The Image of God Corrupted)

1. Read Gen. 2:16,17.

    a. What did God tell Adam he <u>could</u> do? (vs. 16)

    b. What did God lovingly and clearly command Adam <u>not</u> to do? Why? (vs. 17)

2. Read Gen. 3:1-5.

    a. From what you read here (vs. 1,4,5) and from what you learned about Satan last week, describe his character:

Satan's character is the personification of sin. He is a diabolical, merciless liar, deceiver and murderer! His demonic powers of deception are supernatural—making wrong *appear* right, right *appear* bad, and evil *appear* good and desirable. *There is a way that seems right to a man, but in the end, it is the way of death (Prov. 14:12).* <u>Only the Spirit of God working through the Word of God</u> as we read it, study it, cherish it and obey it, <u>can cut through that kind of demonic deception</u> and keep us safe and secure from Satan's deceptions and sin's allurements (Heb. 4:12; 2 Cor. 4:4). You will hear this statement, or portions of this statement, many times throughout this study. It is repeated because it is imperative that we recognize and apply this Truth continually...*lest as the serpent deceived Eve by his craftiness, your minds should be led astray (2 Cor. 11:3).* Be sure of this, you and I are no match for Satan's demonic powers of deception. Without the clear, unalterable Truth of the Word of God, we will be *led astray* and fall for sin's deceptive temptations every time, and we will experience the awful consequences sin always brings—separation from God, guilt, death. God has given us His Word to show us clearly what is truly *good* (blessings and life) and what is *evil* (sin and death). That is why we need to read God's Word and study God's Word daily...and we need to *hide it in our hearts – Ps. 119:11* (memorize it) so that when Satan comes to us with a lie, we will recognize it immediately for what it is, and we will be able to stand firm against it with the Truth of God's Word (Matt. 4:1–11).

    b. What was Satan's first temptation to Eve? (vs. 1b)

The first thing Satan did was to raise doubt in Eve's mind about the love and goodness of God, and the Truth of His Word. Isn't this the way sin always begins? He wanted, and succeeded, to stir within Eve a spirit of unbelief and discontent so that she began to question God's loving commands: "Why did God make that command not to eat the fruit from the tree of the knowledge of good and evil? Was it because He wanted to withhold something good from me...something that would be better than what He has given me?" By raising doubt in Eve's mind about the love and goodness of God, he also succeeded in turning Eve's attention away from God and onto the forbidden fruit and her own selfish lusts. We do well to remember the deadly potential of falling for this kind of temptation—questioning God's love and goodness, and in that doubt turning our attention away from God and onto our own selfish lusts for the hurtful things God has forbidden. For it is this very temptation that has proven Satan's most effective weapon throughout the history of mankind. He used it successfully on Eve, and you can be sure He will use it to tempt you and me as well. May God help us all to heed this warning.

    c. What was Eve's answer to Satan's question? (vs. 2,3)

It is important to note that Eve clearly understood God's command not to eat of the fruit from the tree in the middle of the garden—the tree of the knowledge of good and evil. *Knowing* God's command was not enough to keep her from falling for Satan's lies. So it is with us. It is not *knowing* what God's Word *says* that keeps us secure in God's love and protection. It is trusting God enough to *obey it* that keeps us from falling.

We would do well to pay attention here also to two fatal mistakes that Eve made that led to her downfall and ultimately to the fall of the human race. And they are the same two mistakes that we, being descendents of Eve, make far too often. Let's look at them.

Eve's first fatal mistake was entering into conversation with the devil. God created us to commune and fellowship with Him. And in this intimate fellowship and communion, we are protected by God from the devil's lies and deceptions. *We cannot commune with the devil and God at the same time.* The moment we turn our attention to the devil and enter into conversation with him, we are, in reality, turning our back on God and we sever our relationship with Him. In this state of separation from God, we are no longer protected by His wisdom, discernment, and power to overcome. We are but helpless pawns for the devil's diabolical lies and deceptions (John 10:10a, 2 Cor. 2:11).

Eve's second deadly mistake was in turning her focus away from God and all that He had given her *richly to enjoy* (Gen. 2:16, 2 Tim. 6:17) to the one thing that she was not to partake of: the *forbidden fruit*. How often do we allow Satan (through our lustful flesh) to cause us to focus upon the *forbidden fruit* instead of all the other good fruit (not just "food" but habits, practices, lifestyle choices, our relationship with God, etc.) that God has given us to enjoy that is always the best for us. We must study the Word of God that we might know what God says, not adding to or taking away from it (Rev. 22:18,19), in order that we will be kept from believing the devil's lies and deceptions, and fall and die. Remember, God's laws are always good and protective, <u>not burdensome</u> *(1 John 1:5)*. It is only when we add to them or take away from them that they become burdensome.

    d. What was Satan's twofold lie as a result of Eve's focus upon the forbidden fruit? (vs. 4,5)

3. Read Gen. 3:6 and 1 John 2:15–17.

In 1 John 2:15–17, we are told of the three basic lusts of a sinful nature that, if allowed to fester, (focus upon, think about) will lead to sin every time. They are: the lust of the flesh (the fleshly cravings of a fallen self-centered rather than God-centered heart), the lust of the eye (discontent, greed), and the boastful pride of life (selfishness, pride, rebellion). Do you see these three basic lusts working in Eve's heart, which led to her fall?

1) The *"lust of the flesh"* - *She saw that the tree was good for food.* Eve did what so many of us foolishly do. She listened to Satan and followed the desires of her selfish, unbelieving heart rather than the voice of her faithful, loving God. She focused upon her fleshly lust and upon its gratification until nothing would stop her from satisfying that lust. She also focused upon the temporary pleasure that satisfying her fleshly craving would bring rather than the long-term consequences. In other words, she knew what she wanted, and what she wanted was immediate gratification of her fleshly lusts. It is that all too common inner rebellion that says: "I want what I want, when I want it, and as much as I want…and I *will have it*—regardless of what God says!"

2) The *"lust of the eye"* - *The fruit was a delight to her eyes.* Next, she looked on the external qualities of the forbidden fruit. How it *appeared* to her deceived, lustful flesh. To her insatiably greedy heart, it *looked* good. *There is a way that seemeth right to a man, but in the end, it is the way of death (Prov. 14:12).*

3) The *"boastful pride of life"* - *The tree was desirable to make one wise"* (as wise—or wiser—than God). Finally, she allowed her pride to convince her that she knew better than God what was best for her! Therefore, she pridefully and rebelliously defied God.

    a. What did Eve do to fulfill her fleshly lusts? (There are two actions listed here. What was the *first* thing she did? (vs. 6b)

Every time I read this story, I am reminded of the deadly consequences of following in the way of Eve: going places I should never go (what was Eve doing sitting in front of and gazing lustfully upon the one thing of which God forbade her to partake?) and dwelling on things I should never dwell on, i.e., the *forbidden fruit of sin's enticements*. Dwelling upon fleshly lusts instead of the riches of God's life-giving promises—and loving, protective warnings—in His Word will inevitably lead to disobedience. Disobedience is sin. Sin separates us from God, and brings on the awful pangs of guilt…and *death*. Studying Eve's *bad example* and the awful consequences her decision cost her, makes me all the more determined to be like the wise psalmist who *cherished God's precious Word, meditated upon it continually, hiding it in his heart, then trusting and obeying it in order to keep his feet from evil (Psalm 119:1–11, 100–105, sel.)*. As I fill my heart and mind with the Truths of God's Word, there will be no empty place for the devil's lies and deceptions to enter. I will be able to immediately recognize the lie and stand strong against it (2 Cor. 10:5).

    b. Looking at the last part of verse 6, what was the second thing that Eve did? (vs. 6b)

Women, we need to take note here of the incredible power of influence we have over the men in our lives. We can influence them for good or for evil. We need to guard this power very carefully, asking God to help us be influencers for good to our husbands, encouraging them in the ways of God and in their role as head of the household and God-appointed leader in our home. (If not married, our power of influence affects our relationships with our fathers, brothers, nephews and other men with whom we associate). Eve's tragic example is but the beginning of many other similar examples in the Bible in which women willfully influenced their men for evil, bringing sin and destruction upon them, their family, and in some cases upon an entire nation. May God help us all to be very careful about how we handle this wonderful gift God has given us—the powerful gift of *"influence"*—that we may use it wisely as God intended, for good and not for evil.

4. Read Rom. 5:12.

    a. What *entered the world* as a result of Adam and Eve's rebellion against God's good, protective law? (two things)

5. Read Rom. 6:23a.

    a. What are the *wages* (penalty) *for sin?*

Write out a Bible verse that had special meaning to you today.

Based upon what you have learned today, write a prayer to God expressing the desires of your heart in applying these Truths to your life.

Chapter 3 — Day 2
The Tragic Fall of Man — Part 2
(Guilt, the Curse)

> *Then the eyes of both of them were opened, and they knew that they were naked; and they sewed fig leaves together and made themselves loin coverings...and they hid themselves from the presence of the Lord God among the trees of the garden (Gen. 3:7,8).*
>
> *Then the Lord God called to the man, "Where are you?" (Gen. 3:9).*
>
> *...to Adam God said...cursed is the ground because of you; in toil you shall eat of it...and cursed is the man who trusts in mankind and makes flesh his strength, and whose heart departeth from the Lord (Gen. 3:17, Jer. 17:5 NASB/KJV).*

Foundational Truth # 8

In addition to spiritual death and separation from God, sin invokes guilt, causes the sinner to attempt to *hide from God* and puts him under a *curse* (the destructive domination of the sin nature). Yet, God, in His love, continues to call out to man, beckoning him to return to Him and enter into a loving, forgiven relationship with Him, where the curse of sin is broken!

Billy Graham included this wise caveat in a number of his messages: "Sin operates on the principle of sowing and reaping as expressed in *Gal. 6:7,8: Do not be deceived, God is not mocked; for whatever a man sows, this he will also reap. For the one who sows to his own flesh (rejects God, sins habitually) shall from the flesh reap corruption.* You always reap a crop that is more than you sowed, matures later than you expected and lasts longer than you want."

The story of Adam and Eve still rings through the ages in confirmation of this tragic Truth. The moment Adam and Eve chose to believe the lies of Satan and to rebel against God, they began to experience the internal conflict of conscience-wrenching shame and guilt that sin always produces. In a vain attempt to ease the pain of this inner torment, they tried to hide themselves from the presence of the Lord. And man, in his sinful state has been attempting to hide himself from the presence of God ever since.

> *And they heard the sound of the Lord God walking in the garden in the cool of the day...Then the Lord God called to the man, and said to him, Where are you? (Gen. 3:9)*

God in His incomprehensible love and mercy called out to sinful, rebellious Adam and Eve, "Where are you?" And God in that same love and mercy has been calling to proud and self-sufficient man ever since to return and to enter into a loving, trusting, relationship with Him.

But stubborn, rebellious man refuses to listen, and he fails to comprehend that even though he may run from God, he cannot hide.

Where can I go from Thy Spirit? Or where can I flee from Thy presence? If I ascend to Heaven, Thou art there; If I make my bed in Sheol, behold, Thou art there…If I dwell in the remotest part of the sea, even there Thy hand…will lay hold of me (Psalm 139:7–10, sel.).

It was this loving hand of God that sought out His fallen children—even after they had rebelled and rejected His love. He could have destroyed them in that terrible moment of their rebellion. But in His tender, compassionate love, He called out to them, then He went after them to bring them back to Him—to repentance and a renewal of their relationship with Him.

"Who told you that you were naked? Have you eaten from the tree of which I commanded you not to eat?" And the man said, "The woman whom Thou gavest to be with me, she gave me from the tree, and I ate. Then the Lord said to the woman, What is this you have done? And the woman said, "The serpent deceived me, and I ate" (Gen. 3:12,13).

With the introduction of sin also came the introduction of the "blame game." Rather than act like a man, confess, and deal with the consequences of his sinful choice, Adam blamed Eve for his sin, Eve blamed the devil, and they both blamed God. And sinful man continues to follow Adam's example, always trying to find an excuse for his sin, someone he can blame so that he does not have to own up to his responsibility for it. And God alone knows the untold pain that this has caused through the ages. Blame-shifting never solves the problem of sin or its painful consequences. It only complicates and magnifies it. Personal responsibility, confession, and repentance are God's (and the only effective) solution. May God help us to avoid the hurtful, deadly trap of blame-shifting and respond to our sinful choices with mature responsibility and true repentance.

And the Lord said to the serpent, because you have done this, cursed are you more than all the… beasts of the field; on your belly shall you go; and dust shall you eat all the days of your life (Gen. 3:14).

God is speaking to Satan, who was immediately cut down to the form of a snake. I'm sure that this did not sit well with this previously strikingly-handsome, charismatic angelic being. And what a picture of sin and its awful, ugly consequences this is. That slimy, repulsive creature slithering around eating dirt and striking at people every chance it gets. Every time I look at a snake now, I see a picture of sin with its slithering demonic deceptions and ugly consequences.

Cursed are you…(there will be) enmity between you (Satan) and the woman, and between your seed and her seed; He shall bruise you on the head, and you shall bruise Him on the heel. To the woman He said…In pain you shall bring forth children…to Adam He said, cursed is the ground because of you; in toil you shall eat of it…both thorns and thistles it shall grow…by the sweat of your brow, you shall eat bread (Gen. 3:14–19, sel.).

Here we are introduced to the tragic ongoing consequence of Adam and Eve's rebellion—*the curse of sin.*

Webster defines a curse as: "an invocation for harm or injury, evil." Man's rebellion against God (willful decision to disobey God) brought upon him an *invocation for harm, injury, and evil.*

There would be continual enmity (strife) between the seed of the woman and the seed of the devil—those who chose to follow God and those who chose to follow the devil. Tensions would erupt into spiritual—and often physical—battles and bloodshed. There would be oppressive guilt. God is letting us all know here that this continual *enmity* is the way it would be in a sin-cursed, fallen world. But the worst result of the curse of sin would be the separation from God—from His love, protection, forgiveness and peace. Please note, however, that already in this verse, at the very introduction of sin and its *curse* upon man—enmity, hardship and death—God introduces His *plan of salvation* to *overcome* the awful curse. He would send a Savior who would pay the price for sin—"death"—and restore man to a forgiven, loving relationship with God. The "He" to whom God refers is Jesus. Through His atoning sacrificial death followed by His victorious resurrection (victory over sin and death) on man's behalf, Jesus would *crush Satan on the head (Gen. 3:15)*. He would deal a death blow to Satan's power to control man and make him sin. In the redemption process, God would allow Satan to *bruise Jesus*, indicating the suffering He would endure for us. All who put their faith and trust in Jesus and what He did to pay the penalty for their sins, would break the curse and would be empowered to live lives of liberty and victory over sin. In the place of the internal conflict and guilt, there would be forgiveness and restoration with God in an intimate, protective relationship. In the security of that relationship would come an abiding, never ending peace, contentment, and joy. It was a beautiful plan.

But before we look more closely at that wonderful plan, we need to back up for a moment and look at the result sin's curse brought upon the now *fallen* image (nature) of man and woman.

> *To the woman He said, "I will greatly multiply your pain in childbirth; in pain you shall bring forth children;…your desire shall be (to rule over) your husband, (but) he shall rule over you (Gen. 3:16).*

We all understand clearly the reality of the first part of the curse of sin upon women—pain in childbearing. But I fear that we take much too lightly the second part—*your desire shall be (to rule over) your husband, (but) he shall rule over you.* Women, we need to recognize here that we have inherited Eve's rebellious, authority-usurping propensity. Our sinful, fallen nature has an insatiable desire to *control* our husbands…and everyone and everything else around us. That's the bad news. But the good news is that Jesus, God's promised deliverer, has already come. He has not only borne the penalty for our sins (death), but He has also broken the curse sin had upon us so that we no longer must live under its control and consequent guilt. In the next few days we will be studying how we can enter into that redemptive saving relationship and never again live under the curse of sin. And as we do, we will find that because Jesus has broken the curse of sin, and because we now rest completely in the security of God's love and victory for us, that formerly driven "need to control" has been dismantled. We can now gladly and willingly submit to our husband's God-ordained protective headship and become for our husbands (and others) what God designed us to be: helpmates, nurturers, and encouragers. God always blesses obedience. As we persevere in perfecting the good, godly character qualities of true biblical womanhood, we will find a new joy, peace and fulfillment that we never knew before, and it will become a delight, not a dread, to submit, support and "rest" in our husband's headship and authority.

I recognize that because of the pervasiveness and the dreadful potential of sin, there are extreme cases in which life-threatening abuse is involved, in which case the woman may be forced—for her protection and the protection of her children—to remove herself from such a situation, at least temporarily. My heart aches for these women. And I pray that they will find encouragement in the clearly proclaimed promise of God that nothing is impossible with Him. God can break even the most rebellious, wicked heart and bring him back to Himself (Matt. 19:26). Let us pray for these husbands—that God will do just that. And let us pray for and encourage the women we know who are facing difficult marriage and home situations to persevere in obedience and being the kind of women God has called them to be and in so doing, very often serve as the instrument through whom God works to bring the wayward husband to Himself. Let us never stop praying for or believing Him for this (1 Tim. 2:4).

> *Then to Adam He said, Because you have listened to the voice of your wife, and have eaten from the tree about which I commanded you, saying, 'You shall not eat from it', cursed is the ground because of you…In*

toil you shall eat of it all the days of your life. Both thorns and thistles it shall grow for you; by the sweat of your brow you shall eat bread (Gen. 3:17–19, NASB/KJV).

In these verses we are introduced to the two-fold effect of the curse of sin upon man. First, there would be a natural propensity to abdicate his God-given responsibility as the physical and spiritual head of the family. As the God-appointed leader, the man, not his wife, was to be the protector and provider of his family, making sure physical and spiritual needs were met. In God's eyes, Adam was ultimately responsible for Eve's sin because of his failure to fulfill his role as her protector from Satan's deception, standing strong against his lies, as he should have (1 Tim. 2:14).

Secondly, because of his devastating failure, Adam would now have to carry out his responsibilities *by the sweat of his brow*. He would continually encounter invading thorns and thistles—trials and difficulties—that would cause problems and interfere with his God-given responsibilities as provider and head of the family. He would have to look to God for the strength and enablement to overcome them.

Please note here once again, women, the tremendous influence we have on our men! Adam wanted to *please* Eve. So rather than stand up to her when she was clearly disobeying God and tempting him to sin, he gave in to her wishes and sinful desires. We women today continue to wield this same powerful influence over our men. We can use this influence in a godly way to build up our men, encouraging them to fulfill their God-ordained role and purposes or, in a selfish and sinful way, we can use it to influence them to give in to our (and their) sinful lusts and demands.

The wise woman builds her house, but the foolish tears it down with her own hands (Prov. 14:1).

Bible Study Supplement

Chapter 3 – Day 2 — The Tragic Fall of Man — Part 2 (Guilt, the Curse)

1. Read Gen. 3:7.

    a. What was the first consequence of Adam and Eve's sinful rebellion against God? (vs. 7a)

    b. How did Adam and Eve attempt to deal with their sinful state? (vs. 7b)

The first tragic consequence of Adam and Eve's sinful rebellion was the loss of innocence—their purity and holiness before God. That beautiful, flawless *image of God* in which they were created had been destroyed. As we discussed last time, this resulted immediately in spiritual death—a separation from God—because holy cannot dwell or fellowship with unholy. Adam and Eve knew this. Guilt and shame overwhelmed them. They were painfully aware that they could no longer stand in the presence of God and fellowship with Him as they had freely done before, for God was holy, and they were now defiled and sinful. It is interesting to note that "nakedness" is used throughout the Bible to refer to the exposure of our sinful condition before God (who is holy). In a desperate attempt to cover their sin, they sewed loin coverings from fig leaves to hide their nakedness from exposure to God's holy perfection. But it did not work. It did not work for Adam and Eve, and it will not work for us, either. Fig leaves (our human attempt to cover our sin apart from God's plan of redemption) will never hide our sin from God. Adam and Eve, just like us, needed a Savior—not fig leaves!

2. Read Gen. 3:8–10.

    a. What was Adam and Eve's response when they heard God *walking in the garden*? (vs. 8)

    b. Why do you think Adam was afraid when God called to him, "Where are you?" (vs. 10)

Adam clearly knew the penalty for sin—death. He had already died spiritually, and now he feared for his physical life as well. There are countless people in the world today who live their lives in fear of death and the judgment that will follow because they have never experienced the precious love and forgiveness of God by entering into a loving, forgiven relationship with Him. Only in such a relationship can any of us experience that wonderful peace—peace with God, with ourselves, and with one another—and the joy that flows from it, that only God can give.

3. Read Gen. 3:12,13.

    a. How did Adam respond to God's probing question: "Have you eaten from the tree of which I commanded you not to eat?" (vs. 12)

    b. How did Eve respond when the Lord asked her, "What is this you have done?" (vs. 13)

As mentioned earlier, rather than accepting personal responsibility for their sin—rebellion and willful rejection of God's command—Adam and Eve played the blame game: "The woman whom Thou gavest to me, she gave me from the tree…The serpent deceived me, and I ate" (Gen. 3:12,13). Tragically, we live in a society that insists on continuing on in this kind of selfish, irresponsible behavior: blaming others for our sins. That is, in itself, a form of rebellion against God who says that we are each one personally accountable for our sin (Ezek. 18:1-4; Lev. 5:1-7, 14-19). The real tragedy of the blame game is that as long as we continue to blame others (my husband, my parents, my "genes," the devil, society, or even my own "natural weaknesses"), refusing to take personal responsibility, there is no hope for true forgiveness and restoration to a right relationship with God. We will continue to live in a self-destructive world of deception, lies, excuses, and habitual sin that takes us ever deeper into shame and guilt and a sense of failure. God cannot heal a sick soul that refuses to acknowledge its own rebellious depravity.

God alone knows the full tragic toll of destruction that has resulted from the prevailing "psychologized" mindset that no longer acknowledges sin for what it is but calls it by new, politically-correct labels, offering people an excuse for their sin but never the true repentance and forgiveness they so desperately need. Without forgiveness, people are left with no real hope that things will ever get any better. They are told they must *live with* their problem and *learn to cope*. That is not freedom. That is *bondage*. And it is from this kind of bondage that Jesus came to set us free. *Excuses will never take away the guilt, shame, fear, inner turmoil of sin, or the ultimate penalty that it requires—death.* Only repentance through the love of God made possible by the price Jesus paid for sin's penalty will do that. People do not need excuses for their sins; they need forgiveness. They need a Savior. May God help us all to avoid this very dangerous and deadly trap: looking for an excuse for our sin rather than looking to God for forgiveness and His merciful love and grace to overcome it.

4. Read Gen. 3:14,15.

    a. What was the first curse affecting man that came as a result of his rebellion? (vs. 15a)

    b. What else does God clearly announce to Satan (and to Adam and Eve) after He told of the enmity that would now exist between God's "seed" (the followers of God) and Satan's "seed" (the followers of Satan)? (vs. 15b)

The enmity that God spoke of would not only affect relationships among men who would remain faithful to God and those who would choose to follow after Satan, it would also affect every man and woman personally, as there would now be two natures resident within them. There would be ongoing strife (conflict, turmoil) between man's former perfect holy nature and his now fallen sinful nature, his sin-sick soul. This internal battle, called *the conflict of the two natures*, would go on throughout the earthly lifetime of fallen man. But the good news is that God, in His unfathomable compassion and mercy, already had a plan in place to *overcome* this curse. God introduced His plan right there in the very same moment that Adam and Eve faced the curse they had brought upon themselves.

5. Read Gen. 3:16.

    a. What were the two main curses of sin specifically upon woman?

We've already talked about the second component of this curse, but it bears repeating here that we women take far too lightly the destructive potential of this aspect of our fallen nature and thus are often ill-prepared to stand against and overcome it by faith and obedience to God—the curse of *desiring to rule over our husbands*, to usurp their God-given role as leader and head of the household. How many homes today suffer untold strife and contention because the woman fails to overcome the curse of wanting to *control/lead*. But when the woman confesses this sin and turns to God, trusting and obeying Him in following His good instructions for true womanhood, she finds her greatest joy in fulfilling her role as nurturer and encourager in support of her husband's God-ordained "headship." Thus, she becomes a blessing and not a curse to her husband and to her family (Prov. 31:10–31, Titus 2:3–5).

When I first became a Christian, this was one of the hardest of all sin's curses that I had to overcome. I was by nature a strong, enterprising, achievement-oriented woman. And I had lived in a female-dominated society (as our society remains today) for so long that not only condoned female dominion ("headship," authority) but also extolled it as our right as women. I was sure this was the way it was *supposed* to be. I craved and thrived on control, success, positions of authority, and the attention these got me. I was most definitely the self-appointed "head" of our household and the ultimate decision-maker. The result: A most miserable existence for both my husband and me, where contention and strife ruled daily. Disobeying God's good rules of order always brings strife, chaos, and discontent. I had so much to learn and apply. But as I continued in God's Word and recognized my sinful attitude and behavior in this, I repented, and I began to willingly (and joyfully!) relinquish the control of our home to the one to whom it had rightfully been given by God, my husband. I say joyfully, as I was now able to recognize the incredible burden that I had placed upon myself—through my disobedience—that God never intended me to bear. As I began to obey God's good instructions concerning biblical womanhood, an amazing miracle of transformation took place. God replaced the former strife and contention with a sweet, Christ-centered love, joy, and peace that now permeates our hearts and our home.

This God-ordained role of the headship of men applies in every other relationship, not just husband and wife. The man is clearly commanded in God's Word to hold the position of leadership with the woman serving in a support role as a completer. Primarily, this involves nurturing (building up) and encouraging. The violation in obeying this God-given rule of order concerning male/female roles is rampant in our society, and the results have been predictable: strife and conflict in relationships, organizations, businesses, a divorce rate of nearly 60%!, mass gender confusion, and the destruction of the family.

Of course it is not *all* the woman's fault. Men have abrogated their God-given roles as leaders—spiritual and physical heads of the home and society—creating a huge gap that has put untold pressure on women to somehow *fill*. We can't "fix" that, but we can *pray* for our husbands and other men in our lives that God will intervene and help them to understand their God-given role and give them the courage to accept it and carry it out in a godly, Christ-honoring way. And we can be obedient to what God calls us. Remember the power of influence that we have with men: to influence them for good or to drive them further from God through our stubbornness in demanding our way, continual criticism and unbiblical usurping of their authority. I love 1 Peter 3:1–3, which talks about the beauty of a *quiet and gentle spirit* that influences a woman's husband and children for good and godliness. As our husbands see and experience our Christlike love and encouragement, they will be convicted in their own hearts to begin to live up to their responsibilities. What a difference we women who do know and desire to obey God's Word can make as we, through the power of the Holy Spirit in us, overcome this curse of desiring to rule over our husbands—and other men in our lives—and begin to build strong families according to God's good plan.

There is far more involved in this important subject of true biblical womanhood than we have time to get into here, but I just want to close with a couple of encouraging thoughts. Jesus had a very high regard for women, and they were an essential and vital part of His ministry while on earth and continue to be so. God created the woman to fulfill a very valuable role within the home, church, and society at large. Prov. 31 is all about a woman who clearly understood this and demonstrated it consistently as she managed well her household (Prov. 31:10–27).

> *Strength and dignity are her clothing and she smiles at the future. She opens her mouth in wisdom and the teaching of kindness is on her tongue. She looks well to the ways of her household, and does not eat the bread of idleness. Her children rise up and bless her; Her husband also, and he praises her, saying: "Many daughters have done nobly, But you excel them all." Charm is deceitful and beauty is vain, But a woman who fears the Lord, she shall be praised (Prov. 31:25–30).*

6. Read Gen. 3:17–19.

   a. What curse befell man as a result of his sinful disobedience? (vs. 17b,19a)

It's a huge responsibility being the spiritual and physical head of the household! Because of sin's curse, it is tough for most men to get up and go to work day after relentless day, whether they *feel* like it or not, in a land of *thorns and thistles*. We need to pray for our men. They need an extra measure of God's grace and they need our daily encouragement and support if they are to successfully carry out their tremendous God-given responsibility.

However, we as redeemed men and women must never forget the *good news* in the midst of life's "fallen" realities:

> **Jesus has broken the curse of sin, and when we enter into a forgiven, accepted, loving relationship with Him, then care for and support one another in our God-ordained roles, His righteousness replaces the conflict and turmoil and our homes become a haven of His love, peace, contentment and joy.**

Write a Bible verse that had special meaning to you today.

Based upon what you have learned today, write a prayer to God expressing the desires of your heart in applying these Truths to your life.

Chapter 3 — Day 3
Without the Shedding of Blood...

An Introduction to the Sacrificial System of Redemption

> *And the Lord God made garments of skin for Adam and his wife, and clothed them (Gen. 3:21).*
>
> *Without the shedding of blood, there is no forgiveness (Heb. 9:22).*

Foundational Truth # 9

The wages of sin is death (Rom. 6:23). Therefore, there can be no forgiveness and reconciliation with God without the shedding of blood. (Death is the sin debt that must be paid to free the sinner).

The shedding of blood. It is not a very pleasant subject. So it is usually avoided in our conversations and also in our Bible studies. We hurry quickly past it to get to the gospel of the love and grace of God in Jesus. It's a serious error. It is impossible to even begin to understand, appreciate, and rejoice in the gospel of the love and grace of God in Jesus apart from embracing the central theme—the redeeming blood. And, sadly, lest we offend, we do the very same thing when we share the gospel with others—avoid the blood. This has even greater potential for harm because, in reality, we may be giving people a false gospel. Until one understands that *the wages of sin is death,* and that all the bloodshed in all the world from the very beginning has been the result of <u>sin</u>, he very likely will not recognize the destructive power of sin in his life or his need for a *Savior* and *true* (sincere, heart and life-changing) *repentance.* It was <u>sin</u> that cost God the very life blood of His own beloved Son and it is still <u>sin</u> that continues to wreak havoc upon the fallen human race. Without a clear comprehension and acceptance of this, any repentance or salvation experience one may have may not be genuine—real. (Just as mine was not real throughout my teen and early adult life). It is a very serious issue we must address.

God had clearly instructed Adam: *And the Lord God commanded the man, saying, "From any tree of the garden you may eat freely; but from the tree of the knowledge of good and evil you shall not eat, for in the day that you eat from it you shall surely die" (Gen. 2:16,17).*

As we learned yesterday, the moment Adam and Eve sinned by rebelling against God's loving, protective command, they died spiritually; they were immediately separated from God because God is holy, and holy and unholy cannot dwell together. Separation from God always results in *death* because God is the source of life itself and everything that is good and loving in it.

And the Lord God made garments of skin for Adam and his wife, and clothed them (Gen. 3:21).

Here we are introduced to the dichotomy of divine holy love and justice. Holy justice demanded the penalty for sin—*death*. But God, in His merciful, compassionate love, paid the price for man's sin in order to restore him to fellowship with Him. The terrible price for Adam and Eve's selfish act of rebellion was the life of an innocent, spotless (defect-free) animal, most likely, a lamb. And that was only the beginning of the shedding of blood for the redemption of sinful, selfish man. The blood of thousands of animals throughout the Old Testament and into the New would be shed. And even more tragically, later, the very blood of the spotless Lamb of God would be poured out to pay the penalty for man's rebellion against God, <u>sin</u>! May God help us to never forget this fact so that we never again look upon sin lightly or fail to engage in resolute, unwavering, never-give-up-until-it-is-conquered battle against it! It is what Paul referred to as the *good fight (2 Tim. 4:7)*.

> *Now the man had relations with his wife Eve, and she conceived and gave birth to Cain…And again, she gave birth to his brother Abel. And Abel was a keeper of flocks, but Cain was a tiller of the ground. So it came about in the course of time that Cain brought an offering to the Lord of the fruit of the ground. And Abel, on his part also brought of the firstlings of his flock and of their fat portions. And the Lord had regard for Abel and for his offering; but for Cain and for his offering He had no regard (Gen. 4:1–5).*

When I first began studying the Bible, I found this story very troubling. It seemed so unfair: God's regard for Abel's offering and not Cain's.

But as I continued to study, I could clearly see that it was *not* unfair. God had given to both Cain and Abel the same loving opportunity that He had given to their parents: A close, intimate, relationship with Him! Even after the fall, God still desired to have this fellowship with His children as demonstrated by His direct intervention in paying the price for their sin: death. It was God who slew the animal and atoned for Adam and Eve's sin externally with the skins of the animal and internally with its blood, the payment for sin—death—so that the relationship could be restored (Gen. 2:17; Rom. 6:23). And we can be sure that God *clearly* instructed Cain and Abel concerning the atonement offering—what it was to be, when and how it was to be offered. [We know this from the principle of the nature of God. He is *not the author of confusion - 1 Cor. 14:33*. When God gives an instruction for response (obedience) it is always clearly stated - Gen. 2:17; Rom. 6:23 - and hundreds of other like verses]. Cain understood perfectly the kind of offering that God required, but in rebellion against God, he defiantly offered what he wanted to offer rather than what God had instructed. It is called "my will, not Thine," or rebellion. It didn't work for Cain, and it won't work for us as we'll see again tomorrow and throughout the rest of this study. God is still God, the sovereign ruler of the universe, and He has a plan for the redemption of fallen man and only His plan will achieve that redemption and eternal life with Him. To their blessed hope, He had already promised that one day He would send a Savior who would pay this price once and for all. The perfect, holy, spotless *Lamb of God* (Jesus) who alone was *without sin* and thus qualified to make this atonement, would shed His blood for the redemption of the world (Gen. 3:15; John 3:16). In the meantime, these animal sacrifices—a foreshadow of Jesus' sacrifice—would atone for the people's sin and enable them to remain in fellowship with God and receive His loving blessing, provision, and protection.

So it is not a matter of God being partial to Abel; that He loved Abel more than Cain. It was that Abel *chose* to walk with God in humble and loving obedience. He *chose* to live in intimate relationship with God, listening carefully as God spoke to Him, then obeying with a glad, surrendered heart. Cain, on the other hand, continued on in the rebellious ways of his parents. He pridefully and contemptuously disobeyed God, going his own way, away from God.

> *When Cain saw that God had regard for Abel's offering and not for his, Cain became very angry and his countenance fell. Then the Lord said to Cain, "Why are you angry? And why has your countenance fallen? If you do well, will not your countenance be lifted up? And if you do not do well, sin is crouching at the*

door; but you must master it"…(but) Cain (refused to listen and) went from the presence of the Lord and settled in the land of Nod (Gen. 4:7).

In these verses, and the verses that follow in Genesis 4, (as well as references in the New Testament), we see that Cain made no attempt to *master his sin* but defiantly boasted of it and continued to walk according to his ungodly lusts, rebelling against God. He *chose* to *leave the presence of God*, and caused his children also to sin and follow in his destructive ways.

Now these things happened…as examples for us, and they were written for our instruction, that we should not crave evil things, as they craved (1 Cor. 10:11).

When we choose to go the way of Cain, not listening to God and allowing a spirit of rebellion to fester in our hearts, we open the door to sin, we fall, and we experience the agony of guilt and separation from God, and with it, a fallen countenance. If we continue in this pattern, willfully disobeying and sinning against God, we develop a hard heart that takes us even further into rebellion in a determined effort to quiet the nagging guilt. Soon we are very far from God. If the rebellion continues, the conscience will eventually be seared (completely shut off from God, from *life*). It *dies*. In this sad state we can no longer *hear* the voice of God. It is a very dangerous pattern. That is why God urges us to stay close to Him and to walk in trusting obedience, because God is a good and loving God, and He will always protect us and keep us from Satan's lies and sin's allurements and the pain and destruction—both present and eternal—they cause.

Our relationship with God must always be built upon faith in the goodness and love of God so that we respond as Abel responded in humble, loving obedience.

Now Cain said to his brother, Abel, "Let's go out to the field." And while they were in the field, Cain attacked his brother Abel and killed him. Then the Lord said to Cain, "Where is Abel your brother?" And he said, "I do not know. Am I my brother's keeper?" And He said, "What have you done? The voice of your brother's blood is crying to Me from the ground. And now you are cursed from the ground, which has opened its mouth to receive your brother's blood from your hand. When you cultivate the ground, it shall no longer yield its strength to you; you shall be a vagrant and a wanderer on the earth"(Gen. 4:8–12, NIV/NASB*).*

And so we see the awful consequences of sin once again. And everyone who willingly chooses to go the way of Cain will find himself a frustrated, unfulfilled vagrant—far from God and far from peace. We see this pattern repeated over and over throughout the Bible.

For the sons of Israel walked forty years in the wilderness, until all…who came out of Egypt, (except Moses, Joshua and Caleb, who believed and obeyed God) ***perished because they did not listen to the voice of the Lord*** *(Josh. 5:6).*

May God help us to comprehend the awful, terrible, *painful* consequences of sin, the result of *failing to listen to the voice of the Lord*.

Bible Study Supplement

Chapter 3 – Day 3 — Without the Shedding of Blood...
An Introduction to the Sacrificial System of Redemption

We learned last time, and reviewed again today, the sad, but important Truth that *the wages of sin is death (Rom. 6:23)*. Keep this in mind as you answer the following questions.

1. Read Gen. 3:21.

    a. Who paid the penalty for Adam and Eve's sin...How?

Here we are introduced to *death* for the first time in the history of the universe—the result of Adam and Eve's rebellion. Here we see also the love of God that paid the penalty for the rebellion (sin) as God, Himself, slew the animal and clothed Adam and Eve out of His merciful compassion.

2. Read Gen. 6:5–9.

    a. What was the condition of the world as a result of sin just a few generations after Adam and Eve first rebelled against God in the beautiful Garden of Eden? (vs. 5)

    b. Describe what this did to God's heart. (vs. 6b)

    c. What kind of man was Noah? Describe his relationship with God (vs. 9)

I love this verse. *Noah was a righteous man, blameless in his time...Noah walked with God.* If we choose to *walk with God*, in humble, loving, obedient fellowship, we, too can be like Noah—*righteous, blameless in (our) time).* It is my daily prayer.

    d. How did God respond to this? (vs. 8)

Chapter 7 of Genesis gives us the account of the great flood—the consequence of blatant universal disregard and rebellion against God. But God, in His mercy, saved eight people from the destruction, just as He will save all who walk with Him in loving trust and obedience.

3. Read Gen. 8:1-4, 15-22.

    a. What did Noah do as soon as he came out from the ark? (vs. 20a)

    b. What did he offer up? (vs. 20)

    c. How did the offering come up to God? (vs. 21a)

4. Read Gen. 22:1-3.

    a. What did God asked Abraham to do? (vs. 2)

    b. How did Abraham respond? (vs. 3)

We will not read the details of the rest of this story. Most of you know it well. Abraham *believed* and *obeyed* God. God had told him that through his son, Isaac, would come descendants as numerous as the stars, and also the Savior (Gen. 15:2–6, 18:7). So if God asked him to offer up his son as proof of his faith, he would do it because he *believed* that God was able to *raise him from the dead (Rom. 4:17–21)*.

In obedience to God, Abraham did take Isaac to the top of Mount Moriah, built an altar, tied his son to it, raised the knife to kill him, at which time he was stopped by *the angel of the Lord* who said to him: *"Do not stretch out your hand against the lad, and do nothing to him; for now I know that you fear God, since you have not withheld your son, your only son, from Me." Then Abraham raised his eyes and looked, and behold...a ram caught in the thicket by his horns; and Abraham went and took the ram, and offered him up for a burnt offering in the place of his son. And Abraham called the name of that place, The Lord Will Provide (Gen. 22:12–14).*

What a beautiful story of the faith and trust of Abraham and the loving provision of God in response.

Here, again we see a hope-instilling demonstration of things to come: a prototype of what God would indeed do to attain the salvation of the world. He would provide the Lamb—His only Son—allow Him to die, to pay the penalty for the sins of all mankind, then raise Him up from the dead to reign victoriously over sin and death, forever!

Later in Genesis we read that Abraham's descendants (Abraham's grandson, Jacob, and his children), migrated to Egypt in search of food because of a great famine. There they were provided and cared for by Jacob's son, Joseph, whom God had placed in a position of authority. I love the way God uses real people throughout His Word to teach us important lessons. He continually gives us human examples, "types," who point us to Jesus and help us understand His nature and character—the very nature and character of God, Himself (Heb. 1:3). Joseph is one of these. It is beautiful to see this expression of God's tender love woven throughout Scripture. I hope you are beginning to see the connection between the exercise of unwavering faith, trust, and obedience to the blessing, favor, and provision of God. God loves to bless and provide for His faithful, trusting children who walk in humble, surrendered obedience to Him.

> *The children of Israel enjoyed the best of the land until many generations passed (four hundred years) and there arose a new king over Egypt, who did not know Joseph. This wicked king was a cruel taskmaster and greatly oppressed the children of Israel. He made their lives bitter with hard labor in mortar and bricks and all kinds of labor in the fields and he set unreasonable quotas for them, and when they could not make these, he beat them mercilessly...And the people cried out to God and God sent them a deliverer, His servant, Moses who...delivered the people from the cruel oppression of the Pharaoh of Egypt (Ex. 1:6–14, 2:23–3:10, 5:5–14, 12:40,51).*

Most of you know well the story of the deliverance of the children of Israel from the bondage of Egypt: Moses' meetings with Pharaoh and the demonstrations of God's power—Aaron throwing his staff to the ground and it becoming a snake, the Nile River turning to blood the moment Moses struck it with Aaron's restored staff, the ten horrific plagues, and finally:

5. Read Ex. 12:3-13.

   a. What kind of lamb were the people to take? (vs. 5)

   b. What were they to do to the lamb on the fourteenth day? (vs. 6)

   c. What were they to do with the blood? (vs. 7)

   d. What would happen that night? (vs. 12)

   e. What would the blood applied to the door posts of the house do? (vs. 13)

   f. What happened at midnight? (see vs. 29)

The Passover was a foreshadow of the most dramatic, history-altering event that would ever take place in the course of mankind and his relationship with God. We'll look tomorrow at this incredible event in which the light of God's glorious redemptive love burst upon the darkness of sin's destruction and death and obliterated its power! It's the most beautiful *love story* ever written.

Write out a Bible verse that had special meaning to you today.

Based upon what you have learned today, write a prayer to God expressing the desires of your heart in applying these Truths to your life.

Chapter 3 — Day 4
Behold the Lamb of God

> *But when Christ appeared as a high priest of the good things to come, He entered through the greater and more perfect tabernacle, not made with hands... and not through the blood of goats and calves, but through His own blood, He entered the Holy place once for all, having obtained eternal redemption... For Christ also died for sins once for all, the just for the unjust, in order that He might bring us to God (Heb. 9:11,12; 1 Pet. 3:16).*
>
> *Greater love hath no man than this, that he lay down his life for his friends (John 15:13, NASB/KJV).*

Foundational Truth # 10

Jesus willingly laid down His life, suffering an agonizing painful death on the cross in order to pay the penalty for our sins—death. It was the only way the holy justice of God could be vindicated without violating the free will of man. It was also the greatest demonstration of love the world would ever know!

Let's take just a couple of minutes here to review what we studied yesterday, because it is so important to understand this in order to fully comprehend the magnitude of what Jesus did for us!

The Bible tells us that even before He created us, God *knew* that we would rebel and that our sin would separate us from Him because God is holy, and holy and unholy cannot dwell or fellowship together. Not then, not now, not ever. Heaven is a holy place and only what is holy will be there. Aren't you glad that there will be no *sin*—and the sorrow, pain and suffering sin brings—in heaven?

God knew full well the price holy justice demands for rebellion (sin)—*death (Rom. 6:23; Rev.13:8; Heb. 9:22)*. God made this clear to His children from the very beginning, and He continues to make it clear to us today. In the third chapter of Genesis, in Leviticus, Deuteronomy and again in chapter nine of Hebrews, God tells us that because He is holy, the only acceptable payment for sin is the *shedding of blood—death (Gen. 2:17; Lev. 17:10–14; Heb. 9:22)*.

It was man's willful choice to rebel—SIN—that caused the bloodshed, <u>not God</u>!

And it is still that choice of man *to sin*—<u>not God</u>—that continues to wreak havoc and cause *bloodshed* (pain and suffering) in its many forms, today: strife and contention between a husband and wife, and in other relationships, (because of selfishness, pride, stubbornness), the breakdown of the family (same sins), violence, wars, poverty, pornography, pedophilia, and a host of other wicked perversions. All of it is because of *sin* not the *cruelty of God.* How often we get that all mixed up and blame God instead of repenting and taking responsibility for our sins and the hurt and pain they cause, then fighting to eradicate sin from our lives and helping others do the same. It is so important that we understand this in order to begin to grasp how great the mercy and love of God was in sending Jesus to take upon Himself the suffering, pain, and death our rebellious sin required and *we deserved*.

In the Old Testament redemption system, there were endless sacrifices to meet the requirement for the "atonement," (payment for mans' sins—death). A defect-free, unblemished lamb, along with a number of other animal and grain offerings, were brought to the high priest daily. The unblemished lamb was killed and its blood sprinkled upon the altar. The blood represented not only the giving up of a life for the payment of sin but also purification from sin (The defect-free lamb had paid the penalty for sin so that through his shed blood the sinner would be purified, made holy and acceptable to God). Once a year, on the Day of Atonement, the most prized, unblemished, spotless lamb was brought to the temple, slaughtered, and his blood carried into the Holy of Holies where it was sprinkled upon the Mercy Seat above the Ark of the Covenant, which represented God's presence—His holiness. This was symbolic of the day that Jesus would come and give Himself—a once-for-all sacrifice—for the redemption of the world. But until then, because the people's hearts were so proud, so selfish and so fickle, they would continue in their sins and, therefore, perpetual sacrifices had to be made daily to cleanse and purify them and enable them to remain in fellowship with God, enjoying His blessings and protection. So there was an endless cycle of sin, sacrifice (shedding of blood), atonement, sin, sacrifice, atonement. It was a laborious, painful and never ending system until…

…when the fullness of time had come, God sent forth His son, born of a woman, born under the law to redeem them that were under the Law…Behold the Lamb of God that takes away the sin of the world (Gal. 4:4; John 1:29).

But God…being rich in mercy and grace, demonstrated his love toward us, in that, while we were yet sinners, Christ died for us…For God so loved the world that He gave His only begotten Son that whosoever believeth in Him might not perish, but have eternal life (Rom. 5:8; John 3:16).

When Christ appeared as a high priest of the good things to come, He entered through the greater and more perfect tabernacle, not made with hands…and not through the blood of goats and calves, but through His own blood, He entered the Holy place once for all, having obtained eternal redemption…For Christ also died for sins once for all, the just for the unjust, in order that He might bring us to God (Heb. 9:11,12; 1 Pet. 3:16).

And so God the Son (Jesus), the Creator and sustainer of the universe, *by whom and through whom all things were made (Col. 1:17)* emptied Himself of all His divine glory, power and position to become a lowly, humble, bond-servant and ultimately the perfect, spotless, sinless *Lamb of God that takes away the sins of the world!*

…who, although He (was God), did not regard (His position as) God a thing to (hold on to), but emptied Himself, taking the form of a bondservant, being made in the likeness of men…He humbled Himself by becoming obedient to the point of death, even death on a cross. (Phil. 2:6–8)

Pause for a moment here and ask God to help the reality of so great a love sink deep into your soul. Read the above verse again, slowly, meditating upon the unfathomable sacrificial humility and love of Jesus *(Phil. 2:6–8).*

Jesus willingly emptied Himself of all His divine rights and power in order to become like one of us. He then, in unfathomable love, *died* (poured out His blood) on a cruel Roman cross, taking upon Himself the penalty for selfish, stubborn, rebellious man's sin and sinful man's guilt.

Greater love has no one than this, that one lay down his life for his friends…I am the good shepherd; I lay down My life for the sheep. No one takes it from Me, but I lay it down on My own accord (John 15:13, 10:14,18, NASB/NIV).

No wonder *the word of the cross is foolishness to those who are perishing (1 Cor. 1:18)*.

There is no place in human logic and sinful pride to comprehend (or allow thoughts of) so great a love. Because we all, in our fallen state are so proud and so selfish by nature, we do not want to get near that kind of love, knowing that its holy, sinless, purity will penetrate quickly our phony claims to goodness and expose our hypocritical, *self*-centered, *self*-serving, *self*-absorbed love.

…in whose case the god of this world has blinded the minds of the unbelieving, that they might not see the light of the gospel of the glory of Christ, who is the Image of God. (2 Cor. 4:4)

Yet, for even these, Jesus died:

For God did not send the Son into the world to condemn the world, but that the world, through Him, should be saved. He who believes in Him is not condemned; he who does not believe has been condemned already, because he has not believed in the name of the only begotten Son of God. And this is the condemnation, that the Light is come into the world, and men loved the darkness rather than the light; for their deeds were evil (John 3:17–19).

That is why we need to pray fervently for our lost loved ones, friends, and neighbors that God would be merciful and send His Holy Spirit to open their eyes that they might recognize their need for Jesus and for the reconciliation He offers us through His shed blood on Calvary. It is only the Spirit of God that can enable any of us to even begin to comprehend the purity of God's holiness that demanded such a price and the magnitude of God's love that paid it!

This is the first step of faith that we all must take. We must believe God that His plan was the only way back to Him and to fellowship in His holiness. This was not easy for me. It seemed so cruel and so *bloody*. Why? Why would God, the sovereign and omnipotent God of the Universe—the One who was over all and could do whatever He wanted—make such an awful, cruel, *bloody* plan of redemption? He could have just declared that because of His mercy and Grace, all sinners were forgiven. They needed only to ask His forgiveness whenever they sinned and He, being merciful and gracious, would forgive them. He could have spared all the shedding of blood—especially the blood of His own Son. Surely…It just did not compute in my analytical, sin-tarnished mind—or emotions. It was in the middle of a very intense struggle with this conflict, that God brought into our lives a pastor—a wonderful, dedicated, humble servant of God, whom I respected highly and who did much to encourage and spur me on in my walk with God. I heard him so often explain about this from the pulpit and one day it finally *sunk in*. God loved His only Son Jesus more that any of us love our children. God's love for Jesus was pure, holy, selfless and sinless; while our love for our children is often impure, unholy, tainted with selfish motivations. Yet we would do anything to spare our children from harm, and certainly from death. Therefore, we can be sure that *if there were any other way God could have achieved the redemption of the human race—without violating man's free will, or His holiness and the divine justice it required—He would surely have chosen it*. But there was no other way to pay the awful price of sin—*death*— no other way back to God, to His perfect love and holiness, without the shedding of the blood of Jesus, who was the only qualified spotless, perfect, defect-free (sinless), Lamb.

Behold the Lamb of God, that takes away the sin of the world; He (Jesus) is the propitiation (payment) for our sins; and not for ours only, but also for the whole world…God was in Christ reconciling the world to Himself…He made Him who knew no sin to be sin on our behalf, that we might become the righteousness of God in Him (John 1:29; 1 John 2:1; 2 Cor. 5:21).

In God's unfathomable, perfect plan, Jesus bore the penalty for all our sins and all our guilt so that as we put our faith in Him—in what He did for us on the cross—we receive the gift of Christ's righteousness—His holiness—and thus we are able to stand in the presence of our holy Father once again.

...knowing this, that Christ Jesus died for our sins according to the Scriptures...having canceled out the certificate of debt which was hostile to us; He has taken it out of the way, having nailed it to the cross (1 Cor. 14:3; Col. 2:13,14).

Hallelujah! The awful *curse of sin* was broken. The debt we could never pay, was paid in full. But even with such a sacrifice, the redemption was not yet complete. Had Jesus stayed in the grave, there would have been no victory over death and, consequently, no redemption from sins. The sins would remain. Jesus would have died in vain. But, Jesus did not remain in the grave.

On the first day of the week, at early dawn, they came to the tomb, bringing the spices which they had prepared. And they found the stone rolled away. When they entered, they did not find the body of the Lord Jesus... While they were perplexed about this, behold, two men suddenly stood near them in dazzling apparel; and as the women were terrified and bowed their faces to the ground, the man said to them, "Why do you seek the living One among the dead? He is not here, He has risen. Remember how He spoke to you while He was still in Galilee, saying that the Son of Man must be delivered into the hands of sinful men, and be crucified, and the third day rise again." And they remembered His words (Luke 24:1–8).

Truly it is impossible to fully comprehend with our finite, sin-corrupted minds, the holy purity and depth of God's love for us! *For one will hardly die for a righteous man...But God demonstrates His love toward us, in that while we were yet sinners*—in willful, proud, defiant rebellion against Him—*Christ died for us! (Rom. 5:7,8).* The depth and purity of God's love is—and always will be—*beyond human comprehension (Is. 55:8,9; Rom. 11:33)*. It takes faith to begin to see the greatness of God's love for us and to receive His most gracious and loving gift.

The wages of sin is death, but the gift of God is eternal life through Christ Jesus, our Lord...For as many as received Him to them gave He the right to become children of God! (Rom. 6:23; John 1:12).

Thanks be to God for His unspeakable gift! (2 Cor. 9:15).

Bible Study Supplement
Chapter 3 — Day 4 — Behold, the Lamb of God

One of the most beautiful and powerful scriptures in the entire Bible is the prophetic account of Jesus' atonement for our sins found in Isaiah 53. Written more than 700 years before Jesus' birth, God gives a clear account of the coming of the Messiah, the Savior of the World.

1. Read Is. 53:2-6.

    a. Describe Jesus' appearance as He walked this earth. (vs. 2b)

Note: I find this verse incredibly comforting. Jesus was not a strikingly handsome man that commanded attention because of His perfect features, tall stature, and flawless outward appearance. He *had no stately form or majesty that we should look upon Him, nor appearance that we should be attracted to Him.* He was just an ordinary, common looking, man, like most of us. I think it is incredible that Jesus *chose* to come in this appearance, as He certainly could have come as the most handsome man the world would ever see. After all, He was the Creator of man and every feature of man. He could have chosen the best in which to wrap His human soul, but instead, He chose to come as one with physical flaws and weaknesses like we all have. Would that we would learn from Jesus' pure, loving, and selfless humility.

    b. What was life like for Jesus; how was He treated? (vs. 3a)

Note: Be sure, Jesus *understands* when we are going through times of hurt, rejection, heartbreak and suffering. He's *been there* and He is there *with us* when we go through such times (Heb. 4:15, 2:18).

    c. How did we respond to the way Jesus was treated? (vs. 3b)

Aren't you thankful that Jesus does not respond to us in the same way that we treat Him?!

    d. What did Jesus do for us? (six things - vs. 4a,5)

    e. What have we done? (vs. 6)

    f. What has God done concerning our iniquity? (vs. 6b)

Keep in mind that we are by nature sheep-like creatures, prone to wander. That is why it is so important to keep close to our Good Shepherd, through the reading and studying of God's Word and prayer, that we might ever hear His voice, and follow Him rather than, in our sinful, selfishness, greed, and prideful rebellion, listen to the lies of the enemy and obey him, as Eve did (John 10:27; Gen. 3:6).

2. Read 1 Pet. 3:18.

    a. What did Christ do? (vs. 18a)

    b. What did He accomplish in that act? (vs. 18)

3. Read Heb. 9:11–14.

    a. What did Jesus do for us? (vs. 12)

    b. What else does the *blood of Jesus* do for us? (vs. 14)

4. Read Heb. 9:22,24.

   a. What is necessary for the remission of sins? (vs. 22)

   b. Where did Jesus enter? (vs. 24)

Note: The Bible tells us that Jesus is, even now, in Heaven, at the right hand of God *interceding for us* (Rom. 8:34). What a Redeemer, what a Savior!

5. Read John 1:29.

   a. What did John the Baptist announce regarding Jesus—Who was He and what had He come to do?

6. Read Phil. 2:5–8.

   a. What did Jesus do—for you and for me? (7a,8)

I pray that you are gaining a deeper comprehension of the awfulness of sin and the terrible price Jesus paid for it. May we ponder this often, for the more we stand at the foot of the cross the greater will be our appreciation of and joy in receiving His *unspeakable gift!* (2 Cor. 9:15).

In order to help us do this, we will read the account of the greatest love story ever told. But we are not going to do that today because you have already studied long and diligently, and your mind is probably about as *full* as it can be at the moment. Therefore, because this is what the *good news* of the gospel is all about—the incredible, unfathomable love and redemption of Jesus—it warrants our reading it when our minds are fresh and really focused upon what *really* transpired in these most crucial hours on that first *Good Friday* and that glorious *Resurrection Day!* Please read this text sometime this week—perhaps Saturday morning or some evening before you retire when you have a few extra minutes and are not rushed or distracted by other pressing needs. And please try to read it at least one other time before the end of the study, for it is at the heart of who you are as a redeemed, blood-bought child of God. Before you read, pause for a moment and ask God to help you read this matchless love story with a whole new awareness of, and gratitude for, the unfathomable magnitude of Jesus' love, that paid such a price for your sin, salvation, loving fellowship, and eternal life with God in Heaven—forever!

Here is the text that you will be reading - Matt. 26:36–75; Matt. 27, 28.

Truly, the story of Jesus' life, sacrificial death and resurrection is the greatest love story ever told! Because of Jesus' once-for-all sacrifice on the cross for our sins, there will never again be the necessity of sacrificing innocent lambs to pay our sin debt, no more perpetual atonement…NO MORE BLOOD! Praise God…it is finished. Sin and death have been conquered! Jesus paid it all!

> I hear the Savior say/Thy strength indeed is small
> Child of weakness, watch and pray/Find in Me thine all in all
>
> Lord, now indeed I find/Thy power and Thine alone
> Can change the leper's spots/And melt the heart of stone.
>
> For nothing good have I/Whereby Thy grace to claim
> I'll wash my garments white/In the blood of Calvary's Lamb
>
> And when, before the Throne/I stand in Him complete
> Jesus died my soul to save/My lips shall still repeat.

Jesus paid it all/All to Him I owe;
Sin had left a crimson stain/He washed it white as snow.

Write out a Bible verse that had special meaning to you today.

Based upon what you have learned today, write a prayer to God expressing the desires of your heart in applying these Truths to your life.

Chapter 3 — Day 5
You Must Be Born Again

> *Truly, truly I say to you, unless one is born again, he cannot see the kingdom of God (John 3:3).*
>
> *God has given us eternal life, and this life is in His Son. He who has the Son has life; he who does not have the Son of God does not have life (1 John 5:11,12).*
>
> *I am the Way, the Truth and the Life; no one comes to the Father except through me (John 14:6).*

Foundational Truth # 11

There is only one way back to God—one way of salvation by which anyone is *saved* from the penalty of sin—*death*—and welcomed back into fellowship with God. It is through repentance, then, by faith, accepting what Jesus did through His sinless, holy life, sacrificial death on the cross, and resurrection from the grave, obtaining victory over sin and death. The moment a person *repents,* *believes* and *receives* God's free gift of salvation, he is *born again (born from above, spiritual rebirth)* and becomes a child of God, inheriting eternal life with God and all believers in heaven forever.

My heart breaks every time I think of so many in my life that I love deeply who have fallen victim to one of the greatest and most tragic deceptions ever foisted upon humankind (2 Cor. 2:11; John 8:44). It is the popular and blindly accepted tenet of tolerance: "All 'truth' is relative, there are no absolutes", along with all the other deceptions it has spawned: "All paths lead to 'God;' all 'good people' will go to Heaven; we must allow people to think and do as they feel right to think and do. The power of demonic deception is seen once again in the fact that even highly intelligent people have been blinded by this crafty lie, even though it is in itself, self-contradicting in nature. The one who says: "All truth is relative, there are no absolutes", has, in reality, just made an absolute statement! But, blind to the contradiction, the argument continues: Since there are no absolutes, all moral, spiritual and ethical issues are merely personal opinions and one person's opinion carries no more weight than any other person's opinion. None of us has a right to impose *his opinion* on anyone else.

But *thus saith the Lord*, is not my opinion or the opinion of any preacher, denomination, or any other human institution. It is the sure and unalterable Word of God. And about this most crucial of all subjects—the eternal destiny of man, God's Word could not be simpler or clearer:

> *Truly, truly I say to you, unless a man is born again, he cannot see the Kingdom of Heaven. And Jesus said to them: I am the way, the Truth and the life. No one comes to the Father except through me…There is salvation in no other; for there is no other name under Heaven given among men whereby we must be saved…For God so loved the world that He gave His only begotten Son that*

whosoever believeth in Him should not perish but have everlasting life (John 3:3, 14:6; Acts 4:12; Matt. 7:13,14; John 3:16).

Refusing to accept God's clear Word given here, arguing against it, or denying it does not change one iota of the absolute Truth concerning God's only acceptable means of salvation, forgiveness of sins, peace with God, and eternal life with Him in Heaven.

In those brief moments when I would drop my cold, determined guard, and open my heart to the wooings of God's gentle and loving Spirit *(Job 36:15,16)*, when I would humble myself enough to look *beyond myself* and my rebellious intellectual arguments and rationalizations concerning salvation, eternal life, etc., I could see how absolutely absurd was the *wisdom of the world (1 Cor. 3:19)*; for indeed, the further man got from God and obedience to His life-giving Word, ignoring his need for salvation, the more rampant became the wickedness, crime, war, mental and emotional problems, personal and interpersonal conflicts and crises, divorce, broken homes, broken hearts. I could see, in those moments of *true* enlightenment (from God), that those foolish people who had given their lives to Him and were followers of Jesus—Christians—were the happiest, most secure, most truly enviable people in all the world. I knew that they had what I so desperately needed.

Finally, after years of rebellion against the convictions that came often to my conscience, in a God-ordained moment of near fatal desperation, by the grace of God, the impenetrable wall was cracked. The light of God's Truth filtered in and I began, with an open heart, to examine what the Bible says about that *Name given among men by which we must be saved (Acts 4:12)*.

But the angel said to him, "Do not be afraid, Zacharias, for your petition has been heard and your wife Elizabeth will bear you a son, and you will give him the name John…for he will be great in the sight of the Lord, and he will be filled with the Holy Spirit…And he will turn back many of the sons of Israel to the Lord their God. And it is he who will go as a forerunner before Him…to turn the hearts of the… disobedient to the attitude of the righteous; so as to make ready a people prepared for the Lord (Luke 1:13–17).

It is clear from the importance that the Bible places upon the ministry of John the Baptist (and many other related passages) that being *born again* begins with the heart—not the head. John the Baptist was called and commissioned by God to be the forerunner of Jesus. He was to go ahead of Jesus to *prepare the hearts of the people*—to turn them from an attitude of disobedience and rebellion to humility, repentance and righteousness.

And he (John the Baptist) came…preaching a baptism of repentance for the forgiveness of sins… Make ready the way of the Lord…Behold the Lamb of God which takes away the sins of the world (Luke 3:3; John 1:29).

There must be a heart preparation/change for true repentance and acceptance of Jesus (genuine faith/belief) to take place. One must see himself for what he really is: a poor, wretched sinner in need of a Savior, and in that light, be willing to humble himself in order to fully accept what God has done for him in Jesus.

Unless you humble yourself and become like (a) child, you shall not enter the kingdom of Heaven (Matt. 18:3,4).

Therefore having overlooked the times of ignorance, God is now declaring that all men everywhere should repent performing deeds appropriate to repentance (Acts 17:30).

Repent…and believe on the Lord Jesus for the remission of your sins (Acts 2:38; 16:31).

Today, John the Baptist's work continues through those who know Jesus and minister the Truths of God's Word to prepare hearts to receive Jesus as personal Lord and Savior and thus be *born again.* So what does Scripture teach about the importance of repentance in *saving faith?*

For the sorrow that is according to the will of God produces a repentance without regret, leading to salvation; but the sorrow of the world produces death. (2 Cor. 7:10)

In this passage we are clearly warned that there are two kinds of sorrow: a sorrow that is according to the will of God that produces *a repentance...leading to salvation,* and a *sorrow of the world that produces death.*

It is so crucial to understand the difference, for life and death—eternal life and death—are held in the balance. Let's examine first: godly sorrow/true repentance.

Godly sorrow (true biblical repentance) involves two parts: 1) confession, 2) repentance.

If we confess our sins, He is faithful and just to forgive us our sins and to cleanse us from all unrighteousness. (1 John 1:9, KJV, NASB).

The Greek Word translated *confess* here is *homologeo* and means "To say the same thing as" or to "agree with." In this case it means to "agree with God" regarding our sins. We see our sins as God sees them: that which *rebels against Him and rejects His love, brings shame and reproach to His holy name, denies His sovereignty and His goodness, and, most grievously, cost the life of His precious Son.* Once we truly comprehend this and come to the place where we agree with God about our sins *in our hearts,* resulting in humble, genuine contrition over what our sins have cost God, our sorrow is godly and produces a *repentance without regret* leading to *true salvation* and the assurance of life eternal with God in Heaven.

Now let's look at the second part of godly sorrow: repentance. The Old Testament word translated *repentance* is *shub,* meaning, "to turn," and was used to refer to turning from idols to God or turning from evil to obey God's commandments. The New Testament word for repentance is the Greek word, *metanoia,* which means "change of mind/heart that results in a change of behavior" *(Luke 3:8; Acts 26:20, 17:30).*

If any man be in Christ, he is a new creature; old things pass away, behold new things come (2 Cor. 5:17).

Genuine repentance, therefore involves a change of mind/heart, which results in a change in affections/behavior. It involves turning away from idols (anything we love more than God) to God in grateful love and obedience. Jesus was continually calling the people to abandon their rebellious idolatrous living and return wholeheartedly to God—to godly righteousness and obedience, where they would experience the fullness of God's blessing, grace, and peace.

Along with godly sorrow, the Bible tells us that to be born again our repentance must be linked to genuine *faith* that *believes on the Lord Jesus Christ.* We must personally believe what Jesus did for us on the cross: *Christ died, the just for the unjust...He, Himself is the propitiation* (payment) *for our sins (2 Cor. 5:21, 1 John 2:2).* Jesus took upon Himself the punishment for our sin, paying it —in full!—by His death on the cross, then rose again from the dead as victor over sin and death, giving us eternal life. We validate this belief by a public profession of faith.

...that if you confess with your mouth Jesus as Lord, and believe in your heart that God raised Him from the dead, you shall be saved, for with the heart man believes, resulting in righteousness, and with the mouth he confesses, resulting in salvation (Rom. 10:9,10).

Let's review: One is genuinely *born again* when he personally, by a volitional choice of His will:

1. *Repents* of his sins from the heart - Experiences authentic *godly sorrow (2 Cor. 7:10).*

2. *Believes God* - Accepts, by faith, what Jesus did for Him on the cross for His salvation (John 3:16; Rom. 6:23, 10:9,10).

3. *Confirms* this decision by a *public profession* of faith. In this public affirmation, the genuinely repentant person proclaims that he has, by faith, received Jesus as his personal Lord and Savior. (He has accepted what Jesus did for him on the cross—dying for His sins— then rising from the grave, victorious over sin and death so that he now has eternal life with God in Heaven).

4. *Gives evidence* of his salvation through a change in his desires and behavior (2 Cor. 5:17). At the moment one is sincerely *born again* by a genuine profession of faith, God gives him a *new heart and a new spirit (Ezek. 36:26),* which results in a profound change in mind, emotions, will, and behavior. This profound change is marked by new desires, new behavior, and new attitudes toward God and others. There will also accompany it a new, Holy Spirit- inspired *love, peace, and joy (Rom 14:17).*

   Then you will say on that day, "I will give thanks to Thee, O Lord; For Thou…hast done excellent things. I will trust and not be afraid; for the Lord God is my strength and song, And He has become my salvation." Therefore, (I will) joyously draw water from the springs of salvation. (Is.12:1–3,5)

Bible Study Supplement

Chapter 3 — Day 5 — You Must Be Born Again

The theme of repentance and salvation is found throughout the Word of God. It is at the core of the gospel. God welcomes all who come to Him in genuine repentance, then accepts what He has done for them in Jesus (John 3:16). He forgives their sins and invites them to enter into a loving, protective, eternal relationship with Him.

1. Read Jer. 3:12,13, 22,23,25.

    a. What is God crying out to His children to do? (vs. 12a,13a,22a)

    b. What does He promise if they do this? (vs. 12b, 22a)

    c. What does the prophet Jeremiah urge the people to do? (vs. 25a)

    d. Why? (two reasons - vs. 25)

2. Read Jer. 4:14-18.

    a. What does God lovingly plead for His wayward children to do? (vs. 14)

    b. Why are the cities of Judah in so much trouble and turmoil? (vs. 17b)

    c. Describe what has happened. (vs. 16b,17a)

    d. Why has this happened? (vs. 17b,18)

We see again the theme of repentance in the opening pages of the New Testament. In Matt. 4, we are given Jesus' first words when He began His public ministry.

3. Read Matt. 4:17.

    a. From the beginning and throughout His earthly ministry, what was the central message of Jesus' teaching? (vs. 17)

4. Read Acts 26:19,20.

    a. What did Paul faithfully declare (preach)? (three things - vs. 20b).

Note: True repentance will result in a change in attitude, heart, and behavior.

5. Read 1 John 1:9.

    a. What does God promise if we come to Him in sincere humble confession? (two things)

6. Read John 3:1-6.

What did Jesus tell Nicodemus was necessary to enter the kingdom of God? (vs. 3,5)

Note: Verse 5 says: *Truly, truly, I say to you, unless one is born of water and the Spirit, he cannot enter the kingdom of God.* Throughout the Old Testament, as well as in the New Testament, water is symbolic of cleansing, purifying. It refers to a washing, or purification from one's former way of life and sinful desires as expressed in Ezek. 36 and Eph. 5: *Then I will sprinkle clean water on you and cleanse you from filthiness and you will be clean…that He might sanctify her having cleansed her by the washing of water with the Word* (Ezek. 36:25-27; Eph. 5:26). So being *born of water* refers to repentance as an integral part of *saving faith*—the cleansing and renewing of our heart from rebellious, sinful desires to new desires for holiness and righteousness. This we receive *by faith in what Jesus accomplished for us on the cross*, purging away our sin and giving us a new heart that desires to live godly and righteously. *He became sin for us that we might become the righteousness of God in Him* (2 Cor. 5:21). To be *born of the Spirit*, therefore, also involves welcoming the Spirit of God into our repentant hearts that He might empower us to live new, righteous lives for the Glory of God, for our good and joy, and the good and joy of others we love and with whom we share God's good news (Eph. 1:13,14; Rom. 8:28; John 15:11; Matt.28:19,20).

7. Read Acts 16:29–31.

    a. What did Paul tell the Philippian jailer he must do to be saved? (vs. 31)

Note: To believe in the Lord Jesus means to believe not only in what He did for us on the cross but also to believe what He teaches us in His Word. (Remember what we learned in Chapter 2, Day 1—Jesus is the Word of God incarnate). If we truly believe what Jesus taught about Himself, about God, our heavenly Father, and about the Holy Spirit, we will want to obey Him, and in so doing, we make Jesus not only our Savior, but also our Lord.

8. Read Rom. 10:9,10 (Below).

    …that if you confess with your mouth Jesus as Lord, and believe in your heart that God raised Him from the dead, you shall be saved; for with the heart man believes, resulting in righteousness, and with the mouth he confesses, resulting in salvation (Rom. 10:9,10).

    a. Based on this verse, the verses we studied above and in today's meditation, describe how one is *born again*.

9. Read John 14:6 and Acts 4:12.

    a. How many ways are there to Heaven?

    b. What is this way?

10. Read Is. 1:16, 18-20.

    a. What does God instruct us to do? (vs. 16)

Note: We wash ourselves and make ourselves clean through true biblical confession and repentance.

    b. What invitation does He give us? (vs. 18a)

    c. What does He promise us if we do this? (vs. 18)

    d. What will happen if we consent and obey? (vs. 19)

Note: Do you see God's heart for *relationship* here? The invitation is personal, warm, gentle. *Come, let us reason together.* God wants us to come to Him, to commune with Him (reason with Him) as we read His Word and talk with Him in prayer. It is such a precious invitation from the heart of an infinitely loving God.

Write out a Bible verse that had special meaning to you today.

Based upon what you have learned today, write a prayer to God expressing the desires of your heart in applying these Truths to your life.

Chapter 4

Memory verse: *Seek ye first the kingdom of God and His righteousness and all these things shall be added to you (Matt. 6:33).*

Bonus memory verse: *This is life eternal, that they may know Thee, the only true God, and Jesus Christ whom Thou hast sent (John 17:3).*

Day 1
The Sabotaging of Salvation
Demonic Deceptions that Keep People from Entering into a True Saving Relationship with God

Day 2
Examine Yourself — Proofs of Salvation — Part 1

Day 3
Examine Yourself — Proofs of Salvation — Part 2

Day 4
Progressive Sanctification
The Holy Image of God – In Restoration

Day 5
I'm Not OK, You're Not OK
Coming to Grips with our Stubborn, Rebellious Nature

Chapter 4 — Day 1
The Sabotaging of Salvation

Demonic Deceptions that Keep People from Entering into a True Saving Relationship with God

> *Not everyone who says to Me, 'Lord, Lord,' will enter the kingdom of Heaven; many will say to Me on that day, 'Lord, Lord, did we not prophesy in Your name, and in Your name cast out demons, and in Your name perform many miracles?' And then I will declare to them, depart from Me, I never knew you" (Matt. 7:21-23).*

Foundational Truth #12

Not everyone who says to Me, 'Lord, Lord,' will enter the kingdom of Heaven (Matt. 7:21). **Satan, the great deceiver, has exercised his greatest powers of deception in this most crucial area—the salvation and eternal destiny of man. Many who have never sought out the Truth of God's Word, have fallen for the lies, and though they faithfully occupy the pews of churches Sunday after Sunday, or live noble honorable lives outside the church, they are lost, and bound for a Christless eternity in hell. It is a sobering Truth based upon the clear teachings of God's immutable Word.**

And Jesus answered and said to them, "See to it that no one misleads you. For many false Christs and false prophets will arise and will mislead many" (Matt. 24:4,5,24).

Jesus warned that in the last days there would be false Christs and false prophets who would deceive the people and *mislead many (Matt. 24:4,5,24).* Since man's eternal soul is at stake, we can be sure that Satan will literally stop at nothing in his attempt to deceive and keep sinners estranged from God—from understanding and accepting the true gospel of salvation. Jesus went on to warn that the deception would become so great in the last days that even the elect would be deceived if they did not remain vigilant in their study of God's Word, the only source of true wisdom, which has the power to cut through demonic lies and deception.

We need to heed this caveat now more than ever in light of yet another warning from God:

The devil, knowing that his time is limited is already at work with all power and signs and false wonders, and with all the deception of wickedness for those who perish, because they did not receive the love of the Truth so as to be saved. And for this reason they (will be given over to) a deluding influence so that they...believe what is false...(because they) did not believe the Truth, but took pleasure in wickedness. (Rev. 12:12b; 2 Thess. 2:7–12 selected.)

Be sure that the devil is on a rampage like never before because he knows his time is limited—the end is near—and he is bound and determined to take as many as he can with him to his self-appointed destiny—

hell, the lake of fire (Rev. 20:15). We need God and the wisdom and discernment of His Word now more than ever. We need to heed the warnings throughout Scripture concerning the inevitable succession of events that always takes place when people *forsake God*. The first thing that happens is a disregard for God's Word, which results in spiritual blindness, demonic deception, disobedience, and eventually, the judgment of God. We see evidence all around us that we are well into this cycle once again. Because we have rejected God's merciful cry to return to Him, a spirit of delusion now prevails in the whole world. And we are not immune from that influence. It has invaded even our sacred sanctuaries—our churches…and our homes. That is why we need to be in God's Word consistently because only the Truth in God's Word can cut through this kind of demonic deception so that we can recognize the delusions that come to us from every side and can stand strong against them. *May God help us to see the urgency here.*

Demonic Deception – What Exactly Is It?

Demonic deception is a spiritual blindness or deception that is so strong that the one who is under its influence is "deceived beyond an ability to comprehend that he is deceived." Demonic deception is, therefore, a powerful weapon against which there is no intellectual defense, for the deceived are not able to recognize that they are…deceived.

Only the Word of God can cut through the blinding, delusional power of demonic deception.

So all who are without the Truths of the Word of God have no defense against demonic deception.

How does demonic deception occur? By three means:

1. Satan: through direct temptations and enticements through our mind, just as he tempted Eve.

2. Our own lustful, deceitful hearts which are, by nature, (our fallen nature), in rebellion against God until we are reconciled to Him and looking to Him (His Word/Holy Spirit) for guidance.

3. False teaching!

We talked about the first two ways demonic deception comes upon us in last week's studies, so today we will deal with false teaching, especially as it relates the most crucial subject of salvation. May God help us to heed His warnings.

And Jesus said to them, "Watch out! Beware of the leaven of the Pharisees and Sadducees… (today's anti-God academic intellectuals and self-appointed, "spiritual leaders") for (they) are like whitewashed tombs which on the outside appear beautiful, but inside are full of all uncleanness. Outwardly (they) appear righteous to men, but inwardly are full of hypocrisy (Matt. 16:6).

Your dwelling is in the midst of deceit; Through deceit (you) refuse to know Me, declares the Lord. (You) practice a discipline of delusion. (Jer. 9:6, 10:8)

*For the time will come when they will not endure sound doctrine; but wanting to have their ears tickled, they will accumulate for themselves teachers in accordance to their own desires; and will turn away their ears from the Truth, and will turn aside to **myths**. (2 Tim. 4:3,4).*

What are some of these deadly myths (demonic deceptions) concerning salvation many are turning aside to today?

Myth (false teaching) number one: There is no Heaven and no Hell. This life is all you have, so eat, drink, and be merry. When you're dead you're dead. But God's Word says there is a very real Heaven and a very real Hell. And we all will go to one place or the other when we die, there to live eternally.

Let not your heart be troubled; believe in God, believe also in Me. In My Father's house are many dwelling places; if it were not so, I would have told you; I go to prepare a place for you. And I will come again, and receive you to Myself; that where I am, there you may be also." (John 14:1–3)

It is appointed unto man once to die and after this, the judgment...Then He will say to those on His left, "Depart from Me, accursed ones (who refused to believe) into the eternal fire which has been prepared for the devil and his angels" (Heb 9:27; Matt. 25:41).

And if anyone's name was not found written in the book of life, he was thrown into the lake of fire . . . that place where there shall be weeping and gnashing of teeth...where their worm does not die, and the fire is not quenched (Rev. 20:15; Matt. 8:12; Mark 9:43–48).

Myth number two: All good people who are kind to others and make society a better place in which to live will go to Heaven. Therefore, it is not so much what you believe that will get you to Heaven, it is what you *do*. (This is also referred to as salvation by works.) This is, undoubtedly, the most widespread—and believed—demonic lie. Because of this we need to examine this one very closely. Let's look at some of the carefully construed, ever so enticing deceptions, then examine God's Word to see what God says about these seductive lies.

You've heard this carefully construed demonic lie dozens of times and so have I: God is love, therefore, God would never send a good person to hell.

One of Satan's most effective tools is to mix a little Truth into every lie making it unarguably rational from an intellectual standpoint. For the Christian, he carries the demonic deception one step further with misplaced (out of context) Scripture to make the argument *appear not only believable, but, biblical.* And so he has done here. Let's look at the deceptive *mixing* in this nearly universally accepted myth: There are two parts to the lie.

Part 1: God would never **send** a good person to hell.

Part 2: God would never send a **good** person to hell.

Biblical answer to Part 1: It is true! God doesn't *send* anyone to hell.

For God so loved the world that He gave His only begotten Son that whosoever believes on Him shall be saved...God would (desires) that all be saved and come to a knowledge of the Truth...As many as received Him, to them He gave the right to become children of God (John 3:16 KJV,1 Tim.1:4, John 1:12).

Not one person will be in hell because God *sent* him there. Every man and every woman who wakes up in hell one day will be there because they *chose* to reject God's loving offer of grace: forgiveness of sins and salvation through faith in the sacrificial death and resurrection of Jesus.

For those who have never heard the true gospel of Christ, the Bible makes it clear that God has revealed Himself to them—to everyone!—through His creation and through their own *conscience (Rom. 1:18–20).* Every person, therefore, is responsible for what they did with the revelation they were given.

In this country there will be no excuse for not responding to the gospel. We are a nation replete with opportunities to hear the gospel: a plethora of Bibles and other gospel teaching books, tapes, videos, Bible-teaching churches in nearly every community, radio, television, personal witness of others, including people that every person knows who has a personal relationship with God and that they (anyone who does not know) could ask for further guidance if needed, etc.

Biblical answer to Part 2: God would never send a *good* person to hell. So the question is: How good is good enough? Exactly how good does man have to be to merit Heaven?

Every one of them has turned aside; they have all become corrupt; There is no one who does good, not even one. All of us like sheep have gone astray, each of us has turned to his own way; For all of us have become like one who is unclean, And all our righteous deeds are like filthy rags (Ps. 53:3; Is. 53:6, 64:6 KJV/NASB).

Man judges everything by his own fallen, sinful standards. God's standard is absolute, perfect, unflawed holiness. Nothing less will enter Heaven. There is not one person who has ever walked the face of this earth (apart from Jesus) who meets this standard, for: *All have sinned and come short of the glory (holiness) of God (Rom. 6:23).* How then, can any man be saved?

He made Him who knew no sin to be sin on our behalf, that we might become the righteousness of God in Him (2 Cor. 5:21).

By faith in Christ's completed work for us on the cross, Christ's righteousness is imputed (given to, "put on") every believer. Therefore, when God looks at the true believer, He no longer sees his sinful imperfections, but Christ's holiness, and that is the only way anyone will enter the portals of Heaven, because Heaven is a holy place and only holy people will live there.

Myth number three: One is assured a place in Heaven by 1) attending church regularly, 2) having his name on a church roll, 3) getting baptized, 4) making a *public profession* of faith. Though people who are saved will make a public profession of faith, get baptized, join a church, and attend church regularly, none of these will in themselves save anyone—if there has been no heart change, true repentance. Combined with the false teaching concerning salvation by good works, these common lies have deceived a myriad. It truly breaks my heart to realize that there are people who sit in pews in churches faithfully every Sunday who, because of the demonic deception of these lies, are perishing. Tears still come to my eyes as I think how close I came to believing these —all the way to hell! And my heart aches for all the precious, sincere, well-meaning people who remain under its cloud, for the Bible clearly and lovingly warns:

Not everyone who says to Me, 'Lord, Lord,' will enter the kingdom of Heaven . . . many will say to Me on that day, 'Lord, Lord, did we not (sit in church every Sunday, get baptized, have our name on a church roll, take Holy Communion, or live sincere, noble, "good" lives, helping people) And I will declare to them, 'I never knew you; depart from Me' (Matt. 7:21–23).

Myth number four: All roads lead to the same place (Heaven/Nirvana); there are just different ways of getting there. But God's Word says:

I am the Way, the Truth and the Life; no one comes to the Father except through Me (Jesus)…Enter by the narrow gate; for the gate is wide, and the way is broad that leads to destruction, and many are those who enter by it…(but) the gate is small, and the way is narrow that leads to life, and few are those who find it (Matt. 7:13–14).

Truly, truly, I say to you, he who does not enter by the door into the fold of the sheep, is a thief and a robber. But he who enters by the door…to him the doorkeeper opens…I am the door (Jesus); if anyone enters through Me, he shall be saved (John 10:1,2,9).

Myth number five: It really doesn't matter what "name" you use to refer to God: Allah, Buddha, Hari Krishna, a universal positive force (New Age), Sheeva (or the thousands of other gods of the Hindus. They are all the same, and it doesn't matter which one you worship as long as you are sincere.

However, Creator God says:

I am the Lord, and there is no other; Besides Me there is no God…I am the Lord, and there is no other, the One forming light and creating darkness, causing well-being and creating calamity; I am the Lord who does all these…And there is salvation in no one else; for there is no other name under Heaven that has been given among men, by which we must be saved (Is. 45:5–7, Acts 4:12).

This God, the one and only true God, the Creator, and sustainer of the universe, has lovingly revealed Himself to us in the pages of His Holy Word, and He still calls out to all who do not yet know Him.

For God so loved the world, that He gave His only begotten Son, that whoever believes in Him should not perish, but have eternal life...Repent... and believe in the Lord Jesus, and you shall be saved (John 3:16; Acts 16:31).

Now, therefore, fear the Lord and serve Him in sincerity and truth; put away (false) gods...And if it is disagreeable in your sight to serve the Lord, choose for yourselves today whom you will serve: whether the (false) gods of your fathers or those (in the culture which surrounds you); but as for me and my house, we will serve the Lord (Josh. 24:14,15).

Bible Study Supplement

Chapter 4 — Day 1 — The Sabotaging of Salvation

1. Read 2 Cor. 4:3,4.

    a. To whom is the true Gospel of Christ veiled? (vs. 3)

    b. Why? (vs. 4)

2. Read 2 Timothy 4:3,4.

    a. What will happen in the end times, just prior to Jesus' return? (vs. 3)

    b. What will these people do? (vs. 4)

May God help us all to remain faithful to His Word and to the teaching of sound doctrine.

3. Read Acts 20:29-32.

    a. What did Paul warn would come in after him? (vs. 29)

    b. What would these people do? (vs. 30)

    c. What did Paul instruct God's true disciples to do? (vs. 31a)

    d. What is the *Word of grace* able to do? (vs. 32)

4. Read 2 Pet. 2:1,2,12-19.

    a. What is Peter's clear and fervent warning here? (vs. 1a)

    b. What will these false prophets—and the people who follow them—do? (vs. 1b,2)

    c. What will these wicked people do to those who are not well grounded (discerning) in the Truths of God's Word? (vs. 14,18,19a)

5. Read Jer. 14:13,14.

    a. What did God say about the prophets who were promising the people lasting peace while they continued in their wicked ways? (vs. 14)

What a loving, much-needed, warning God has given us for our world today. There are prophets (teachers, educators, televangelists, and other self-proclaimed "preachers") who are proclaiming that "all is well" and telling us to ignore God's clear warnings given to us in His Word. They are also telling us that it is not necessary to read and study God's Word for ourselves; that this is the job of the pastor or priest and we can "get" all the "Bible" we need in church on Sunday mornings or on a tape or video or watching Trinity Broadcasting Network's plethora of "religious programs". Sadly, there is as much false teaching on these programs as Jeremiah faced with the false prophets of his era. But, because people do not know God's Word they become easy prey for false teachers and fall for their lies through their own deceptive hearts.

6. Read Ezek. 22:25-30.

    a. What is happening among the prophets of the land? (vs. 25)

    b. What did God search for? (vs. 30)

May God help us all to remain vigilant and obedient to His Word, so that when His eyes search for a man to *build up the wall* and *stand in the gap* before Him, His eyes will fall on us, and He will find us faithful, building up the walls of Truth that have fallen because of false prophets.

7. Read 1 John 4:1.

    a. What does God instruct us to do? (1 John 4:1)

Note: We *test the spirits* by holding up what they are teaching against the Truth of God's Word. If their teaching in *any way* violates Scripture, we can be sure they are false teachers and need to be avoided lest our own minds become contaminated and we open ourselves up to demonic deception.

8. Read 1 John 2:18,19,21.

    a. What has already arisen? (vs. 18)

    b. Why did these people go out from God's people? (vs. 19)

    c. What can never be found in God's Word, the Truth? (vs. 21)

We need to be so, so careful of infiltrators that pretend to be *of us* but are, in reality, ravenous wolves that will eventually *go out from us* taking as many as they can with them!

9. Read 1 John 4:6.

    a. What will people who know God do?

Write out a Bible verse that had special meaning to you today.

Based upon what you have learned today, write a prayer to God expressing the desires of your heart in applying these Truths to your life.

Chapter 4 — Day 2
Examine Yourself — Proofs of Salvation — Part 1

> *Therefore if any man is in Christ, he is a new creature; the old things passed away; behold, new things have come (2 Cor. 5:17).*
>
> *I will give you a new heart and put a new Spirit within you...and I will put My Spirit within you and cause you to walk in My statutes (Ezek. 36:25-28).*

Foundational Truth #13

The Bible gives many *proofs of Salvation*—verses that confirm the inward and outward change that takes place at the time of every genuine new birth. We are commanded to *examine ourselves to make sure we are in the faith (2 Cor. 13:5)*. It is the most important examination we will ever make, for indeed our eternal destiny is at stake.

"Don't talk to me about God! I was brought up in the church. I've been going to church since I was a child so I know what it's all about!" The woman's eyes glazed in bitter anger. She turned and stomped away in a final gesture of defiance. I stood, trembling in her wake. What had I said to elicit this kind of response?

My husband and I owned a Christian bookstore, which we had dedicated to the Lord as an evangelistic outreach to the community. Lonely, hurting, searching people came in weekly and we were able to minister God's love and the wonderful good news of Christ's salvation to them. On that particular morning, God had given me the glorious joy of leading a woman to saving faith in Jesus. I was so excited I could hardly wait to share the wonderful news with someone. The first person to come in after that was the woman described above. She had been a frequent visitor in the bookstore and held a prominent position in her church. Naturally, I assumed she was a Christian. I was but a few sentences into sharing the wonderful good news when, at the first mention of a personal relationship with Jesus, the savage words stopped me cold, and before I knew it, I was standing alone. Sadly, I realized what had just taken place. I'd been there myself not so long ago. I went to the back room, got down on my knees, and began to pray for this woman who was so hurting inside and so desperately in need of receiving the love and forgiveness of Jesus.

If any man has not the spirit of Christ he is none of His (Rom. 8:9b).

I once heard a preacher say, "Conviction without repentance brings anger...and a whole lot of downright misery!" And it is true.

But the wicked are like the tossing sea, for it cannot be quiet; Its waters toss up refuse and mud... 'There is no peace,' says my God, 'for the wicked' (Is. 57:20,21).

Remember what we said earlier—"wicked" in the Bible refers to all who are outside of a personal relationship with God or not walking in His will. That dear woman in the bookstore was not alone in her internal embattlement. There are a lot of discontent, bitter, miserable people in the world today—people who are under conviction from the Holy Spirit (John 16:8), but refuse to turn back to God. Some do it out of willful, rebellious pride and defiance. But there is, tragically, an even greater number who have never come to a saving faith in Jesus because they are deceived by the enemy or filled with deep hurt or fear. Some have had a really hurtful experience in a church or perhaps at the hands of someone who *claimed* to be a Christian. Others are paralyzed in fear because they've heard a false gospel and they really don't understand the true nature of God and the greatness of His love, mercy, and grace. Because of demonic deception and false teaching, many have come to see God as a mean, cruel dictator who will take away everything that is enjoyable or brings pleasure if they become a Christian. Though nothing could be further from the Truth, for it is only through a personal relationship with Jesus that we can even begin to experience all the wonderful blessings, peace, and joy God longs to give us, the demonic deception is so powerful, they remain bound in fear. It is for these that my heart aches the most, because I've been there and I understand how deceptive and how paralyzing demonic fear can be. In fact, I am convinced that of all of Satan's lies, this one—the fear factor—keeps more people from coming to true saving faith in Jesus than any other, even pride and rebellion. It was certainly the case with me. And God alone knows how many more yet remain estranged from God because of this awful demonic fear. Because of the devastating potential of this, I will devote a separate lesson later to the paralyzing power of fear through demonic deception and how, through the Truths of God's Word and the enabling of the Holy Spirit, it can be gloriously and victoriously overcome.

The Bible teaches that a beautiful "spiritual metamorphosis," a miraculous inner change from something old to something new, takes place in the heart and soul (mind, emotions, will) of every person who is born from above of the Spirit of God. This is what Jesus referred to as the new birth, or being born again that we studied a couple of days ago. It is similar to the metamorphosis of that sluggish slow, ugly, gray, earthbound caterpillar who, under God's direction, spins around itself a chrysalis, then, dies. His body literally dissolves into a thick, murky substance. A few weeks later, in the miraculous workings of God, the thick, murky substance begins to take shape again into a completely different form. The sluggish, ugly, gray, earthbound caterpillar has become a beautiful, colorful, vivacious butterfly, able to spread its wings and, with beauty and grace, fly!

Earlier, I shared with you just a brief snapshot of that metamorphosis in my own life when, after years of fighting against God, I finally surrendered my heart and soul to Him. I'll never forget that day as long as I live. I can't fully describe it. I wish I could. I suppose it's different for everyone because it is a personal encounter with God, and you just can't adequately describe that! But one thing I've found in talking to many others who have experienced it: A definite change takes place inside, just as the Bible says.

> *If any man is in Christ, he is a new creature; the old things passed away; behold, all things have become new...But God, being rich in mercy, because of His great love with which He loved us, even when we were dead in our transgressions, made us alive together with Christ (2 Cor. 5:17; Eph. 2:4,5).*
>
> *I will give you a new heart and put a new Spirit within you...and I will put My Spirit within you and cause you to walk in My statutes (Ezek. 36:25–28).*

There is a very real and profound change that occurs in the soul. Something that was dead comes alive! I guess that is why Jesus called this miraculous event the "new birth." God breathes into our soul His life, and our formerly dead-in-sin spirit comes alive; that part of us that can know, and enjoy personal, intimate, fellowship with God!

The Bible clearly instructs that a person is only deceiving himself if he thinks he has been *born again* when there is no change in his attitudes, desires, or behavior. He will surely fail the test of true salvation when he stands before God.

> *…or do you not know that the unrighteous shall not inherit the kingdom of God? Do not be deceived; neither fornicators, nor idolaters (habitually placing anything before, or loving anything or anyone more than God), nor adulterers, nor effeminate, nor homosexuals, nor thieves nor the covetous, nor drunkards, nor revilers, nor swindlers, shall inherit the kingdom of God. And such were some of you; but you were washed, but you were sanctified, but you were justified in the name of the Lord Jesus Christ, and in the Spirit of our God (2 Cor. 6:9).*

The most important test that God commands all of us to take, therefore, is found in *2 Cor. 13:5:*

> *Test yourselves to see if you are in the faith; examine yourselves! Or do you not recognize this about yourselves, that Jesus Christ is in you—unless indeed you fail the test (2 Cor. 13:5).*

Bible Study Supplement

Chapter 4 — Day 2 — Examine Yourself — Proofs of Salvation — Part 1

There are many verses that confirm the inward and outward change that takes place at the time of every genuine new birth. So let's take a few minutes here to obey God's important command to: *Test yourselves...to see if you are in the faith*. We will examine several of these tests today and finish up with the rest tomorrow.

1. Read 2 Cor. 13:5.

    a. What are we commanded to do and why?

2. Read 1 Cor. 6:9-11.

    a. Who will not enter the kingdom of God? (List them - vs. 9,10)

    b. Verse 11 says that many people who come to Jesus were once like this, but what happened? (vs. 11)

Note: It is important to note here that idolatry (listed in verse 9) involves loving or worshiping *anything* more than we love and worship God. This could mean actual idols of wood and stone, or more commonly, idols of the heart—money, material things, fame, fortune, food, popularity (the praise of man), and a thousand and one other possibilities. We need to be very careful about this sin (idolatry), and the others mentioned here, because God gives similar warnings in Gal. 5:19-21; Eph. 5:5,6; 1 John 3:6-10; Rev. 21:8,27, 22:14,15). God loves us and He wants to protect us from the disillusionment, powerlessness and eventual destruction that idolatry always produces because idols can never help us or give us real, lasting joy and contentment.

3. Read Ezek. 36:25-28.

    a. What does God do for us when we genuinely repent of our sins and accept Jesus into our hearts? (vs. 25-27a)

4. Read 2 Cor. 5:17.

    a. What happens to every true *born again* believer?

5. Read Eph. 1:13,14.

    a. What does God give us as confirmation that we have truly been born again?

6. Read Rom. 8:16.

    a. Who bears witness with our spirit?

    b. About what does He bear witness?

7. Read 1 John 2:3.

    a. What will we want to do after we are saved?

Note. One of the first things that happens to every born again believer is a new devotion to the Word of God. He loves the Word of God and hungers to know it better so that He can obey it. By this he proves His love for God and expresses gratitude for His salvation.

8. Read 1 John 3:14,15.

    a. How do we know that we have passed out of death into eternal life *(born again)*? (vs. 14)

    b. What is the one who hates his brother? What does he not have? (vs. 15).

We need to take very seriously these *biblical proofs of salvation*. Our eternal destiny is at stake.

We'll look at the rest of the *proofs* tomorrow.

Write out a Bible verse that had special meaning to you today.

Based upon what you have learned today, write a prayer to God expressing the desires of your heart in applying these Truths to your life.

Chapter 4 — Day 3
Examine Yourself — Proofs of Salvation — Part 2

They went out from us, (because) they were not really of us; for if they had been of us, they would have remained; but they went out, in order that it might be shown that they all are not of us (1 John 2:19).

Who is the liar, but the one who denies that Jesus is the Christ (1 John 3:22).

Our study today will be a bit different. In order to maintain the continuity with yesterday's lesson—*Proofs of Salvation—Part 1*, we will do the Bible Study first, then finish with the meditation and a summary of the Biblical Proofs of Salvation.

It is interesting to note that the entire epistle of John is dedicated to the doctrine of salvation—what it is, how one is saved, and the proofs of salvation that will follow every genuine salvation experience. It's clearly very important to God that we understand these "proofs" and verify our salvation with them.

1. Read 1 John 2:22.

    a. Who is a liar?

Note: The born again believer has a deep love and devotion to Jesus who is not only "the Christ"—the Messiah, the Savior and redeemer of the world—but also his personal Lord and Savior. He loves to talk about Him and express his gratitude for what He has done for him. He would rather die than deny him. So whenever you hear someone *deny Christ* by not wanting to even talk about Him, or dishonoring Him through irreverence or blasphemous remarks, there ought to be serious concern over his salvation.

2. Read Matt. 7:17-23.

    a. How will other people recognize that we have been born again? (vs. 20)

    b. Who will enter the Kingdom of Heaven? (vs. 21b)

    c. What will Jesus say to those who *claim* to know Him but have never been genuinely *born again*? (Repented from the heart and received Him as personal Lord and Savior) (vs. 23)

3. Read John 10:27.

    a. What do Jesus' sheep hear?

    b. What do they do?

4. Read Heb. 12:5–8.

   a. What do all loving fathers do for their children? (7b)

   b. Why should you be concerned if you never experience the loving discipline of God? (vs. 8)

5. Read Eph. 5:1–8.

   a. What can we know with certainty? (vs. 5)

   b. What happens to those who pay no heed to God's loving warnings and continue to walk in disobedience? (vs. 6)

   c. What are we now and how are we to walk? (vs. 8)

Before we close this very important lesson, we must address briefly two issues that have caused confusion and doubt in the mind of some who truly have been born again. These issues are: the role of emotions in the salvation experience and being able to name a specific day/time in which the salvation experience took place. We live in a "touchy, feely" world where so much of our experiences are ruled by emotions. But saving faith is not an emotion. It is an intelligent, volitional act of the mind, the heart and the will. God very beautifully describes in John 3 the way the Holy Spirit works to bring about the salvation experience.

The wind blows where it wishes and you hear the sound of it, but do not know where it comes from and where it is going; so is everyone who is born of the Spirit. (John 3:8)

The Holy Spirit—like God the Father and God the Son—is a very real and distinct individual in the Godhead. He sees each of us as the unique individual we were created to be. He knows each of our unique personalities because He created them. Therefore, He works in different ways in different people to draw them to Jesus and into His kingdom. Some people have a very dramatic emotional salvation experience while others are *born again* in a very quiet, calm (unemotional) way. I've seen both—and just about everything in between. I do not doubt in the slightest the genuineness of the faith of any of these truly *born again* believers as I have seen the evidence of salvation in the beautiful and consistent *fruit* they bear (Matt. 7:20). But their salvation *experiences* were as different as night and day.

Regarding being able to name an exact date and time of conversion, for those who came to faith in Christ in adulthood, there will almost always be a very specific dramatic experience—that distinct moment when one recognizes his rebellious, lost condition, repents of his sins, and turns his heart to God. He comes to the end of his self-rule (controlling his own life and living for self rather than for God), and gladly puts his life under the Lordship of Jesus, His Savior, **knowing** He will do a much better job of managing it than he has. It involves a complete change in heart/desires/will and nearly all will be able to tell you the exact time and date this dramatic event took place. And well they should, for the Bible clearly says:

Therefore if any man is in Christ, he is a new creature; the old things have passed away; behold, all things have become new (2 Cor. 5:17).

That is pretty clear. New creature; old things passed away. All things—new. If one is suddenly a new creature, he will be quite aware of the moment that miraculous transformation took place.

However, children who are born into a strong Christian family where faith and trust in God is modeled twenty-four hours a day and Jesus is the center and focus of all activity, may not be able to name a specific time and date when they were actually *born again*. Salvation for them was a gradual experience from the day they were born. They were taught the things of God and grew to know, love, and trust in Him. I have known a number of people who have come from this kind of strong Christian heritage who cannot remember an exact date or time when a unique salvation experience actually occurred. As far back as their memories will reach, through the strong, consistent teaching and modeling of their parents, they realized they were sinners in need of a Savior, that Jesus died for them on the cross and rose again from the dead to save them from their sins. They "always" knew this, believed this, and accepted it as their only way to Heaven. And they have desired to live for Jesus, to be obedient and fulfill His will for their lives.

The Bible does, however, teach that once the child has reached the *age of accountability* (intellectual reasoning and understanding), it is important that he make a public profession of faith in Jesus to confirm his repentance and acceptance of Jesus into his heart as his personal Lord and Savior, then follow this confession with believer's baptism.

Elizabeth Elliot Gren stands out in my mind as a beautiful example of this. She was born into a very strong Christian home where daily Bible reading, prayers, and hymn singing were the focus and the priority of every day's activities. When asked to give the date that she actually accepted Jesus into her heart, she responded that she could not remember "not being a Christian". From the beginning, following her mama and papa's godly examples, she had always accepted Jesus as her Lord and Savior. In other words, hers was a slow, gradual process from the day she was born, while others are often much more sudden and dramatic. It is as the Bible says: *The wind blows where it wishes and you hear the sound of it, but do not know where it comes from and where it is going; so is everyone who is born of the Spirit* (John 3:8). Sometimes the wind blows in ever so soft, gentle breezes. At other times it comes as a mighty rushing gale. So the experience is not nearly so important as the fruit that does or does not follow.

The point is that *whoever* has been truly born again will demonstrate the *proofs of salvation* consistently in his life, because the Holy Spirit now lives in him to produce this fruit.

Since this is at the heart of whether or not we will spend eternity in Heaven with God and all others who have genuinely accepted Jesus as Lord and Savior, or in Hell, a place of eternal torment and suffering, we need to take the test very seriously to see if indeed we are *in the faith*. Please turn to the next page for a summary of the Biblical Proofs of Salvation. (You may want to make copies of this to share with friends who may be deceived by teaching about salvation by good works or "easy believism.")

Biblical Proofs of the New Birth

1. *I will give you a new heart and put a new Spirit within you…and I will put My Spirit within you and cause you to walk in My statutes)…if any man be in Christ, He is a new creature, old things passed away, new things have come…that they who live should no longer live for themselves but for God (Ezek. 36:25–28; 2 Cor. 5:17,15).*

The born again believer who is in the faith will have a new heart and new desires to know, love, and obey God. He will no longer seek his own will but God's will for his life and he will set his affections upon pleasing Him and fulfilling His good plans day by day.

2. *You also after you believed were sealed in Him with the Holy Spirit who is given as a pledge of our inheritance…you are not in the flesh but in the Spirit, if indeed the Spirit of God dwells in you. But if anyone does not have the Spirit of Christ, he does not belong to Him" (Eph. 1:13,14; Rom. 8:9).*

The moment a genuine confession is made, the Holy Spirit comes immediately to indwell the born again believer. His very real presence serves as a *seal* of salvation. This is that unshakable assurance in the heart that says: I know that I know that I know that I am a child of God. I have a personal, forgiven, growing relationship with Him now and will enjoy *Life Eternal* with Him in the glorious paradise of Heaven one day.

3. *And by this we know that we have come to know Him, if we keep His commandments (1 John 2:3; see also 1 John 3:6–9; John 14:21,23).*

The repentant sinner will have a love for and a desire to obey the Word of God. He recognizes that it is impossible to obey the Word of God if he does not know the Word of God. Therefore, he has a hunger and thirst for God's Word, spending time consistently in it that he might please His heavenly Father and bring honor and glory to Him by upholding and obeying His commands.

4. *We know that we have passed out of death into life because we love the brethren. He who does not love abides in death. Everyone who hates his brother is a murderer; and you know that no murderer has eternal life abiding in him (1 John 3:14,15).*

God's love (John 3:16) and hate cannot live together in the same heart. Hate must go. The *born again* believer will repent of any residual hatred or bitterness towards his brothers and sisters and offer to them the same forgiveness that has so graciously been extended to him by God.

5. *Who is the liar but the one who denies that Jesus is the Christ (1 John 2:22).*

The born again believer will not deny or refute the deity or the Lordship of Jesus. He believes all God says about him in His Word and lives his life accordingly, bringing honor and glory to Him.

6. *Not everyone who says to me, 'Lord, Lord,' will enter the Kingdom of Heaven; but he who does the will of My Father…even so, every good tree bears good fruit…So then, you will know them by their fruits (Matthew 7:17–23).*

Those who are *born again* seek with all their hearts to know and do the will of God, gratefully, joyfully bearing fruit for God and for His kingdom (John 15:8).

7. *My sheep hear My voice, and I know them, and they follow Me (John 10:27).*

God's true sheep *hear* (listen to, recognize) His voice and they earnestly seek to *follow Him*.

8. *My son, do not regard lightly the discipline of the Lord, nor faint when you are reproved by Him; for those whom the Lord loves He disciplines…God deals with you as sons; for what son is there whom his father does not discipline? But if you are without discipline, then you are illegitimate children and not sons (Heb. 12:5,8).*

True sons of God will welcome the discipline of their loving, heavenly Father, knowing that it is *for their good*, that they may *share in His Holiness…becoming partakers of the divine nature…(yielding) the peaceful fruit of righteousness*. The person who can sin without any sense of conviction or discipline from God has every reason to be greatly concerned about his sonship (Deut. 10:13; Heb. 12:10,11).

These proofs of the Lord's love for us given through the precious gift of salvation are just the beginning of our vast blessed inheritance in Christ (Eph. 1:1–21, 2:1–6; 1 Pet. 1:1–9; 2 Pet. 1:3–10, 2:9,10; 1 Cor. 2:9–13, etc.). God has so, so much more for all who receive Jesus as their personal Lord and Savior which we'll look at in upcoming chapters. No wonder Jesus said to His disciples when they returned from their first evangelistic outreach, Do not rejoice that the spirits are subject to you, but rejoice that your names are recorded in Heaven! (Luke 10:19,20).

That is why I am praying, even as I write this, that if there is anyone who fails these tests of true salvation or for whom there is any doubt in his mind about his relationship with Jesus and his eternal destiny, that he will not wait one more day to settle this issue once and for all. Please seek out a Pastor or Christian friend whom you know to be truly *born again*, who will gladly answer any questions and walk with you through the steps of the new birth so that you, too, can enter into a personal relationship with Jesus and be assured of not only life eternal with Him in Heaven one day, but of a new and fulfilling, blessed and rewarding life here on earth (Ps. 25:12; 1 Pet. 1:5; Deut. 28:1–13; Rom. 6:4; Ps.16:11, etc.).

> *…and the Spirit and the Bride say "Come" and let the one who hears, "come." Let the one who is thirsty, "come" and take of the Water of Life. Come unto me all who are weary and heavy laden, and…you shall find rest for your souls (Rev. 22:17,20; Matt. 11:28,30).*

Write out a Bible verse that had special meaning to you today.

Based upon what you have learned today, write a prayer to God expressing the desires of your heart in applying these Truths to your life.

Chapter 4 — Day 4
Progressive Sanctification
The Holy Image of God — In Restoration

> *But we should always give thanks to God for you, brethren beloved by the Lord, because God has chosen you from the beginning for salvation through sanctification by the Spirit and faith in the truth. And it was for this He called you through our gospel, that you may gain the glory of our Lord Jesus Christ. (2 Thess. 2:13,14)*

Foundational Truth # 14

God has chosen you from the beginning for salvation through sanctification by the Spirit...for whom He foreknew, He also predestined to become conformed to the Image of His Son (2 Thess. 2:13,14; Rom. 8:29). The second step in the salvation process (after justification—the *new birth*) is sanctification. This is the process whereby we are *set apart for God's Holy purposes*. As we walk in obedience to God's good plans for our lives daily, God is ever at work conforming us to the Image of Jesus—that beautiful holy image that was destroyed in the fall. It's a glorious process *(2 Cor. 3:18)*.

I remember it as if it were yesterday: We were seated in the plush auditorium of the luxury beachfront Fontainebleau Hotel in Miami. A regal, royal-blue velvet curtain shimmered in the background of the spacious stage as dozens of spotlights danced across it in anticipation of the special awards soon to be announced. In a few moments, I was enveloped in those same lights as the announcement was made of my being selected IBM System Support Specialist of the year. (IBM was at that time the leading computer technology, sales and service company in the nation). A list of lofty achievements was read as enthusiastic applause echoed through the auditorium. I had dreamed of this recognition since my first awards banquet as the System Support Specialist for our region just one year earlier, and only two years after joining IBM. So quickly I had achieved this most coveted award. It should have been a moment of exhilarating joy and celebration. But even the grand fanfare, spotlights and the applause on the outside could not ease the tormenting turmoil inside as my mind churned with plaguing thoughts: how can I top this next year? How many systems will I have to configure/sell? How many overtime hours will be required? How many weekends will I have to sacrifice? I could not enjoy for even a few minutes a sense of real, inner satisfaction, contentment—peace.

I didn't know God then, so I didn't understand that there would be no real or lasting peace, no matter what I achieved. Sadly, many years would pass before I would understand this fundamental Truth: All real and lasting peace begins with peace with God found in a forgiven, personal relationship with Him, through faith in Jesus and His redeeming work on our behalf on the cross. But that is only the first step. God has a beautiful plan for each of our lives and until we are actively involved in pursuing the fulfillment of that plan—God's plan—all our dreams and schemes (and even lofty achievements) will be just as the Bible says in *James 4:14: like a vapor that quickly disappears* leaving us empty and ever striving for more but never finding the true fulfillment, and contentment for which we so desperately long and were created to enjoy.

> *For we are His workmanship, created in Christ Jesus for good works, which God prepared beforehand, that we should walk in them. (Eph. 2:10)*

Contrary to popular acceptance in a tragic number of churches today, God does not save anyone to occupy a pew on Sunday morning then go out and do his own thing all through the week, come back to church the next Sunday, sit and soak, go back into the world, do his own thing again, return and repeat the cycle over and over again until he dies and goes to Heaven, never experiencing any change in his thinking, motivations, or behavior, or bearing any fruit for the kingdom of God. God created us all to be *set-apart, sanctified, useful vessels, fulfilling **His** good will and purposes, bearing fruit for Him (2 Tim. 2:21; John 15:8; Rom. 12:1,2; Eph. 2:10; John 13:5–14; John 17:4).*

> *But God has chosen you from the beginning for salvation through sanctification by the Spirit and faith in the Truth, and it was for this He called you through our gospel, that you may gain the glory of our Lord Jesus Christ (2 Thess. 2:13,14).*

God tells us clearly here that the new birth is but the first step in God's special plan for our lives. The next step is *sanctification.*

Sanctification comes from the Greek word, *hagiasmos: Set apart for God's Holy purposes.* It is a glorious ongoing work of God's grace by which the believer is set apart (separated) more and more from sin and becomes more and more like Jesus. This is accomplished by the Holy Spirit working through the Word of God (Rom. 8:3,4; John 17:7). Sanctification results in holiness and purification from the guilt and power of sin.

In other words, we are, through the redemptive work of Jesus, purified from all past sin and guilt, then empowered by the Holy Spirit to live sanctified, righteous lives as we continue in faith and obedience (John 8:31,32). Sanctification is, therefore, an ongoing, progressive, work in which our spirit, our *new nature,* cooperates with the Spirit of God, in conforming us into the image of Christ, recapturing that once perfect image of God that was lost in the fall.

It may be helpful to think of it this way: The fall was the image of God, lost. Sanctification is the image of God, regained (or, more specifically, "being" regained through a progressive purification as our love for and obedience to God grows and old sinful habits are *put off* and new righteous ones are *put on – Eph. 4:22–24).* If only we would fully embrace and, by faith, *live* in the magnitude of this glorious truth! There would be a lot more "joy in the journey".

The Old Testament sacrificial system created the backdrop for understanding the New Testament doctrine of sanctification. Daily, the priests who were to offer the sacrifices had to be consecrated, *set apart,* and ceremonially purified before they could participate in the holy worship of sacrificial duties. Even the instruments used in the offering and the altar itself had to be purified. It was a holy venture—all for the purpose of making atonement for the sins of the people. Yet all of these ceremonial laws, intricate and complex as they were, could not actually take away sin; they could only serve as a temporary "covering" *(Heb. 9:13),* similar to the garments God made for Adam and Eve in the Garden.

Jesus' blood of the New Covenant goes so much further! Far beyond mere ritual purification, and the temporary covering of sins, Jesus' perfect sacrifice on our behalf is able to *cleanses us from all unrighteousness and to purge our conscience from dead works to serve the living God (Heb. 9:14).* Our sanctification, like our justification comes to us through faith in the promises of God which we are now empowered to *live* through the Holy Spirit that comes to us the moment we *believe.*

Justification and sanctification are symbolically represented in baptism: buried with Christ through death, (justification), raised to new life in Christ (sanctification) (Rom. 6:4; 1 Cor. 1:2; Acts 20:32; 1 Cor. 1:30; 6:11).

Therefore, having been justified by faith, we have peace with God through our Lord Jesus Christ through whom we have obtained our introduction by faith into this grace in which we stand; (Rom. 5:1,2).

Sanctification is the second step in the *continuation of grace* in the salvation process: Justification, Sanctification, Glorification.

You have been chosen according to the foreknowledge of God the Father by the sanctifying work of the Spirit, that you may obey Jesus Christ…For whom He foreknew, He also predestined to become conformed to the image of His Son (1 Pet. 1:2; Rom. 8:29).

The process of sanctification may be summarized as follows:

1. Being set apart for God's holy purposes
2. Fulfilling His good and perfect will for our lives (Eph. 2:10; Rom. 12:1,2; Jer. 29:11–14).
3. Becoming conformed to the image of Jesus (Rom. 8:29).
4. Serving as God's ambassadors, sharing His love and truth with others that they, too might be *born again,* become children of God, and enter into the sanctification process (2 Cor. 5:15–20).

In so doing we bring honor and glory to God for we are living the purpose for which He created us.

As obedient children, do not be conformed to the former lusts which were yours in your ignorance, but like the Holy One who called you, be holy yourselves also in all your behavior; because it is written, "You shall be holy, for I am holy." (1 Pet. 1:14–16)

This process of sanctification (being set apart for God's holy purposes, becoming like Jesus) is that *upward call* in Christ to which Paul refers in that beautiful third chapter of Philippians:

Not that I have already obtained it, or have already become perfect, but I press on in order that I may lay hold of that for which also I was laid hold of by Christ Jesus. Brethren, I do not regard myself as having laid hold of it yet; but one thing I do; forgetting what lies behind and reaching forward to what lies ahead, I press on toward the goal for the prize of the upward call of God in Christ Jesus (Phil. 3:12–14).

Personally, I find this glorious process of sanctification incredibly liberating. No longer am I bound by the pressures and confusing dictates of human goodness—trying desperately to be a good person. How good is good enough? It is impossible to be good enough to merit the acceptance and favor of God whose standard is perfect holiness. However, when I put my faith completely in Jesus and His finished work on the cross, His righteousness and His holiness become my righteousness and holiness (2 Cor. 5:21; 1 Pet. 3:18; Rom. 5:6–18). I am no longer a good person, but I have become *in Jesus,* a holy person. It is my greatest joy, through the power of the Holy Spirit resident within, to reflect that holiness and righteousness as the image of Jesus is being formed more and more in me.

*For we are His workmanship, created in Christ Jesus for good works, which **God prepared beforehand,** that we should walk in them (Eph. 2:10).*

I will never forget the huge burden that fell from my shoulders the day this precious truth penetrated my soul. For the first time in my life, I realized that God really did have a beautiful plan for my life. So I no longer had to strive to *find it* or to *achieve it*—doing that which would merit God's (and others!) favor and approval through my own striving labors. My responsibility was merely the joy of walking in *God's* beautiful plan in the power of the Holy Spirit, moment by moment, day by day. With this realization came the additional freedom of knowing that there was only one person I now had to please and that was God—who was endlessly loving, merciful, and gracious. No longer did I have to *prove my worth* to countless, endless others, as I had so desperately striven for so long to do.

For not he who commends himself (or is commended by others) is approved, but **whom the Lord commends**...*well done, good and faithful servant; enter into the JOY of your Master (2 Cor. 10:18; Gal. 1:10; Matt. 25:23).*

Now, may the God of peace Himself sanctify you entirely; and may your spirit and soul and body be preserved complete, without blame until the coming of our Lord Jesus Christ (1 Thess. 5:23).

Bible Study Supplement

Chapter 4 — Day 4 — Progressive Sanctification — The Holy Image of God — In Restoration

1. Read Eph. 2:1–9.

   a. What were we before God, by His mercy and grace, redeemed us? (vs. 1)

   b. What did God do for us? (vs. 4,5)

   c. How have we been saved? (two parts – fill in the blanks below) (vs. 8)

   For by _____ you have been saved, through _____,... it is the gift of God not of works lest any man should boast.

   d. By whom (have we been saved)? (vs. 4,8b)

2. Read Eph. 2:10 (Please use the NASB translation below to answer the questions that follow).

   For we are His workmanship, created in Christ Jesus for good works, which God prepared beforehand, that we should walk in them (Eph. 2:10).

   e. Who were we created in (through our new birth)?

   f. For what purpose were we created?

   g. Who prepared these?

   h. What is both our privilege and our joy? (vs. 10b)

3. Read Rom. 8:28,29.

   a. To whom do all things work together for good? (two qualifications - vs. 28)

   b. What is God's desire (purpose) for all of us who love Him? (vs. 29)

4. Read 2 Cor. 5:15,17–21.

   a. What happens to everyone who is genuinely born again? (vs. 17)

   b. How will he now live? (vs. 15)

   c. What ministry has God given to all of us? (vs. 18)

   d. What are we now (our main spiritual vocation)? (vs. 20a)

   e. What are we to become, live out? (vs. 21)

5. Read 1 Pet. 2:9,10. (I love these verses! They are a beautiful picture of our blessed inheritance in Christ as redeemed, sanctified, set apart, children of God).

   a. What are we now that we have been saved and are being sanctified? (four things - vs. 9a)

    b. or what purpose? (vs. 9b)

    c. Who are we now? (vs. 10a)

    d. What have we received? (vs. 10b)

Note: 1 Peter 2:10 is, in a nutshell, the biblical solution to the sad, empty, unbiblical teaching of *self-esteem* that we will be looking at next week. Before Christ, we had no real identity or acceptability. We were, as the world so often labels us, "nobodies" with no real value, purpose or belongingness. But after receiving Christ as our personal Lord and Savior, we became the *children of God*. And we can't possibly receive any greater value or acceptability than that!

6. Read 2 Thess. 2:13,14.

    a. For what has God chosen you? (vs. 13)

    b. How does He accomplish this? (two ways - vs. 13b)

    c. What will be the result if we are obedient to God in pursuing this purpose? (vs. 14b)

7. Read Jer. 29:11-13. (Please use NASB here to answer the questions below).

    11. "For I know the plans that I have for you," declares the Lord, "plans for welfare and not for calamity to give you a future and a hope.

    12. Then you will call upon Me and come and pray to Me, and I will listen to you.

    13. And you will seek Me and find Me, when you search for Me with all your heart" (Jer. 29:11–13).

    a. What kind of plans does God have for you? (vs. 11)

    b. How can we be sure that we will find God's good plans for our lives? (vs. 13)

Write out a Bible verse that had special meaning to you today.

Based upon what you have learned today, write a prayer to God expressing the desires of your heart in applying these Truths to your life.

Chapter 4 — Day 5
I'm Not OK, You're Not OK
Coming to Grips with Our Stubborn, Rebellious Nature

> *The heart is more deceitful than all else and is desperately wicked; Who can understand it? (Jer. 17:9, KJV/NASB)*
>
> *You have been rebellious against the Lord from the day I knew you; You neither believed the Lord, nor listened to His voice (Deut. 9:23,24).*
>
> *You, too have done evil, even more than your forefathers; for behold, you are each one walking according to the stubbornness of his own evil heart, without listening to Me (Jer. 16:12).*

Foundational Truth # 14

I am *by nature*—my fallen sinful nature—stubborn, rebellious and disobedient to God. My heart, in its natural state, is full of selfishness, pride, deception, and is defiantly opposed to God and the things of God. *In me, that is in my flesh dwells no good thing (Rom. 7:18).*

When I was working on my Master's in counseling, a very popular book that was required reading in one of my counseling theories classes was a book entitled: *I'm OK. You're OK.* Its basic premise was that we are all inherently good inside, so our job as counselors was to get people to look inside themselves for their inherent good and to let that guide them.

What tragic counsel! Nothing could be further from biblical Truth—and from *reality*—as we witness the long-term devastating results of this kind of teaching, which is still at the heart of much counseling today.

What does God have to say about our *inherent good* within?

The heart is more deceitful than all else and is desperately wicked; Who can understand it? (Jer. 17:9, KJV/NASB)

For I know that nothing good dwells in me, that is, in my flesh; for the wishing is present in me, but the doing of the good is not. For the good that I wish, I do not do; but I practice the very evil that I do not wish. But if I am doing the very thing I do not wish, I am no longer the one doing it, but sin which dwells in me (Rom. 7:18–20).

The first step in progressive sanctification is to recognize that: *in me, that is in my flesh, dwells no good thing (Rom. 7:18)*! Apart from Christ we are all, by nature (our fallen, sinful nature), inherently bad, not good. We are stubborn and rebellious, sinful, people, and the only *good* in us is the residual *image of God* that yet remains. But even that has been corrupted and defiled. That is why we need the regenerating power of new birth (rebirth) and the purification it brings. And that is why we need the ongoing work of grace in sanctification, in which the Holy Spirit quickens our minds, creating within them, righteous discernment/desires. This is accomplished as we read and study God's Word which exposes the deception and wickedness in our hearts and renews our mind so that we begin to think new, righteous, holy thoughts that desire to know and obey God's *good and perfect* will (Rom. 12:1,2).

As I began to study the Old Testament, I was amazed at how similar my life and attitudes were to those of the children of Israel. We can learn much from God's dealings with this stubborn and rebellious, stiffnecked lot. Most of us are very much like them.

> *For thus says the Lord of hosts, the God of Israel: "Behold, I am going to eliminate from this place, before your eyes and in your time, the voice of rejoicing and the voice of gladness, the voice of the groom and the voice of the bride." Now it will come about when you tell this people all these words that they will say to you, "For what reason has the Lord declared all this great calamity against us? And what is our sin which we have committed against the Lord our God?" Then you are to say to them, "It is because your forefathers have forsaken Me," declares the Lord, "and have followed other gods and… bowed down to them; but Me they have forsaken and have not kept My law. You too have done evil, even more than your forefathers; for behold, you are each one walking according to the stubbornness of his own evil heart, without listening to Me. So I will hurl you out of this land into the land which you have not known; and there you will serve other gods day and night (Jer. 16:9–13).*

We briefly mentioned earlier a principle that is clearly taught throughout the Word of God—and again here—and that is this: If we stubbornly insist on having it our way, there comes a time when God says: "OK, have it your way." And He steps aside and lets us serve those other gods to which we have looked to satisfy and fulfill us. What a terrible place to be! It is exactly the place that the children of Israel found themselves in Egypt—in bondage to a cruel and heartless taskmaster, which is what every other "god" apart from our loving heavenly Father will be.

> *No one can serve two masters; for either he will hate the one and love the other, or he will hold to one and despise the other. You cannot serve God and mammon (Matt. 6:24).*

There are ultimately only two masters in the world: God and Satan. God is *loving, compassionate and merciful (Gen. 3:16; 1 John 4:8; Lam. 3:22,23);* Satan is a *liar (deceiver), robber, killer, and destroyer (John 8:44, 10:10).*

The fact that anyone would *choose* to serve Satan rather than God only proves the depravity, pride and stubbornness of our own wicked and deceptive hearts.

As I continued to study the fickle, unfaithful, idolatrous children of Israel (Ex. 16–20, 32–34; Num. 11–25), I became more and more painfully aware of the degree to which I had already developed so many of their same stubborn, rebellious patterns:

> *You have been rebellious against the Lord from the day I knew you…You have neither **believed the Lord**, nor **listened to His voice**. (Deut. 9:23,24)*

> *The Lord has a case against the inhabitants of the land, because there is no faithfulness, or knowledge of God in the land…they direct their desire toward their iniquity, because they have stopped giving heed to the Lord. A spirit of harlotry is within them; they have played the harlot continually and (have been) led astray… departing from God; **Israel is stubborn, like a stubborn heifer** (Hosea 4:18,10b, 5:4,12b, 4:16).*

When I read: *Israel is stubborn, like a stubborn heifer*, it was one of those proverbial moments when the words seemed to jump off the page. What an apt description—of me! I was no different than those stiffnecked, rebellious people who refused to give heed to the Lord but instead ran after every "god" that came to my lustful flesh promising pleasure, satisfaction, and freedom. I needed to confess my sin of stubbornness and rebellion (disobedience) and idolatry (spiritual harlotry) and come back to God, submitting myself in humble love, devotion, and obedience to Him, knowing that He is a merciful and loving God who always delivers on His good promises (2 Cor. 1:20; Josh. 23:14). It was the beginning of new godly wisdom, transforming of my mind and healing of my soul.

> *Wash your heart from evil, that you may be saved; How long will your wicked thoughts lodge within you? Like watchmen of a field, they are against her round about, because she has rebelled against Me, declares the Lord. Your ways and your deeds have brought these things on you, This is your evil, How bitter! How it has touched your heart (Jer. 4:14,17,18).*
>
> *Therefore, thus says the Lord , if you return, then I will restore you, before Me you will stand… and I will redeem you from the grasp of the violent…return O faithless ones, I will heal your faithlessness (Jer. 15:19,21).*

The sooner we recognize that our heart is indeed *deceitful and desperately wicked* and that, in us, that is, *in our flesh, dwells no good thing,* and turn to God for the cleansing and renewing Truths of His Word, the sooner we will begin to experience the real and lasting healing that comes through the sanctification process. God's Word provides the discernment and power we need to recognize and stand against the lies and deceptions of not only the devil, but also our own lustful, fallen flesh and deceitful heart. As we come to it daily, and invite the Holy Spirit to cleanse and renew our hearts and minds through its Truths, we are sanctified and empowered to walk in God's protective, liberating Truth. This is what the Bible calls the *believer's rest (Heb. 4:11)*, the "resting place" of true inner *peace, contentment and freedom* (from sin's destructive power, guilt and bondage) *(Heb. 4:11; John 8:31,32; Phil. 4:7, 11)*.

> *So they shall no more walk after the stubbornness of their evil heart…I (will) set you among My sons, and give you a pleasant land, the most beautiful inheritance of the nations! And you shall call Me, My Father, and not turn away from following Me…And I will be a Father to you; and you shall be sons and daughters to Me, says the Lord Almighty (Jer. 3:17,19; 2 Cor. 6:18).*
>
> *…(and so) we all, with unveiled face beholding as in a mirror the glory of the Lord, are being transformed into the same image from glory to glory (2 Cor. 3:18).*

Bible Study Supplement

Chapter 4 – Day 5 — I'm Not OK, You're Not OK —
Coming to Grips with our Stubborn and Rebellious Nature

Note: Keep a bookmark in Jeremiah as we will be returning to it several times today.

1. Read Jer. 17:9. (Please use NASB/KJV below to answer the question)

   The heart is more deceitful than all else and desperately wicked; who can understand it? (NASB/KJV).

   a. What is the condition of our fallen hearts?

Please note that our inherited-from-Adam, sinful, fallen hearts are deceptive, and wicked to the core. In its natural state the heart is continually in rebellion against God. It is full of pride and selfishness and refuses to submit in obedience to God's protective loving plans. Left alone—unwashed, uncleansed, unpurified—it will persist in following the destructive desires of its own rebellious, sinful lusts rather than the will of God…all the way to hell.

In spite of this, we continually hear many people—"experts" on radio and television, in magazines and newspapers, even well-meaning friends—telling us: "Just listen to your heart and do what it says." That is very bad advice and gets us into a ton of agonizing trouble. We need to listen to the Word of God and do what it says. It is so, so important to let the reality of Jer. 17:9 sink deep into our souls: *The heart is more deceitful than all else, and is desperately wicked; Who can understand it?* Only when we are fully aware of this, will we be careful to continually cleanse it with the purifying waters of repentance and Truth from God's Word. Even then, we can never be sure that we have removed *all* the deception and wickedness. We can be sure, however, that there will never be deception in the pure, holy, infallible Word of God.

2. Read Jer. 2:4-8, 11–13.

   a. What did our fathers do? (vs. 5)

   b. What has happened to God's land? (vs. 7)

   c. What two sins have God's people committed? (vs. 13)

Note: To hew/dig for themselves cisterns means to create their own "gods" that they go to for help, fulfillment, contentment, peace; gods that are broken and powerless to help them.

3. Read Jer. 16:9-13.

   a. What is going to be eliminated (brought to an end) from the land? (vs. 9)

   b. Why? (vs. 11)

   c. What are the people walking according to, instead of listening to God? (vs. 12)

   d. What will be the result? (vs. 13)

Note again here the biblical principle of free will and reaping and sowing. If we stubbornly insist on having it our way, God will let us have it (Rom. 1:21-28). So if our desire is to walk in stubborn rebellion against God, He will allow us to do that, and we will reap what we have sown: bondage to the very gods for which our lustful hearts yearned. But they will be worthless, deceptive gods that cannot and will never deliver on their promises! And because they are false gods empowered by Satan, they will be cruel taskmasters.

4. Read Isaiah 30:1-3. Note: Egypt is the "world" with all its excessive, sensual lusts, pleasures, and enticements. Pharaoh represents all the "gods" (idols of the heart) that we run to for help, fulfillment, satisfaction.

   a. What does God warn against? (vs. 1)

   b. What does He say we do every time we do this? (vs. 1b - the very end of the verse)

   c. What did the rebellious people do? (vs. 2)

These verses warn us about stubbornly pressing on to have it our way: to continue to execute a plan that is not God's plan because we have failed to truly seek Him and to surrender our life in trusting obedience as His will is revealed to us through His Word and the leading of the Holy Spirit. God does have a beautiful plan for each of our lives, and it is only in following Him in the fulfillment of this plan day by day that we find true peace and contentment and avoid the painful consequences of *adding sin to sin*.

5. Read Hosea 4:16a.

   a. What is Israel like? (Can you relate?)

6. Read Jer. 9:12-14.

   a. Why is the land ruined? (three reasons - vs. 13,14a)

7. Read Jer. 6:16-19.

   a. What does God plead for us to do? (vs. 16a)

Note: The "ancient paths" are Truths found in the infallible, immutable, Word of God.

   b. What will you find if you do this? (vs. 16b)

   c. How did the people of Jeremiah's day respond to God's loving invitation? (vs. 16b,17)

   d. What was the result, and why? (vs. 19)

May God help us not to make the same tragic mistake but rather to gladly stand by the ancient paths and *walk in them* (Jer. 6:16) that we might experience the protection, provision, and unending blessing of a loving and intimate walk with God.

8. Read 1 Samuel 7:3,4,12–14.

   a. What did God promise if the people returned to Him and directed their hearts to serve Him alone? (vs. 3b)

   b. Did God keep His promise? (vs. 13,14)

The Book of Jeremiah is one of the saddest books in the Bible. It tells of God's continual loving call to His rebellious, wayward children to *return* and *repent* and stay close to Him that He might guide them, protect them, and bless them. But time and time again, Israel turns a deaf ear and refuses to heed God's loving plea. They persist in walking *after the stubbornness of their own rebellious hearts, without listening to God*. And eventually, because of the holiness of His Name which they continually *defiled among the nations*, God had to act. He had to bring judgment against the blatant, rebellious sins of the people.

We see this illustrated in the many beautiful invitations from God to His people in the book of Jeremiah. For example, Jer. 3:19: How I would set you among My sons and give you a pleasant land. The most beautiful inheritance of the nations! And I said, 'You shall call Me, Father, and not turn away from following Me. But, sadly the invitations are invariably followed by: "but they would not". They refused to listen to God or accept His loving invitation. May God help us to learn from the inevitable tragic results of such a life of rebellion that we might be rather like Samuel and the house of Israel in his day who carefully, joyfully *served the Lord only*, experiencing the victory, restoration and rest that a life of obedience always brings.

God still wants to be *Our Father*. He wants us to come to Him daily; to seek His forgiveness and cleansing, wisdom and counsel, protection and blessing.

> *Blessed is the man who trusts in the Lord, and whose trust is the Lord. For he will be like a tree planted by the water, that extends its roots by a stream. (He) will not fear when the heat comes; but (his) leaves will be green. And he will not be anxious in a year of drought, nor cease to yield fruit...And Jacob shall return and be undisturbed, and secure, with no one making him tremble (Jer. 17:7,8, 47:27b).*

Write out a Bible verse that had special meaning to you today.

Based upon what you have learned today, write a prayer to God expressing the desires of your heart in applying these Truths to your life.

Chapter 5

Memory verse: *This is life eternal, that they may know Thee, the only true God, and Jesus Christ whom Thou hast sent (John 17:3).*

Bonus memory verse: *I will destroy the wisdom of the wise; And the cleverness of the clever I will set aside...for the wisdom of the world is foolishness before God (1 Cor. 1:19, 3:19).*

Day 1
Priorities: The Quintessential Priority of Knowing God
The Biblical Principle of First Fruits

Day 2
God's Inexorable Gift of Free Will
Choose You Today . . . the Blessing or the Curse

Day 3
Man's Wisdom vs. God's Wisdom

Day 4
The Psychologization of Sin

Day 5
Beware! The Deceptiveness of Sin

Chapter 5 — Day 1
Priorities: The Quintessential Priority of Knowing God
The Biblical Principle of First Fruits

> *This is life eternal, that they might know Thee the only true God and Jesus Christ whom Thou has sent (John 17:3).*
>
> *Seek ye first the kingdom of God and His righteousness and all these things (provision for our physical needs, love, peace, joy, contentment) shall be added to you (Matt. 6:33).*
>
> *You shall observe the Feast of the Harvest of the First Fruits (Ex. 23:16).*

Foundational Truth # 15

Seek ye first the Kingdom of God and His righteousness and all these things shall be added to you (Matt. 6:33). **At the core of the sanctification process is the conforming of our fallen nature to the Image of Jesus. We must *know* this Image before we can be transformed into it. The more we look upon Jesus and study His nature, the more His nature will be formed in us. It is essential, therefore, that we make this our number one priority: to know Him, so that we obey Him and become like Him.**

Not long after we opened our Christian Bookstore, God brought across our path a precious, godly man who loved the Lord with all his heart and radiated the love, peace, and joy of Jesus. It was a blessing just to be around him. One day as we were talking, I asked him how he could be so consistently full of joy and contentment. He did not hesitate for a moment, responding: "In one of the most beautiful prayers in all of Scripture, Jesus said: 'This is Life Eternal, that they might *know* Thee, the only true God and Jesus Christ whom Thou hast sent.' I have made that my *life verse*, because the more I seek to know God, the more I love Him, and the more I love Him, the more I want to please Him, and the more I want to please Him, the more of Himself He reveals to me, and the more of Himself He reveals to me, the more I become like Him, and the more I become like Him, the more I experience the bounty of His blessings and grace, and the more I experience the bounty of His mercy and grace, the greater my joy, and the greater my joy, the more I want to tell others about all God has done for me, bringing yet more JOY…and peace.

I never forgot that good exhortation and I am so thankful for it because ever since that day, I, too, have made the pursuit of knowing God my number one priority and my heart's greatest desire. The bountiful blessings of God's mercy and grace that I have experienced as a result have been far beyond anything *I could have hoped or dreamed (Eph. 3:16–20).* I have discovered time and time again that life—real life—that is both presently and eternally significant each and every day, can only be found in a personal, obedient, growing relationship with God through His Son, Jesus Christ.

When I first became a Christian, I was encouraged to stick to the New Testament. The Old Testament, I was told, was no longer in effect, so I should concentrate on the New Testament. What poor, unbiblical counsel that was! We need the *whole counsel of God's Word (Acts 20:27)* if we are to understand and develop the heart, mind and character of God as we are instructed to do *(1 Pet. 1:13–16)*. The teaching of the Old Testament serves as the foundation for understanding not only the character of God, but also every doctrine taught in the New Testament. Reading the New Testament apart from reading and understanding the Old Testament is like trying to build a house from the roof down, or building a house with no foundation. A house built upon that kind of weak, faulty undergirding will never stand when the torrential winds and rains of life's trials beat upon it (Matt. 7:25). It will fall . . . and *great will be its destruction (Matt. 7:27)*.

The Old Testament is rich with God's revelation of Himself—His holy and just nature, perfect love, eternal goodness. It also unfolds His beautiful plan for man. The Old Testament is rich in history as it chronicles all the major events that have transpired *from the beginning*—from even before the creation of the universe. It is the world's oldest, most detailed and accurate history book ever written. Furthermore, it establishes the foundation of all the doctrines of the Bible which are built upon in the New Testament.

A central doctrine in the Old Testament, which we studied earlier, is the sacrificial system of redemption, and at the heart of this system was a focus upon first fruits—the first born of the household, the first (best) of the flock, the first of the grain harvest—all of which were consecrated (sanctified), set apart for God's holy purposes. The animals and certain grains, oils, and spices were offered as a fragrant and acceptable offering to God (Lev. 2–6). Because God had been present with the people giving them the first fruits of His love, provision, and protection, in joyful gratitude the people were to offer back to Him the first fruits of their love and labors.

In the New Testament this same theme is followed in the coming of Jesus, who was the first fruit of the expression of God's love to His people: *For God so loved the world that He gave His only begotten Son. That whosoever believed in Him might not perish, but have everlasting life" (John 3:16; cf. James 1:18; Rev. 14:4; 1 Cor. 15:20,23)*.

In the Book of Revelation, we read about those who *follow the Lamb wherever He goes…These have been purchased from among men as first fruits to God and to the Lamb (Rev. 14:4)*. It is a beautiful picture of God and man in relationship lovingly, gratefully giving their best (first fruits) to one another. Jesus was the very best that God could offer us. Does it not seem only fitting that we should do no less in offering back to God the first fruits of our love and affection?

It is impossible to know and love someone without spending time with them.

As I continued to study the doctrine of first fruits, I realized that time is one of God's most precious gifts to us. He gives us twenty-four hours every day. How could I do less than offer back to God the *first fruits* of this precious gift?

> *…and in the early morning, while it was still dark, He arose and went out and departed to a lonely place, and was praying there (Mark 1:35).*

Jesus is our example. I so often have been struck with the reality of how Jesus' ordered His day—His clear priorities. Spending time with His Father was always His number one priority. Don't you think that if Jesus, the perfect, sinless Son of God found it desirable and even necessary to rise early in the morning in order to spend uninterrupted time with His Heavenly Father in prayer and fellowship with Him, it must be all the more necessary for us? I believe that our Heavenly Father eagerly waits for us to come to Him in this kind of *first fruit* spirit. He longs for us to just *be there, with Him,* lifting our hearts in praise, thanksgiving, and love, then quietly listening as He speaks to us. This kind of loving, interactive communion with His children is at the heart of God's purpose in creating us *in His image (Gen. 1:26; John 17:21, etc)*.

But, as we learned earlier, there is an enemy of our soul that relentlessly fights against such communion with God because he knows that it is through this fellowship that we receive the *mind of Christ (1 Cor. 2:16)* and the *power of Christ (Eph. 3:16–20, 1:18–21)* to overcome his lies and temptations. So he will do all he can to convince us that we are saved, redeemed children of God and, therefore, we don't really need this kind of daily *ritual*. After all we don't want to become legalistic. So we ought to just rest in the assurance that we are *saved and going to Heaven*. This unbiblical lie, if followed, will lead only to the weakening and eventual *shipwreck of our faith (1 Tim. 1:19)*.

I know this is true, because I fell for the lie, and I experienced the inevitable tragic result. After an initial season of hungering and thirsting for God's Word, it grew harder and harder to sit at my quiet time table for any length of time for the sole purpose of communing with God by reading and studying His Word and fellowshipping with Him in prayer. I can remember ever so clearly the nearly constant battle I had with practicing the principle of *first fruits* priorities. First of all, I was not a "morning person". I could, and often did, sleep late into the morning. Then, by the time I got up, I was already very behind on daily responsibilities and all that needed to be done. Even when I was working full time, I would sleep until the last possible moment before I had to get up and hurriedly dress in order to get out the door to make it to work on time. There just wasn't time to "non-productively" *sit at Jesus' feet*—read His Word, pray, praise, listen …

Later, when that just was not working and I finally realized that I needed to be spending time in God's Word daily, I vividly remember the thoughts and accusations that bombarded my mind every morning as I sat down to study: thoughts about all that needed to be done that day and how far behind I was on so many things—housework, correspondence, meal planning and preparations, baking, people that needed visiting, church related activities—all screaming for attention. So often the devil had me fully convinced that merely sitting there, reading the Bible and praying, was a monumental waste of time, especially when I took the time to do it first thing in the morning. Surely it would be better to get some of the other work done first. Then I would feel better about taking time for reading and studying God's Word, and I would be able to concentrate better. And after all, I was a Christian, and I was faithful in church attendance. Surely that was enough. I would get more serious about reading the Bible when things settled down a bit.

But things never settled down, and by the time I got through the day, I was so exhausted, I could barely crawl to bed. My brain was as tired as my body, so I could not concentrate, and I often fell asleep before I got through the first few verses of Scripture. I eventually saw the futility of this and just gave it up. As this practice of neglect continued, my heart began to grow hard and more and more selfish and soiled by many idolatries, unending worldly influences, and pleasure-seeking encroachments. There was no discernment, divine guidance, or God-directed purpose. God was getting the crumbs of my time and affections, rather than the first fruits. Such a sinful lifestyle of misplaced priorities began to wreak its inevitable havoc upon my personal life and inner peace. And, naturally, that affected my relationship with others, especially my dear husband. Stress-related irritability and anger was often unleashed against him. My life demonstrated what the Bible warns about so often: such a *too-busy-for-God* and *distracted by many things* lifestyle will always produce inner turmoil and outer conflict. *(Luke 10:41)*. It will also result in spiritual barrenness: little, if any, real lasting fruit for the kingdom of God *(John 15:4–8)*. My life had become a dry desert of existence rather than a vibrant, never ending river of love, joy, and peace flowing from the source of Jesus' inexhaustible love and provision *(John 7:38)*. How it must have grieved the heart of my Savior who gave not only the first fruits of His life…but His very life, itself! And I could not even *watch with Him one hour?! (Matt. 26:40)*.

Finally, after a much too long season of such neglect and scant, insignificant fruit for the kingdom of God, I realized that all those rationalizations were very strategically well planned and perpetrated deceptions from the enemy for which I fell nearly every time because of their appeal to the undisciplined, insatiable lusts of my own proud, selfish heart and because my mind was not being renewed daily by the Truths of God's Word to have the discernment I needed to recognize the lies for what they were.

> *Heed instruction (God's Word) and be wise, and do not neglect it. Blessed is the man who listens to me, watching daily at my gates, waiting at my doorposts… for he who finds me finds life, and obtains favor from the Lord. But he who sins against me (neglects me) injures himself (Prov. 8:33–36)*.

How foolish I had been in failing to heed this instruction. I needed the wisdom of God, the discernment of God, the power and strength of God, the guidance of God if I were to know and obey His good plans for my life. I repented of my sin of misplaced priorities and neglect of the *one thing needful (Luke 10:42)*, and recommitted my life to make knowing, loving, and serving God my number one priority. As I was faithful in this commitment, I found that God blessed the obedience in ways far greater than the small sacrifice of those first fruits of my time. I became more focused and began to accomplish more in less time with more energy, and certainly more joy. Soon I found myself rising earlier and earlier just so I would have a little more uninterrupted time with the Lord, and it was not long before this precious time became my greatest joy and delight, and I could hardly wait to get to my quiet-time corner every morning. It was a time when I knew that God would meet me there. He would *forgive my sins, restore the joy of my salvation,* and *hear my cries for help, comfort, healing (1 John 1:9; Ps. 51:12, 40:3, 34:6, 23:2,3)*. He would refresh my languishing soul with the life-giving manna of His Word, and He would fill me with His wisdom and Truth and *instruct me in the way I should go (Ps. 25:12)*. And so it happened. And continues. My early morning quiet time has become the most treasured time of the day for me. I can't even imagine starting my day without it.

And I have found through the years that when I am the very busiest and under the greatest pressure with *humanly* overwhelming challenges and demands—deadlines to meet, many people for whom I am caring, extra responsibilities with family, church, etc.—I need time alone with God more than ever in order to quiet my soul, find refuge and refreshment, and draw necessary wisdom, strength, and encouragement from His precious Word and from fellowship with Him in prayer. Just as when Moses asked God to *teach me your ways*, God replied: *My presence shall go with you, and I will give you rest (Ex. 33:14)*. Going out with the sweet assurance of God's wisdom, guidance, presence and provision truly does *restore my soul!*

The reality is: We will have time for what we choose to have time for. It is a matter of priorities. If we are being obedient to Jesus' command to *seek first the kingdom of God and His righteousness*, our relationship with Him will be our number one concern and pursuit. We will gladly and eagerly order our priorities in order to be able to spend uninterrupted time with Him before the activities of the busy day begins. If God is not given the first fruits of our time, He will be relegated to whatever time is left over at the end of the day, which will be but the crumbs (leftovers) of our time and energies. We will most likely be too tired and too weary to think clearly or to do any serious study of His Word or fervent prayer. And, as mentioned earlier, if God is not number one in our lives, we are loving and worshiping something else more than we are loving and worshiping Him, and God calls this idolatry—a terrible sin which, like all sin, separates us from God and from His peace and joy. I cannot stress how important it is for all of us to take a serious look at our priorities. God knew that we would need this time—in His Word and prayer daily—to receive the wisdom, discernment, and strength we need to meet all the problems, difficulties, and decisions that come to us. It is crucial to our spiritual health and well-being, for if our spirit and soul (mind, will, emotions) are weak and sickly from lack of solid, biblical nourishment, everything in our life will be weak and sickly.

I love the story of Mary and Martha and how Jesus commended Mary for choosing the *one thing needful,* just as He does all of us who begin each day in prayer and *sitting at His feet* as we study His Word and allow the Holy Spirit to speak to us through it.

May God help us all to follow Mary's good example—to always choose *the one thing needful* above all else—God Himself—giving Him, not the leftovers of our life and service, our time and talents, our praise and worship, but the *first fruits.*

> *In the morning, O Lord, Thou wilt hear my voice; In the morning I will order my prayer to Thee and eagerly watch…How lovely are Thy dwelling places, O Lord of Host; My soul longed, even yearned for the courts of the Lord… My heart and my flesh sing for joy to the living God. How blessed are those who dwell in Thy house! They are ever praising Thee…Lord, Thou has been our dwelling place in all generations…in Thy presence is fullness of joy; at Thy right hand there are pleasures forevermore! (Ps. 5:3, 84:1,2,4, 90:1,16:11).*

> *Let me hear Thy lovingkindness in the morning; for I trust in Thee; Let Thy good spirit lead me… (Ps. 143:8).*

Bible Study Supplement

Chapter 5 — Day 1 — Priorities: The Quintessential Priority of Knowing God

1. Read Lev. 23:10-14.

    a. What were the people to bring to God of their crops? (vs. 10)

    b. What were the people not to do until they had offered their first fruits? (vs. 14a)

In this special text regarding the *offering of first fruits*, we read that the people were not to *eat* any of the grain—roasted or baked in the form of bread—until they had first offered to the Lord their worship and praise and *first fruit* sacrifice. I found this instruction to have special meaning in my own personal quiet time study and worship. I began to make it a practice to not put anything into my mouth until I had first offered worship and praise to God and nourished my soul on the heavenly manna of His Word. It was amazing how much better (more focused and intimate) my quiet time became after this. I was no longer distracted by the preoccupations of food—thinking about it, preparing it, partaking of it, cleaning up after. Free of all that, it was much easier to focus my mind and heart upon God and His Word.

2. Read John 17:3.

    a. What is *eternal life (life eternal)*? (vs. 3)

It is impossible to *know God* and *love God* without spending time *with God*—in His Word and prayer. It is there that God reveals Himself to us—His true nature and character. And the Bible tells us that the more we *behold the glory of the Lord*, the more we are changed by it and *transformed into the same image—from glory to glory* (2 Cor. 3:18).

3. Read Matt. 6:33.

    a. What did Jesus command us to seek first? (two things - vs. 33a)

    b. What promise does He give us if we will do this? (vs. 33b)

    c. What do you think Jesus meant by this?...What does it mean to you?

4. Read 1 Peter 2:2.

    a. Who should we be like regarding our love for the Word of God? (vs. 2)

    b. What will happen if we do this? (vs. 2b)

5. Read Mark 1:35-39.

    a. When did Jesus pray and spend time alone with His Father? (vs. 35)

    b. What was everyone else doing while Jesus was praying? (vs. 36,37)

    c. What did Jesus tell Simon when he (Simon) found Him? (vs. 38)

It is interesting to note that the people were impatiently clamoring for Jesus, looking here and there and fluttering about. But Jesus was purposely and quietly away by Himself spending time with His Father.

It was there that Jesus received His instructions *from His Father* for the day—not while listening to the people, trying to please them, or planning His agenda according to their clamorings—or even his own *human* (fleshly) desires. He only wanted to know and do the Father's will. It is a beautiful example for all of us. When we take time to be with the Lord early in the morning as Jesus did, relinquish our own sinful lusts and desires, and allow the Lord to "plan our day", we will know God's will, and we will be led and empowered by the Holy Spirit to fulfill it. Then, as we walk in obedience through our day, we will experience God's blessing and the confidence and joy that always comes with being in the center of our Father's will (John 15:7–11).

6. Read Ps. 42:1–2a.

    a. Describe the psalmist's love for the Word of God.

Do you have this kind of inner hunger and thirst for the Word of God? If not, ask God to help you to develop this. It is very spiritually healthy to have this inner longing for the Word of God.

7. Read Luke 10:38-42.

    a. What was Mary doing? (vs. 39)

    b. What was Martha doing? (vs. 40)

    c. How did Jesus lovingly rebuke Martha for her misplaced priorities? (vs. 41)

    d. What did He say about Mary's priorities? (vs. 42)

Jesus rebuked Martha for her many distractions. He praised Mary for choosing *the one thing needful*—time with Him. What do you think Jesus would say to you as He observed your activities on a typical day? (Which He certainly does, anyway). Who are you most like as you begin and go through your day, Mary or Martha? Who would you like to be like? In your prayer today, ask God to help you to become more like Mary in her character and priorities.

Write out a Bible verse that had special meaning to you today.

Based upon what you have learned today, write a prayer to God expressing the desires of your heart in applying these Truths to your life.

Chapter 5 — Day 2
God's Inexorable Gift of Free Will
Choose You Today...the Blessing or the Curse

> *See, I am setting before you today life and prosperity, and death and adversity—the blessing and the curse; in that I command you today to love the Lord your God, to walk in His ways and to keep His commandments...that the Lord your God may bless you...But if your heart turns away and you will not obey, but are drawn away and worship other gods and serve them, I declare to you today that you shall surely perish (Deut. 30:15,18, 11:26).*
>
> *So choose life in order that you may live, you and your descendants. (Deut. 30:19).*

Foundational Truth # 16

An essential aspect of the image of God in which we have all been created is volition—free will. God created us to be free moral agents with the right and the responsibility to *choose* whom we will love, serve and obey and how we will respond to every situation in life—in godly righteousness or in anti-God disobedience and rebellion. **God will never violate this aspect of our nature—the right, the privilege and the responsibility to *choose*.**

I see them all the time, often in nursing homes or struggling with a degenerative disease that has left them debilitated, housebound, and ever so miserable: people who have stubbornly (or ignorantly or fearfully) refused to look to God and pursue *His* good plans for their lives, and they come to the end of their days filled with bitterness and a painful sense of loss and regret.

How often my heart has been broken as I watched close friends and relatives become deceived by the lies of Satan into thinking that they really could go through life *kicking against the goad (Acts 9:5, KJV)* (ignoring or rebelling against God's good purposes for their lives) with no consequences. You will not find this idea—that a redeemed child of God can live his life however he wishes giving no thought to God's plans and purposes—in the Bible anywhere. God is merciful and God is gracious—so gracious. And He is longsuffering, *not treating us as our sins deserve (Ps. 103:10)*. But there comes a time in every man's, every woman's life when, *for the sake of God's holy name,* He must act *(Ezek. 36:17–22)*. Stubbornness and rebellion must be dealt with—now, on this earth—because there will be none of that in Heaven where we all who have been truly *born again* will one day live with God. This time, there will be no satanic or Adamic rebellion as there was the first time. The choice to *know, love, and obey God (John 17:3; 14:21,23)* will be made here on earth, and only those who *choose* to do so (know, love, and obey God by entering into a loving, trusting, growing, obedient relationship with Him) will be there—in Heaven—eternally (1 Cor. 6:9–11; Gal. 5:19–21).

God's Word is so lovingly clear about this. Just as we have learned, God created us to be in relationship with Him. He also created us to fulfill a very special purpose for our lives (Eph. 2:10; Jer. 29:11–14). It is only when we are faithfully and obediently involved in the carrying out of God's *before-ordained purposes (Eph. 2:10)* that we will experience the true peace, joy, and fulfillment for which we all long and which God desires that we enjoy. When we neglect or rebel against this pursuit, our lives will be filled with turmoil and discontent, because we have violated the very reason for which we were created (Deut. 6:4,5; Matt. 22:37; John 17:3, etc.). And you can be sure we will add to unnecessary pain and turmoil the longer we persist in this pattern. We will *continue* to make wrong, destructive choices, because only God's Holy Spirit working through His Word can cut through the demonic deception that is both in our fallen hearts and in the fallen world all around us (Jer. 17:9; 1 John 2:15–17). Only God knows the safe and secure way through the maze of choices these deceptions present to us daily, and He will lead us accordingly, keeping our *hearts steadfast and our feet from stumbling (Prov. 3:23,26).*

The more I walk with God and the more I minister to others, the more acutely I am made aware of the devastating results that a stubborn and rebellious spirit always brings, not just for the individual but for all those whose lives that individual touches. Most of the people who come for counseling are in the midst of incredibly heartbreaking personal pain and conflict precisely because this pattern of rebellion against listening to and obeying God was established in their hearts at a young age and was never broken. So, instead of becoming more like Jesus, holy and pure in their thinking, attitudes and behavior, they drift farther and farther away. And the farther away from Jesus they go, the greater the conflict, distress, and turmoil, because, just as the Bible says, *He holds all things together" (Col. 1:17).*

Remember Jesus' exhortation to Saul on that providential day when the light of Heaven broke upon his world: *Saul, Saul, why are you persecuting Me?* (by continually rebelling against me and stubbornly going your own way). *It is hard to kick against the goad" (Acts 26:14).*

That's why, from the beginning, God continually instructed His children concerning the tremendous, consequential power of choice that He had given them:

See, I have set before you today life and prosperity, and death and adversity; in that I command you today to love the Lord your God, to walk in His ways and to keep His commandments…that you may live and multiply, and that the Lord your God may bless you in the land where you are entering to possess it. But if your heart turns away and you will not obey, but are drawn away and worship other gods and serve them, I declare to you today that you shall surely perish. I call Heaven and earth to witness against you today, that I have set before you life and death, the blessing and the curse. So choose life in order that you may live, you and your descendants, by loving the Lord your God, by obeying His voice, and by holding fast to Him (Deut. 30:15–20).

God cannot lie (Titus 1:2). And He has promised to *bless* all who *love Him, walk in His ways, and keep His commandments (Deut. 30:16).* In other words, when we make knowing Him, loving Him, and obeying Him our number one priority, He will, just as He has promised, take care of *everything else that concerns us (Matt. 6:33; Ps. 138:8).*

"For I know the plans that I have for you," declares the Lord, "plans for welfare and not for calamity, to give you a future and a hope. Then you will call upon Me and…pray to Me, and I will listen to you…you will find Me, when you search for Me with all your heart" (Jer. 29:11–13).

That is good news for all of us! God longs for His rebellious children to return to Him (Jer. 15:19), to repent and to begin a fresh new, loving, obedient relationship with Him. God promises that when we do this, He will fill our days with true meaning, purpose, and *showers of blessing (Jer. 29:11–13; Ezek. 34:25,26).*

If you return, then I will restore you…and I will gather you from all the nations and from all the places where you have been in exile…and I will make a covenant of peace with (you) and eliminate harmful beasts from the land, so that (you) may live securely…and I will cause showers to come down…they will be showers of blessing (Jer. 15:19; Ezek. 34:25,26; also Deut. 30:16).

God loves to bless His obedient children. And He wants to protect them because He knows what sin does; it robs and kills and destroys all that is truly good and life-producing. So that is why there is rejoicing in Heaven whenever a broken, sin-torn soul *chooses* to come home with a humble, repentant heart: *Father I have sinned against Heaven and in your sight; I am no longer worthy to be your son" (Luke 15:21).*

Remember the story of the prodigal son? Rather than respond in righteous anger and indignation as He so justly could have done, scolding and punishing his rebellious, runaway son, the father (God) *ran to meet him, embraced him*, and said to his slaves: "*Quickly bring out the best robe and put it on him, and put a ring on his hand and sandals on his feet; and bring the fattened calf, kill it, and let us eat and be merry; for this son of mine was dead, and has come to life again; he was lost, and has been found. And they began to be merry" (Luke 15:22–24).*

I have witnessed this great miracle again and again. I have seen our gracious heavenly Father restore into beautiful oneness and fellowship with Him countless repentant sinners so that they enjoyed from that moment on, productive, joyful, and purposeful days. I know several of these now, and their lives are a continual source of beauty, encouragement and inspiration to me!

The reality of this God-given gift—the right to choose—is one of the most liberating Truths of Scripture. What a joy to realize each moment that we live, that we can *choose* God's blessing by choosing to trust and obey Him. Or, just as surely, we *choose* the curse of sin with all its destructive consequences, if we, in defiant disobedience and rebellion or just plain laziness and apathy, refuse to do this. If I choose to obey God, I know that He will give me the wisdom and strength not only to complete every task He gives me, but to complete it with joy, experiencing the reward of knowing that I have pleased Him and brought *Him* joy in the process also.

I have no greater joy than this, to hear that my children are walking in the Truth (3 John 1:4).

Just a side note here. This, of course, does not mean that loving and obeying God will exempt us from trials and tribulations, pain and suffering. We live in a fallen body with a fallen nature (heart, mind, will, emotions) in a fallen world in which pain and problems are a daily reality. Having a personal relationship with God and walking in obedience to Him does not exempt us from problems, but it does assure us that we will never have to walk through them alone or without God's presence, comfort, and enabling strength to overcome them. *True joy and blessing are not found in the absence of pain and problems but in the presence and peace of God in the midst of them.*

We need to seriously ponder the dynamics of this wonderful gift of choice that God has given to all of us. Every time, *every time*, something happens to us, we can choose how we will respond: in trusting obedience to God, bringing the smile of God and His blessing, or in fear, doubt, or anger, bringing upon ourselves the curse of sin with all its painful consequences.

Think about this the next time you face a difficult or even painful circumstance: I can choose to trust and obey God. I can choose to thank God because I know that He loves me and He has promised that *all things work together for His glory, my good, and the good of those I love most*— even if I don't understand it at the moment *(Rom. 8:28; 2 Cor. 1:3–7)*. If I choose to trust and obey, I can be assured of the blessing of God's presence and His enabling strength, comfort, and peace (Col. 1:27; Eph. 3:16–20), come what may!

God loves us with an everlasting, perfect love. Therefore, He has our very best interest in mind at all times, and He longs to bless us as we walk in trusting, surrendered obedience in the fulfilling of all His good plans—His very best for us (Jer. 29:11–13; Rom.12:1,2). The choice is ours: obedience to God or stubborn and rebellious disobedience against Him. The results are sure: *the blessing or the curse.*

Bible Study Supplement

Chapter 5 — Day 2 — God's Inexorable Gift of Free Will

1. Read Deut. 30:1–10, 15–20.

    a. What does God set before us today (and every day)? (vs. 15,19)

    b. How can we choose God's blessing? (three things - vs. 16)

    c. What does God clearly warn us to guard against? (three things - vs. 17)

    d. What will be the consequences if we fail to heed God's warning? (vs. 18a)

    e. What does God plead with us to do? (vs. 19b)

    f. How can we do this? (three things - vs. 20)

In Deut. 28 and 29, God gives us a graphic picture of the stark contrast between the lives of those who choose to obey God and those who stubbornly refuse and choose to walk in their own willful stubbornness and rebellion.

2. Read Deut. 28:1–25.

    a. What will come upon those who choose to obey the voice of the Lord? (vs. 3)

    b. What will come upon those who choose to rebel against God by not heeding (obeying) His commandments and statutes? (vs. 15)

3. Read Deut. 28:27–35.

    a. Several specific curses that come upon the disobedient are listed in these verses. What are they?

        • Verse 27:
        • Verse 28:
        • Verse 29a:
        • Verses 29b, 33b:
        • Verse 34:

The Bible is clear here, and in the remaining verses of Deut. 28 about the curses we bring upon ourselves when we abandon God or are not careful to observe the *words of the law that are written in this book*. These are critical warnings for our day. We have not been careful to *observe the words of the law written in this book*, and we are reaping the clearly stated consequences.

> *The Lord will smite you with madness and with blindness and with bewilderment of heart; and you shall grope at noon, as the blind man gropes in darkness, and you shall not prosper in your ways; but you shall only be oppressed and robbed continually, with none to save you…and you will be driven mad by the sight of the things you see (Deut. 28:28,29,34).*

Think of the epidemic of macular degeneration (blindness) in the past few decades…and how many are experiencing *bewilderment of heart, confusion, groping at noon, as the blind man gropes in darkness. Oppression and madness of mind* is evidenced by the pandemic of devastating mental and emotional disorders; and an all-time high in the suicide rate, broken homes, broken marriages, broken lives.

Ever-striving for the material but never prospering is seen in the equally devastating epidemic of overspending, financial disasters, bankruptcies, and foreclosures.

> *If you are not careful to observe all the words of this law which are written in this book, to fear this honored and awesome Name, the Lord your God, then the Lord will bring extraordinary plagues on you and your descendants, even severe and lasting plagues, and miserable and chronic sicknesses. And He will bring back on you all the diseases of Egypt of which you were afraid, and they shall cling to you. Also every sickness and every plague...not written in the book...the Lord will bring on you until you are destroyed...because you did not obey the Lord your God... So your life shall hang in doubt before you; and you shall be in dread night and day and shall have no assurance of your life. In the morning you shall say, "Would that it were evening!" And at evening you shall say, "Would that it were morning!" (Deut. 28:58–62, sel.).*

At no time in the history of the world has *extraordinary, severe, and lasting plagues* (ie., rampant, devastating sexually transmitted diseases, AIDS) and *miserable, chronic sicknesses*, maimed and debilitated more people than in our present age. According to the National Organization of Rare Diseases, there are over five thousand rare chronic diseases for which there is no known cause or cure. And think of the additional awful blight of cancer, heart disease, diabetes, eating disorders of every nature and all the devastation these have caused! So endless and so relentless, is the pain of the afflictions that *in the morning, they say, "Would that it were evening!" And at evening, "Would that it were morning!"* (Deut. 28:67).

We have sown the wind, we are reaping the whirlwind (Hosea 8:7).

5. Read Deut. 28:45,47,48.

   a. Why do all the curses that God lists in Deut. 28 come upon the people? (vs. 45)

   b. What happened to those who refused to serve the Lord with joy and a glad heart? (vs. 48)

This is a beautiful verse to remind us of the importance of keeping a thankful and joyful heart.

6. Read Psalm 106:4–25, 32–43.

   a. What did the people do? (four things - vs. 13,14)

   b. What was the result? (vs. 15)

   c. What did the people do again, even after God had mercifully turned His wrath from destroying them? (four things - vs. 24,25)

   d. What did the people fail to do when they came into the pagan, wicked lands? (vs. 34)

   e. What did they do instead? (vs. 35,36a)

   f. What was the result? (36b)

   g. What even more heinous sin against God did they commit? (vs. 37,38)

Here we see a graphic picture of the scourge of abortion, the result of our modern defiant rebellion against God. The sacrificing of our children is the inevitable result of disobedience and rebellion against

God. It is the children who always suffer the most when parents disobey God and abandon a close and obedient walk with Him. May God be merciful!

    h. Because the people continued to rebel against God in spite of His many merciful interventions and pleadings to "return," what did they bring upon themselves? (vs. 41)

    i. What was the result? (vs. 42,43b)

I hope that we are all beginning to see the power of choice that God has given us and the blessing or the curse that is inextricably linked to it. We really are free to choose the quality of life that we will enjoy—or painfully endure—while we are upon this earth (Deut. 30:15–20).

7. Read Josh. 24:14,15.

    a. What does Joshua lovingly command the people to do? (three things - vs. 14)

    b. Joshua, speaking for God, offers the people a choice. What is it? (vs. 15)

    c. Joshua then tells the people of his choice for him and his family. What was it? (vs. 15b)

What would be your response to Joshua (God) today? Whom have you decided to serve? It's an important question we ought to ask ourselves every day when we first arise. Remember, the choice is ours; the result is sure: the blessing or the curse. It is my prayer that we will all follow Joshua's example who boldly proclaimed: "As for me and my house, we will serve the Lord!"

Write out a Bible verse that had special meaning to you today.

Based upon what you have learned today, write a prayer to God expressing the desires of your heart in applying these Truths to your life.

Chapter 5 — Day 3
Man's Wisdom vs. God's Wisdom

> *For it is written, I will destroy the wisdom of the wise; And the cleverness of the clever I will set aside…Where is the wise man? Where is the scribe? Where is the debater of this age? Has not God made foolish the wisdom of the world? (1 Cor. 1:19,20).*
>
> *For the wisdom of this world is foolishness before God (1 Cor. 3:19).*

Foundational Truth # 17

There are two separate and very distinct kinds of wisdom: 1. God's wisdom 2. The wisdom of the world. Which wisdom you choose to follow will determine not only the significance, meaning and value of life that is enjoyed—or endured—here on earth, but also your eternal destiny.

As my desire to be pleasing to God in all I did grew in the sanctification process, I was, naturally, drawn into a deeper, more thorough study of the Word of God. One day as I was reading Jesus' warnings to the Pharisees, my heart was struck by a certain verse:

> *You hypocrites, rightly did Isaiah prophesy of you, saying, This people honors Me with their lips, but their heart is far from Me. In vain do they worship Me, <u>teaching as doctrines the precepts of men</u> (Matt. 15:7–9).*

I could see that, having lived in the world and been very much a part of the world for so many years, I had taken in a cadre of *precepts of men* that I accepted as *doctrine*. Because I had no solid biblical discernment, I was like the novice prospector, unable to tell the difference between real gold (the ageless, infallible wisdom of God) and fool's gold, (worldly wisdom) that looked like and sounded very much like the real thing (2 Cor. 11:13–15).

I prayed that God would quicken my mind to greater discernment so that I would be able to recognize error and replace it with godly biblical thinking. As the mind of Christ (Biblical Truth) began to develop within me, I became more and more aware of the deception that permeated our culture—not only today but in the years when my own personal presuppositions (belief system, assumptions of truth) were being formed.

Man-centered humanism, the present, nearly universally accepted demonic belief system, had already become firmly entrenched and was the predominant philosophy of western culture by the time I reached college. Its psychological indoctrinations were thorough and incredibly deceptive. As a conscientious and diligent student (but not yet a Christian), it was impossible for me to escape the influence of this anti-god, anti-biblical philosophy that places man at the center (control) of the universe. It was everywhere: in the classroom, on television, in the movies, in everyday conversations with other students, family, and friends.

Since man was considered the center of the universe, education, science, and technology were deified, becoming revered *gods*, the source of wisdom and authority to which people flocked for their answers to the problems and sicknesses of the world—not God. The more degrees a person could amass, the greater the respect and *esteem* he/she commanded (and the greater was considered his/her wisdom). One's *identity* was often inextricably linked with how much education he had, making it (the amassing of degrees) a very appealing trap into which to fall, just as I did. It is a dangerous trap, however, because the modern public education system is in rebellion against God and diametrically opposed to the teachings and authority of Scripture.

As a new Christian, however, I did not realize this. And, because I was already struggling with an *identity* problem, I did not want to appear uninformed or intellectually inferior. (My *identity problem*, in reality, was a host of sin problems that I could not see due to the unbiblical psychological indoctrination). So I jumped on the bandwagon with countless others who tried to mesh them together. It was called *integration:* Psychology was *integrated* with the Bible. But it didn't work; it will never work, because God is holy, and He is building a kingdom of holiness and righteousness, totally free of sinful man's tainted worldly thinking and selfish ambitions—the heart of modern humanistic psychology. (More on this tomorrow).

Note! I am not saying here that there is no place for medicine, doctors or the vast information that science gives us. It is all from God and He, in His loving sovereignty and provision, uses these things to be a blessing and to help us in this fallen world. I am just saying that we must make sure that we keep God at the head of it all and worship Him (the Creator) and not doctors, medicine or science (the creation). We will get into this topic in more depth in Book Three when we examine a biblical approach to modern medicine and science.

God is the ruler of the universe and the only and final authority, no matter how advanced and sophisticated the *wisdom of the world* becomes. It is God's wisdom and God's wisdom alone that has stood the test of time and has remained unshaken throughout the ages, and it will continue to do so: *Forever, O Lord, your Word is established...and it will stand...from generation to generation (Ps. 119:89).*

The Bible warns us that *the wisdom of the world is foolishness to God (1 Cor. 3:19).* But it is a foolishness that, because of demonic deception, appears intellectually sound, unarguably logical, and, as the forbidden fruit, *desirable to make one wise (Gen. 3:6).* Its tantalizing temptations, which appeal to the natural, unsanctified lusts and desires of our fallen nature, so often make it virtually *humanly* impossible to counteract or resist. Only the Truths of the Word of God can cut through its seductive lies and give us the wisdom and discernment we need to stand firm against this kind of powerful demonic deception.

For example: We have all heard the very logical statement: "All 'truth' is God's Truth". Is this a true statement or not?

Let's examine it according to the principles found in God's Word.

Father, sanctify them in Truth. Thy Word is Truth...the sum of Thy Word is Truth, and every one of Thy righteous ordinances is everlasting (John 17:17; Ps. 119:165).

We must always ask: What is the source of the 'truth' that is claimed to be *God's Truth*? Is it a textbook? Even a "godly" textbook of a seminary course? Is it a quote from a renowned, respected intellect, author, inventor, religious leader? The bottom line is this: Regardless of the intellectual fame, rank or respect of the one who espouses it, if the purported 'truth' violates Scripture in any way, then it is not *God's Truth* and therefore not real 'truth' at all. It must be rejected.

The Word of God must always be the plumb line against which all 'truth' is judged *(Amos 7:7,8)*.

We must be very careful about this because demonic deception is very powerful and it is easy to fall for subtle misrepresentations of 'Truth'. There is a lot of worldly wisdom coming at us every day, and it is easy to be deceived, because it very much looks like 'truth', sounds like 'truth', and everybody and his brother is touting it as 'truth'. But, again, if any part of what is being proclaimed is not in agreement with the Word of God, then we must take a stand against it—popular or not—because it is the Truth alone (God's Truth) that sets people free, and if we love them, as we are called to do (1 John 3:14), we will lovingly, gently, but clearly, tell them.

We must not only know *about* God's Truth, but we must continually be taking it in—reading it, studying it, meditating upon it—that our minds might be renewed and transformed from worldly thinking to new, righteous thinking and obedience.

And do not be conformed to this world, but be transformed by the renewing of your mind, that you may prove what the will of God is, that which is good and acceptable and perfect (Rom.12:2).

This we must do daily because we are creatures of short retention. We forget so easily! A Truth learned today can easily be forgotten "tomorrow" if it is not reviewed, renewed, and reinforced on a regular, ongoing basis.

There is a way which seems right to a man, but its end is the way of death (Prov. 14:12).

Most temptations that effectively cause us to stumble (sin) come masked as 'truth', usually in the form of worldly wisdom that always appeals to the natural lusts of our sinful flesh and desires: it "seemeth" *so* right! Remember Satan's most effective tactic of deception—mixing a little Truth with error to deceive and to cause the lie to be accepted without question or opposition. There is only one way to protect ourselves from falling for these attractive, very believable and universally accepted 'truths' and to recognize the lies behind them. It is to be so saturated with the Word of God that nothing can come into us that does not pass through the purifying filter of the absolute and incontrovertible Truth of God's Word. For only the Word of God has the power to cut through the kind of demonic deception that permeates worldly (as opposed to godly) wisdom. That is another reason it is so important to study and meditate upon the Word of God daily so that the *sum of God's Truth (Ps. 119:160)* protects our hearts and minds from error and we are able to stand firmly against worldly lies and deceptions just as Jesus did (Matt. 4:1–11).

We are going to get into specific deceptions of worldly wisdom in the rest of this chapter and again next week, but for today, let's ask God to help us understand the importance of discerning between *worldly wisdom* and *true biblical wisdom*—the wisdom of God—so that we will be quick to recognize and resist destructive demonic deceptions and enticements that come to us in the most attractive and believable temptations.

…and no wonder, for even Satan disguises himself as an angel of light, therefore it is not surprising that his servants also disguise themselves as servants of righteousness (2 Cor. 11:14,15).

Bible Study Supplement

Chapter 5 — Day 3 — Man's Wisdom vs. God's Wisdom

1. Read 1 Cor. 1:18-30.

    a. What is the message of the cross to those who are 1) perishing…2) being saved? (vs. 18)

    b. What did God say that He would do? (vs. 19) and what has He done? (vs. 20b)

I smile every time I read these verses. Think of all the modern, advanced scientific research of today that is continually making great, *new* discoveries, only to have the findings of another comprehensive research project just a short time later debunk that *wisdom*, coming to a completely different, often contradictory conclusion. If the scientifically proven finding were really true, every test that followed would come to the same conclusion. But they don't, and for those who have put their faith and trust in modern medicine and science, it gets mighty confusing trying to figure out exactly what to believe.

Do you remember that for many years we were told that to have healthy bones and teeth we should drink at least two cups of milk every day? (And you will still find this recommendation on many official, doctor recommended "healthful diet" programs). A few years ago, a new study declared that such a habit is very dangerous and causes calcium buildup, kidney stones, and plaque in the arteries. Other *reliable, scientific studies* also revealed that the pasteurization process destroys— renders completely unabsorbable—the nutrients in the milk so that no calcium is being absorbed anyway. You must get your calcium from another source, (supplements) we were told. Yet another study declared that all cow's milk was bad for human consumption, destroys the immune system, and causes cancer. So much for two cups of milk every day!

And we can learn about an endless succession of other contradictions as we read the newspaper or listen to daily news reports. It doesn't take long to observe how truly foolish so much of the world's ever changing wisdom is! But the Word of God does not change. It is *the same yesterday, today, and forever* (Heb. 13:6). And it is just as true today as it was four thousand years ago: *Forever, O Lord, Thy word is settled in Heaven. Thy faithfulness continues throughout all generations; Thou didst establish the earth, and it stands* (Ps. 119:89-90).

    c. What was God well-pleased to do? (vs. 21)

    d. What do the Jews demand…and what do the Greeks look for? (vs. 22)

Note: "The Jews" was a term used frequently in the New Testament to refer to the unbelieving within the Jewish community—those who rejected Jesus. "The Greeks" were the intellectual aristocracy within the Greek culture, who considered the mind as "god" and continually sought to expand their (worldly) wisdom and develop superior intellect. These were the skeptics, agnostics and so called "atheists" of that day, just as we have today.

    e. What simple message did Paul preach and what was that to the Jews…the Greeks? (vs. 23)

    f. What is Christ to those who are called by God and born again? (two things - vs. 24)

    g. What kind of people did God call to do His work? Most of them were not… (vs. 26)

h. What has God chosen to carry out His work…and why did He do this? (vs. 27–29).

I find it incredibly encouraging that God so often called (and continues to do so) not the wealthy or noble—but common, hard working, oft rejected by society's elite, men and women like fishermen, tax collectors, poor widows, prostitutes, humble servants and faithful mothers to be His chosen "vessels of honor" to carry His message.

i. What has Jesus become for us? (vs. 30)

This is such an important text to help us get our eyes off the world with its flawed wisdom and deceptive enticements and back onto God in whom alone is found real wisdom, power, meaning and purpose. It is only in following God in all the good plans He has for us that we are able to avoid the deceptive, destructive foolishness of the world and find true fulfillment and the peace and joy it brings.

2. Read 1 Cor. 3:19,20.

a. What is the *wisdom of this world* in God's eyes? (vs. 19)

3. Read James 3:13–18.

a. What will characterize the life of a truly wise person? (two things - vs. 13)

b. What does worldly wisdom produce? (two things - vs. 14,16)

c. Describe the wisdom that is from above (vs. 17)

Please note that the wisdom from above is *first of all—PURE*. It is holy, set apart, unstained by the wisdom of the world. It is a clear warning not to mix (attempt to integrate) worldly wisdom with God's wisdom. It just doesn't work and makes a mockery of God's Word. May God help us to be careful to seek *pure* wisdom from above (God's Word) and to conduct our lives according to it, not the tempting, unholy (and ultimately destructive) compromises with the world.

Verse 18 tells us that those who live by godly wisdom (wisdom that is from above) will be peacemakers—*sowing seeds of godliness in peace and reaping harvests of righteousness*. It's a beautiful picture of the outworkings (fruit) of the *wisdom of God* in practical day to day living.

4. Read Prov. 2:1–13.

a. What will happen to the one who seeks God's wisdom as looking for a treasure? (vs. 5)

b. Who gives wisdom…and what comes from His mouth? (vs. 6)

c. To the one who is faithful in His pursuit of wisdom, what does God promise? (vs. 10)

5. Read Prov. 3:13–26.

a. Who is blessed? (vs. 13)

b. Describe the value of gaining godly wisdom and understanding. (vs. 14–17)

c. What other advantages come to the one who chooses to live by sound wisdom and discernment (discretion)? (vs. 22a,23,24)

    d. What are we not to fear? (two things - vs. 25)

    e. Why? (two reasons - vs. 26)

6. Read Prov. 4:18,19.

    a. How is the *path of righteousness* (walking daily in Godly wisdom) described? (vs. 18)

    b. Describe the *way of the wicked*. (two characteristics - vs. 19)

Here we see again the problem of demonic deception that comes to all who refuse to *heed instruction* and *seek the wisdom of God*. People who are thus deceived do not even recognize what *makes them stumble*.

May God help us to recognize the incalculable value and joy of knowing and living according to the unchanging, sure and secure Truths of His infallible Word—wisdom that is *from above*.

Write out a Bible verse that had special meaning to you today.

Based upon what you have learned today, write a prayer to God expressing the desires of your heart in applying these Truths to your life.

Chapter 5 — Day 4
The Psychologization of Sin

Behold, they have rejected the word of the Lord, and what kind of wisdom do they have? Lies and not Truth prevail in the land; they do not know Me, declares the Lord. And they heal the brokenness of My people superficially, saying, 'Peace, peace,' but there is no peace (Jer. 8:9, 9:3, 8:11).

In no area is the encroachment of worldly wisdom into our lives and our approach to problem solving more prevalent today than in the area of psychology.

This is, as you know from reading my testimony, a subject of deep, personal concern. Having experienced "psychological" problems from the time I was a child, I naturally sought all the wisdom I could find to help deal with these and have victory over them. Then, as now, psychology was touted to hold the answer to such problems. Therefore, the study of this subject became paramount in my educational pursuits beginning as early as high school, then college where I majored in it, and after that, as I went on to earn post-graduate degrees and certifications. I ever so faithfully studied every "expert" on the subject, every theory, and psychological methodology of dealing with problems found in the textbooks and latest professional journals. After I became a Christian, the Holy Spirit, working through the Word of God, revealed to me the error in this approach to dealing with these kinds of problems, which are, in reality, problems of the soul.

Psychology comes from the Greek word *psyche*, or *pseuche*, which means "soul" and *logia*, "study of." It is, therefore, by its own definition the study of that which affects the soul of man. The soul consists of mind, emotions, and will. Bear in mind that from the beginning of the history of mankind until the late 1800s, when Sigmund Freud came upon the scene, there was no such thing as "psychology". Problems of the *pseuche* (mind, emotions, will) were recognized for what they were, soul problems, and they were dealt with as such. In the earliest days, God Himself addressed issues of the *soul* as He spoke directly to His servants, the prophets, who then spoke to the people concerning these problems and how they were to be resolved. Later, Jesus brought further instruction from God concerning the proper godly care and maintenance of the soul. He taught us many things that would enable us to achieve and maintain the health and well-being of our souls as we followed His good instructions. After He returned to Heaven, He left us the Word of God, His Holy Spirit, and His "body", the priesthood of believers, to continue to help us deal with our various "pseuche"—and other—problems.

The solution to soul-related problems in the Christian community throughout these many centuries until the late 1800's, involved identifying related sin issues (inappropriate, unbiblical response to various problems of life), confessing and repenting of these, and replacing them with appropriate godly thinking and behavior. Of course we recognize that, because of the fallenness of man, this did not always happen appropriately, and there were abuses to be sure, but in true Bible-believing, preaching, teaching churches, believers dealt with their soul problems in this manner quite effectively.

Tragically, because we have allowed the world to set the standards for behavior, sin is so often no longer called sin but a *disease* or *disorder*. This is very sad, because it robs people of the hope for real and lasting help and healing. Throughout my schooling, I was taught that I should never even remotely allude to the possibility of healing to my counselees. That would present to them a false hope. Rather, I was to teach them to accept their *incurable disease* and learn to live with it through the various drug therapies and coping techniques psychology could offer.

This same "psycho" therapy was, naturally, applied to my own personal problems. For so many years, I was told that I had an eating disorder. It was a "disease," and I was taught various coping techniques—behavioral modification, visualization, goal setting which included a number of rigid rules that could not be violated. That only made the matter worse because I could never keep all the rules. But when I began to study the Word of God, I could see that the disorder was not an *incurable disease* at all, but *sin*: gluttony. It involved the seductive, sinful lust for fleshly indulgence and pleasure—a form of idolatry and sensuality spoken of in *Phil 3:18,19, Eph. 4:19,* and *James 1:14.* As I began to confess and sincerely repent of my sin, hope was born in my heart. I soon came to see that, indeed, there is power in the blood of Jesus, in His purifying Word, and in the enabling of the Holy Spirit to redeem and release the sin-sick soul from enslavement to the tormenting cycle of sin and guilt. As opposed to coping techniques, the Word of God offers forgiveness and freedom for all who are willing to confront sin, genuinely confess, repent, and forsake it. What liberation to realize that I was no longer a slave to my insatiable fleshly appetite, but rather it now had become a slave to the Lordship of Jesus under whose authority I now rested. (Jesus reigns and rules over all principalities and powers, including the power of the sin of gluttony…and every other sin – *Eph 1:19–21, 2:6, Rom. 6:4,,Eph. 3:16–20,* etc.). I'll never forget that glorious day when I awoke and, for the first time in my life, realized that I now had a *choice* regarding my appetite. I no longer had to give in to its seductive temptations, relentless accusations, and badgering demands, suffering each time the painful consequences of sin—guilt, death *(Rom. 6:23)*. I was now free to choose to obey the Bible's life-giving command to *eat for strength and not for gluttony (Eccles. 10:17b)*…and many other wonderful Scriptures regarding good diet and health practices. And oh, what a difference that made in the well-being of, not just my soul, but my body and spirit as well *(1 Thess. 5:23)*.

I could also help other people by taking them to Scripture and showing them what the Bible says about their particular undealt-with sin areas, so that they, too, could *put off* hurtful, sinful habits, and replace these with godly, healthful, habits (Eph. 4:22–24). As I did this and witnessed, time and time again, the power of the Holy Spirit in setting people free of the torment of bondage to a never ending cycle of sin and guilt, I no longer wanted to have anything to do with the foolishness of the world that refused to confront sin for what it is: rebellion against God's good, protective laws which always leads inevitably to destruction and death. By giving people an excuse for their sin rather than dealing with it biblically, we only bind them even more tightly in the shackles of the sin/guilt cycle, robbing them of the hope to ever be truly free (John 8:31,32,36).

Though we won't have time to investigate it thoroughly here—that we will do in Books Two and Three—I feel compelled by the Spirit of God to at least mention here just one area in which the integration of psychological theories into church teachings and practices have wreaked havoc in the Christian community, leaving an incalculable number of God's soldiers sidelined—debilitated and unable to participate in fulfilling God's special call upon their lives. In so doing, they have been stripped of all real hope and joy. That is the area of depression.

Depression comes in many forms and is referred to by various practitioners as clinical depression, chronic depression, manic depression, or bipolar, depending upon its specific manifestations, length and degree of severity. It is defined as: a lingering state of low spirits, gloom, dejection, sadness. A sense of hopelessness, of being pressed down to the point of being unable to function. In the case of bipolar, the episodes of "low spirits, gloom and dejection" are separated by periods of extremely high emotional exhilaration and sense of well-being. These "highs", however, are usually brief and pass quickly in comparison to the lingering periods of low spirits and gloom. These vastly variant, inexplicable "mood swings" can occur without warning and often without any specific outside causational event. (A compilation of definitions from various textbooks and dictionaries).

Having *lived there* for the greater part of my life, I have a tender heart for all who suffer from bipolar/chronic depression because I *understand* the hellishness of it—the indescribable pain and confusion. Truly, there are no words to adequately express this state. To me, it felt like what I imagine hell to be like, a place of agonizing, never-ending pain and torment.

Bipolar, and chronic, clinical depression are very complex afflictions. They are often (usually!) accompanied by strange, inexplicable, oft excruciating physical pain, which makes them even more confusing, for it is often impossible to identify the source of the pain. Is the depression causing the pain or the pain causing the depression? Sometimes it is truly impossible—by human evaluations—to determine. It is certainly not a simple matter of "snapping out of it".

Because this subject involves more than we have time to deal with adequately today, I won't go further with it here, but I just had to share with those who suffer from this very real and very painful affliction that there is hope and there is healing—not in the bankrupt *coping techniques* or myriad *drug therapies* of modern psychology, but in the Word of God, the redemption of Jesus and the power of the Holy Spirit, for even such a hellish affliction as this. Nothing is impossible with God. As one who is completely drug free and living a stable and productive life, (and there are hundreds more among the redeemed who can testify to this as well), I just want to offer real hope and encouragement. As we move into a deeper understanding of God's solution to the problem of bipolar and clinical depression (in Book 3) I know that God, by His rich redemptive mercy and Grace will deliver many more from this awful, painful bane (Ps. 107:20).

I waited patiently for the Lord; and He inclined to me, and heard my cry. He brought me up out of the pit of destruction, out of the miry clay; He set my feet upon a rock making my footsteps firm. And He put a new song in my mouth, a song of praise to our God; many will see and fear, and will trust in the Lord (Ps. 40:1–3).

This is my never ending song and prayer.

I'm including in the appendix an article that Mel and I were asked to write for the Psychoheresy Awareness Ministry newsletter. Please read this as a supplement to today's meditation. Psychoheresy Awareness is a ministry dedicated to exposing the lies and deceptions of modern psychology, including that which has infiltrated the church. See "Resources" in appendix for more information on the ministry.

May God help us all who know the Truth and love the Truth and have tasted of the freedom that comes from obeying the Truth to stand together in this critical area, ministering hope to those whose lives have been broken by sin's devastating lies and deceptions, that they may be truly set free through the liberating Truths of God's Word, not superficially healed by psychology's powerless coping techniques.

From the prophet even to the priest, everyone practices deceit. And they heal the brokenness of My people superficially, saying, "peace, peace"…but there is no peace (Jer. 8:10b,11).

Bible Study Supplement

Chapter 5 — Day 4 — The Psychologization of Sin

1. Read Ps. 32:1-5.

    a. Who is blessed? (vs. 1,2)

Please note that last qualification of blessedness: "in whose spirit is no deceit (guile)". True blessedness—freedom and liberation—begins with honesty before God and others. It involves accepting responsibility for our sins, genuinely confessing and repenting of them, then accepting God's mercy and total forgiveness, and going on in that power to overcome future temptations. .

    b. What happened to the psalmist when he kept silent (did not repent of his sin)? (vs. 3,4).

Note: "Bones wasting away" refers to basic, inner physical strength and stamina. It's a kind of relentless sapping of energy (life) as deep as "the bones".

    c. What did God do when the psalmist confessed his sin? (vs. 5b)

Note here that God did not only forgive his sin, He forgave even the guilt that accompanies sin.

2. Read Is. 41:28,29 - Please use NASB below to answer questions.

    (28) But when I look there is no one, and there is no counselor among them who, if I ask, can give an answer.

    (29) Behold all of them are false. Their works are worthless, their…images are wind and emptiness.

    a. For whom was God looking? (vs. 28) Did He find this person? (vs. 28)

    c. What did He find instead? (vs. 29)

God was looking for a true, godly counselor who would minister His righteous, life-giving Truth and salvation to His people, but He could find no one. I'm sure that as God looks out upon His Church today, He sees much the same barrenness of true biblical wisdom in understanding His Word and gladly ministering it effectively to others. I am so thankful that you are among the precious few who desire to do this. God longs for all of us to answer His very special call in Is. 41:27b: *I will send a messenger of good news.* So many have been hurt far too long by the devastating effects of the *psychologization of sin*. We can help them by giving them real, lasting hope and healing found in the Truths of the Word of God ministered through the Spirit of God.

4. Read Jer. 8:8–11.

    a. Why are the *wise men* put to shame? (vs. 9)

Note: Today, these "experts" would include counselors, psychologist, psychotherapist, who do not rely upon the pure Truths of God's Word for dealing with problems of the soul.

    b. For what is everyone greedy? (vs. 10b)

Note: Common rates for *one hour* of psychotherapy today is eighty to one hundred fifty dollars!

Psalm 38 is a classic psychological case study of a man greatly oppressed and weighed down by his own sin and guilt. We've all been there, haven't we? I'm so glad that the Bible is a book that shows us life as it really is in a fallen world. This honest portrayal gives me something with which I can identify and from which I can move into the encouraging assurances of God's compassionate love, forgiveness, and always sufficient and abundant healing grace (Lam. 3:22,23; 2 Cor. 12: 9,10; John 10:10; Hosea 6:1,2). As you read this Psalm, please keep in mind that it was written by David as he wrestled with a *besetting sin* in his life concerning which he had failed to deal with adequately. It is a very graphic and realistic picture of the awfulness of habitual sin and its terrible consequences. No wonder Paul urges us to *fight the good fight* in order that we might eradicate completely every habitual sin from our lives. As we, with God's help, do this, we will find ourselves in that sweet, blessed state of total forgiveness, abounding grace, and peace with God, others and ourselves.

5. Read Ps. 38:1–22.

   a. Why was David in so much anguish? Why did his bones have no soundness? (vs. 3b)

   b. What has overwhelmed him (gone over his head)? (vs. 4a) How does it feel? (vs. 4b)

   c. Why do his wounds fester and refuse to be healed? (vs. 5) Use NIV below to answer.

   My wounds fester and are loathsome because of my sinful folly (Ps. 38:5).

   d. What are some other physical manifestations of his undealt with sin? (vs. 6–8,10,11)

   e. What is David's hope? To whom does he turn? (vs. 21,22)

6. Read 1 John 1:9.

   a. What will God do every time we come to Him in sincere confession and repentance?

No wonder David wrote after his extended exile from God and long-overdue confession:

> *How blessed is the man whose transgression is forgiven…and in whose spirit there is no deceit. Create within me a pure heart, O God, and renew a steadfast spirit within me…restore to me the JOY of your salvation (Ps. 32:1,2, 51:10,12).*

Write out a Bible verse that had special meaning to you today.

Based upon what you have learned today, write a prayer to God expressing the desires of your heart in applying these Truths to your life.

Chapter 5 — Day 5
Beware! The Deceptiveness of Sin

> *But encourage one another day after day…lest any one of you be hardened by the deceitfulness of sin (Heb. 3:13).*
>
> *There is a way that seemeth right to a man, but its end is the way of death (Prov. 14:12).*

Foundational Truth # 18

There is a way that seemeth right…but its end is the way of death (Prov. 14:12). **Sin is deceptive—always! It comes to us through our fallen nature looking like *good* and *life* but producing *evil* and *death*! Beware of the deceptiveness of sin! Only God's Word—knowing it and obeying it—can keep us safe from sin's demonic deceptions and allurements.**

What a dangerously deceptive age we are living in, just as Jesus warned (Matt. 24:5,24; 2 Thess. 2:7–12)! As I think back on those early years of my Christian walk, I remember so well being made aware of, for the first time, the all-encompassing deception in my own selfish, stubborn heart. As I read and studied God's Word, the light of His Truth began to shine upon dark places, exposing *hidden sins and sinful motivations (Ps. 19:12, 139:23,24).* Yet, so often, I could not follow through with what I knew God was asking me to do: to repent *from the heart*, and turn away from these sins. There were so many and they had become so much a part of who I was. Though the conviction of idolatry was strong at times—that there were many idols in my heart that I really did love more than God—the deception was so powerful that I could not see them (the idolatries) as real *sins* that needed to be dealt with. They just did not seem *that* bad that they actually needed to be abandoned. "After all," the voice of deceptive reason rationalized within me, "These little sins are no big deal. You are under grace now. God understands. And if you do sin, your sins are covered by the blood of Jesus. And besides, everyone else is doing the very same things. If it is OK for all of those other *good* Christians, then surely it is OK for you, too. Just ignore it (the conviction), and it will go away."

That is very, **very** dangerous, deceptive thinking! The truth of the matter is: There is no such thing as an innocuous, no-big-deal sin! Every sin, no matter how insignificant it may seem, is still a sin that separates us from God, causes distress, hurts others, and gets us off course from knowing and doing God's will for our lives (Is. 59:2; James 4:1–4; Heb.3:12–19). Not to mention that all sin grieves the heart of God and causes a blight upon His holiness that we as His ambassadors are to reflect in the world (1 Pet. 1:13–16; Phil. 2:15). But there is another danger we need to heed very seriously as stated in today's focus verse above, *Heb. 3:13 – lest your hearts be hardened by the deceitfulness of sin.* Every time we sin and refuse to recognize it as *sin* and repent sincerely of it, our conscience is dulled (less alert), our heart grows a little harder and the sin stronghold is reinforced. If this pattern continues, we may be headed for that very tragic condition which the Bible refers to as being *given over to a reprobate mind,* and eventually, hell

(Rom. 1:18–30). Because of the grave seriousness of this, we'll devote a full day to studying the dangers associated with a hard heart in Chapter 7, but for today, I urge you, to please heed the warning: All sin is serious and must be dealt with biblically, lest our hearts become hardened and we fall into the vicious habitual sin/guilt cycle from which there will be no escape.

For me, the sin issues that I faced were not small or innocuous on any scale. They involved very serious idols of the heart that I really did love more than God, yet I was totally convinced that there was no way I could live without them. That is the power of the deception of sin. We can't even recognize that the thing we think we can't live without is the very thing that is destroying us and keeping us bound in a vicious cycle of sin and guilt. Such a destructive cycle (habitual sin) will inevitably result in a fermenting bitterness against God because He will not give us what our lustful flesh demands, or because He does not just automatically take it away without any discipline or diligent perseverance on our part. This fermenting bitterness all too frequently erupts into outbursts of anger against those nearest and dearest to us. How it must grieve not only those we hurt but also the heart of God, for it makes a mockery of what Jesus did for us on the cross: suffering and dying for our sins, then rising victorious over them so that we, by faith and obedience, can do the same. We no longer have to sin habitually and suffer sin's inevitable consequences over and over. We have the wisdom of God that comes to us through His Word, that cuts through the deception of sin, and we have the power of God that is resident within us through the Holy Spirit to enable us to remain strong and resistant, standing firm against sin's temptations, bringing blessing and joy to our hearts and to the lives of those we love.

Deeply entrenched, habitual sin issues (addictions and compulsions) are called, biblically, "sin strongholds" and are the most difficult to bring down because they involve a powerful system of *demonic deception (Mark 5:9)*. That is why psychological counseling, with no acknowledgment of spiritual factors—our fallen, sinful-to-the-core nature, the power of demonic deception, along with all our fleshly excuses and rationalizations for sin and guilt—is powerless and of virtually no lasting value when dealing with this kind of demonic control that has been working through many lies over many years. Addictions and compulsions are *sin* problems. And people in bondage to sin need a Savior—not an excuse.

As I look out upon the present condition of our world in which crass sin, selfishness and rebellion, along with a heartbreaking irreverence for God and His righteous holiness are accepted as the *norm* and *OK*, my heart is grieved to its very core. We are no different than the apostate children of Israel in the days of the judges when idolatry, immorality, and a blatant, blasphemous disregard for God prevailed throughout the land: *Every man did what was right in his own eyes (Judges 17:6)*. Lust reigned. Sin was ignored. Godlessness ruled. What a heyday it was for Satan and the forces of hell!

And what a heyday it is for them today! I am reminded of the many heartbreaking cries of God:

> *I called and you refused; I stretched out My hands to a disobedient and obstinate people all day long, crying out to them to return…but they would not…the Lord has sent to you all His servants the prophets again and again, but you have not listened nor inclined your ear to hear (Is. 65:2,3; Prov. 1:24,25; Jer. 3:12; Jer. 25:3,4)*.

It is only because of the longsuffering patience and mercy of God that *we have not all been consumed (Is. 33:14)* in this age of rampant wickedness, apostasy, and disregard of sin. And, sadly, we are *all* guilty of allowing our unbridled lusts and cravings for sensuality and pleasure to slowly erode our commitment to remain, as we have been called, *set apart, for God's holy purposes (2 Thess. 2:13)*. We have, as the Bible says, all *gone astray* and *become defiled (Ps. 53:2,3; Is. 51:6; Jer. 16:12)*.

There comes a day—there always comes a day—when God, for the sake of His Holy Name, must act:

*When the house of Israel was living in their own land, they defiled it by their ways and their deeds… therefore, I poured out My wrath on them for the blood which they had shed on the land, because they had defiled it with their idols…they profaned My Holy name, but I had concern for My Holy name which the house of Israel profaned…therefore, I will vindicate the Holiness of My great Name…**then the nations will know that I am God**! (Ezek. 36:17–23; Ezek. 20:38,39 sel.).*

The judgment of God fell upon the wayward, disobedient children of Israel, and you can be sure that it will fall upon us as well if we continue down this rebellious, self-seeking, God-defying path, for God's Holy Name is at stake (Judges 6:1–6a).

Whenever there is apostasy (a falling away from God), there is always a rebellious disregard for sin. Rather than acknowledging sin for what it is—rebellion against God and His love and a violation of His holiness that cost the life of His precious Son—the apostate continues on in his defiant disobedience, moving farther and farther away from God until he calls *right wrong, and wrong right (Is. 5:20)*. Just as we are doing in our society today! (Abortion, homosexuality, pornography, adultery, etc!). May God have mercy!

The body of Christ as a whole is no less guilty. In the name of tolerance, the Church has allowed every kind of idolatry for the fulfillment of fleshly lust imaginable to infiltrate its preaching, teaching, and fellowship. And we are reaping the inevitable results: dissension and discord in personal relationships and within churches, marital conflict and the breakdown of the family, a divorce rate that is equal to, and in some areas, higher than that of the non-believing world—all a terrible blight on God's Holy Name. That is why we so desperately need the plumb line of the Word of God in our own hearts, so that we can discern right from wrong and true biblical Truth from the error of worldly wisdom and demonic deceptions, so that we truly can—and *do—come out from them and be separate*, living holy and righteous lives that bring honor and glory to God, and draw others to Jesus (2 Cor. 6:16–18; 1 Pet. 1:14–16).

God alone knows the full toll that has been wreaked upon individuals, families, and upon the reputation of the body of Christ as a whole because we have allowed our attitudes and our behavior to be dominated by worldly thinking and the psychological way of excusing ungodly behavior as sickness or a psychological disorder, refusing to deal with it for what it is: sin. It takes a lot of courage to confront so colossal and powerful an enemy: our own fallen, sinful, selfish-to-the-core self and to help others do the same. It is much easier (or so it deceptively seems at the moment) to do what I did all those long years of rebellious disregard for God and for His Word: *choose* to accept the idolatrous sin as an incurable disease so that I always had a ready excuse and didn't have to deal with it. What I failed to recognize in such a deceived state is that this is the greatest lie of all. It is precisely because I refused to deal with it that the idolatrous sin issues continued to wreak their heavy toll of suffering and destruction in my life and in the lives of those around me against whom I often lashed out in guilt and anger.

May God help us all to see the danger of this kind of failure to deal with the sin in our lives, lest we become like the Laodiceans who were so totally deceived by their long-term idolatrous living they could not perceive their own deplorable state for what it was.

Because you say, "I am rich, and have become wealthy, and have need of nothing," and you do not know that you are wretched and miserable and poor and blind and naked (Rev. 3:17).

Such is the inevitable state of all who refuse to acknowledge God or to obey His Word, including confessing their sins and dealing with them biblically.

God in His infinite love has made a way for us to experience freedom from the lies and deception of sin and its inevitable painful consequences—guilt, death—in the redemption found in the cross of Christ through genuine and honest confession, repentance, and forgiveness, followed by willing and joyful obedience to the Word of God. (Remember that genuine confession and repentance involves agreeing with God about our sin's awfulness—what it did to Jesus—and that it is willful rebellion against God and our responsibility to honor Him, reflecting His pure holiness). As we *hide the Word of God in our hearts* that we might know it and obey it *(Ps. 119:11)*, we are empowered to be brave and courageous warriors, who are not afraid to face the enemies of our soul (sin issues) and to overcome them with the purity and power of God's Truths in the strength of the Holy Spirit. For then and only then will we be truly free to *be about the Father's business*, fulfilling His good purposes for our lives, winning souls to His kingdom of peace and joy, and strengthening those already in the body of Christ.

> *How blessed is he whose transgression is forgiven, whose sin is covered [atoned for by the blood of Jesus]. How blessed is the man in whose spirit there is no deceit! (Ps. 32:2).*

Bible Study Supplement

Chapter 5 — Day 5 — Beware! The Deceptiveness of Sin

1. Read Prov. 14:12.

    a. Describe the "way of sin" (vs. 12a).

    b. To what does following that way lead every time? (vs. 12b)

I urge you to please memorize this short, but powerfully important verse. It is one of the best warnings concerning the deceptiveness of sin in the Bible. Sin always *seemeth right.* But just as surely, it leads to destruction and death every time. Perhaps not immediately, but you can be sure, *the wages of sin is death*—every time!: death to our relationship with God, death to a free and clear conscience (guilt), death to our joy, peace, contentment (Rom. 6:23). That is as certain a spiritual law as the law of gravity in the physical world. Let this Truth sink deep into your soul: *The wages of sin is death*—every time: That is just the nature of sin! We must, therefore deal with it boldly, courageously and decisively, refusing to give in to its never ending sweet deceptive enticements that *seemeth so right.* A good rule that I have found of incalculable value, sparing me from sin's deceptive snares so often, is this: If something *looks or sounds too good to be true, it probably is!* In most cases, we do well to flee from it immediately. In the very least it requires serious prayer and careful investigation into the Word of God to confirm its agreement with, or opposition to, the Truth (God's Word). Anything that violates Scripture in any way is sin and needs to be avoided, or in the case when sin has already been committed, it needs to be dealt with through genuine confession and repentance. (Agreeing with God about it, then obeying His Word in overcoming it—forsaking it and casting it from our lives).

2. Read Judges 6:1–10.

    a. What did the Lord allow to happen because of the continual sinning of Israel? (vs. 1)

Here again we see the principle of being *given over to our own sinful lust (Rom. 1:28)* when we rebel and insist on doing things our way instead of obeying God. May God indelibly impress upon our hearts the grave danger—and loving warning—here: If we insist on stubbornly rebelling against God (sinning), He will *give us over to the desires of our hearts (Rom. 1:24,28).* He'll give us what we are clamoring for: our own way. Our loving God will not force us to love Him or obey Him. That would be coercion, not love. He will let us go our sinful, rebellious way. Soon we will be ensnared by the very thing we set up as our "god" to which we run to have our fleshly desires met. But all "gods" other than the one true God who created the heaven and earth, are controlled and empowered by Satan himself and through this power become demanding taskmasters that we serve as powerless slaves unable to escape to freedom.

    b. What was the result of the captivity of the Israelites by the Midianites? (vs. 4,5b,6a)

Because of their disobedience and insistent rebellion against God, the children of Israel were given over to the Midianites by God. In other words, they got what they demanded: freedom from God's loving, protective laws. And, being left alone by God (at their own demand), they were defenseless against the far greater number and power of their enemies who continually harassed and oppressed them—coming upon them in hoards, innumerable and powerful, to totally devastate. *Thus, Israel was brought very low* (vs. 6a). That's where sin always takes us!

When we are feeling especially low for long periods of time, we need to get down on our knees and ask God, through His Holy Spirit, to *search our hearts and see if there be any wicked way* (unconfessed, undealt with sin) *in us (Ps. 139:23,24)*. Is there any stubborn rebellion that we have not yet dealt with honestly and decisively (in true repentance) before God? Is there any area in which we have failed to listen carefully to and obey the Word of God? We should welcome this kind of illumination so that we can identify the sin that is causing the oppression, repent, and be restored to the *joy of our salvation* (Ps. 51:12).

   2. Read Heb. 3:1,2,12–18.

     a. Who are we now that we are saved and have become children of God? (vs. 1a)

     b. What were both Jesus and Moses in their ministries? (vs. 2)

     c. What are we to take care *not* to allow to happen? (vs. 12)

     d. What does God instruct us to do? (verse 13a) Why? (vs. 13b)

Note here once again, the warning regarding the *deceitfulness of sin*. One of sin's chief characteristics is its demonically powerful deception in making good appear as bad/evil (not desirable) and evil/bad look good (desirable). Remember the Garden—the temptation? Did not Satan appeal to the lust of the eyes and the lust of the flesh, making a tragically evil act of disobedience appear as innocuous and even good? May God help us all to remember this characteristic of sin when our lustful hearts are tempted. Also note that another very dangerous aspect of failing to deal with sin biblically—genuine confession, repentance—is the inevitable hardness of heart that follows. The more we resist God's Holy Spirit (convicting us of sin and pleading with us to repent and turn in obedience to God), the harder and more resistant to change our hearts become. A hard heart is one of the most dangerous conditions there is, for a hard heart that refuses repeatedly to obey the voice of the Lord will be given over to the sin it so craves—the sin that, if not repented of, will eventually destroy it (Judges 6:1–10; Heb. 10:26–29).

     e. How do we become partakers of Christ (share in Christ)? (vs. 14)

To become a partaker of Christ means to partake in His very character and nature—to take it in and allow it to become our very nature and character. Jesus had a pure, holy, trusting, obedient character and so will we as we *partake with Him* in loving, trusting obedience to God. In so doing we will also have Jesus' mind, discernment, and power to recognize and to stand against the deceptions as He did when He was tempted (Matt. 4:1–11).

     f. What does this Scripture warn us not to do? (vs. 15)

     g. With whom was God angry? (vs. 17)

     h. To whom did He swear that they would not enter into His rest? (vs. 18)

Does this not encourage us all to get a lot more serious about dealing with the sin in our lives and replacing it with godly behavior?

   3. Read Heb. 11:24–27. (This is one of my favorite Bible passages dealing with how we can have victory over sin in our lives).

     a. What did Moses give up? (vs. 24)

Think about what this means. Moses had an incredibly prosperous and powerful future in front of him. Comfort, recognition, prestige. All would be his as the adopted grandson of the ruler of one of the greatest, most powerful nations on earth. He would have a palace for a home, servants, chariots, a name that would be recognized, respected, admired everywhere he went. What a heart for God Moses had, to be willing to give all that up in order to obey God's calling on his life! It's a beautiful example for all of us.

Please use the NASB here to answer the next two question:

(Moses) chose rather to endure ill-treatment with the people of God, than to enjoy the passing pleasures of sin (Heb. 11:25).

b. What did Moses choose over the riches of the Egyptian empire? (vs. 25a)

c. What secret regarding sin did Moses fully understand that enabled him to walk in obedience to God, even if it meant hardship for a season? (vs. 25b)

It is critical to note here that Moses understood the deceptiveness of sin to always promise what it cannot and will never deliver—lasting pleasure and contentment. Whatever pleasure sin may deceptively hold out, you can be sure, it will be very temporary and short lived with the ultimate result being what sin always produces—suffering, guilt, death. And usually the suffering is more painful and severe than the sinner ever considered. May God help us to be fully aware of the serious consequences of giving in to the *passing pleasures of sin.*

d. What was Moses looking forward to, in which he found joy and courage? (vs. 26b)

e. How was Moses able to endure? (vs. 27)

Write out a Bible verse that had special meaning to you today.

Based upon what you have learned today, write a prayer to God expressing the desires of your heart in applying these Truths to your life.

Chapter 6

Memory verse: *For He delivered us from the domain of darkness, and transferred us into the Kingdom of His beloved Son (Col. 1:13).*

Bonus memory verse: *If anyone wishes to come after Me (be my disciple), let him deny himself, and take up his cross daily, and follow me (Luke 9:23).*

Day 1

Thy Kingdom Come

Out of the Darkness Into His Marvelous Light

Day 2

The Problem of Self-Esteem

Day 3

God's Solution to the Self-Esteem Problem

Day 4

The Very, Very Serious Sin of Idolatry

Day 5

The Person and Ministry of the Holy Spirit: Part 1

Who Is the Holy Spirit? What Does He Do?

Chapter 6 — Day 1
Thy Kingdom Come

Out of the Darkness Into His Marvelous Light

> *The time is fulfilled and the Kingdom of God is at hand; repent and believe in the gospel (Mark 1:15).*
>
> *For He delivered us from the domain of darkness, and transferred us into the Kingdom of His beloved Son (Col. 1:13).*

Foundational Truth #19

Jesus came not only to die for our sins and to rise victoriously over sin and death, but also to establish a new kingdom rule of God in men's hearts. Through His redemptive death and resurrection, we can now be delivered from the domain of darkness—evil, sin, death—and translated into the kingdom of God—light, love, forgiveness, peace and joy. Every individual, by his own God-given freedom to choose, decides to which kingdom he will belong, the kingdom of God (light) or the kingdom of Satan (darkness).

In the beginning, there was only one kingdom in heaven and on the earth—the kingdom of God. When Satan rebelled against God, he, and those who rebelled with him, were cast out of heaven to the earth. It was there he connived in his heart that he would build his own kingdom and eventually take over the rulership of the universe. Since the only inhabitants on the earth at that time were Adam and Eve, it is to them that he went in order to seduce them away from God and into his kingdom. Satan craftily deceived Adam and Eve into believing his lies and following him in rebelling (sinning) against God. He did this by raising doubt in their minds about the love and goodness of God, then he offered them godlike status in his kingdom—independence and autonomy, complete control of their lives, freedom from God's rule. The moment Adam and Eve believed Satan's lies and rebelled against God's protective law, sin entered their hearts and the beautiful image of God was destroyed. They fell from holiness and thus from fellowship with God. They would have perished eternally in their sin had God not in His unfathomable love made a way for them to be reconciled to Him in forgiveness and restoration.

Since *the wages of sin is death (Rom. 3:23)*, that "way" (of forgiveness and restoration) was initially through the sacrificial offering of an animal to pay the penalty for sin (death). Through the blood shed, God forgave their sins and reestablished the broken relationship with His children. And so it went for many generations as God taught the people about His kingdom of love and how they could live in it through trust in Him and obedience as He led them daily. But man's heart was so rebellious and so wicked, he would not listen, but continually turned his back on God, going on in his wicked rebellion. Had it not been for the longsuffering compassion of God, the entire lot of rebellious man would surely have been wiped out. But God was merciful, and he found in a man named Noah, a heart of righteousness that loved Him and desired to walk with Him in humble, trusting obedience. Through this man and his family, God preserved the human race, starting over again. But, once again, man's heart quickly turned again from God, and wickedness and evil prevailed causing every kind of distress and suffering—as sin always does. When the people got so oppressed by their sin and the awful consequences it brought, they cried out to God, and God once again mercifully listened and delivered them. But they never made any effort to change their hearts and turn them to God. They just kept going back to their sin…*like a dog returns to its vomit (2 Pet. 2:22)*. Then God became silent. He said nothing—for 400 years! He had to give the people time to realize the awful, terrible consequences they had brought upon themselves through their blatant, rebellious sinning and rejection of Him. Finally, they could see the utter futility and hopelessness of their miserable existence. And once again, they began to cry out to God. Then…

> *…in the fullness of time…(when everything on God's timetable was in perfect order according to the plan He established before the foundation of the world), God sent forth His Son, born of a (virgin) woman, (by the power of the Holy Spirit), that He might redeem those who were under the law (curse of sin), that they might receive adoption as(God's) sons (Gal. 4:4).*

And so entered…Jesus, *God in flesh* to reestablish God's Kingdom rule in the hearts of man, and the rebuilding of the image of God.

> *Jesus came into Galilee, preaching the gospel of God and saying, "The time is fulfilled, and the kingdom of God is at hand; repent and believe in the gospel" (Mark 1:15).*

"It's here!" Jesus is proclaiming. "The kingdom of God is no longer out there, in the future, far away. It is *at hand*, among you! I am the promised Messiah, the anointed one, the Savior that God said He would send to deliver His people from sin and give them eternal life with Him in heaven. Repent and believe the gospel (good news)." It was a glorious day in the history of mankind! The kingdom of God had come to earth. Jesus, God's Messiah, had come to deliver God's people from the *domain of darkness* and to transfer them into His marvelous kingdom of light. Jesus would teach the people how to enter into this wonderful kingdom and what living in God's kingdom was all about. He would explain things to them that no earthly ears had ever heard about God's glorious kingdom and power and glory. And He, Himself, would be *the way* into God's kingdom through His perfect life, sacrificial death and victorious resurrection. Jesus wanted them (and us!) to be a part of this wonderful kingdom.

> *For He (the Father) delivered us from the domain of darkness and transferred us to the kingdom of His beloved Son (Col. 1:13).*

So, what about these two kingdoms…and the people in them? What are they like?

The kingdom of darkness can be described best by three words: *deception, destruction and self*. It is a kingdom driven by pride (rejection of God), selfishness, and greed. It is self-obsessed, self-possessed and self-consuming. Its demands can never fully be met nor is it ever capable of being satisfied: *The eyes of man are never satisfied…the wicked are like the tossing sea for it cannot be quiet. Its waters toss up refuse and mud…there is no peace…for the wicked (Prov. 27:20b; Is. 57:20).* It's a kingdom in which all who dwell can never be truly satisfied because they are devoid of their God-created purpose and, even more tragically, estranged from the very presence of God Himself, who is the source of all real and lasting love, meaning, and blessing. The kingdom of darkness (Satan's kingdom) is full of evil—rebellion, violence and wickedness of every kind. But far more sadly, it is also full of very well-meaning, kind, loving, giving people who through demonic deception have come to believe that they are "good people" who "have no need of God." Those in this group who accept the reality that there is life after death believe they will go to heaven, nirvana, or be reincarnated into a higher and higher form until they receive godlike status because of their "goodness." That is really sad because God is holy and we (all) are sinful—*all have sinned and come short of the glory (holiness) of God*

(Rom. 3:23). Not one single human being will make it to heaven (a holy place) on his own merits. He can only go there through Jesus—who was holy and died for our sins and gives to all who put their faith and trust in Him, forgiveness (holiness) and eternal life with Him in heaven. There is a third group of people who occupy Satan's kingdom and that is the modern day hedonist who believes that this life is all there is so "grab all the gusto you can get because when you're dead, you're dead." It's sad because the power of demonic deception in every one of these cases is so great that those ensnared cannot even recognize their bankrupt, meaningless state:

> *Because you say, "I am rich and have become wealthy, and have need of nothing," and you do not know that you are wretched and miserable and poor and blind and naked (Rev. 3:17).*

And what about the *kingdom of light*—God's kingdom. What is it like?

First of all, the kingdom of God about which Jesus spoke, is not a physical kingdom. (Though it certainly will be one day). For now, it is a spiritual kingdom—a kingdom that rules in the heart of man. Therefore, the kingdom of God for the moment is "now," and "not yet." It is "now" because the moment we turn our hearts to God in genuine repentance, the Holy Spirit comes to live in us and establishes God's kingdom rule of wisdom, love, assurance and peace. But it is "not yet" because the glorious consummation of Jesus' return and physical reign over every other kingdom and every heart has *not yet* happened. Yet it is as certain as the air we breathe. It is this sure, secure *blessed assurance* of Jesus' return and our glorification with Him that burns ever more brightly in every kingdom of God child (Prov. 4:18!).

So what about the present "now" kingdom? What does it look like? It looks like the original plan! Jesus came to reclaim that beautiful *image of God*, to build it back into the souls of every one who would *repent, believe,* and *follow Him*.

> *But as many as received Him, to them gave he the right to become children of God (John 1;12).*

> *I will dwell in them and walk among them. And I will be their God, and they shall be My people. Therefore come out from their midst and be separate, says the Lord. And do not touch what is unclean and I will welcome you and I will be a father to you. And you shall be sons and daughters to Me, says the Lord Almighty (2 Cor. 6:16–18).*

> *If anyone loves Me, he will keep My Word; and My Father will love him and We will come to him, and make our abode with Him… I will love him and will disclose Myself to him (John 14:23,21).*

> *I pray that the eyes of your heart may be enlightened, so that you may know what is the hope of His calling, what are the riches of the glory of His inheritance in (the kingdom of God), and what is the surpassing greatness of His power toward us who believe…(for) God being rich in mercy because of His great love with which He loves us, made us alive together with Christ…and raised us up with Him and seated us with Him in the heavenly places in Christ Jesus…far above all rule and authority and power and dominion (Eph. 1:18–21, 2:4,5).*

> *The Lord (Himself) is my portion and my cup.. because He is at my right hand, I will not be shaken… Christ in you, the hope of Glory (Ps. 16:5,8b; Col. 1:27).*

I think we are all beginning to get the picture now. What Jesus is telling us in these passages—and many more like them—is that He came to establish a *new kingdom*. Not a temporary one like the one over which Satan rules for the moment, but one that will endure forever. Only those who come to God and enter by the narrow gate can be a part of this wonderful, glorious kingdom. The narrow gate is "Jesus" (Matt. 7:14; John 14:6; John 10:7–17, 27,28; John 3:16). It is trusting in what Jesus did for us on the cross—dying for our sins—then rising victorious over sin and death. It involves repenting of our sins and, in overwhelming gratitude for what Jesus did for us, turning from our idols and our rebellious self-rule in Satan's kingdom of darkness to serve the *true and living God (1 Thess. 1:9)*. This new kingdom—the kingdom rule of Christ in our hearts—is a very real kingdom, completely different and separate from the worldly kingdom in which we physically reside. It is the new, set apart, holy kingdom of God (Mark 1:15; Col. 1:13).

The unregenerate world, apart from Christ, cannot understand this. Their eyes have been blinded by the demonic schemes of Satan to believe the age old lie that independence *from* God offers far more than a relationship *with* God (2 Cor. 4:4). But that is the biggest lie of all because all life that is any life at all begins with a personal relationship with God because HE IS LIFE and the source of all that is life-giving. That's what kingdom living is all about—*life, and that more abundantly (John 10:10)*. ·

There is so much that Jesus delivers us from when we accept Him as our Lord and Savior and are translated from the *kingdom of darkness into His marvelous light (Col. 1:13)*, but I am convinced that the greatest freedom of all is freedom from the demanding, self-obsessed, self-consuming, **self**-life ruled by Satan and our own sinful, insatiable flesh that can never be satisfied or find true contentment and peace. Jesus knew that the self-life was a destructive life that possessed its possessor, robbing and maiming and consuming him until, eventually, everything he valued was destroyed—his sense of fulfillment and purpose, dignity and worth—leaving him empty and devoid of *real,* (satisfying, lasting) inner peace and joy and *life*. It is from this kind of rapacious, consuming, never satisfying life that Jesus sets every kingdom child *free (John 8:31,32,36)*.

This is the beauty and the glory of life in the kingdom of God. We are free from the dictates of the world with all its taskmasters and endless demands, and, even more liberating, we are free from Satan's rule through our insatiable flesh. Free to love, to trust, to obey, to serve, to bear fruit, to rest, to minister and be ministered to (in a proper, godly way), free to lie down in the green pasture of God's love and always sufficient, always abundant provision, free to refresh ourselves in His presence beside the still waters of a humble, repentant heart and a clear and guilt-free conscience, free to experience the reviving purification of the living waters that flow ceaselessly from the throne of grace through the Holy Spirit now living in us (1 John 4:19; Prov. 3:5,6; Deut. 28:1–13; Matt. 20:26–28; John 15:8; Heb. 4:10,11; Prov. 11:25; Ps. 23:1–3; Jer. 31:3; 2 Cor. 12:9,10; Ps. 16:11, 23:2; 1 Tim. 1:5; John 7:38).

No wonder Jesus said, *"Blessed are the eyes which see the things you see, for I say to you, that many prophets and kings wished to see the things which you see, and did not see them, and to hear the things which you hear, and did not hear them" (Luke 10:23,24)*.

And what were those *special things* envied and sought after by kings and prophets? It was the beautiful, inexhaustible blessings and joys of the kingdom of heaven that now lives *in* you and me and every *born again* believer's heart that will be with us and *in us* forever! (John 14:16)

For the kingdom of heaven is not eating and drinking, but righteousness and peace and joy in the Holy Spirit…These things I have spoken to you, that My joy may be in you and your joy may be full! (Rom. 14:17; John 15:11).

Bible Study Supplement

Chapter 6 — Day 1 — Thy Kingdom Come
Out of the Darkness Into His Marvelous Light

1. Read Col. 1:13–17.

    a. From what have we been delivered/rescued? (vs. 13a)

    b. To what have we been transferred (brought into)? (vs. 13b)

    c. Who holds all things together? (vs. 17)

Note: Verse 17 (question "c" above), refers to Jesus, as clarified in verses 13–16.

The *kingdom of heaven* is used synonymously with the *kingdom of God*. They both refer to God's kingdom rule—the rule of God's Word—in our hearts.

2. Read Matt. 13:44–52.

    a. What is the kingdom of heaven like? (vs. 44a) What did the man who *found it* do? (vs. 44b)

    b. How is the kingdom of heaven described in the next two verses? (vs. 45,46)

    c. What is Jesus telling us regarding the value of this kingdom in these verses?

    d. How is the kingdom of heaven describe in the next verses? (vs. 47,48)

    e. To what does Jesus compare this? (vs. 49,50)

    f. To what does Jesus compare every one who has been instructed about the kingdom of heaven? (all who have become disciples, followers of Jesus) (vs. 52)

Jesus considered the kingdom of heaven/kingdom of God a most important subject for he talked a lot about it…

3. Read Mark 4:26–32.

    a. What is the kingdom of God compared to in vs. 26?

    b. What happens to the *seeds* that are planted? (vs. 27,28)

Isn't this encouraging? Jesus is saying here that if we are faithful in planting the seeds of the kingdom (God's Word), in people's hearts, God will cause those seeds to grow and to produce a harvest. Doesn't that encourage you to be a kingdom *seed planter*?

    c. To what is the kingdom compared in vs. 31? (I love this one—it's my favorite Kingdom illustration.)

    d. How large is this seed when it is planted? (vs. 31b)

    e. What happens to this seed when it matures and what does it become for the birds? (vs. 32)

8. Read Luke 10:1,17-24.

   a. In what state of being (attitude, disposition) did the 72 disciples return? (vs. 17)

   b. In what did Jesus say that the disciples should really rejoice? (vs. 20)

   c. Whose eyes are blessed? (vs. 23)

   d. What do you think Jesus meant in verse 24?

Write out a Bible verse that had special meaning to you today.

Based upon what you have learned today, write a prayer to God expressing the desires of your heart in applying these Truths to your life.

Chapter 6 — Day 2
The Problem of Self-Esteem

For the time will come when they will not endure sound doctrine; but wanting to have their ears tickled, they will accumulate for themselves teachers in accordance to their own desires; and will turn away their ears from the truth, and will turn aside to myths (2 Tim. 4:3-4).

I have prayed long and fervently, and spent untold additional hours in the Word over the past several months seeking God's heart—true biblical wisdom—regarding this subject. I know that the issue of self-esteem is a very sensitive one because of all the attention focused upon it in the past 25 years. In all honesty, I much prefer not to broach the subject because of the strong personal emotion and allegiance connected to it and to the experts who espouse it, several of whom have come to command a near god-like reverence. However, to do so—avoid this topic—would clearly be a willful act of disobedience regarding God's call on my life in writing this study. Therefore, I must, in obedience to God, share the burden God has placed upon my heart concerning this subject that affects all of us in very powerful ways throughout our lifetime.

My people perish for lack of knowledge (true biblical wisdom) (Hosea 4:6).

Of all the factors that played into both the intensity and the duration of those long, agonizing years of mental torment and emotional instability, the one that contributed the most, by far, was believing and applying to my life the very appealing, albeit deceptive and unbiblical teaching of self-esteem. And God alone knows how much pain and suffering others have endured because of the same error. Many families have been destroyed (as ours nearly was), and inestimable damage has already been done to the cause of Christ and to the witness of the Church because God's people have embraced this self-centered (as opposed to God-centered) unbiblical teaching, leaving them weak and absorbed in the pursuit of *self-esteem* (feeling good about themselves) rather than esteeming Christ and bringing honor and glory to Him by loving and obeying Him, and sharing His love with others (Matt. 20:25–28; Phil. 2:3, cf. 4–8).

For decades now, even as early as grammar school, this unbiblical teaching has influenced how teachers teach and parents parent in the exercising, or lack thereof, of proper (biblical) discipline. For fear of negatively impacting a child's development, parents were told and teachers were taught that all care must be exercised to avoid damaging fragile Jimmy or tender Suzy's self-esteem. Later, as fragile Jimmy and tender Suzy entered high school, then college, the childhood training was reinforced by further teaching that promoted attention to self and "looking out for #1."

When I was in graduate school studying for my master's in psychology, the teaching of self-esteem permeated nearly every psychological methodology and technique I studied. In fact, we were taught that nearly all mental, emotional, and psychological problems were inextricably linked to low self-esteem. The main thrust, therefore, was to use our professional psychological training to build up the counselee's self-esteem until they came to a place where they *felt good about themselves* because only those who *feel good about themselves* are able to take control of their lives and overcome their problems. In my field training and supervised counseling situations, I continually heard: the problem with (now adult) proud, defiant Jimmy and mentally and emotionally unstable Suzy is a low self-esteem. The cure was always the same: do whatever it takes to nurture and build up the damaged self-esteem. And so that is what I always tried to do, being totally blind to the fact that I was not helping Suzy at all, but actually playing into the devil's hand to set her upon a course that would lead her farther and farther away from mental stability, true freedom and peace.

God created us to have a personal relationship with Him and in and through this relationship to fulfill His good plans for our lives and solve our problems. We are not "in control." God is "in control" and only God has the wisdom, the power and the resources to deal with our problems in a way that brings real victory and lasting peace. It's precisely because we *can't* handle all the problems and heartaches of life in a fallen world that we don't *feel good about ourselves,* so we need to turn to God in trusting faith and dependence on Him, rather than vainly attempting to pump up our own sinful, weak, inadequate, *self-*esteem. It is, in fact, because of a much too elevated self-esteem that most emotional and psychological problems develop, not a lack of it. But the proud, fearful (of losing control) self does not want to hear that, so it turns away to myths and the doctrines of man in order to avoid dealing with the real underlying problems—sinful, unbiblical behavior, disobedience, estrangement from God.

For the time will come when they will not endure sound doctrine; but wanting to have their ears tickled, they will accumulate for themselves teachers in accordance to their own desires; and will turn away their ears from the Truth, and will turn aside to myths (2 Tim. 4:3–4).

The concept of self-esteem as a solution to our soul (psychological) problems is an unbiblical myth. After I was saved and began seriously studying God's Word in search of *God's* wisdom and solutions to my psychological (soul) problems, conviction came to my heart again and again concerning the deceptive fallacies in the self-esteem belief system. I knew that God's Word was clearly instructing me to abandon this system that greatly impeded my growth into true Christlikeness and humble, submissive obedience. It was not an easy endeavor. When "self" has ruled for so long, it is not easily dethroned. But I knew that unless Christ truly ruled over my heart, my will and my emotions, there would never be any lasting peace or solution to any of my "psychological" problems. So I prayed every day that He would help me do what I knew was impossible for me to do alone. And He, through His Holy Spirit, began to do this. Sin issues were faced and dealt with biblically and rivers of peace began to flow, quieting the torrents of turmoil and inner fleshly rebellions (John 7:38).

As I witness the continuing erosion of true biblical discipleship in deference to the integration of worldly philosophies—such as the teaching of self-esteem, and a cadre of other unbiblical teachings—my heart is deeply saddened. I am still stunned by the degree to which the self-esteem movement has penetrated our Christian institutions of education—from grade school through graduate programs. We see it and hear it everywhere—on Christian radio, in Christian magazines, books, and videos. "Experts" laud it, preachers preach it, retreats and seminars promote it. There are even Bible studies to help build one's *self-*esteem! It has truly become, as Paul so clearly warned against: *another gospel (Gal. 1:6).* No longer are we hearing the clear gospel message of sinners in need of a Savior (repentance, salvation, sanctification). We are hearing instead *another gospel* of "sick" or "wounded" people in need of self-esteem. (The *disease model* of excusing sin for sickness).

You too have done evil, even more than your forefathers; for behold, you are each one walking according to the stubbornness of his own evil heart, without listening to Me (Jer. 16:12).

Scripture clearly teaches that we are all born with a selfish, proud and stubborn nature which is in rebellion against God (refusing to listen to and obey Him). This nature has corrupted our once perfect soul (heart/mind, emotions, will) through which we have fellowship with God. So the more we encourage people to build up their *self*-esteem, the stronger becomes their selfish, proud nature corrupting all the more their soul and hindering their growth and relationship with God. It is only to the extent that we overcome the selfishness, pride and rebellion in our own soul (through genuine repentance) that we are able to enjoy a loving, growing, trusting relationship with God—the only place where true and lasting joy, peace, and fulfillment can be found.

It took some time before I was able to see this in my own life, because, as we have studied, sin is very deceptive, and especially to the one bound by it. We are rarely able to recognize it for what it is, but see it only as it deceptively presents itself to our proud, rebellious nature, as something good and desirable. But, in time, as I continued in my studies, the sword of God's Truth—God's Word (Eph. 6:17)—began to cut through the layers of deception that had, in the course of those long years of believing the lies of Satan (and pampering my own selfish flesh), hardened my heart and formed a protective shield that was nearly impenetrable. Little by little, I was able to recognize the spirit of rebellion (*self*-esteem) in my own heart. I could clearly see that all the self-condemnatory remarks that so often and so bitterly flowed from my lips (that I was told was the manifestation of a poor, low self-esteem), was, in truth, the manifestation of a spirit in rebellion against God: a spirit filled with anger because life had not gone the way I had wanted it to go so many times. My self-esteem did not need to be built up; it needed to be brought down—broken and put into humble, loving, willing submission to God, who alone is worthy to be *esteemed*.

The proof text used as the basis for most self-esteem teaching is Matt. 22:39.

You shall love your neighbor as yourself (Matt. 22:39).

So the argument became that we must love ourselves before we are capable of loving others. But this is clearly *not* what Jesus meant (as verified over and over throughout the *whole counsel of God's Word – Acts 20:27*). Jesus knew our fallen, sinful hearts were selfish and self-centered to the core. He knew that we always, by nature, love ourselves and look out for our own personal interests (Eph. 5:29; Phil. 2:4). There is plenty of evidence for that throughout the Bible: Adam and Eve, Cain, Lot, Jacob, the rebellious and disobedient children of Israel, Rehoboam, Ahab, Jezebel, Nebuchadnezzar, the Pharisees, Simon the magician, Ananias and Sapphira, the prodigal son, the rich young ruler, Judas, etc., etc. And there is just as much evidence of this same kind of deeply ingrained *self*-centeredness throughout our world today—in our schools, our businesses, our government, our churches, our homes, and in our own hearts. When you get a new phone book, whose name do you look up first? When the pictures come back from the last family reunion, whose face do you look for first? We are self-centered by nature! (Gen. 6:5).

What Jesus was really saying in Matt. 22:39 is that we need to start looking out for our neighbor in the same way that we are careful to look out for ourselves.

That sheds a whole different light on the meaning of this Scripture, doesn't it? If we spent as much time thinking about, praying for, and loving our neighbor as we do thinking about, praying for, and loving ourselves, a lot more people would see the love of Jesus shining through our lives. But we don't do that, do we? We are too busy looking after our own self-interests, comfort and "esteem." And what is the result? We lose the very thing we are seeking so hard to gain—meaning, purpose, the joy of being a blessing to others…*life*.

He who has found his life (developing a strong self-esteem by continually seeking after the approval and applause of man – oft at the expense of many others), shall lose it (blessing, peace), and he who has lost his life (abandoned the pursuit of his own <u>self</u>-esteem in service to God and others) shall find it (Matt. 10:39).

The more I *lose myself* by focusing upon God and His love and all that He has done for me (John 3:16; 2 Cor. 5:21), and out of a heart overflowing with gratitude for that, find my greatest delight in loving and obeying God and sharing His love with others, the more I *find life*, and *that more abundantly (John 10:10)*. I can vouch for this and so can you. The times we have set aside the quest for *self*-esteem, and *self*-gratification and given ourselves to a humble, trusting, obedient walk with Jesus—loving and serving Him and others—have always been characterized by joy and blessing, and they have been the richest, most fulfilling, most rewarding times of our lives.

> *But Jesus called them to Himself, and said, "You know that the rulers of the Gentiles lord it over them, and their great men (self-appointed "experts") exercise authority over them. It is not so among you, but whoever wishes to become great among you shall be your servant, and whoever wishes to be first among you shall be your slave; just as the Son of Man did not come to be served, but to serve, and to give His life a ransom for many." (Matt. 20:25–28)*

You just can't find anything here—or anywhere else in the Bible—to support the popular gospel of self-esteem. In fact, what is clearly taught throughout the Word of God, is exactly the opposite. We are told that we must *die to self, humble ourselves, think of others more highly than ourselves, serve others, be obedient to God, even if that means going all the way to the cross as Jesus did (Luke 9:23; James 4:10; Phil. 2:3; Matt. 20:26–28; John 13:4; Phil. 2:7,8).*

Jesus didn't save us to "feel good about ourselves." He saved us to be holy—to walk daily in a loving, trusting, purifying relationship with Him, bringing Him honor and glory as we find our greatest delight in fulfilling His good plans for our lives and sharing His wonderful love with others. That is where real joy and peace will always be found.

The Bible warns us over and over of God's hatred of pride and selfishness (which are, in reality, at the heart of *self*-esteem), because He knows what destruction these wreak in the lives of His children (James 4:6,16; Jer. 50:29–32; Ps. 36:11,12; Prov. 6:16,17; Prov. 16:5; Deut. 8:3–14, etc.). God is a loving Father who wants to protect us—*from ourselves*, our *selfish, sinful nature*. In my case, as in the case of others who accept and seek to apply the very wrong, unbiblical teaching of self-esteem, it led me into a restless, driven, unending quest to satisfy every lust and desire of my insatiable, selfish flesh. But that will never happen, because the self is never satisfied—*The eyes of a man finds no satisfaction (Prov. 27:20b)*. What invariably happens is that the one who erroneously thrusts himself into the pursuit of *self*-esteem becomes disillusioned and ends up in a miserable state of joyless discontent, self-pity, and bitterness. And this state is just one short step from chronic depression.

It is my prayer that sharing the Truths of God's Word here regarding the destructive potential of the pervasive and popular unbiblical teaching of self-esteem, will help others avoid some of the same pitfalls and unnecessary pain—both self-inflicted and inflicted on others—it always brings into the lives of those who embrace and pursue it.

> *I urge you not to…teach strange doctrines, nor pay attention to myths which give rise to mere speculation rather than furthering (the cause of Christ)…But the goal of our instruction is love from a pure heart and a good conscience and a sincere faith…And this I pray, that your love may abound still more and more in real knowledge and all discernment, so that you may approve the things that are excellent, in order to be sincere and blameless until the day of Christ; having been filled with the fruit of righteousness…to the glory and praise of God (1 Tim. 1:3–5; Phil.1:9–11).*

Bible Study Supplement

Chapter 6 — Day 2 — The Problem of Self Esteem

1. Read Matt. 22:37–39.

    a. What is the first commandment? (vs. 37)

    b. What is the second commandment? (vs. 39)

    c. What did Jesus mean when He said that we are to love our neighbor *as ourself*? (vs. 39)

2. Read Eph. 5:29a.

    a. What does man *naturally* do regarding his own body/flesh?

God is saying here that we all, by nature, cherish our own bodies and make sure they are taken care of. So in Matthew 22 when Jesus talks about loving our neighbor *as ourselves*, He is <u>not</u> saying we must love ourselves first before we can love our neighbors, but rather, we already *love ourselves*, and now we are to extend that love beyond ourselves to our neighbor. In other words, we are to have the same love and care for our neighbor as we do for ourselves. What a wonderful world this would be if everyone obeyed this one simple command.

3. Read Matt. 20:25–28.

    a. What was the heart attitude of the Gentile leaders/rulers? (vs. 25)

    b. What is the way to greatness for disciples of Jesus? (vs. 26)

    c. How do Jesus' disciples become first? (vs. 27)

Note: Jesus often used the term "slave" to illustrate the ultimate position of humility and service to others. It also illustrates total dependence upon the Master. If we truly love God and others we will lovingly, willingly, and joyfully serve them knowing it brings joy to them and joy to the heart of God as well. In so doing we, too, are filled with joy and satisfaction: *He who waters will himself be watered (Prov. 11:25)*.

    d. What did Jesus *not* come to do? What did He come to do? (vs. 28)

    e. Since Jesus is our example to follow, what should we be about as His disciples? (vs. 28)

Note: Do you see the clear teaching of Jesus here that is completely antithetical to the psychological self-esteem teaching? People with high *self*-esteem find it incredibly difficult, if not impossible, to be true servants, bondslaves of Jesus (or anyone!). And so they exist in a miserable, empty, rewardless state of self-absorption and discontent.

4. Read John 12:24–26.

    a. What must first happen before a grain of wheat *bears much fruit*? (vs. 24)

    b. Contrast what happens to the one who *loves* his fallen, sinful, worldly life with the one who *hates* it. (vs. 25)

    c. What will the Father do for those who choose to love and serve His Son? (vs. 26b)

A similar text is found in Matt. 10:39:

He who has found his life shall lose it, and he who has lost his life for My sake shall find it.

As we come to God in humble repentance and ask Him to forgive us for our prideful attention to ourselves—satisfying *our* wants, *our* needs, *our* selfish lusts—and ask Him to help us turn away from that kind of self-absorption and get our eyes back upon Jesus—knowing Him, following Him, obeying Him, sharing His love with others, He will certainly *hear from heaven, forgive (our) sin, and heal (our) land (2 Chron. 7:14)*. Then we will truly *find life…and that more abundantly.*

Write out a Bible verse that had special meaning to you today.

Based upon what you have learned today, write a prayer to God expressing the desires of your heart in applying these Truths to your life.

Chapter 6 — Day 3
God's Solution to the Self-Esteem Problem

And He was saying to them all, "If anyone wishes to be my disciple, let him deny himself, and take up his cross daily, and follow Me" (Luke 9:23).

And Mary said, "Behold, the bondservant of the Lord; be it unto me according to Your Word" (Luke 1:38).

Thank you so much for your courage in facing this really tough subject so bravely with me. I know that this is not a pleasant or easy topic for any of us. We have all inherited that selfish sin nature that was at the heart of Adam and Eve's rebellion against God. And I'm sure we all get quite weary at times of the battle against it. Satan knows that, too. I see his hand in introducing the wide-spread, very appealing—and nearly universally accepted—teaching of *self-esteem*. It serves well to justify what we so naturally are. That makes it easier. But we all know that sin is very deceptive and every time we give in to it, we only strengthen its stronghold, causing us to sin further, bringing more pain and heartache as it encroaches determinedly to dominate our life.

That is what self-esteem does. By getting us to continually focus upon ourselves—our wants, our desires, our comfort—we really do lose sight of what we are really here for: to magnify the awesome wonder and glory of God, to become conformed to the image of Jesus, and to share His love and the wonderful good news of His salvation with others. And whenever we are not actively involved in this pursuit, all that we do will be pitifully disappointing at best and lead us to eternal separation from God at worst. So yes, it is a huge problem, and the fight will not be easy to dethrone this "god" of self that, for many of us, has dominated our lives for so long, but dethrone him we must if we are to know the real freedom and joy that Jesus gave His life to purchase for us, and in this joy, reflect the magnitude of God's love and salvation all the more that others might "see and believe." This journey to freedom from the domination of our own sinful self is, in reality, a life-long process, for *self* will be with us until we are with Jesus. But the good news of the gospel is that it is not only possible, but God's desire that we walk in victory over our fallen sinful nature as we look to God and obey His Word in the power of the Holy Spirit. There is far too much of God's wisdom concerning this crucial subject than we have time for here today. We'll have to save that for later. But I believe God wants to plant seeds of hope in our hearts that will encourage us in our journey to liberation from the greatest enemy of all—our own sinful self. So with open, receptive hearts let us turn our attention off of our petty pursuit of *self*-esteem for a few moments and sit at Jesus' feet once again to hear what He has to tell us that will strengthen us in the battle against this destructive, joy-robbing bane.

And He was saying to them all, "If anyone wishes to come after Me, let him deny himself, and take up his cross daily, and follow Me" (Luke 9:23).

I remember so vividly the first time I came face to face with this verse in a way that clearly tested my faith and level of commitment and obedience. Mel and I were attending a very thorough, in-depth, year long discipleship Bible Study course which had as its central theme, this pivotal verse. I recall just as vividly the very real and very intense pain those words…*let him* **deny himself**…initially evoked deep in my soul. To *deny self* (also referred to in the Bible as *dying to self*) means to give up every right of my own "self"—my desires, my wants, my fleshly cravings and lusts—in order to be totally under God's authority and rule. Though I knew it was of utmost importance in my spiritual progress as a disciple of Jesus to obey this command, everything in me recoiled at the sound of it. Deny (die to) the "self" I had worked so hard to "build"…the self I had come to love, cherish and *esteem* so much? The thought nearly paralyzed me in fear. It seemed so huge, so all-encompassing, so overwhelming! So utterly impossible—this total surrender and the laying down of the *control* of my life and all my well-laid plans, my goals, my selfish (self-centered, self-controlled as opposed to God-centered, God-controlled) ambitions. It could no longer be, "my will be done, and please bless it, God" but rather "Thy will be done"—even if it hurts for the moment as my selfish flesh does battle against relinquishing the control it has claimed so long. I felt weak, frightened and totally inadequate for the battle. Yet I knew that God's Word taught and time had proven that only God knows what is best for us at all times, and it is only in relinquishing control and walking in humble, trusting obedience that we experience that deep, secure, peace and contentment (Phil. 4:7). So obey Jesus and face this enemy, I must.

Thus began the very difficult, oft painful process—painful, not because I had a low self-esteem, but because, in reality, I had a much too elevated *esteem* of myself and my abilities to manage my own life. I truly believed that I knew better than God the way my life should go and what my goals for the future ought to be. Learning the good spiritual discipline of *denying self* and walking consistently in humble trusting obedience to God is rarely an easy or painless undertaking quickly mastered by any of us, because everything we are by nature—proud and selfish to the core—fights against it. And that battle (spiritual warfare) is continually fueled from the outside by relentless and powerful *self*-promoting propaganda. We see and hear it everywhere—in our schools, on television, in magazines, on billboards; it is clamored from our peers, politicians, psychological practitioners, and sadly, even from the pulpits of many of our churches. "You must love yourself before you can love others; look out for "number one"; take control of your life, do your own thing (as opposed to seeking God's will for your life); you have a right to be happy and healthy, to seek pleasure, to have what you want, so *dream big*, and go for it…"

It is this kind of man-centered inner spirit of rebellion and self-absorption that self-esteem always fosters—an attitude that is already deeply entrenched in most of us. For me, personally, I had no idea at the outset, the intensity of the war into which I had voluntarily entered when I, in obedience to God, decided to do battle against my own cherished, highly-esteemed self (2 Timothy 2:3). There were times the conflict became so intense and the inner agonies of the "dying" process so painful, I was sure I could not endure another moment. I wanted to quit so badly and resign myself to being a "Sunday Morning Christian," saved and going to heaven and that was enough. But what would I say to Jesus when I stood before Him with nothing to offer but my one talent that I had buried and failed to use to serve Him and to fulfill His purpose for my life?

Because the self-esteem gospel had ruled over my heart, desires, and goals through all those years and was so deeply entrenched into the very core of my being, progress was slow, and there were far more setbacks and failures than successes in those early years. The old man does not die easily, and the longer it is left in control, the harder the heart becomes and the more resistant to change and to the breaking process, especially when it has been pampered and coddled by the unbiblical teaching of self-esteem over many years. That is why the Bible instructs parents to *bring up their children in the discipline and instruction of the Lord (Eph 6:4)*. Parents are to discipline their children—biblically—and instruct them to be God-centered, not self-centered when they are young and their hearts are yet tender and can be gently and lovingly brought into submission to the Lordship of Jesus, thus sparing them of the much *much* more painful ordeal that comes when *God* must break the resistant, rebellious spirit when it is older, set in its ways, (selfish and hardened) and stubbornly resistant to change as mine was.

But God was ever so patient with me, holding me tightly, yet tenderly and mercifully in the grip of his never failing grace (Ps. 37:24). Day by faithful day, He led me on the path of righteousness and obedience in overcoming the many *self*-centered sin strongholds in my life. And with every victory came greater freedom and deeper joy. As mentioned earlier, there is far too much to share here about all the precious life-giving lessons learned. (We'll do that in Books Two and Three). But let me mention briefly three basic Truths that helped so much in those early years of the breaking/restoration process.

The first has to do with the core verse mentioned earlier that is at the heart of God's solution to the self-esteem problem.

And He was saying to them all, "If anyone wishes to come after Me, let him deny himself, and take up his cross daily, and follow Me" (Luke 9:23).

We've already talked about the meaning of the first part of this verse—deny self—but what does it mean to *take up our cross daily*, and follow Jesus?

It means first of all to identify completely with Jesus—with His mission and purpose. When Jesus came to earth, He had one goal and one goal only in mind—to *do the will of His Father (John 17:4).* Not for one second did He veer from this goal. He followed God's will all the way to the cross. And so I, too, must set my heart to have this same attitude—to follow my Savior wherever He leads me, no matter the cost, and even if it means—a *cross*. But that's not the end of what it means. There's a second part to this *taking up our cross daily*. The cross represents not just the dying and death of Jesus, it is also inextricably and inseparably linked to His resurrection and His glorious *victory over sin and death*. So if we follow Jesus all the way to the cross, we will also follow Him into resurrection glory. Practically speaking, that means that as we come to God each day and in a spirit of humility and sincere contrition, confess our sins (accepting God's forgiveness and Christ's righteousness—1 John 1:9), then relinquish the control of our lives to God's Holy Spirit, we can, and joyfully will, go out in the power and strength of that beautiful cross that <u>has already</u> accomplished for us victory over sin and death and every other obstacle raised up against us! (Is. 54:17; Eph. 1:18–22).

The second major breakthrough in the journey to liberation from the destructive domination of self, came one beautiful spring day in April when God took me to a precious promise in the book of Isaiah:

Is this not the fast (religious practice) that I choose: To loosen the bonds of wickedness, to undo the bands of the yoke, and to let the oppressed go free. Is it not to divide your bread with the hungry, and bring the homeless poor into the house; when you see the naked, to cover him…Then your light will break out like the dawn, and your recovery will speedily spring forth (Is. 58:6–8).

As I placed this verse up against what I had already learned in *Matt. 22:39: you shall love your neighbor as yourself*, along with *Phil. 2:5: do nothing from selfishness or empty conceit, but with humility of mind, let each of you regard one another as more important than himself, do not merely look out for your own personal interests, but also for the interest of others*, I could clearly see God's solution to the *self*-esteem (sin) problem: obedience to these precious promises.

I soon discovered that as I set my heart to obey Is. 58, just as it promised, a beautiful new *light broke out like the dawn* and *my recovery (began) to spring forth*. Looking back on how God worked in doing this,

I see so clearly the Holy Spirit's guiding hand. At first, I was too weak and yet far too *selfish (self-esteemed)* to totally and fully *abandon all*. So, under the guidance of the Holy Spirit, (Is. 28:10), I just set aside 3–4 hours per week to reach out with Jesus' love in some special way. Praying about it, then led by the Holy Spirit, I would visit a widow or shut-in or make a meal for someone who was sick. On other occasions I invited someone who was hurting or lonely into our home for a relaxing lunch or "tea." And I prayed each time for opportunities to share the gospel. God always honored that prayer and several of these precious souls came to saving faith in Jesus—which always brought overwhelming joy! I also discovered that every time I practiced this small "dividing of bread," I was energized and joy flowed in refreshing streams. It was wonderful and the more I did it, the more I truly **wanted** to do it—more! It was like a blessing that just kept giving. There is always joy and blessing in obedience and in sharing God's love with others! (Deut. 30:15–20; Deut. 28).

A third glorious revelation followed adding to the emerging new freedom and joy *(Ps. 30:5)*.

I have been crucified with Christ; and it is no longer I who live, but Christ lives in me…Christ in you, the hope of glory (Gal 2:20; Col. 1:27).

Oh, glorious Truth! My identity would never again be linked to how much selfish, trivial, *self*-esteem I could muster through my achievements or the strokes of approval I received from others. I now had a new identity, *Christ in (me), the hope of glory! (Col. 1:27)*. As I turned my eyes off of myself and onto Jesus and His perfect love, obedience, sacrifice and all that this meant to me—full forgiveness and complete acceptance with the Father, life eternal and everlasting joy—I realized that I now possessed a priceless *new identity* that no man or circumstance could ever again take away from me. And it became my greatest delight to share this glorious good news with as many as I could. I wanted everyone to have what God had so mercifully, so graciously given to me—a totally new, blood bought, fully alive, redeemed, forgiven, clothed in the righteousness of Jesus, identity. It would never again be *self*-esteem that made me valuable; it was "Christ-esteem" (Jesus living in me in all His perfection and resurrection glory!) that made me priceless in the eyes of God (Rom. 5:8; Is. 43:4a).

In gratitude, and overflowing joy, I lifted my hands and my heart to Heaven in praise to God:

Behold, the bondslave of the Lord; be it unto to me according to your Word (Luke 1:38).

Bible Study Supplement

Chapter 6 — Day 3 — God's Solution to the Self-Esteem Problem

1. Read Luke 9:23.

    a. What must all who wish to be Jesus' disciple do? (three things)

    b. In your own words, explain what Jesus meant by this.

Isaiah 58:6–11 is one of the most beautiful, practical promises in Scripture regarding true discipleship and the rewards of obedience. Before we read this text, let's take a moment here to review the context in which it was written.

God is speaking to the apostate children of Israel. (*Apostate* means fallen away from God, from loving and obeying Him.) They have been busily engaged in many religious rituals like fasting and public prayer, but their hearts were far from God and far from what He had instructed them to do. And things weren't going so well for them. So they began to grumble and complain that God was not being fair. After all, here they were being good little righteous people, doing all their religious rituals—doing "good deeds," calling on His name freely, offering sacrifices, fasting, etc.—so why wasn't He blessing them? But God told them that they were selfish, spoiled hypocrites who only did these things for attention and to get a blessing from God. But their hearts were not with God or for God. Their hearts were in getting what they wanted, when they wanted it, and as much as they wanted. That's why the blessings had stopped. Then God, being ever so patient and merciful, promised that if they would repent of their sins, return to Him, and in His strength and joy be about what they were called to be about—loving and helping people and befriending the lonely and the poor—then He would hear, heal, and bless them once again.

Verses 6–8 speak of some of the ways God suggested that they could genuinely share His love with others. They could minister to those under the bondage of sin—encourage them, pray *for* them and *with* them, and tell them the Truths of Scripture that would help them find victory and freedom. They could be hospitable and share their bread with others, or bring someone who had no home or place to go into their home; they could give clothes to those who were needy. The point is, they had to get past their consuming preoccupation with and focus upon themselves in order to see the needs of others and respond in obedience as God led and gave direction. Then God gave them some beautiful promises if they would do this.

2. Read Is. 58:6–11.

    a. What did God say He would do for the people if they repented of their selfishness and began to take a sincere, loving interest in those around them? (four things - vs. 8)

    b. What did He promise to do when they called to Him? (vs. 9)

    c. What other blessings did He promise them? (seven specific blessings - vs. 10,11)

3. Read Matt. 9:13, using the NASB below.

    But go and learn what this means, 'I desire compassion, and not sacrifice,' for I did not come to call the righteous, but sinners (Matt. 9:13).

a. What does God desire?

Oh, that God would give us all hearts of compassion like Jesus had. God doesn't want all our sacrifices of self-motivated, self-seeking, religious "do-goodism." He just wants our hearts. And if He has our hearts, we will become people of compassion who joyfully seek to be about the Father's business, freely and liberally sharing the love of God just as Jesus did.

4. Read Matt. 19:29,30.

    a. What will all who have left houses, brothers and sisters, and father and mother for Jesus' sake receive? (vs. 29)

    b. Who will be first?...last? (vs. 30)

I am totally convinced that if we all really understood and *believed* this verse we would not only find our greatest joy and delight in being a true, humble servant, we would be scrambling to be "last." We would never again strive to *be served* or recognized for our good deeds and accomplishments, knowing that by doing so we receive all the reward we will get (Matt. 6:5). We would, instead, be *storing up treasures in Heaven*—loving and serving others in Jesus' name in gratitude for and out of the overflow of His love for us, knowing that in so doing we will *receive our reward from the Father! (Matt. 6:1–4, cf. Col. 3:24; Rev. 22:12; Luke 6:38).* It would be *pure joy (James 1:2)*, to follow Jesus' example as a loving, compassionate, giving servant, knowing that one day, one glorious day, those who so lived their lives while here upon the earth will indeed be first in the Father's house *for all eternity!*

5. Read John 13:3-5,12-17.

    a. What did Jesus do? (vs. 5)

    b. What has Jesus given us in this beautiful story? (vs. 15)

    c. What promise does He give to all who obey His command to take up the towel and "do as I have done?" (vs. 17)

6. Read Prov. 11:25 noting especially *25b*.

Note: "To water" (KJV/NKJV/NASB) means to "refresh." Please use "refresh" in place of "to water" in your answer:

    a. What happens to those who water/refresh others (share the love of Jesus with others)?

Along with Luke 9:23 that we discussed earlier *(denying self, taking up cross...)*, Phil. 2:3–8 is a pivotal passage in helping us develop a disciple's heart. It is, in fact the practical outworking of Luke 9:23 and should always be linked to it as we seek to develop a true disciple's heart. Luke 9:23 tells us *what* a true disciple does—*denies self, takes up cross daily and follows Jesus*—and Phil. 2:3–8 tells us in practical terms *how* we do this by looking to the example of Jesus.

7. Read Phil. 2:3–8.

    a. What are we not to do? (vs. 3a)

    b. What kind of heart and mind attitude are we to have? (Please read vs. 3 again, then choose from the two answers below).

        1. Proud, selfish, concerned about "my" needs

        2. Loving, humble, compassionate, concerned about the needs of others

    c. How should we regard others? (vs. 3b)

    d. What are we to look out for? (vs. 4)

    e. What kind of attitude are we to have? (vs. 5)

    f. Describe that attitude. (vs. 6–7)

This beautiful picture of discipleship (being a true follower of Jesus) totally debunks the *self-esteem* doctrine. Jesus was God. He had the right to all the privileges, the honor, and the glory of God. Yet, He never tried to grasp this, to claim what was rightfully His. Instead He *emptied Himself* of all His rights in order to be a humble bondservant of His heavenly Father. It's impossible to find even a trace of *self*-esteem in that. Are we willing to follow this precious example of true, humble, faithful, servant obedience?

    g. How far did Jesus go in His commitment to serve the Father in humble obedience? (vs. 8)

What a beautiful example God has given us in Jesus!

God used these verses in Philippians 2 as a real battering ram in bringing down the stronghold of the sinful, selfish, self-centered (as opposed to God-centered) *self-esteem* idolatry in my life. It is a powerful weapon for this purpose. If you are battling a resistant, strong will that refuses to relinquish control in order to fully love, trust and obey Jesus and reach out to others, you will find that reading, meditating upon, praying about and asking God to help you to obey these verses (along with those we studied in Is. 58) will do much in bringing down that stronghold. I have found this practice of inestimable value in keeping my heart soft, my spirit humble and more compassionate, and my will and desires purer, sensitive to the Holy Spirit's convictions and instructions. In such a state, the spirit of *self-**less**-ness* (less of self, more of God and others like Jesus always displayed) is liberated, takes wings and flies ever higher and freer.

May God help us all to become true disciples of Jesus, motivated and spurred on by a heart of compassion, humility, and surrendered, joyful obedience. Such is the life of those who live and move and have their being—*in Jesus*—in the glorious and beautiful *kingdom of God* (Rom. 14:17; Acts 17:28).

Write out a Bible verse that had special meaning to you today.

Based upon what you have learned today, write a prayer to God expressing the desires of your heart in applying these Truths to your life.

Chapter 6 — Day 4
The Very, Very Serious Sin of Idolatry

I am the Lord Your God…You shall have no other gods before Me. You shall not make for yourself an idol, of any likeness…you shall not worship them or serve them (Ex. 20:2–5).

And you will defile your graven images overlaid with silver…you will scatter them as an impure thing, and say to them, "Be gone!" (Is. 30:22).

Foundational Truth #20

I am the Lord Your God…You shall have no other gods before Me. You shall not make for yourself an idol, of any likeness…you shall not worship or serve them. **God talks much about the sin of idolatry in the Bible because it violates the main purpose for which we were created—to know, love and glorify Him. He also warns us about it because He loves us and He wants to protect us from the devastation idolatry always brings to those who practice it.**

Idolatry: Anything or anyone we desire, love, worship, honor or serve more than God.

I am the Lord Your God…You shall have no other gods before Me. You shall not make for yourself an idol, of any likeness…you shall not worship them or serve them (Ex. 20:2–5).

The following is an excerpt from a reflection I wrote a number of years ago while I was still enslaved to the futility and devastating consequences of idolatry, to illustrate how deceptive, destructive, and powerful the sin of idolatry is. The bracketed inserts [ ] are comments given for clarity or added later after gaining wisdom from God's Word.

It had gone on so long: The pain of the affliction [Lupus/CFIDS/Fibromyalgia] along with the awful, merciless, emotional torment that always accompanied it. To escape the pain and confusion of it, I turned to food for comfort. Food became my god to which I ran for help, relief…and many other reasons. When the pain was especially bad, I ate. When I was happy, I ate. When I was sad, I ate. When I was frustrated, I ate. When I was confused, I ate. When I was angry, I ate. I ate and ate in an unrestrained binge, and when I could eat no more I lay in the miry misery of my willful choice: stomach painfully distended, emotions flooded with guilt and an oppressive sense of failure and gloom. But as soon as the pain subsided, the irresistible lure came once more. And with the lure, total amnesia of the pain. All I could remember was the immediate luscious pleasure of every succulent bite. [That is the nature of demonic deception—it produces an overpowering drive for immediate gratification of a sinful lust accompanied by a total blindness—oblivion—to the fleeting nature of the pleasure and the devastating pain that invariably follows]. There was no resisting such a lure. And so, another binge, more guilt, more failure. To relieve the pain, I ran quickly once again to my god of comfort. Yet another binge, more guilt, an even greater sense of futility and failure. The vicious, destructive, cycle could not be stopped—pain, guilt, another binge to relieve the emotional pain of the guilt, which it did not, but only added to it! So, another binge. And on and on it endlessly went…

I did not eat to live, I lived to eat! [The Bible calls it gluttony].

I felt so alone. So trapped. So ashamed. I thought about suicide—often. I made a number of attempts, but somehow I couldn't even succeed at that. I was a total failure; and by that time, a very fat failure, which brought on more anger because I hated being fat! [Sinful selfish pride and vanity].

Though I tried desperately to control it, the sinful obsession with food [idolatry] controlled me. I remember waking up every morning knowing that I had but two dismal choices—both painful, both miserable. I could eat what I wanted, which would mean a total unrestrained binge, self-hatred, and condemnation for losing control and getting fatter, or I could refuse to eat and be absolutely miserable, because as the day wore on, I truly was hungry, and my body needed nourishment. I hated myself for not being able to control the compelling drive inside, and I hated life because no matter what I chose, I was abjectly and utterly miserable.

I sought professional psychological help for this problem off and on for fifteen years, including two years of intense psychotherapy (with its prolific use of drugs). The psychotherapy was superficial and powerless and sent me into an even deeper sense of frustration and failure, anger, and guilt—depression! And the drugs only added to the problems with their endless side-effects and altering of the natural chemistry of my body, resulting in increased emotional instability.

This destructive cycle continued, even after my salvation. As a Christian, I was all the more aware of the wrongness (sinfulness!) of it—that what I was doing was blatant defiance and rebellion against the first commandment (and many other commands of the Bible). And I knew also what I had to do to change the destructive pattern:

1. *Repent!* Turn away from my sinful addiction to food (idolatry) and turn to God in faith and obedience, trusting Him to satisfy all my legitimate needs (1 Thess. 1:9).

2. *Eat for strength and not for gluttony (Eccles.10:17).* Eat wisely and temperately following God's good instructions for healthful nourishment that gives strength to serve Him in carrying out His good purposes for my life (1 Cor. 9:25; Titus 1:8; Gen. 1:29; Lev.11; Deut.14).

Yet, even with this knowledge, I could not do what I knew in my head was right. The binges continued. Less frequently, but nonetheless, they continued, especially in times of stress, failure, or disappointment.

How often my heart cried with Paul, *wretched man that I am; who will set me free from this body of death? (Rom. 7:24).*

Realizing what a terrible reproach I was bringing to the Holy name of God that I now carried as His child, I went to my knees before God pleading for the wisdom, faith, and grace I needed to truly *repent from the heart* and turn from my wicked idolatry. And God was so, so faithful in hearing and answering my cry (Ps.18:6). I was not instantly *healed*. At first this was hard (to be patient) because I so desperately longed to be free of this bondage so that I could serve and glorify God more fully, but now I can see God's wisdom in overcoming this sin in His best way and time. There was so much God needed to teach me that He could not have done any other way (Ps. 119:67,71). As I *continued in His Word (John 8:31),* He taught me many things that I needed to apply to my life so that I could more carefully and consistently overcome my sin, bring glory to Him and fulfill His good purposes for my life. We will not have time to look at all of the lessons here—that we will do in Book Two—but I want to share just a few briefly here to help us all to be more alert to the danger of idolatry and the absolute need to deal with it decisively.

1. *You shall have no other gods before me…Whether, then, you eat or drink or whatever you do, do all to the glory of God (Ex. 20:21; Cor. 10:31).* The most egregious of the many transgressions against God's Holy ordinances that the sin of idolatry involves is the violation of the very first commandment—our main purpose and reason for our creation -- to bring honor and glory to God and to find our greatest joy and satisfaction *in Him*. He is most glorified when we are most satisfied—*in Him*—not in food, football, T.V., computers, videos or soap operas! (Is. 43:7; 1 Cor. 10:31).

2. *For the sorrow that is according to the will of God produces a repentance without regret, leading to salvation; but the sorrow of the world produces death (2 Cor. 7:10).*

It was during this time that I learned the precious life-giving discipline of *godly sorrow*. Up to this point, I had a sorrow *according to the world* that led to a deceptive, insincere (false) repentance. I was sorrowful because of the pain that my sin caused me! I was not, as true godly sorrow causes, sorrowful because of the pain that my sin caused God—the death of His only begotten Son and the defaming of His Holy Name *(John 3:16; 2 Cor. 5:15,20)*. I had never truly repented from the heart, as manifested by *fruits of repentance (Acts 26:20)*.

3. *But I say, walk by the Spirit, and you will not carry out the desires of the flesh (Gal. 5:16).* God's Word showed me that I was attempting to repent and to change my way of responding to the temptation to satisfy my fleshly lusts in my own strength, rather than relying upon the strength and power of the Holy Spirit. (We will talk more about how we do this over the next three days).

4. *For God knows that in the day you eat from it…you will be like God (Gen. 3:6)* God opened my eyes to see that the main "*god*" I had erected in my heart was the god of *self*. Food was merely a deceptive idol formed *by self* to *serve self*. It all goes back to that original sin: *I will make myself like the Most High (Is. 14:14)*. I will be my own *god*, I will have what I want, when I want it, and as much as I want!

An idol is anything we set up in our heart that we desire—and look to—more than God to meet and satisfy our needs. What we desire, we will love, and what we love, we will trust, and what we trust, we will worship, and what we worship, we will serve.

That is exactly what I did. Rather than setting my affections on God—on knowing Him, loving Him, trusting Him, and looking to Him to fulfill my needs and deepest God-given longings—I sat up many idols after my own fashioning to which I ran for satisfaction.

This idolatrous worship of self—satisfying selfish fleshly lusts apart from God—was at the heart of the first rebellion that cast Lucifer out of Heaven, destroyed the Holy image of God in Adam and Eve, and brought sin and death to all mankind.

No wonder God hates idolatry!

God is love—perfect, holy love. Perfect, holy love nurtures, provides, protects, perfects. It also separates—the Holy from the profane so that the Holy will not be defiled and consumed by the profane. How could perfect love ever embrace that which destroys. It is not possible.

And the Word of the Lord came to me saying, "Son of man, these men have set up idols in their hearts and have put right before their faces the stumbling block of their iniquity…Therefore speak to them and tell them, Thus says the Lord God, 'Any man of the house of Israel who sets up idols in his heart…then comes to the prophet, I, the Lord, will be brought to give him an answer in the matter in view of the multitude of his idols, in order to lay hold of the hearts of the house of Israel who are estranged from Me through all their idols" (Ezek. 14:2–5).

For they have turned their back to Me, and not their face; But in the time of their trouble they will say, 'Arise and save us.' But where are your gods which you made for yourself? Let them arise, if they can save you in the time of your trouble; For according to the number of your cities are your gods, O Judah (Jer. 2:27–29).

> *Therefore say to the house of Israel, 'Thus says the Lord God, "Repent and turn away from your idols, and turn your faces away from all your abominations" (Ezek. 14:6).*

God's Word could not be clearer. Idolatry is a wicked abomination against God—against His loving, sovereign (good and protective) rule in our lives.

There is another subject that I want to touch briefly on today and that is the subject of generational curses, for they are very real, powerfully destructive, and intricately linked with the serious sin of idolatry. We need to heed the warnings of God regarding these terrible curses.

> *You shall not make for yourself an idol of any likeness…you shall not worship them or serve them; for I, the Lord your God, am a jealous God, visiting the iniquity of the fathers on the children, on the third and fourth generations of those who hate Me (Ex. 20:4,5).*

Generational curses always wreak a heavy toll in the lives of many! They are devastating. I have both experienced and seen in countless other lives the tragic consequences when God's warnings were not heeded nor His Word obeyed regarding these tormenting vexations.

The word translated "hate" here in Ex. 20:5 (as in other places in the Bible) means "to love less than." When we love God less than anything else, we fall into the trap of idolatry with all its worldly lusts and affections. We begin to worship other people or objects more than God. Our children see this, and they imitate our behavior, falling into the very same idolatrous, unholy, love affair with sin, invoking the curse of sin upon their lives as well. If only parents realized the *power of their example!* But the good news is, Jesus came to break the curse of all sin, including generational sins. They, like all of our sins, were nailed to the cross (Col. 2:14). We don't have to continue living *under the curse*. If we return to God, repent from the heart of these sins of our fathers (that we, following after them, are now committing), put our faith completely in Jesus, making Him Savior and Lord, the curse will be broken. That is an even more important reason why we must be careful that God and God alone is the object of our affections and the one to whom we look for help and the satisfaction of our needs. Then, instead of passing a curse onto our children, we will pass along a blessing (Deut. 30:15–20).

> *Be sure to observe what I am commanding you this day; watch yourself that you make no covenant with the (idolatrous) inhabitants of the land into which you are going, lest it become a snare in your midst. (Ex. 34:11,12)*

Idolatry always becomes a *snare*, trapping its deceived victim in its grip and robbing him of the freedom and joy Jesus came to give us (John 10:10).

May God, through His Word and through His Holy Spirit now living in us, open our eyes today to see the reality and the destructive power of idolatry. And may He help us *to repent from the heart (Rom. 6:17)*, restore God to His rightful position as Lord of all, and in the power that He gives us through His Holy Spirit, *cast away every impure thing raised up against our knowledge of God and obedience to Christ* (God's righteous rule in our hearts) *(Is. 30:22; 2 Cor. 10:5)*.

> *Return to Him from whom you have deeply defected, O sons of Israel. (Is. 31:6)*

> *Therefore, the Lord longs to be gracious to you…He waits on high to have compassion on you…How blessed are all who long for Him…who return to Him and put their trust in His salvation (Is. 30:18; Jer. 3:22; cf. Is. 12:2; Ps. 9:10, 40:4, 62:8, 65:5, 115:9–11, 125:1).*

> *O people in Zion, inhabitant in Jerusalem, you will weep no longer. He will surely be gracious to you at the sound of your cry; when He hears it, He will answer you…And you will defile your graven images…You will scatter them as an impure thing; and say to them, "Be gone!" (Is. 30:19–22, sel.).*

Bible Study Supplement
Chapter 6 — Day 4 — The Very, Very Serious Sin of Idolatry

1. Read Ex. 20:1-6.

   a. What is the first commandment of God? (vs. 3)

   b. In your own words, what does this mean?

   c. Why do you think God made this the first commandment?

   d. What is the second commandment? (vs. 4,5)

Have you ever stopped to consider why God deemed it necessary to make a second commandment warning us against idolatry when He had already told us clearly to have no other gods before Him? We need to think seriously about this and ask God to help us comprehend His concern regarding idolatry because He understands the power and the destruction of the deception associated with it (remember the temptation in the Garden of Eden: *hath God said...* and *the fruit looked good to the eye)*. How easy it is to justify the worship of idols in our heart to satisfy the relentless appetites of our flesh. May God help us to develop a spirit of discernment that cuts through the deceptions of idolatry's many lures.

2. Read Deut. 4:23 (Please use NASB here).

   Deut. 4:23 - So watch yourselves, lest you forget the covenant of the Lord your God, which He made with you, and make for yourselves a graven image in the form of anything against which the Lord your God has commanded you.

   a. What does God warn us about concerning *graven images*? (vs. 23)

A *graven image* is anything we *engrave upon our hearts* to which we look to satisfy us instead of God. It is anything we love and worship more than God. We call these graven images, *"idols of the heart."* An idol of the heart is not only something we love more than God, it is also something that controls us (dictates how we spend our time and the choices we make).

   b. Do you have any *idols of the heart*? If so, list them.

One cannot worship God and an idol at the same time. Remember Jesus' words: *No man can serve two masters* (Matt. 6:24). We must choose every day—and moment by moment through the day—which master we will serve: the devil (through the many idols he tempts us to set up in our hearts), or the *true and living God* (1 Thess. 1:9).

3. Read Deut. 11:16-23.

   a. What is God's loving and clear warning to us? (vs. 16)

   b. What will happen if we disregard His warning? (vs. 17)

   c. What should we do with these *words of God*? (Be very specific - vs. 18–20)

   d. Why? (vs. 22,23)

These are wonderful instructions. The people were to saturate themselves with the precious promises and Truths of God's Word so that there would be no room for the devil's lies and deceptions. They were to impress the Word on their hearts (memorize them); talk about them to their children as they *sat in their houses, walked along the road, when they lay down at night, and when they rose up in the morning* (vs. 19). In other words, all of life was to center around the Word of God—knowing it, loving it, obeying it. They were even to post Scripture verses around the house so they would be surrounded by the Word, a symbol of protection and a reminder of God's faithfulness through His promises. They were to keep the Word of God before them at all times as those who wore frontals. The NIV omits the word "frontal" in *verse 18*. That is an unfortunate oversight as a good deal is lost by this omission. A *frontal or frontlet* (also referred to as a "phylactery" - NASB) was a small box containing Scripture that the people attached to their foreheads with a headband to ever remind them of the central importance and value of the Word of God, keeping it ever before them, *between the eyes* – Deut. 11:18; Ex. 13:16; Deut. 6:8.

4. Read Deut. 7:1-9.

    a. What were the children of Israel to do to the enemies that God would give into their hands? (three things - vs. 2)

    b. What else were they not to do? (vs. 3)

    c. Why? (vs. 4a)

    d. What further instructions were the people to carry out regarding idols? (vs. 5)

    e. Why? (vs. 6)

    f. What had the Lord done for them (and all His redeemed children!)? (vs. 8)

    g. What are we to know? (vs. 9)

    h. How will knowing this and remembering this, help us in our daily walk?

5. Read Jer. 32:28-35.

    a. What provoked God to anger? (vs. 29b, 30a, 33, 34)

    b. What should this knowledge encourage us to do?

Knowing that idolatry hurts God (defames His Holy name) and provokes Him to anger should send us to our knees in godly sorrow. It should also empower us, through the Holy Spirit now living in us, to be careful not to allow any idols to be engraved upon our hearts to which we run for comfort, pleasure, guidance, instead of God. Let's take a moment to review how we can know if something has become an idol in our lives.

Something has become an idol when:

1. We desire, long for, love, or seek it more than God. It is anything to which we look to satisfy our needs rather than God.

2. Our love for and loyalty to this *person, object, desire, or passion* distracts us from fulfilling God's purpose for our lives or causes us to disobey the Word of God. For example, an idol in the form of a

person, could be a husband, wife, boyfriend, girlfriend, children, an actor or actress, etc. An idolatrous *object* might be cigarettes, alcohol, drugs, food, TV, videos, cars, sports, our body—how we look, our physical fitness, or athletic abilities. *Desires* that have become idolatrous might include a sinful lust for money, material possessions, popularity, fame. Similarly *passions* can take on any of innumerable forms (graven images): an obsessive drive to excel, to be successful in the eyes of the world in order to win the approval of man. It may also be a consuming quest for worldly pleasure, such as hobbies that we pursue more than God and His glory, i.e., sports (golf, tennis, football), travel, participation in luxury spas or health clubs that pamper the flesh, anything that is pursued to satisfy the appetites of the flesh as opposed to pleasing God, etc. [Note! None of the things above are necessarily sinful in or of themselves. *God gives us all things, richly to enjoy!* (1 Tim. 6:17). But they most certainly do become idols when we begin to treasure (seek after) them more than we treasure God, His glory and the fulfilling of His will for our lives].

Please hear God's heart in all this. Idols are false gods that deceive, distract, and destroy by getting our eyes off God and His good purposes. They also defile the holy image of God within us. Idols can never help us or add anything to our lives. They only cause us to sin and break our precious fellowship with God, who is the source of all that is truly good, profitable, and fulfilling. Remember our study of how God created us in His image to have a loving, growing relationship with Him, and that in and through this relationship, we bring glory to Him and fulfill His good plans for our lives (Eph. 2:10; Jer. 29:11-14). It is only in desiring God, clinging to Him above all else and following Him that these special purposes for which we were created are fulfilled. The result: He gets the glory, and we get the JOY (John 15:11, 17:18).

Write out a Bible verse that had special meaning to you today.

Before you write your prayer today, go back to question 2b. Confess any graven idol that may yet occupy a place in your heart and ask God to give you the biblical wisdom and Holy Spirit-enabled power to *cast them out and scatter them as an impure thing... that you may prove yourselves to be blameless and innocent, children of God above reproach in the midst of a crooked and perverse generation, among whom you appear as lights in the world, holding fast the Word of Life* (Is. 30:22; Phil. 2:15,16).

Chapter 6 — Day 5
The Person and Ministry of the Holy Spirit: Part 1
Who Is the Holy Spirit? What Does He Do?

And I will ask the Father, and He will give you another Helper, that He may be with you forever, that is, the Spirit of Truth (John 14:16,17).

Foundational Truth #21

God is Triune. "Tri" – three, "Une" – one. Three persons, one God: God the Father, God the Son, God the Holy Spirit. All are co-equal in nature and power but function in different roles. God the Father serves as the authority figure providing protection, provision, and order much the way the husband/father functions in the family. God, the Son, is the Savior/Redeemer—the means of salvation through whom others are brought into the family of God. The third person is the Holy Spirit, who lovingly *draws* men to God by bringing conviction of sin and the awareness of a need for God through the conscience. He is also the one who performs the miracle of regeneration (new birth), then empowers the *born again* believer to live a new, righteous life, enjoying the bounties of God's blessings and provision.

Writing in his book, *The Full Blessing of Pentecost*, Andrew Murray says: "The church of today is suffering for the lack of one thing only, the heavenly enduement of power (through the Holy Spirit) which made the apostolic Church triumphant." (*How Can I be Filled with the Holy Spirit?*, Armin Gesswein, Christian Publications, Inc., Camp Hill, PA, 1999, p. 4).

And I will ask the Father, and He will give you another Helper, that He may be with you forever, that is, the Spirit of Truth…and you shall receive power when the Holy Spirit has come upon you (John 14:16,17; Acts 1:8).

God never intended His children to go through life in this fallen, sinful world beset with trials and tribulations, turmoil and troubles, alone. That's why He gave us the wonderful gift of the Holy Spirit to indwell us and secure us in God's never failing love, joy, and peace and to strengthen and guide us with His wisdom, power and provision (Gal. 5:16–25; John 7:38).

One of the saddest realities in the body of Christ today is a lack of solid (accurate) biblical preaching and teaching concerning the person and ministry of the Holy Sprit. Because of this failure, the body of Christ is spiritually weak and ill-equipped for the intensity of today's spiritual warfare. And we are surrounded by the tragic results: personal and interpersonal conflict, the breakdown of the family, chronic physical and spiritual debilitation, fruitlessness.

To illustrate, let me share another event from my own spiritual pilgrimage. The year was 1993. I had been a Christian about ten years. I was no less enthusiastic about studying the Word of God at this point than I had been in the beginning. In fact, the hunger and thirst for the things of God was even greater because the more I studied and learned, the more I realized I did not know. The vast riches of God's wisdom as revealed in his Word truly are *inexhaustible, sweeter than honey* and *more precious than gold (Rom. 11:33; Ps. 19:10)*. I eagerly completed a number of in-depth Bible studies. I also attended biblical training seminars and devoured countless books, commentaries, teaching tapes, and videos on the Bible and the Christian walk. Then something very dramatic happened to me. I think it is worth sharing.

"You don't know what we are talking about, Gloria. You can't understand it because you have never experienced it. You will never know the fullness of joy and power that we know until you experience *the Second Blessing*. You can stay where you are in your boxed-in, fundamental beliefs if you want, but not me. I'm going for it. I want it all and don't try to stop me!" With those words spoken in bitter tones and a look of condemnation in her eyes, Mandy turned and walked away. I was left trembling in confusion and hurt. At this point in my life, Mandy was my best friend and confidant: The one with whom I had talked and shared and laughed and cried, had tea parties, lunches and dinners (along with our husbands) and done all sorts of other things that build friendship and love. We even got together every Friday morning and studied the Bible together. We'd been through a lot together these past five years—good times and hard times that had drawn us close. We were best of friends, we really cared about one another until . . .

Mandy had recently met another girl in town who had invited her to her church. She had accepted the invitation and attended with her new friend for the past several Sundays along with accompanying her to some other *special meetings*. At one of these meetings, Mandy got "baptized with the Holy Spirit." Something in that experience changed her dramatically. It was like she was a different person. The soft and gentle sweetness that I had always admired in her had been replaced by an unrecognizable arrogance and critical spirit. She boasted of a new power and a fuller spirituality. The close relationship we had known for the past five years couldn't bridge the gap between the new Mandy and me. And she made it clear that she had something I did not; therefore, it would be impossible for us to maintain the friendship we had before, because we could no longer communicate; we no longer spoke the same *language*. This was totally confusing to me. I could not understand what had changed so suddenly and so drastically that we could not even be friends any longer. I still spoke the same language that I had always spoken—one that Mandy had no trouble understanding before…and I hers. Surely, we could still be friends. I went to visit Mandy to try to talk it out. After all, we were both Christians and we loved the Lord and that hadn't changed. But Mandy was not interested. She was afraid I would try to pull her down from her new climb to "higher" spiritual ground. After repeated attempts and just as many failures, it seemed Mandy was right. We could no longer communicate. The beautiful relationship that we shared all those years was suddenly destroyed. It hurt deeply.

This was not the first time I had been accused of being a second-class Christian, incomplete and missing the essential power of the Christian life: the power that comes through the *baptism of the Holy Spirit*. In my deep desire to understand this better that I might become all that God had saved me to be, I had read scores of books about the person and ministry of the Holy Spirit, the Spirit-filled life, etc. I sincerely and earnestly sought the fullness of the Spirit's indwelling presence and control. I had attended special, "anointed" services where the baptism of the Holy Spirit was taught and "given." I had had hands laid on me as I and all those around me prayed for this *Second Blessing* experience. Yet, I never "got it"; I never spoke in tongues or received special revelations. In recent months, a number of charismatic Christians had confronted me—some not too kindly—with their concern over my incomplete, impotent spirituality. Because I did not speak in tongues and because I had problems in my life over which I was not demonstrating total victory continually, it was clear that I had never received the *Second Blessing*. I was, in their words, "spiritually weak, incomplete, and ineffective." With each accusation I grew more and more confused and discouraged. I did want the fullness of all God offers that I might fully glorify Him.

Was I a second-class Christian? Was I walking in only partial power and victory? The experience with my friend Mandy was the final event in the long series of difficult, oft painful experiences that drove me into a deeper search into God's Word for His Truth about this critical subject: the person and role of the Holy Spirit. I knew that God was not *the author of confusion* and that if I *searched diligently, with all my heart*, He would *teach me* and I would *know His Truth* and *His Truth would, once more, set me free* (1 Cor. 14:33; John 14:26; Jer. 29:13).

I mention this story because I think there are many today who find themselves where I was at that particular time in my life—confused, discouraged, feeling very much like a second-class Christian and spiritual failure. So let's break the Bread of Life once more and clear up some of the confusion about this very important Person in the Godhead—the Comforter, Friend, and Power from on High—that Jesus promised He would send to us to help us and empower us for ministry (John 14:16,26). What does the Bible say about the Holy Spirit? Who is He? What role does He play in the Christian's life? Is there a "Second Blessing"? What is the *baptism of the Holy Spirit*? How can I be filled with and walk in the fullness of the Holy Spirit—moment by moment, day by day?

In the beginning, God created the heavens and the earth…and the Spirit of God was moving over the surface of the waters (Gen. 1:1,2).

First of all, the Holy Spirit is "God." He is the third person of the Trinity—God the Father, God the Son, and God the Holy Spirit. He was present and participated in the creation of the *heavens and the earth*. He is, therefore, a "He," not an "it" or a mysterious "universal force." He is an individual personality as unique and distinct in character as God the Father and God the Son.

And I will ask the Father, and He will give you another Helper, that He may be with you forever; that is the Spirit of Truth, whom the world cannot receive, because it does not behold Him or know Him, but you know Him because He abides with you, and will be in you (John 14:16–17).

The Greek word for "Helper" (also translated "Comforter") is *Parakletos* and means "one of the same kind, called alongside to assist." This means that the Holy Spirit would be of the same kind as Jesus. He would be exactly like Jesus, having all the characteristics and nature of Jesus. In other words, Jesus was God in flesh, the Holy Spirit is God in Spirit, whom God would send to indwell us after Jesus returned to Heaven. Therefore, the very likeness and Spirit of Jesus would be in all who make a genuine profession of faith and received Jesus as their personal Lord and Savior. That's what is meant by *Christ in you the hope of glory (Col. 1:27)*, for indeed, through the indwelling Holy Spirit, Christ *is* in every born again believer. Because the *Parakletos* has been given to come alongside to help, or assist, He does not work apart from, instead of, or in spite of us, but He works *with* us, *in* us, and *through* us.

In His commentary on John 14, Warren Wiersbe says concerning the Holy Spirit:

> Our English word for comfort comes from the Latin words meaning "with strength." We usually think of "comfort" as soothing someone, consoling him or her; and to some extent this is true. But true comfort strengthens us to face life bravely and keep on going. It does not rob us of responsibility or make it easy for us to give up. Some translations call the Holy Spirit "the Encourager" and this is a good choice of words. (Wiersbe, *The Bible Exposition Commentary*, Vol. 1 p.352)

We will be looking at this role (comforter) and other characteristics of the Holy Spirit in the Bible Study Supplement today and again next week. I hope that you find this study of the work and ministry of the Holy Spirit as exciting and encouraging as I always do!

Before we close our meditation today, however, let me just go back to the story I shared with you at the beginning about my friend, Mandy. This was such a sad experience for me. But it did *work for good (Rom. 8:28)*, as it drove me into a much deeper study of the Word of God concerning the ministry of the Holy Spirit. And I learned so much that has been of priceless value in my Christian walk. As I studied, I was reminded again and again of the danger of seeking a sign, wonder, or manifestation of power. Jesus warned:

> *An evil and adulterous generation seeks after a sign; and a sign will not be given it...for false Christs and false prophets will arise...with all the deception of wickedness...that is, the activity of Satan and will show power and great signs and false wonders, so as to mislead, if possible, even the elect (Matt. 16:4, 24:24; 2 Thess. 2:9,10).*

Whenever we seek a supernatural sign or manifestation of power, we open ourselves to demonic activity in the spirit realm where Satan is always at work with all *deception of wickedness.*

I wish I could say the story of Mandy had a happy ending. It did not. Shortly after this experience, Mandy got involved with another man, divorced her husband, and moved away to another part of the country. I never heard from her after that.

Sadly, what Mandy "got" must have been a deceptive false spirit because the Holy Spirit would never divide brothers and sisters. He is, rather, always at work *uniting* God's people so they can be more effective in ministry and better honor and glorify God (John 13:34,35, 17:21–23). Also, the Holy Spirit never manifests Himself in a proud or arrogant way. Jesus was the most humble man that ever walked the face of the earth (Phil. 2:7,8). And the Holy Spirit is like Jesus, in character and nature (John 14:16). Thirdly, the Holy Spirit would never lead any one in a way that contradicts God's Word (i.e., divorce—because God loves his people and he knows the awful hurt and pain divorce always causes). Let's heed Jesus' warnings and be careful not to seek "the gift" (signs, wonders, manifestations of power), but rather let us seek the Giver of all gifts: "God" in His triune majesty and glory, God the Father, God the Son, and God the Holy Spirit. Then we will find, not just a temporary sign or wonder but a glorious, never ending *river of living water.*

> *Now on the day...of the great feast, Jesus stood...saying, "He who believes in Me, as the Scripture said, 'From his innermost being shall flow rivers of living water'" (John 7:37,38).*

Bible Study Supplement

Chapter 6 — Day 5 — The Person and Ministry of the Holy Spirit: Part 1

1. Read Genesis 1:1,2.

    a. Where was the Holy Spirit when the earth was created? (vs. 2)

2. Read Gen. 1:26.

    a. What did God say? (vs. 26a)

    b. From what we studied earlier and from Gen. 1:2, that you just read, who is "Us"?

The story of Ananias and Sapphira is a pivotal text confirming the *deity* of the Holy Spirit.

3. Read Acts 5:1-4.

    a. To whom did Ananias lie? (vs. 3)

    b. Who does the Bible clearly say He (the Holy Spirit) is? (vs. 4b)

So the Holy Spirit is not an *it* or an impersonal *force*. The Holy Spirit is a person—the third person of the Holy Trinity of God ("Trinity" is the noun form of the adjective, Triune, meaning three persons, one God). He is as much "God" as God the Father and God the Son.

4. Read Matt. 3:16,17.

    a. What did Jesus see immediately when He was baptized? (vs. 16)

    b. What did the voice from Heaven say? (vs. 17)

Here we see once again the Trinity of God revealed: God the Father and God the Holy Spirit joining together to confirm God the Son.

Now let's look at the various roles the Holy Spirit plays in the world at large and later in the life of every believer.

5. Read John 16:8.

    a. What is the Holy Spirit continually doing in the world?

The Bible tells us that the Spirit of God is always *at work* in the world *convicting men of sin and righteousness and judgment*. That is, before a person comes to accept Jesus as his personal Lord and Savior, the Holy Spirit, in compassionate, unconditional love, speaks to the conscience, bringing an awareness (conviction) of sin and of the person's separation from God and need for salvation. He then works to *draw him to God* through various reminders of God's presence and love. For example, through glorious displays of God's awesome creation—those breathtaking sunrises and sunsets, a star studded night, the incredible beauty and creative genius found in the thousands of species of birds, sea creatures, animals, flowers and flora. Or it may be through the kindness and witness of a caring friend or relative. The Holy Spirit is always at work...*drawing men to God* (John 6:44). After this He works in redeemed hearts to make them like Jesus (righteous, holy). He also makes known in the conscience the coming judgment of God—for the Christian a continual source of hope and joyous anticipation; for the unbeliever, fear and dread.

6. Read John 3:3-6.

   a. What must happen to a person in order to enter the kingdom of God? (vs. 3)

   b. Who does this work? (vs. 5b,6)

Here we see the primary role of the Holy Spirit: the role of regeneration. Remember that ever since the fall, all people are born with a "dead"—sinful, separated from God—soul. Whenever anyone listens to the gospel message with an open, receptive heart, then responds by confessing his sin, asking for forgiveness and inviting Jesus into His heart to be His Lord and Savior, the Spirit enters the spiritually "dead" soul and quickens it—breathes life into it so that it is made alive once again and reunited in fellowship with God, just as God originally breathed the "breath of life" into man's body at the time of creation in the Garden of Eden. It is this restored *breath of life*—the indwelling Holy Spirit—that causes the person to experience the awesome miracle of the spiritual new birth, to be *born again, or born from above* (John 3:3-6; 1 John 3:1).

7. Read Eph. 1:13,14.

   a. What happens the moment we believe and accept Jesus into our hearts? (13b,14a)

Note: In biblical days the official seal of a King was of utmost importance. It confirmed the authenticity/ownership of the contents of a letter or package. It *proved* unarguably that what was contained inside the envelope was coming directly from the one whose identity was made clear in the seal. In this case the "seal" is *the Holy Spirit Himself* who comes into the heart of every genuine *born again* believer proving the authenticity of his birth into the Kingdom of God. It is the validation from God that says: "This child belongs to Me; He is *My son...My daughter*. This validation for the believer is manifested as that rock-solid, indisputable, unshakable assurance that affirms: I know that I know that I know that I am a child of God; I have been *born again* into the Kingdom of God and I will spend eternity with God in Heaven.

   b. Do you have this seal of the Holy Spirit?

Immediately following our regeneration and the sealing of our eternal destiny within our hearts, the Holy Spirit begins another critical work in our lives that continues until our translation into full glory in the *heavenly* Kingdom of God.

8. Read 2 Thess. 2:13,14. (Please use NASB here to answer the questions).

   13 But we should always give thanks to God for you, brethren beloved by the Lord, because God has chosen you from the beginning for salvation through sanctification by the Spirit and faith in the Truth

   14 And it was for this He called you through our gospel, that you may gain the glory of our Lord Jesus Christ.

   a. For what has God chosen us? (vs. 13)

   b. How is this achieved in our life? (through two means) (vs. 13b)

   c. Who does the work of *sanctification?* (vs. 13b)

   d. In what will this work result? (vs. 14b)

Jesus had much to say about the Holy Spirit—His role on the earth and in each of our lives—while He was on the earth. The Holy Spirit was the main topic of His discussion with His disciples in the upper room the very night He was betrayed and willingly went to the cross for our redemption. Jesus was preparing the disciples for the difficult days ahead of them.

9. Read John 14:16,17.

   a. What did Jesus say that He would ask the Father to do? (vs. 16)

   b. How long would this Person be with the disciples (and all believers)? (vs. 16)

   c. What two names does Jesus give the Holy Spirit? (vs. 16b, 17a)

In this beautiful discourse about the role of the Holy Spirit, Jesus gives Him two names: "Comforter" (or "Helper") and "Spirit of Truth." (Note: the NIV translates "Comforter," as "Counselor." Though this is definitely a role of the Holy Spirit, in this case "Comforter" is a more accurate translation here.

10. Read John 16:7.

    a. What did Jesus say would be an *advantage*...and why do you think he said this? (vs. 7)

When Jesus was on the earth physically, He could only be in one place at one time, but when He went back to His Father in Heaven and sent the Holy Spirit, He (the Spirit) would dwell in every person's heart individually and would, therefore, be personally with each of them at all times giving love, joy, peace, comfort, strength.

The other Word ascribed to the Holy Spirit by Jesus is *Spirit of Truth*. Let's look at what God tells us about this aspect of the ministry of the Holy Spirit.

11. Read John 16:13,14.

    a. What will the "Spirit of Truth" do for all *born again* believers? (two things - vs. 13)

    b. What else will He do? Please turn back to John 14:26 to answer this question.

    c. What will His main purpose be in all that He does? (John 16:14a)

It is so important to remember that one of the main purposes of the Holy Spirit is to glorify Jesus. And because He now lives in us, that is what we will desire to do as well.

It is the Holy Spirit who illumines the Word in our hearts, and comes alongside to enable us to understand and to obey the Word of God and thus have fellowship with the Father, with the Son, with Himself...and with one another! The Holy Spirit is our comforter, our friend, our teacher, and our guide who leads us into all Truth. How can we ever thank God enough for this precious gift—the gift of the Holy Spirit, living in us, empowering us and sealing upon our hearts our eternal destiny as children of God forever! The reality of all that God has given to us in the person of the blessed Holy Spirit sank into my heart like never before as I was preparing these lessons, and I found myself singing over and over with heartfelt gratitude and joy:

> Blessed assurance, Jesus is mine! O what a foretaste of glory divine!
> Heir of salvation, purchase of God, born of His Spirit, washed in his blood.
>
> Perfect submission, perfect delight; visions of rapture now burst on my sight.
> Angels descending, bring from above, echoes of mercy, whispers of love.

Perfect submission, all is at rest; I in my Savior am happy and blest
Watching and waiting, looking above; filled with his goodness, lost in his love.

This is my story, this is my song: Praising my Savior all the day long;
This is my story, this is my song: Praising my Savior all the day long.

Today would be a good day to sing this song again…*Praising our Savior all the day long*.

Write out a Bible verse that had special meaning to you today.

Based upon what you have learned today, write a prayer to God expressing the desires of your heart in applying these Truths to your life.

Chapter 7

Memory verse: *Be filled with the Spirit…walk by the Spirit, and you will not carry out the desire of the flesh (Eph. 5:18; Gal. 5:16).*

Bonus memory verse: *Come, let us go up to the mountain of the Lord…that He may teach us His ways and that we may walk in his paths (Micah 4:2).*

Day 1
The Person and Ministry of the Holy Spirit – Part 2
Living a Spirit-Filled Life: What Does It Mean? How Do I Do It?

Day 2
The Person and Ministry of the Holy Spirit – Part 3
Clearing Up Confusion about the Baptism of the Holy Spirit, Water Baptism, Quenching the Spirit

Day 3
The Unpardonable Sin…Beware! Take Heed! Grave Danger Ahead
The Tragedy of a Reprobate Mind

Day 4
The Very Real Pain and Problem of…FEAR

Day 5
Come, Let Us Go Up to the Mountain of the Lord

Day 6
Closing Thoughts and a Preview of Things to Come

Chapter 7 — Day 1
The Person and Ministry of the Holy Spirit: Part 2
Living a Spirit-Filled Life: What Does It Mean? How Do I <u>Do It</u>?

> *Be filled with the Spirit...walk by the Spirit, and you will not carry out the desire of the flesh...Now those who belong to Christ Jesus have crucified the flesh with its passions and desires. If we live by the Spirit, let us also walk by the Spirit (Eph. 5:18; Gal. 5:16,24,25).*

And they said to one another, "Were not our hearts burning within us while He was speaking to us on the road, while He was explaining the Scriptures to us?" (Luke 24:32).

As I was working on these meditations on the Holy Spirit, I felt my heart *strangely warmed* so often like the disciples on the road to Emmaus when they were joined by Jesus and He *opened the Word of God to them* in ways they had never before understood *(Luke 24:27,45)*. To think that God Himself now *dwells in me* in the form of the Holy Spirit is a reality that is too great and too wonderful to fully comprehend. But I know that it is true because God says it is true (John 14:16,17) and *God cannot lie (Titus 1:2)*. And I know that it is true because every day I feel the warmth, the assurance and the joy of His abiding Presence and I know that He will never *leave me nor forsake me (Heb. 13:5)*. I experience His Presence in a special way also, as I come to the Word of God and listen as He, the *Spirit of Truth guides me into all Truth (John 16:13)*. No wonder the Holy Spirit is called the *Comforter*. But there is another aspect of the Holy Spirit I am just now beginning to understand and, by faith, live.

And behold, I am sending forth the promise of My Father upon you...And you shall receive power when the Holy Spirit has come upon you; and you shall be My witnesses both in Jerusalem, and in all Judea and Samaria, and even to the remotest part of the earth (Luke 24:49; Acts 1:8).

The word translated *power* is *dunamis* from which we get our word dynamite. It means mighty power, extraordinary ability, strength, abundance, supernatural capabilities. Jesus sent that *power from on high* in the form of the Holy Spirit on the day of Pentecost, fifty days after Passover, and just seven days after He ascended back to His Father in Heaven. That very same power, the Holy Spirit, remained here on earth to indwell every born again believer since.

It is the Holy Spirit that gives us the power to live the Christian life and to fulfill all God's good plans for us with divine wisdom, confident assurance, and overcoming strength and joy.

But in a practical sense, how does this happen? Does being filled and empowered by the Holy Spirit just happen—automatically—or must I *do* something to make it a reality in my life?

Do not get drunk with wine, for that is dissipation, but be filled with the Spirit (Eph. 5:18).

Here is the answer to the filling/empowering of the Holy Spirit. We are commanded by God to *be filled* with the Holy Spirit. So, being filled is *not* an automatic thing. We must obey God's command to *be filled*. It is not a matter of "getting" the Holy Spirit. The Bible is clear that all who have received Christ *have* the Holy Spirit living in them (Acts 2:33; 1 Cor. 12:13; Eph. 1:13; Rom. 5:5; 2 Tim. 1:14; Titus 3:5,6). It is a matter of allowing the Holy Spirit to "get"—*have control of*—us, that He might *fill us* from the inside. This He will gladly do as we yield our lives to Him, and, in faith, with a heart towards obedience, *ask* Him *(Luke 11:13)*. In other words, God is not going to fill us with dunamis power to do *our thing*. He will, however, gladly fill us with dunamis power to accomplish all *His good purposes* for our lives. So if we want to live a truly joyous, fulfilling, Spirit filled and empowered life, we must set our hearts toward heaven and being about the *Father's business*.

It is also interesting to note that the command to *be filled* with the Holy Spirit is associated with getting drunk with wine. In the latter case, the one who is totally inebriated is so full of wine that he loses control. It is the wine that now controls him. But *wine is a mocker that leads to dissipation*—foolishness and embarrassment *(Prov. 20:1; Eph. 5:18)*. On the other hand if we allow the Holy Spirit to *fill us* to the point that we are no longer in control, but rather *He* is in control, then we will be imbued with *power from on high*—love and joy, peace, strength and all those good qualities that the Holy Spirit *is* and produces in all who are filled with *Him*.

But you can't fill something that is already full. It you try to do this, all the new will only spill out, being of no value to the vessel that is already full. In this case, what we are full of is our old sinful nature and desires which filled (controlled and directed) our lives completely until we were born from above and received our new nature which is controlled by the Holy Spirit. So now we have two natures very much alive within us: the old fallen nature (self); and the new redeemed nature: the image of God that is being restored. So it is a surrender and control issue. Whichever *nature* we are surrendered to (yielded to, obedient to, allowing to rule) is the one that we will be full of and, therefore, the one that will be in control.

We can't be filled with (controlled by) our sinful nature (fallen fleshly lusts and desires) and the Holy Spirit at the same time. Be sure these two are always in conflict *(Gal. 5:17)*. We must *choose* which one we will yield to and obey. Next to our salvation, this daily decision is one of the most important we will make for the rest of our lives! The Bible is clear about the results:

For the one who sows to (yields to and obeys) his own flesh shall from the flesh reap corruption, but the one who sows to (yields to and obeys) the Spirit shall from the Spirit reap…love, joy, peace, blessing, confidence, contentment, a clear conscience…and eternal life (Gal. 6:8, 5:22; Deut. 28:2–6; Heb. 10:35; 1 Tim. 1:5. 2, 6:6; cf, Deut. 30:15–20; Eph. 1:2–21, 2:1–6, 3:16–20).

If we want to be one of those precious productive, fruitful *vessels of honor* spoken of in 2 Tim. 2:21, we must continually be sowing to the Spirit, trusting and obeying Him as He leads us and pours into us righteousness, wisdom, and *power from on high*.

Therefore, if a man cleanses himself from these things (sinful, fleshly desires and lusts of the old nature), he will be a vessel for honor, sanctified, useful to the Master, prepared for every good work (2 Tim. 2:21).

So the word *filled* in *Eph. 5:18*, more accurately could be translated "surrendered and yielded to, completely under the control of." And whomever we are surrendered to and completely under the control of, we obey, and whom we obey, we serve, and whom we serve, we worship, and whom we worship, we love. Don't ever lose sight of the fact that the Holy Spirit *is* <u>God</u>. So when we yield to Him and trust and obey Him, we are loving and serving God. Likewise, when we rebel against the Holy Spirit's control, we are, in reality, rebelling against God (Acts 5:1–5).

It is important to note also that this imperative verb *be filled* is in the aorist tense, which means a continual (as opposed to completed) action. We are to *be filled* and *keep on being filled* continually. That is what the Bible means by walking by the Spirit. It means that as I go through my day, I must continually yield myself to the control of the Holy Spirit—listening carefully, trusting, obeying—as *He* leads. At first this will be very difficult, because the flesh is very strong; it *wars against the Spirit* and is *continually in opposition to it (Gal. 5:17)*. But the more I practice this good discipline—dying to self, continually yielding to, trusting and obeying the Spirit—the more victory I experience and the stronger becomes my regenerated new godly nature. I begin to long for a greater and greater filling—surrendered dependency upon the Holy Spirit—knowing that by so doing, I am empowered to do all God's good purposes. And it is only when I am fully engaged in that—being about *the Father's business (Luke 2:49)*—that I experience those provisional waters of the Holy Spirit flowing in unending streams of love, joy peace…wisdom, strength, endurance.

> *Now we have received, not the spirit of the world, but the Spirit who is from God, that we might know the things freely given to us by God…Thy Word is a lamp unto my feet and a light unto my path…For the Word of God is living and active and sharper than any two-edged sword (1 Cor. 2:12–14 ; Ps. 119:105; Heb. 4:12).*

The Holy Spirit speaks to us—leads us and guides us—primarily through the Word of God. He takes the Word of God and quickens it (makes it alive) in our hearts so that we can understand it, and He then gives us the power to obey it (1 Cor. 2:12–14; Heb. 4:12; Eph. 3:16–20).

Therefore, we can be sure that:

God's Holy Spirit will never lead us in a way that contradicts God's Word!

So, now that we are filled, what are we to do?

> *…speaking to one another in psalms and hymns and spiritual songs…singing and making melody with your heart to the Lord;…giving thanks for all things in the name of our Lord Jesus Christ to God (Eph. 5:19–21).*

With thanksgiving and joy, Spirit-filled people share God's love and wonderful good news with others. *Hymns and spiritual songs* were the Word of God put to music. We can't *speak to one another in psalms and hymns and spiritual songs* if we do not know the Word of God. It is the Word of God—knowing it, obeying it—that puts the song in our hearts that we love to share and sing with others—the song of God's great love, salvation and glorious eternal future.

There is another way that God leads us by His Holy Spirit:

> *Then He said, "Go out, and stand on the mountain before the Lord." And behold, the Lord passed by. And a great and strong wind tore into the mountains and broke the rocks in pieces before the Lord; but the Lord was not in the wind; and after the wind an earthquake; but the Lord was not in the earthquake. And after the earthquake a fire; but the Lord was not in the fire; and after the fire a still small voice (1 Kings 19:11,12, NKJV).*

The Holy Spirit is a gentle comforter and guide. He does not shout or rail. He leads us in a quiet, soft, voice. So we can be sure, if we are hearing shoutings and railings, it is not the Holy Spirit speaking to us. It is another spirit, and we'd best beware and stand strong against it (1 John 4:1).

It is so encouraging to be reminded once again in the above Scripture (1 Kings 19) of God's perspective of life. Life in a fallen world will involve times when great and strong winds blow against us (the railings of the enemy through the temptations of the world and the lusts of the flesh), but take comfort, God is not *in them*; they are but wind over which God has full control (Mark 4:35–41). And what about those earthquakes—those sudden onslaughts of trials and tribulations orchestrated by the devil to shake our confidence and stir up fret, fear and worry? God is not *in them* either. Like the wind, they too must obey His commands (Mark 4:39; Psalm 119:91b). Then there are those flames that threaten to burn up all that we hold dear? God is not *in them* either. He is, rather, the *fourth man in the fiery furnace* protecting His own so that not a hair on the head is singed! (Dan. 3:24–28). That is why it is so critical to have a daily quiet time with God every day, so that God's Holy Spirit may quiet our soul and open our eyes and ears to the Words and Ways of God—*God's perspective* on life. We really do need to *be still, and know* that God is still God and *He holds all things in His sovereign, loving power (Psalm 46:10; Is. 46:9,10)*. Each day as we read and study God's Word and as we fellowship with Him in prayer, God's still small voice comes to us through the Holy Spirit comforting, reassuring, and directing us in God's good plans for our life.

But I say, walk by the Spirit, and you will not carry out the desires of the flesh…from your innermost being will flow rivers of living water (Gal. 5:16; John 7:38).

What a precious promise! As we walk in surrendered obedience to (filled with) the Holy Spirit, we will not *carry out the destructive desires of the flesh*. Rather, God's love and joy, wisdom and discernment, will continually flow into and through us like *rivers of living water (John 7:38)*.

So the secret to living the *dunamis* (mighty power, extraordinary strength, abundant) *Spirit-filled life* is simply to *be filled* and *keep on being filled* with the Holy Spirit. This we do by yielding our lives to the Holy Spirit's control, and asking Him to fill us to overflowing with His dunamis love, joy, peace, patience…wisdom, power, strength, etc., then walk in trusting obedience as He leads. There will be joy in the journey as long as we do this because we are no longer relying upon our own strength and provision, but upon the limitless resources of the Spirit of God who has promised to supply *all that we need according to His riches in glory in Christ Jesus (Phil. 4:19; cf. Luke 11:9–13; Eph. 3:16–20).*

So the church throughout all Judea…enjoyed peace, being built up; and, going on in the fear of the Lord and in the comfort of the Holy Spirit (Acts 9:31).

Bible Study Supplement

Chapter 7 — Day 1 — The Person and Ministry of the Holy Spirit: Part 2
Living a Spirit-Filled Life: What does it mean? How do I <u>Do It</u>?

1. Read Acts 1:8.

    a. What did Jesus promise the disciples would receive?

2. Read Acts 2:1–11.

    a. What rested upon the heads of the disciples as the wind filled the house? What did this represent? (vs. 3,4)

    b. What were they able to do as a result of the Holy Spirit's empowerment? (vs. 4,6,8,11)

Note: What is spoken of here is not some strange "angelic" or mystical "Holy Ghost" language that no one understood. It was clearly languages and dialects of other countries that the disciples had never learned through formal education or personal study. Do you see God's heart for evangelism here? He cared about every soul that gathered that day and He made sure they all heard the gospel in their own heart language. What a beautiful way to begin the evangelization of the world.

3. Read Acts 4:23–31.

    a. What did the disciples ask God to do for them? (vs. 29b)

    b. What characterized the disciples after they were filled with the Spirit (vs. 31b)

4. Read Eph. 5:15-18. Please use the NASB translation here to answer the questions below.

    (15) Therefore be careful how you walk, not as unwise men, but as wise

    (16) making the most of your time, because the days are evil.

    (17) So then do not be foolish, but understand what the will of the Lord is.

    (18) And do not get drunk with wine, for that is dissipation, but be filled with the Spirit.

    a. How are we to walk? (three characteristics - vs. 15,16)

    b. What does God say we are not to be? What are we to understand? (vs. 17)

    c. What is God's will for us? (vs. 18b)

Let's close by reading the classic Scripture that best illustrates the Spirit-filled life and how that is achieved.

5. Read Gal. 5:16–25.

    a. What will happen if we walk by the Spirit? (vs. 16)

    b. What goes on in the inner man once the Spirit takes up residency? (vs. 17)

This is such a crucial verse. We must recognize that the flesh (our fallen nature) is continually in rebellion against God. Its desires are always destructive. That's why Scripture lovingly warns us here that we can't just do what we *naturally* want, please or wish. We must yield all those lusts and desires of the destructive fallen nature to the Holy Spirit for only the Spirit of God can recognize hurtful, sinful desires and give us the wisdom and power to stand against and overcome it. That is why it is *so* important to be *filled* with the Spirit so that the Spirit is in control and not our deceptive, destructive flesh.

    c. Review the list of the *acts of the sinful nature* in verses 19–21, then write down here any that may be a problem for you and include these in your prayer today, that God would help you to overcome these sin strongholds through the power of the Holy Spirit now resident in you, as you surrender to Him and obey as He leads you.

    d. Please note the stark warning if we fail to do this. What is it? (vs. 21b)

    e. If you are walking in the Spirit, what kind of fruit will be manifest in your life? (vs. 22,23)

    f. What have those who belong to Christ done? (vs. 24) Have you?

    g. If we want to live a Spirit-filled life, how are we to walk? (vs. 25)

6. In your own words, explain what it means to be filled with the Holy Spirit and how this happens.

Are you filled with the Spirit? Do you consistently walk by the Spirit as you go through the day? If not, confess this sin to God (yes, it is a sin because being filled with the Holy Spirit is not a suggestion. It is a loving command from God…*Be filled*…Eph. 5:18), then renew your commitment to do this daily, yielding your heart and will to Him and to His empowerment that your life will be, as the Scripture promises, like a watered garden, never lacking in beauty or sustenance—the power to remain strong and to be a blessing to others, come what may!

> *And the Lord will continually guide you, and satisfy your desire in scorched places, and give strength to your bones; and you will be like a watered garden, and like a spring of water whose waters do not fail (Is. 58:11).*

Write out a Bible verse that had special meaning to you today.

Based upon what you have learned today, write a prayer to God expressing the desires of your heart in applying these Truths to your life.

Chapter 7 — Day 2
The Person and Ministry of the Holy Spirit: Part 3
Clearing Up Confusion About the Baptism of the Spirit, Water Baptism, Quenching the Spirit

For by one Spirit we were all baptized into one body. There is one body and one Spirit, just as also you were called in one hope…one Lord, one faith, one baptism (1 Cor. 12:13; Eph. 4:4,5).

I have many dear friends who sincerely believe that the Bible teaches the doctrine of the baptism of the Holy Spirit as a separate and distinct experience from the initial act of regeneration, the new birth. In other words, one does not "get" the Holy Spirit until the time of the Second Blessing (the baptism of the Spirit, known also as "the anointing"). This experience of the baptism may occur within a few minutes of the initial salvation experience or it could be months, even years later. And some people never experience it, leaving them weak, lacking in power.

I've also read books by great men of faith, mightily used by God in building the Kingdom who also support this doctrine. In every case, those who believe it and those who teach it have all experienced the phenomena known as the Second Blessing. But what exactly does the Word of God say about this? We must, as always, go to the plumb line of God's Word for clarification.

In Him, you also, after listening to…the gospel of your salvation, having also believed, you were sealed in Him with the Holy Spirit…who is given as a pledge of our inheritance (Eph. 1:13–14).

In these verses we are clearly told that the *moment* we received Jesus into our hearts and made Him our Lord and Savior, the Holy Spirit came into our hearts as a seal of our salvation and of our eternal inheritance with Him. So that is when we "get" the Holy Spirit.

For by one Spirit we were all baptized into one body, whether Jews or Greeks, whether slaves or free, and we were all made to drink of one Spirit…Therefore we have been buried with Him through baptism into death, in order that as Christ was raised from the dead through the glory of the Father, so we too might walk in newness of life (1 Cor. 12:13; Rom. 6:3,4).

The "baptism" spoken of in these verses clearly refers to the spiritual baptism we read about in John 3:3–5 [*Unless one is born again, he cannot see the kingdom of God…unless one is born of water (repentance) and of the Spirit he cannot enter into the Kingdom*]. It is that life changing, eternity-altering event that takes place when we, by faith, accept Jesus as our personal Lord and Savior and are *baptized from above* by the Holy Spirit into the Kingdom of God. It does not refer to water baptism which God's Word clearly explains (throughout the Book of Acts, in Romans and Corinthians) as a separate event that takes place *after* spiritual rebirth as a separate, outward public witness to what has already happened on the inside. Water baptism is also done as an act of obedience to God.

Jesus is our example. Jesus was baptized. But He didn't get baptized to be *saved*. He got baptized as an outward sign of His devotion and obedience to the Father *when He began His public ministry (age 30)*. With His baptism, Jesus was publicly declaring His love for His Father and His commitment to the fulfilling of His will (Matt. 3:15; John 17:4). And that is what every new believer since "witnesses to" through his baptism. He is basically saying: I have received Jesus as my Lord and Savior and I am making public my decision and my desire to follow Him and to do the will of my heavenly Father. Water baptism is an outward expression—witness—of what has already taken place inside—spiritual regeneration, the new birth into the Kingdom of God.

Water baptism is also a beautiful symbolic picture of repentance and of our new life in Christ. As we go under the water, it symbolizes the burying of our old sin life; when we come up out of the water, it reflects being raised to a beautiful *new life* in Christ. It is also symbolic of resurrection. Just as Jesus was raised from the dead, so we are being raised from our former spiritual deadness to new—eternal—life with Him. *Buried with Christ…raised to new life in Him (Rom. 6:4)*.

There is one body and one Spirit, just as also you were called in one hope of your calling; one Lord, one faith, one baptism (Eph. 4:4,5).

The Bible makes it clear. There is only one Spirit…and one spiritual baptism. Either you are born again and have, therefore, received the Spirit of God (the seal of salvation), or you are not and you have not. It is as simple as that.

Whether or not one consistently manifests a victorious, Spirit-filled, fruitful life, is not a matter of the *baptism* of the Holy Spirit, therefore, it is, rather, a matter of being *filled* with (controlled by) the Holy Spirit—dying to self, then yielding the mind, emotions, and will to Him, walking in trusting obedience as He leads and guides through the day. However, a caveat is in order:

Jesus answered, Truly, truly, I say to you, unless one is born of water and the Spirit, he cannot enter into the kingdom of God. That which is born of the flesh is flesh, and that which is born of the Spirit is spirit. Do not marvel that I said to you, 'You must be born again.' The wind blows where it wishes and you hear the sound of it, but do not know where it comes from and where it is going; so is everyone who is born of the Spirit (John 3:5–8).

The workings of the Spirit of God are unique in every individual's life. Just as we cannot see the wind—we only see and hear various manifestations of it, the bending of branches, the rustling of leaves as it blows through the trees—so it is with the Holy Spirit. We cannot *see Him* or exactly *how* He is working—in our lives or in others. We can only see and hear various manifestations of what His work is producing: *the fruit*. That is what is important! (Matt. 7:17–23).

It is very dangerous, therefore, to contrive a set of rules concerning how the Holy Spirit works in individual lives, both in the matter of regeneration and sanctification; or to say that the Holy Spirit works in a humanly logical, specific way to bring people to God and to sanctify them in His ways. God is a very personal God. He knows every heart, and He knows every circumstance in every person's life. And God, who *desires that all would be saved and come to a knowledge of the Truth (1 Tim. 2:4)* works in mysterious ways to draw men and women, boys and girls to Himself. We need to leave that divine, spiritual work completely in His hands.

Because of an individual's own personal history, personality, and present circumstances, God may very well orchestrate events that cause him to experience a dramatic "crisis" (referred to as *the Second Blessing*, or *Baptism of the Holy Spirit*), at which point he dramatically and in an utterly life-changing way releases the control of his life to Christ, yielding his body, soul, mind, and spirit in total surrender to the Holy Spirit. He experiences a very real and profound change in his heart and will, which is outwardly manifested in his attitude, behavior, and level of peace and joy. Dramatic as it may seem, however, according to the *whole counsel of God's Word (Acts 20:27)* that is, in actuality, the filling of the Holy Spirit, as a result of his, for the first time, totally yielding his will to the Spirit's control, not a unique *baptism* of the Spirit. God's Word is very clear that all who have received Jesus are *baptized* by the Holy Spirit into Christ *(Eph. 1:13,14; 1 Cor. 12:13; Rom. 6:3,4)*.

> *…but you shall receive power when the Holy Spirit has come upon you; and you shall be My witnesses both in Jerusalem… in Judea… and even to the remotest part of the earth (Acts 1:8).*

Jesus is here establishing the unique and powerful role that the Spirit will play in the disciples' lives, and in the lives of all who follow after them, in fulfilling the ministry to which He calls them. In essence, He is saying, "This task to which I have called you as my disciple—to consistently overcome sin and live a godly life in a difficult, cruel, sinful world, while you are in a weak, fallen body, and to *make disciples* of others, teaching them how to do the same—is much too big for you to do in your own wisdom and power. Therefore, I am sending to you, just as I promised, the Holy Spirit who will be in you and will empower you to do all these things with courage, boldness, and strength." It is the initial *giving* of the Holy Spirit in fulfillment of Jesus promise (John 14:16). That dramatic event took place on the day of Pentecost (and was verified in other similar events in the early establishment of the church) and served as a glorious demonstration to the disciples of the power of the Spirit and of their need for the Spirit in order to fulfill the work to which God had called them. These glorious events were recorded in Scripture for our benefit and instruction as well (1 Cor. 10:6,11), reminding us that none of us can live the Christian life in our own power and strength. It simply is not possible. To attempt to do so will always lead to painful, heart breaking disappointment, failure and discouragement.

> *Ye have not because ye ask not…I say to you, ask, and it shall be given to you; seek, and you shall find; knock, and it shall be opened to you. For everyone who asks, receives; and he who seeks, finds; and to him who knocks, it shall be opened. Now suppose one of you fathers is asked by his son for a fish; he will not give him a snake, will he? Or if he asked for an egg, he will not give him a scorpion, will he? If you then, being evil, know how to give good gifts to your children, how much more shall your heavenly Father give the Holy Spirit to those who ask Him?… But let him ask in faith without any doubting, for the one who doubts is like the surf of the sea driven and tossed by the wind. Let not that man expect that he will receive anything from the Lord, being a double-minded man, unstable in all his ways (James 4:2; Luke 11:9–13; James 1:6–8).*

We must *believe* that God is a loving Father who desires to give us not just "good gifts" but the very best because His love for us is perfect (John 15:13). The Holy Spirit is the best gift God could have given us after Jesus left this world because *He is God* and He now lives *in us*. And because of that we **are** *more than conquerors over every* trial and temptation and we *can* live obedient, Christ-honoring lives characterized by confidence, peace and joy…*if* we *believe!* (Rom. 8:31–37; Matt.. 21:22). Once again, we see that *faith* is the key to *receiving* (activating in our lives) what we have already been given. For example, when I am faced with many temptations and much pressure and stress, instead of becoming anxious and short-tempered (as is the *natural* response to pressure and temptations), I can *choose* to trust the Holy Spirit to guide me and to provide all that I need—the wisdom, the strength, the endurance—to overcome the temptations and difficulties, knowing that *He is God* and He reigns *far above all rule and authority* which certainly includes anxieties, trials and difficulties (Eph. 1:21, cf. 1 Cor. 10:13; Ex. 14:13–31; 2 Chron. 20:15–25, etc.). I will be like David who walked onto the battlefield confidently: *You come to me with a* *sword (and) a spear, but I come to you in the Name of the Lord of hosts (1 Sam. 17:45).* I can also *choose* joy and peace even when difficulties and pain assail me because these are the fruit of the Spirit who now dwells in me producing this fruit continually as I *believe, trust and obey.* I can pray, "Thank you, Holy Spirit that you live in me and you *are* my peace and joy in this difficult situation." And if I *really* believe this, and, by faith, act accordingly, I will *experience* peace and joy because God promised it (John 7:38; Gal. 5:16–25).

Rejoice always; pray without ceasing; in everything give thanks for this is God's will for you in Christ Jesus. Do not quench the Spirit. Do not despise prophetic utterances (1 Thess. 5:16–20).

To *quench* means to *suppress, inhibit, stop the flow of, or extinguish.* We *quench* the Holy Spirit when we neglect to consistently read and study God's Word (for it is through the Word of God that the Holy Spirit speaks to us). We also quench the Spirit when we fail to exercise a thankful, joyful heart. Another way we quench the Spirit is when we refuse to heed instruction from God's Word as it comes to us through preaching, teaching, or the ministry of admonition and exhortation of others. We can also quench the Holy Spirit by interfering with how He is working in another person's life, perhaps causing confusion or discouragement. We need to be very careful about all these things lest we extinguish the very power source of our Christian life.

There is just one final way that we misuse this wonderful gift that God has given us in the Holy Spirit and that is called *grieving* the Holy Spirit. It is very serious and often follows acts of *quenching* the Spirit. Of all the warnings in Scripture, these two, *quenching* and *grieving* the Spirit need to be heeded with greatest solemnity, for disobeying these commands will lead invariably to shipwreck of our faith if we are saved, and for those not yet in the Kingdom of God, to eternal separation from God. Because of the seriousness of the danger involved we will devote special study to this topic tomorrow.

Just a few concluding thoughts about the wonderful person and ministry of the Holy Spirit. The Holy Spirit is gentle; that's why He is called a comforter. But He is also divinely powerful to do *exceeding abundantly above anything we could think or ask (Eph. 3:20).* We must attribute to Him the same respect and holy awe that we do God the Father and God the Son, and we must allow Him the freedom to work in our hearts and in every believer's heart as God so wills. What matters when it comes to the presence of the Holy Spirit in any person's life is not what experience a person has had, but how he conducts his life on a day-to-day basis. Does the life reflect devotion to and reverence for God, obedience to His Word, humility, service to others, love for all? Is it consistently producing the fruit of the Spirit—love, joy, peace, patience, etc.—and boldly proclaiming the gospel? Is it pointing people to Jesus and bringing honor and glory to Him (John 16:14)? Then this person is indeed born again (baptized by the Holy Spirit) and living a Spirit-filled life, regardless of any experience he has or has not had.

Now may the God of hope fill you with all joy and peace in believing, that you may abound in hope by the power of the Holy Spirit (Rom. 15:13).

Bible Study Supplement

Chapter 7 — Day 2 — The Person and Ministry of the Holy Spirit: Part 3

Clearing Up Confusion About the Baptism of the Spirit, Water Baptism, Quenching the Spirit

1. Read 1 Cor. 12:13.

    a. According to this verse, what were we all baptized into? By Whom?

2. Read Eph. 4:4-6.

    a. How many "bodies" are there? (vs. 4a)

    b. How many Spirits are there? (vs. 4a)

    c. How many baptisms are there? (vs. 5)

But what about that *Second Blessing* as a separate and distinct baptism of the Holy Spirit?

A passage that has often been used in teaching a Second Blessing, or separate baptism of the Holy Spirit, is Acts 19:1–6. It's important to consider it.

3. Read Acts 19:1–6.

    a. Had the people received the baptism of the Holy Spirit? (vs. 2)

    b. Why not? (vs. 2b)

    c. What baptism had they received? (vs. 3)

    d. What did John tell the people? (vs. 4b)

    e. After Paul explained this, what did they do? (vs. 5)

    f. What happened next? (vs. 6)

As we studied earlier, one of the most effective tools of Satan is deception. He comes as an angel of light. In this case he had effectively deceived this particular group of seekers into believing that they could somehow be saved by being *baptized into John*. (Just as he continues to deceive people into thinking that they can be saved by good works, going to church regularly, joining a church, or by being "baptized"—as an adult or as a baby with someone else, a sponsor or "godparent," making a profession of faith for them… and a number of other unbiblical teachings regarding regeneration). And the reason they fell for this deception is because they were not properly taught the Truths of God, or perhaps they had been blinded by religious tradition that was so strong at the time (and remains so). These people didn't really understand the true gospel message—that one must be *born again* from above by the Holy Spirit through personal *repentance* and *faith in Jesus*. Nor were they taught about the Holy Spirit and His ministry in their lives. It is a case of Rom. 10:14: *How then shall they call upon Him in whom they have not believed? And how shall they believe in Him whom they have not heard? And how shall they hear without a preacher?*

In this case, Paul corrected the error by teaching the people the true gospel message, then baptizing them after they had made a genuine profession of faith. In the early church, (still practiced in many eastern European countries), it was customary to *lay hands on* new believers immediately after baptism as a means of *commissioning* them for service in God's Kingdom. Throughout these early apostolic days of the establishment of the church, the Holy Spirit often manifested in special ways, i.e., enabling people to speak in previously unknown languages, confirming His role in empowering believers for ministry. He continues to *fill* and *empower* all who come to Him, yield to His control, then walk in obedience as He leads them.

This story should serve as a warning to us all. There is so much going on in our world today that looks like and sounds like "truth," and even has elements of Truth (biblical Truth) in it! That is why it is so dangerous and can, as Jesus said, *mislead…even the elect* (Matt. 24:24). We must be as the Bereans who *received the Word with great eagerness, examining the Scriptures daily, to see whether these things were so* (Acts 17:11). For if we do not, we will be vulnerable to getting caught up in following another person or cause or movement, or religious tradition rather than following Jesus and the pure and holy milk and meat of God's Word, illumined to us by the Holy Spirit as we earnestly, with receptive hearts, read, study and obey it.

4. Read Rom. 8:13-16.

   a. Who are the *sons of God*? (vs. 14)

   b. What have they received? (vs. 15b)

   c. How can anyone know for sure that he has truly been *born again*? (vs. 16)

As we studied yesterday, to be filled with the Spirit, means to be yielded to His control and to walk in obedience to the Word of God, led and empowered by the Holy Spirit. Staying filled with the Holy Spirit is a matter of abiding in or continuing in this practice: reading God's Word, praying for wisdom, then yielding our mind, emotions, and will to the Holy Spirit's control, moment by moment, step by step. Always remember that the Holy Spirit empowers us to obey the Word. So He will *never* ask us to do anything that violates God's Word. Whenever we feel led to do something that violates God's Word, we can *be sure* that this is not from the Holy Spirit but from the great deceiver, Satan. We must reject it and continue to follow the *Holy* Spirit.

5. Read John 7:38,39.

   a. What happens to one who believes in Jesus? (vs. 38)

   b. To Whom was Jesus referring when He spoke of *streams (rivers) of living water*? (vs. 39a)

When we *quench the Spirit*, (through disobedience, ignoring His convictions, or rebelling against His leading), we dam up the river, and the flow of God's life and power to us is cut off. Let us be careful not to quench the work of the Holy Spirit in us.

6. Read Acts 5:32.

   a. To whom does God give the Holy Spirit? (vs. 32b)

To be baptized by the Spirit means that we belong to Christ's body. To be filled with the Spirit means that our bodies, in their totality—body, soul, mind, and will—belong to Christ so that our deepest heart's desire will always be to do that which is *pleasing to Him and brings Him honor and glory because He alone is worthy…majestic in power, working wonders (2 Cor. 5:9; 1 Cor. 10:32; Rev. 4:11; Ex. 15:11).*

As we have learned in this lesson, when we are *filled with* (under the control of) *the Spirit*, we will live our lives with joy, thanksgiving, a submissive spirit, power to resist temptation and to walk courageously and victoriously through trials and tribulations. God has indeed given us so very much in the person and ministry of the Holy Spirit. Let us cease from seeking after the Spirit for what we can *get* from Him, but rather let us *give ourselves* completely to His control so that He may fully possess us and, therefore, mightily use us to tell others the wonderful good news of all that God has done for us in Christ.

> Joys are flowing like a river, since the Comforter has come;
> He abides with us forever, makes the trusting heart His home.
>
> Bringing life and health and gladness, all around this heavenly Guest
> Banished unbelief and sadness, changed our weariness to rest.
>
> Like the rain that falls from Heaven, like the sunlight from the sky,
> So the Holy Ghost is given, coming on us from on high.
>
> See, a fruitful field is growing, blessed fruit of righteousness;
> And the streams of life are flowing, in the lonely wilderness.
>
> What a wonderful salvation, where we always see His face.
> What a perfect habitation, what a quiet resting place!
>
> Blessed quietness, Holy quietness, What assurance in my soul!
> On the stormy sea He speaks ... How the billows cease to roll.

(Blessed Quietness, Manie P. Ferguson, W.S. Marshall, *Sing Joyfully Hymnbook,* Tabernacle Publishing Co., Carol Stream, IL 1989)

Write out a Bible verse that had special meaning to you today.

Based upon what you have learned today, write a prayer to God expressing the desires of your heart in applying these Truths to your life.

Chapter 7 — Day 3
The Unpardonable Sin...
Beware! Take Heed! Grave Danger Ahead
The Tragedy of a Reprobate Mind

> *For even though they knew God, they did not honor Him as God, or give thanks, but they became futile in their speculations, and their foolish heart was darkened..they exchanged the Truth of God for a lie...for this reason God gave them over to the lusts of their hearts...to impurity (and) degrading passions...to a depraved mind, to do those things which are not proper (Rom. 1:21,22,24,26,28).*
>
> *Those (who perish) will believe what is false... because they did not receive the love of the Truth so as to be saved (2 Thess. 2:10,11).*

Today we come to one of the most crucial topics in this entire study, for its potential for destruction, if not heeded, extends beyond time. Please pray with me that the Holy Spirit will give us all an extra measure of discernment and sensitivity to what the Word teaches regarding the dangers of a depraved (reprobate) mind—the result of repetitively ignoring or rejecting the Holy Spirit's loving pleas to *repent and turn to God.*

> *For since the creation of the world His invisible attributes, His eternal power and divine nature, have been clearly seen, being understood through what has been made, so that (all) are without excuse. For even though they knew God, they did not honor Him as God, or give thanks, but they became futile in their speculations, and their foolish heart was darkened. Professing to be wise, they became fools and exchanged the glory of the incorruptible God for an image in the form of corruptible man...therefore God gave them over in the lusts of their hearts to impurity...for they exchanged the Truth of God for a lie, and worshipped and served the creature rather than the Creator, who is blessed forever...for this reason God gave them over to a depraved (reprobate) mind, to do those things which are not proper (Rom. 1:20–28, sel.).*

> *For the mystery of lawlessness is already at work;...that is, the one whose coming is in accord with the activity of Satan, with all power and signs and false wonders, and with all the deception of wickedness for those who perish, because they did not receive the love of the Truth so as to be saved. And for this reason God will send upon them a deluding influence so that they might believe what is false, in order that they all may be judged who did not believe the Truth, but took pleasure in wickedness (rebellion against God) (2 Thess. 2:7–12, sel.).*

At the beginning of this study, I mentioned a very important principle found throughout the Word of God. Because it is such a crucial life/death matter, it behooves us to take a few minutes to review it. It is the biblical principle of being *given over to the desires of our hearts.* It works like this: if we persist in going our own way, stubbornly and rebelliously rejecting the convictions of God's Holy Spirit in our consciences concerning our relationship to God or our lack of obedience to His Word and His will for our lives (grieving the Holy Spirit), there comes a time when God will say, "OK, you want it your way…have it your way." And He *gives us over to the desires of our heart* (those lustful cravings that we desire more than God - *Rom. 1:24)*. Because God will never violate our right to choose, He basically says: "You don't want me around, OK, I won't bother you anymore…I'll leave you alone." And He *departs (1 Sam. 6:14)*. And with His departure goes His loving hand of guidance and protection. He does exactly what we have been demanding: He lets us have *our will*. In this tragic moment, our minds become reprobate—darkened, depraved, cut off from God. It is called having a *seared conscience,* the state in which a conscience no longer functions according to its God-created design—to draw us to and keep us close to God, giving us wise, godly discernment and judgment. In this depraved, separated from God condition, we are no longer able to recognize demonic deception—not on the outside (through the devil's *lies and enticements - 2 Cor. 11:3,14,15)*, nor on the inside (the lustful cravings of our own *deceitful and wicked heart – Jer. 17:9)*. There cannot be a greater tragedy than this, for a reprobate mind is no longer able to discern Truth (real, godly Truth) from error, right from wrong, good from evil, that which builds up and brings joy and peace from that which tears down and destroys.

Thankfully, because of God's rich mercy and patient grace, this process of being given over to a reprobate mind does not happen instantaneously. It is a gradual process that takes place over time and repeated rebellions. That's why the Bible lovingly warns:

Do not quench the Holy Spirit…do not grieve the Spirit (Eph. 4:20; 1 Thess. 5:19).

Every time we ignore, reject or rebel against the convictions of the Holy Spirit as they come to us through nature, our conscience, the Word, or the loving concern of others God sends to minister to us and to urge us back to God, our heart gets a little harder, our mind a little darker….

For even though they knew God, they did not honor Him as God, or give thanks; but they became futile in their speculations, and their foolish heart was darkened…professing to be wise, they became fools… (exchanging) the Truth of God for a lie, and worshiped and served the creature rather than the Creator (Rom. 1:21,22,25).

If we allow this cycle to continue, one day the heart becomes so hard that it is incapable of hearing the voice of the Holy Spirit and God gives us exactly what we have demanded—our own lusts and sinful desires.

God gave them over to degrading passions…to a depraved (reprobate) mind because they did not receive the love of the Truth so as to be saved (Rom.1:21,26; 2 Thess. 2:10).

At this point, the habitual rejecter of God experiences one of the greatest tragedies of all—a seared (dead) conscience and an impenetrable heart. When the conscience becomes completely seared, the Holy Spirit departs *(1 Sam. 16:14)*. The mind instantly becomes reprobate (morally abandoned, depraved). The hater of God has received what he demanded—separation from God. He has taken the final step in *crossing God's deadline* from which there is *no way of return*. This is what the Bible calls *blasphemy of the Holy Spirit,* or the *unpardonable sin.*

Therefore I say to you, any sin and blasphemy shall be forgiven men, but blasphemy against the Spirit shall not be forgiven. And whoever shall speak a word against the Son of Man, it shall be forgiven him; but whoever shall speak against (blaspheme) the Holy Spirit, it shall not be forgiven him, either in this age, or in the age to come (Matt. 12:31,32).

What is this terrible sin God warns us about here that is so awful, so heinous it can never be forgiven and will result in eternal separation from Him…in hell?

Based on this crucial text (Matt. 12:31,32) and other related Scripture, God tells us that some people reject Jesus because they have been deceived and they really don't understand that Jesus is God and that He was sent from Heaven to earth to die on the cross for their sins (paying the penalty—death) in order that they can be reconciled to God and spend eternity in Heaven with Him (John 3:16; Rom. 5:8, etc.). Therefore, they may use His name in vain and they may utter terrible things about Him in ignorance. And this, they may do also regarding God the Father. These people have not committed the unpardonable sin. They are just deceived or uninformed, and they need someone to love them and share with them the true salvation message. But the one who has clearly heard the gospel, and who, through the convicting work of the Holy Spirit in his conscience, knows that Jesus is God's Son and that He died on the cross for our sins, yet continues to blatantly and rebelliously reject this message and the God who sent it, this one…

…tramples underfoot the Son of God, and (has) regarded as unclean the blood of the covenant by which he was sanctified, and (has) insulted the Spirit of grace?…Then they will call on Me, but I will not answer; They will seek Me diligently, but they shall not find Me; Because they hated knowledge, And did not choose the fear of the Lord (Heb. 10:29; Prov. 1:28,29).

I beg you. Do not take this lightly. This "crossing God's deadline" is very real. It is very clearly taught in Scripture, and is the most serious warning in all the Bible. It will happen just as God says: if we continually ignore, reject or rebel against the Holy Spirit's loving convictions, we will get exactly what we ask for—a seared, dead conscience and separation from God. We need to examine our own hearts concerning our sensitivity to the Holy Spirit, and we need to earnestly pray for and warn others who have repeatedly rejected the gospel message of the impending peril ahead—the grave danger of *crossing God's deadline*, after which, there will be no way to turn back and receive the gift of salvation so freely offered (John 3:16; Heb. 6:4–6).

One of the saddest stories in the Bible is that of rebellious Esau, who knowingly, rebelliously sold his own birthright to satisfy his fleshly cravings, then went on to continue in his rebellion against God. Later, when he realized what he had done, the Bible says…*he found no place for repentance, though he sought for it with tears (Heb. 12:15–17).*

Another similar, grave warning comes to us in *Heb. 6*:

For in the case of those who have once been enlightened and have tasted of the heavenly gift and have been made partakers of the Holy Spirit, and have tasted the good word of God and the powers of the age to come, and then have fallen away, it is impossible to renew them again to repentance, since they again crucify…the Son of God, and put Him to open shame (Heb. 6:4–6).

To illustrate the seriousness of this situation, I want to close by sharing a story that still brings tears to my eyes every time I think about it. It is, undoubtedly one of the saddest situations I have ever experienced!

For many years I befriended and shared the gospel with Ed and Veronica. Veronica was open and receptive and soon made a profession of faith. But Ed was hard and rebellious. He always mocked and ridiculed me when I came over or tried to share the gospel with him. A few years later, Veronica died, going home to her Lord whom she had come to love so much. Ed's health began to deteriorate markedly to the point that he could hardly walk. He was very much alone in the world because they did not have any children, and he had no close friends who were there for him in his time of need. (Though I tried to befriend him, taking food to him after his wife died, he asked me not to come anymore because he did not want to listen to any talk about God).

One day as I was praying for Ed, I felt the Holy Spirit impress upon my heart to visit him and minister the gospel to him one more time. I will never forget that day as long as I live! As I sat across from that poor, downcast man, sharing the gospel with him, he looked at me with tears streaming down his cheeks and he said, "I know that what you are telling me is the Truth. I've known it for many years, and I want to do what you are asking me to do (accept Jesus as personal Lord and Savior), but it is too late for me. I can no longer do this…I just can't." I tried to explain that if he realized that what I was saying was true, then all he had to do was repent of his sins, believe the gospel and receive Jesus as His personal Lord and Savior. But the words of repentance, faith and acceptance of Jesus just would not materialize—in his heart or on his lips. He just kept sobbing and crying out, "It's too late. It's too late. It's too late!..."

I saw him only one more time after that. He had just come out of a local restaurant. It was a pitiful sight. He looked so alone and dejected—shoulders stooped, head cast down to the ground. He was barely moving, shuffling his feet only a couple of inches at a time because he did not have the strength to pick them up. In a few days, I read that he had died, still rejecting Jesus because he had *crossed God's deadline*.

This experience had a profound impact upon my life. I could never look at another human being the same after that. I saw in each one a precious eternal soul that would spend eternity in Heaven with God or forever separated from Him in hell, depending upon what he/she had done with Jesus. Had they heard the good news about what Jesus did for them on the cross and how they could have forgiveness of sins, peace with God, and eternal life with Him in Heaven—forever? Had they accepted Jesus as their personal Savior? I became all the more eager to share the good news. Like Isaiah, I cried: *"Here am I, send me!" (Is. 6:8)*. I asked God to prepare hearts, then send me to minister the good news of Jesus to those who had never heard or those who had been hardened by sin's deceptions through the years, before they too, *crossed God's deadline,* and it would be eternally…*too late.*

> *Therefore, just as the Holy Spirit says, Today if you hear His voice, do not harden your hearts as when they provoked me…going continually astray…and they refused to know My Way…And working together with Him (the Holy Spirit), we also urge you (open your heart), for now is the time of God's favor, today is the day of salvation (Heb. 3:7,8,10; 2 Cor. 6:2,3).*

> *Return, faithless Israel, declares the Lord; I will not look upon you in anger. For I am gracious, declares the Lord;…only acknowledge your iniquity, that you have transgressed against the Lord your God…return, O faithless sons, I will heal your faithlessness…Come now, let us reason together, says the Lord; Though your sins are as scarlet, they will be as white as snow, though they be as crimson, they shall be as wool…If you consent and obey, you will eat the best of the land. But if you refuse and rebel, you will be devoured… Truly the mouth of the Lord has spoken… (Jer. 3:12,13,22; Is. 1:18–20).*

> *Whoever will call upon the Name of the Lord will be saved (Rom. 10:13).*

Bible Study Supplement

Chapter 7 — Day 3 — The Unpardonable Sin…Beware! Take Heed! Grave Danger Ahead
The Tragedy of a Reprobate Mind

1. Read Rom. 1:20–25,28.

    a. What has been known since the creation of the world? (vs. 20)

    b. What did some who *knew God, not* do….and what was the result? (vs. 21)

    c. What did they become? (vs. 22)

    d. What did they do with the Truth of God? (vs. 25)

    e. What happened as a result? (vs. 28)

2. Read Prov. 1:20–33. (Note: "Wisdom" is the voice of God that comes to us through His Word, ministered to us by the Holy Spirit).

    a. What is *Wisdom* doing? Where? (vs. 20)

In other words, God's Wisdom is everywhere, all around us—in nature, our consciences, through other people—*crying out* to us. Are we listening?

    b. How did the *naïve (simple ones)*, the *mockers (scoffers)*, and the *fools* (those who hated God's knowledge) *respond* when the Holy Spirit cried out and *stretched out His hand to them*? (vs. 24,25a).

    c. What will be the result because they did this? (vs. 28)

    d. Why? (four reasons - vs. 29,30)

    e. What will be the tragic result? (vs. 31,32)

    f. What will happen to the one who listens? (vs. 33)

3. Read Heb. 10:26-29.

    a. What happens if we go on sinning willfully? (vs. 26,27a)

In verse 28 the writer of Hebrews says that anyone who has set aside (rejected, rebelled against, disobeyed) the Law of Moses (concerning premeditated murder), dies on the testimony of two or three witnesses.

    b. In light of this, what solemn warning does he give in vs. 29?

Remember, Jesus was completely innocent of all crime. He had done nothing to hurt anyone. He willingly laid down His life for the very ones who murdered Him! It is the cry of a loving Father whose love and holy justice cannot just sit by and watch the precious blood of His innocent Son, shed for lost sinners, continually be *trampled underfoot* with no respect or reverence. It was much too high a price.

4. Read Heb. 6:4-6. (Please use NASB here)

For in the case of those who have once been enlightened and have tasted of the heavenly gift and have been made partakers of the Holy Spirit, [5] and have tasted the good word of God and the powers of the age to come, [6] and then have fallen away, it is impossible to renew them again to repentance, since they again crucify to themselves the Son of God, and put Him to open shame. (Heb. 6:4–6)

    a. What happens to those who have been enlightened and have tasted of the heavenly gift, been made partakers of the Holy Spirit and have tasted the good word of God and then have fallen away? (vs. 6a) Why? (vs. 6b)

5. Read Ps. 81:8–16.

    a. What happened when the people continued to refuse to *listen to God*? (vs. 12)

    b. What would happen if they *listened to God* and followed His ways? (vs. 14,16)

6. Read Prov. 29:1.

    a. What will happen to the one who *hardens his neck* (remains stiff-necked and unrepentant) after many rebukes (convictions, reproofs)?

It's called: *crossing God's deadline.* May God help us to heed seriously this warning—not just for us, but for those we love. And if there be any who are approaching this critical line, the passing over of which marks the point of no return, may God help us to pray earnestly for them and to go to them with the good news of the gospel before it may be eternally…too late!

Write out a Bible verse that had special meaning to you today.

Based upon what you have learned today, write a prayer to God expressing the desires of your heart in applying these Truths to your life.

Chapter 7 — Day 4
The Very Real Pain and Problem of...FEAR

> *Since then the children share in flesh and blood, He, Himself likewise also partook of the same, that through death He might render powerless him who had the power of death, that is, the devil...and might deliver those who through fear of death were subject to slavery all their lives (Heb. 2:14,15).*

Fear...For many this simple four letter word conjures up debilitating emotional upheaval, anxiety and a host of other problems. As we near the end of this study, I want to open my heart once more to share with you a little about my own personal battle with this very powerful enemy. I do so with a prayer that it may be an encouragement to others who may be experiencing the oppression of demonic fear. Because this kind of fear leads often to a hardening of the heart for protection, its potential for destruction is very serious. To illustrate, let me share an experience that the Lord used to help me understand this and to pray more earnestly for those affected.

I visited Sharon when she first moved in. I took her some homemade nut bread and warmly welcomed her to our neighborhood. From our conversation that day, it was apparent that she was not a Christian, so I began to pray for her, and a few weeks later, Mel and I invited her to have supper with us. On another occasion, I took her some food when she was sick. We included her in fellowship gatherings that we had in our home with our church family who also expressed genuine Christian love to her. And we continued to pray for her. We prayed that God would help us to live before her in a genuine way, the love, joy, and peace that comes from having a personal relationship with Jesus, and that through this, He might draw her to Himself and open her heart to receive Jesus, too. We also shared our faith directly as God gave opportunity.

One day, as I was praying for Sharon, I felt the Holy Spirit prompting me to put together a package of books and videos that God has used in my life to help me understand many things about the nature and character of God, the creation of the Universe, the accuracy and reliability of the Bible, Jesus' teachings and ministry, etc. So that is what I did.

I sat with her in her living room enjoying a very warm, pleasant conversation. At one point she asked me about how I spent my time, what my personal interests were. As I began to talk about that—helping others, biblical counseling, sharing the good news of the gospel of Jesus (our missionary work)—her countenance began to change. A bitter hardness replaced the congenial smile. I could see anger welling up in her eyes. Suddenly, she stopped me and began to brutally assault my "narrow, bigoted faith." She went on to mock the cross, the need for salvation, the superiority of her own intellect along with all others who did not buy into that kind of "pathological ignorance," and many other hateful, inflammatory accusations. Seething in anger, she asked me to leave and made it clear that I was not welcome in her house as long as I insisted on talking about Jesus, the Bible or anything to do with God.

Tears welled up in my eyes as I walked back home. I remembered ever so vividly times not so long ago, that I held the same impenetrable intellectual hardness as Sharon. I could not help but think of times in my own life when I had responded just as vehemently and lashed out with similar condemnation. And there were times—many times—when my anger was vented against God in moments of conviction when I knew that my life was not right before Him, and that I needed to do something about that. But I was so full of fear that He would destroy everything I had worked so hard to build in my life. (There was so much fear!) Those were always embattled, confusing (painful!) times. When I got home, I knelt down at my quiet time table and thanked God for His incomprehensible longsuffering that patiently endured all those years of my own mockery and rejection. "Thank You, Lord. Thank You for not giving up on me. Thank You for dying on the cross for my sins, for making me your child and for forgiving me for all those times I "spit in your face," by rejecting your love and suffering for me. I'm so sorry…As the tears streamed down my cheeks, I began to pray for Sharon. I could *relate* to her hurt, her pain. I had sensed it earlier as I looked into her eyes. I wasn't sure of the source of it, but wondered if perhaps she'd had some really hurtful experience with people who *claimed* to be Christians …but weren't. That can be very painful. Or perhaps it was with people who really were Christians, but were going through their own deep pain at the time and just were not capable of being as sensitive to the needs of others as they would otherwise be. I asked God to please be merciful and help her to recognize lies and deceptions that had hardened her heart and blinded her eyes so that she could no longer sense God's love or hear His gentle calling to her. I prayed that God would somehow use me to help her understand these things and that she would open her heart to receive Jesus as her own personal Lord and Savior. And I continued to pray for Sharon every day. A few months later, my husband and I moved away from that community and I was no longer able to visit Sharon or extend a helping hand of Christian love. I sent Christmas cards, but she never responded. Eventually, I lost contact with her. I don't know if I will ever see her again to be able to personally talk to her about Jesus, but I still pray for her and I will never stop believing God for her salvation so that I can see her again—if not on this earth, then one day in heaven.

In my own years of prodigal living and rebellion against God, I don't think that deep down inside—I mean really deep down inside—I hated God. I'd seen—and experienced—enough of God's beautiful, awe-inspiring creation and the intricate perfection of design in it. I was not foolish enough to believe that all that just *evolved* with no intelligent design. My analytical mind just couldn't buy that (even though I tried desperately to do so throughout my secular educational pursuits). So the problem was not so much a hatred of God or the people who believed in Him. It was, I can see now, a demonic fear of this unknown thing called Christianity that had to do with a man named Jesus, a cross, and pain and suffering. I had a very tender, sensitive heart. The mere thought of blood for any reason turned my stomach and I did not want any part of that! I, too, had read enough of the Bible to understand that the heart of *the gospel* was the cross of Christ. That was *not* good news to me! And I knew that if I were to even entertain the idea of Christianity I would have to embrace the cross, the bloodshed…and a radical change in my own very controlled, and comfortable life. Because of the demonic fear and deception, I could not do that. The cross itself was too awful, too painful. And the *radical change* idea was overwhelming. I'd never liked change—big changes, little changes. I liked continuity, order, control. I functioned best with structure, well-laid plans, goals—clearly stated, methodically worked towards and achieved! I cringed at the thought of giving all that up to trust a "God" I could not even see or touch and knew so little about. I'd heard so many awful things about "God." I was sure He would take away everything I had worked so hard to achieve. (Demonic fear is so deceptive and so powerful. It makes the very thing we need the most appear hurtful and the thing that hurts the most as something good and desirable).

But the pain gave no rest. It drove me into a deeper consideration of many things—life, death, the purpose for my existence, etc. In these honest, contemplative moments, I recalled that my life had been one of nearly continual pain from early childhood: physical pain along with an internal pain that was too deep and too intense to describe with mere words. Thinking about this now, I am sure there was demonic involvement in that as well. But I did not understand anything about such things—the spirit world, demonic influence and the power these wreak upon unprotected minds and hearts. All I knew was that life was very hard and very painful for me. And the thought of embracing anything else that might add to that (more pain), was beyond my ability to even consider. I'm sure that this was the greatest factor in the development of a hard heart and closed-mindedness to the gospel. Suffering, regardless of its cause or origin, has a way of building a lot of *fear* in those it afflicts. And *fear* always produces hardness as a means of protection…survival. Whatever it takes to ease the pain—drugs, a life-dominating obsession/compulsion (addiction), pleasure, mind games and other intellectual rationalizations—that is what is pursued. For me, (and for many others), the obsession became a drive for significance, to do something that would earn the respect and approval I so desperately longed for…and *needed*—to offset the pain or at least to give meaning to it. If I attained to a certain level of *significance,* all the special talents, that now were fettered because the pain and its accompanying fear had robbed me of so many opportunities, could be far more effectively expressed, benefiting others. And what about all those invaluable *lessons learned* through the suffering that could also benefit so many. If only I had a higher, broader platform from which I could share my talents and wisdom. Enmeshed in all these preoccupations was a driving desire to do something that would go on living long after I was gone. I suppose that was because I *did not want to die!* That was, by far, my *greatest fear.* But if that was going to be unavoidable, then there would just have to be some part of me that remained to keep at least a memory (a part of me) alive before others. I guess that is why reincarnation and some of the New Age evolution/universal spirit belief systems were so appealing to me. It was comforting to think that this wasn't the *end;* that I would merely take on another form and enter into another cycle of life.

The thought of death was increasingly haunting, evoking painful speculations. If I embraced Christianity it would mean a sure and certain "death" (the thing I dreaded most!) immediately: death to the self-rule of my life, death to *my* goals, dreams and aspirations…(or so I so wrongly and deceptively *thought!*) And, of course, there would still be that eventual death to my physical body—then…the judgment of God. I was so deceived at that point, I did not realize that the very thing I feared the most was precisely what I needed to deliver me from fear of death and judgment: the cross of Jesus. Through His sacrificial death on the cross, Jesus paid the penalty for sin—death. By accepting this wonderful gift and putting my faith in what Jesus did for me on the cross, the fear of death would be shattered—swallowed up in the blessed assurance of *eternal life* with God in Heaven and I would never have to face the judgment of God for my sin. Jesus already did that for me! (2 Cor. 5:23; 1 Pet. 3:18, etc). I would only have to face the judgment of God if I rejected God's precious gift of salvation. Demonic deception is so powerful, totally blinding spiritual eyes to the Truth.

So what broke the power of that kind of demonic fear and enslavement that nearly cost me my eternal life and separation from God forever—in hell?

> *First of all, then, I urge that entreaties and prayers, petitions and thanksgivings, be made on behalf of all men…This is good and acceptable in the sight of God our Savior, who desires all men to be saved and to come to the knowledge of the Truth. (1 Tim. 2:1–6 selected)*

God alone knows how many prayers ascended to His throne of grace on my behalf over the years! How thankful I am for all those who loved me enough to pray for me and to never give up in that sacrificial expression of love! I know that those faithful fervent prayers played a huge part in the mercy of God being extended to one so far away, so full of pride, stubbornness, and rebellion, and so bound by *fear.* God, *who desires that all would be saved and come to a knowledge of the Truth (1 Tim. 2:4),* hears the prayers of His saints on the behalf of His lost lambs *(Luke 15:4–7)*. May God bless every one who earnestly contended for my soul before His throne of Grace! (And may God help us all to do the same for others we know who remain outside the family of God).

And what about that fear of the cross and bloodshed and all that? Remember what we learned earlier:

> *For the word of the cross is to those who are perishing, foolishness; but to us who are being saved it is the power of God…But a natural man does not accept the things of the Spirit of God, for they are foolishness to him, and he cannot understand them, because they are spiritually appraised (1 Cor. 1:18, 2:14).*

Demonic fear manifests itself in protective intellectual rationalization so that all that cannot be explained or understood according to human logic and reason is rejected as foolishness. That is why Jesus *called a little child and had him stand among them…I tell you the Truth, unless you become like little children, you will never enter the kingdom of heaven (Matt. 18:1–3, NIV).*

But if demonic fear manifests itself in paralyzing unbelief and intellectual rejection of God's Truth, from where does the *faith to believe*—as a little child—come?

> *How shall they call upon Him in whom they have not believed? And how shall they believe in Him they have not heard? And how shall they hear without (someone to tell them)? (Rom. 10:14).*

> *Now all these things are from God, who reconciled us to Himself through Christ and gave us the ministry of reconciliation, namely, that God was in Christ reconciling the world to Himself, not counting their trespasses against them, and He has committed to us the word of reconciliation, Therefore, we are ambassadors for Christ, as though God were entreating through us; we beg you on behalf of Christ, be reconciled to God (2 Cor. 5:18–20).*

The reason most people reject the gospel, is because they do not *know God* and they have never heard about the magnitude of His love, mercy and grace from someone who has lived on both sides of the cross. To all who have, God has commended *the word of reconciliation (2 Cor. 5:19)*. Just as we were once blind to the things of God, filled with fears and hardness, we understand what that is like and we can take the wonderful gospel to others with a heart of compassion and sincere love—just as Jesus came to us.

We can tell them the Truth about God's wonderful love, mercy and grace and the *good news* of salvation and all that He has done for us in Jesus. We can share our personal testimony of God's patient love and longsuffering in our own lives. It is living *proof* of the power—and desire—of God to redeem and change lives, and bring lasting meaning, purpose and peace. And we can help people to understand that the gospel is not *logical*. The kind of unconditional, selfless holy love that Jesus had for lost sinners that caused Him to lay down His life in incomprehensible suffering, for the very ones who hated him, mocked him, spit in His face, tore locks of hair from his head and from his beard, beat a crown of thorns into his brow, mercilessly ripped the flesh from his back with metal thongs attached to leather whips until his inner organs were exposed, then pounded nails into His feet and hands and hung Him on a cross to die, is far beyond *human logic or understanding*. It must be embraced the only way it can be embraced—*by faith.* That is why we must encourage people to put aside all human intellectual reasoning and rationalizations. We must, relying completely upon the Grace of God and the convicting, drawing work of the Holy Spirit, help them to listen as a little child listens—with a trusting, believing heart—to what God says about the creation of the world, Satan's rebellion, Adam and Eve, God's clear instructions to them, their rejection and disobedience, the penalty for sin—death—and the unfathomable love of God that paid it—the awful price for our sin.

> *He who is without sin among you, let him be the first to throw a stone at her…and when they heard it, they began to go out one by one…And straightening up, Jesus said to her, "Woman where are (your accusers)?*

Did no one condemn you?" And she said, "No one, Lord." And Jesus said, "Neither do I condemn you; go your way…sin no more (John 8:7–11).

Jesus is the only one who comes to the outcast sinner in compassion and love, never condemnation. And Jesus is the only one who can forgive us our sins, restore us to a right, loving relationship with God, give us eternal life and the power to be *more than conquerors* over all our sins and all our fears.

Come, see a man who told me all the things that I have done…(is this not) the Christ?…one thing I do know; I was blind, and now I see (John 4:29, 9:25).

Jesus is the only one who knows all about us, loves us anyway and invites us to have a personal, eternal, loving relationship with Him. He is also the only one who can open blind eyes and heal sin-sick souls.

May God help us all to be willing and eager ambassadors for Jesus, going to all our friends and neighbors as God gives opportunity, and telling them *what great things He has done for us*, that the devil's curse of fear may be broken, lost souls redeemed and brought *out of darkness into His marvelous light (Col. 1:13; 1 Pet. 2:9,10)*.

Before we close today's meditation, let's go back for just a moment to that blood-stained cross. I think the simple childhood song learned in Sunday School and loved by children through many generations, "Jesus Loves Me, This I Know," says it best:

> Little ones to Him belong; they are weak, but He is strong.
> Yes, Jesus loves me…Yes. Jesus loves me…Yes, Jesus loves me…The Bible tells me so.

Remember what we learned in our study on Jesus' life, death, and resurrection. We learned that God loved Jesus more than we could ever possibly love another human being (just as He also loves us!), and if there could have been any other way for God to pay the penalty for sin that His holy justice required without violating the free will He gave to His children, He would certainly have done so! But there was no other way that holy justice could be accomplished. Someone had to pay the penalty for sin—death. That is why there had to be a cross. And the more we come to it and gaze upon its sacred beauty, the more we will recognize it for what it is: God's most precious instrument for the redemption of mankind. And so the hideous awfulness of the cross is swallowed up in the reality that it is, in fact, God's greatest expression of love ever lavished upon fallen man. One who has spent time at the foot of the cross no longer recoils at the mention of it, but rather embraces it with deep, oft tearful, thanksgiving and praise.

> Jesus loves me, He who died. Heaven's gates to open wide,
> He will wash away my sins. Let the little child come in.
> Yes, Jesus loves me…Yes, Jesus loves me…Yes, Jesus loves me…The Bible tells me so.

God is love! (1 John 4:8)

The cross is God's exclamation point to this indisputable fact.

And perfect love casts out fear (1 John 4:18).

And we bear witness that the Father has sent the Son to be the Savior of the world. Whoever confesses that Jesus is the Son of God, God abides in him, and he in God. And we have come to know the love God has for us. God is love…By this, love is perfected with us, that we may have confidence in the day of judgment…There is no fear in love; but perfect love casts out fear, because fear involves punishment, and the one who fears is not perfected in love (has never come to know the wonderful, perfect love of God). We love, because He first loved us (1 John 4:14–19).

Bible Study Supplement
Chapter 7 — Day 4 — The Very Real Pain and Problem of...*FEAR*

Demonic fear is a very real and very devastating problem in our world today. Because it reaches its destructive tentacles into many areas of life, we will devote another day to discussing it in Book Three. In that Bible Study supplement, we will focus upon the biblical solution to bringing down the stronghold it erects in believers' hearts that keep them in bondage to various forms of idolatry, compulsions and obsessions, etc. But for today, I want to focus upon the nature of God concerning His love, mercy, compassion and longsuffering patience, for it is demonically inspired lies concerning the nature of God that keeps more people from opening their hearts to the gospel than any other factor. Lies like: the God of the Bible is a mean, vindictive God who rains down judgment from heaven the moment a person violates His impossible-to-keep laws. He demands total allegiance and obeisance so that all who come to Him must give up everything that is fun or enjoyable. He then straps them with strict, repressive rules that keep them in further bondage, making their lives miserable. He is quick to judge, and turns a cold ear to the one who cries out for mercy and forgiveness. Nothing could be further from the Truth! All are lies. Demonic, deceptive, lies!

1. Read: John 3:16,17. (Please use KJV written here)

    16. For God so loved the world that He gave His only begotten son, that whosoever believeth in Him should not perish, but have everlasting life.

    17. For God did not send his Son into the world to condemn the world, but that the world, through Him might be saved.

    a. How much did God love the world? (vs. 16)

    b. What did God *not* send His Son into the world to do?...but to do what? (vs. 17)

There are so many Bible verses that testify to the love of God and His care and concern for His children. In fact, the entire Bible testifies to God's love. So it just won't be possible in the short time we have today to do justice to this subject, but as we look at just a few verses, I pray that our hearts will be stirred to delve deeper into the rich fields of God's Word for more *treasures* (Matt. 13:44) concerning this central theme of the Bible—God's great love for you and me and all the people in the world.

To give us an opportunity to look at a few more of these today than we would have time for if we looked up each one individually, I will write several of them out here. Please read them prayerfully, asking God to help you really *see* them in a new light today for all that they mean.

Greater love has no one than this, that one lay down his life for his friends (John 15:13).

But God demonstrates His own love toward us, in that while we were yet sinners, Christ died for us (Rom. 5:8).

He made Him who knew no sin to be sin on our behalf, that we might become the righteousness of God in Him...God was in Christ reconciling the world unto Himself, not counting their trespasses against them, and He has committed to us the word of reconciliation. Therefore, we are ambassadors for Christ, as though God were entreating through us; we beg you on behalf of Christ, be reconciled to God (2 Cor. 5:21,19,20).

I am the good shepherd; and I know My own, and My own know Me. And I have other sheep, which are not of this fold; I must bring them also and they shall hear My voice, and they shall become one flock with one shepherd. No one has taken away (My life) from Me, but I lay it down on My own initiative (John 10:14–17, sel.).

Jesus tells a poignant story about God's loving heart for lost lambs in Luke 15. It's about a shepherd who has 100 sheep. One wanders off from the flock and becomes lost. Jesus says that the shepherd leaves the 99 and goes out to search for that one lost sheep and when He has found it: *He lays it on his shoulders, rejoicing. And when he comes home, he calls together his friends and his neighbors, saying to them, "Rejoice with me, for I have found my sheep which was lost!"* He then goes on to say: *"I tell you that in the same way, there will be more joy in heaven over one sinner who repents, than over ninety-nine righteous persons who need no repentance (Luke 15:4–7).*

You just can't find vindictive condemnation or judgment in that!

Throughout Scripture we see that there are two kinds of *fear*. One is destructive. One is necessary, healthy and beneficial in our relationship with God. Destructive *fear* (demonic, unhealthy fear) is synonymous with being afraid or filled with dread that something terrible will happen. Healthy, beneficial fear (good, godly fear) expresses reverence for God, a deeply held respect, holy awe and wonder at His greatness, his goodness and His love. It is good and spiritually healthy—to have this kind of fear.

> *The Lord is compassionate and gracious, slow to anger and abounding in lovingkindness…He has not dealt with us according to our sins…For as high as the heavens are above the earth, so great is His lovingkindness toward those who fear Him. As far as the east is from the west, so far has He removed our transgressions from us. Just as a father has compassion on his children, so the Lord has compassion on those who fear Him…The lovingkindness of the Lord is from everlasting to everlasting on those who fear Him (Ps. 103:8–17 sel.).*

I love this next verse. It is symbolic of the light of Jesus that God's love brings into every believing heart.

> *Then the Lord said to Moses, Stretch out your hand toward the sky, that there may be darkness over the land of Egypt, even a darkness which may be felt. So Moses stretched out his hand toward the sky, and there was thick darkness in all the land of Egypt for three days. They did not see one another, nor did anyone rise from his place for three days,* **but all the sons of Israel had light in their dwellings!** *(Ex. 10:21–23).*

What a beautiful picture. It illustrates that even though all the world around may be in darkness, God's children will always have light in their dwellings because Jesus is the light of the world and has come to inhabit all who accept Him as Lord and Savior.

> *I am the light of the World. He who follows me shall not walk in darkness but will have the Light of life! (John 8:12).*

And then there are all the verses about God's presence and promises to always be with us and to deliver us from the hands of our enemies.

> *I will never leave you nor forsake you (Heb. 13:5)*

> *The righteous cry and the Lord hears, and delivers them out of all their troubles; The Lord is near to the brokenhearted and saves those who are crushed in spirit. Many are the afflictions of the righteous; but the Lord delivers him out of them all…in the world you will have tribulation, but be of good cheer. I have overcome the world (Ps. 34:18,19; John 16:33).*

There are also dozens of verses that contrast the life of those separated from God and those who have entered into a relationship with Him:

Those who love Thy law have great peace, and nothing causes them to stumble…But the wicked are like the tossing sea, for it cannot be quiet, and its waters toss up refuse and mud (all the day). There is no peace, says my God, for the wicked (Ps 119:165; Is. 57:20,21).

For the waywardness of (those who) hated knowledge, and did not choose the fear of the Lord shall kill them, and the complacency of fools shall destroy them. But he who listens to Me shall live securely, and shall be at ease from the dread of evil (Prov. 1:32,33).

Many are the sorrows of the wicked; but he who trusts in the Lord, lovingkindness shall surround him (Ps. 32:10).

The way of the transgressor (the one separated from God) is hard…but the way of the righteous is like the light of dawn that grows brighter and brighter until the full day (Prov. 13:15, 4:18).

These verses, and dozens more like them, cut right through the demonic deception of fear. It is not life with God that is filled with turmoil and destruction. It is life separated from God's love and protection that robs the unbelieving of all the *good things* God has for us *to enjoy* (1 Tim. 6:17). For the righteous, his journey in the light of God's love is safe, secure, and filled ultimately with only *good things*…and joy.

God is love—to the core of His being—and everything He does is done in perfect love. Perfect love is patient and compassionate in nature—it *suffers long* (1 Cor. 13). Other precious qualities of God are His mercy, tenderheartedness and grace—all of which hold his justice and judgment at bay far beyond what any human ever would! Finally, God never asks anyone to give up anything that is *fun* or *pleasurable*. Never! God delights in pleasure and joy (John 15:11, 17:13; Zeph. 3:17) and He wants us to experience as much of it as our finite hearts can contain! Joy is at the heart of worship and worship is at the heart of God's purpose in creating us: to worship Him and to reflect His glory. God longs for this for us because He knows that as we get caught up in the beauty and majesty of His glory, there is *joy inexpressible and full of glory* in our own hearts (1 Pet. 1:8). This beautiful journey into the wonder, the beauty and the joy of God's love and radiant glory begins when we come to God in repentance, then open our hearts to receive His greatest gifts of love—the forgiveness of our sins, victory over sin and death, and a home with Him in heaven, forever. At the moment we do this we enter into the most glorious, the most wonderful, the most rewarding relationship we will ever have—an intimate, personal relationship with the God of the Universe! As we grow in this relationship and as we discover more and more about this wonderful God and how great and awesome He is, our joy only increases.

All that God does in us and through us and for us and with us is formed out of His heart of love. It is good. Joyously and wonderfully good. I can honestly say that when I became a Christian, God did not *take away* one pleasurable thing from me, not one! Nor did He ask me to *give up* anything that brought joy or delight to my heart. In some cases, He opened my blind eyes to show me habits and lusts that were sinful and destructive and He graciously, mercifully changed my desires so that I no longer lusted after these things. I **thank Him** eternally for that! The only things that have gone from my life have been things that were hurtful, inflicting inestimable pain and suffering—not just on me but on those I loved most dearly. I would not want any of these back again—ever! And He brought a lot of new things and new joys into my heart I never had experienced before. He continues to bless in ways far beyond my *human understanding* (Eph. 3:20). I can only lift up a very grateful heart every day and say "Thank you, Lord for Your incomprehensible goodness, mercy and grace." And I assure you that I am not alone in this experience. Every Christian that I know—every one!—shares a similar testimony. It is the rich love, mercy and grace of God that brings meaning and joy to our lives day by faithful day!

This I recall, therefore I have hope…the Lord's lovingkindnesses indeed never cease, For His compassions never fail. They are new every morning; Great is (His) faithfulness. The Lord is good to those who wait for Him. To the person who seeks Him (Lam. 3:22–25, sel.).

There are more than 2,000 promises in the Bible attesting to God's love. May this small sampling serve to give you a taste of just how great and good and loving God truly is! Certainly, it is beyond human understanding, but every time we look at the cross, we *know* that it is true!

I want to close today's special time of looking at the love and goodness of God with one of my favorite Scriptures as it relates to the overcoming power of love over *fear*. May God help us all to live daily in its glorious Truth and assurance.

1. Read Luke 1:68,74,75.

    a. What has God done? (vs. 68)

    b. What has happened to all who have been redeemed? (vs. 74a)

    c. What does this mean for us? (vs. 74b,75)

Write out a Bible verse that had special meaning to you today.

Based upon what you have learned today, write a prayer to God expressing the desires of your heart in applying these Truths to your life.

Chapter 7 — Day 5
Come, Let Us Go Up to the Mountain of the Lord

> *Then they said to Moses, "Speak to us yourself and we will listen; but let not God speak to us" (Ex. 20:19).*
>
> *And a highway will be there, a roadway, and it will be called the Highway of Holiness. The unclean will not travel on it...but all who keep my covenant, those I will bring to My Holy Mountain, and make them joyful in My house (Is. 35:8, 56:6,7).*

There is a story in the Old Testament that I could very much relate to in those early years of my new Christian life. The Lord used it to get my attention and move me into a closer, more trusting, more obedient walk with Him. I think it's worth sharing, with a prayer that it will encourage us all to *keep to the course God has for us... pressing ever onward and upward (2 Tim. 4:7; Phil. 3:12–14)*.

The story is found in Exodus 19 and 20. It had been three months since the children of Israel had left Egypt. They had come through the Red Sea. They had, from the loving hand of God, been provided the rain of manna from Heaven every morning and quail that covered the camp for meat at twilight. They had received water from a rock and experienced the blessing of the Lord at Rephidim in defeating the strong and powerful Amalekites. Now they were camped at the base of Mount Sinai where the Lord would soon give to them the Ten Commandments along with the other ordinances they would need to keep them strong, holy, and victorious over their enemies. The Lord said to the people: *You, yourselves, have seen what I did to the Egyptians, and how I bore you on eagles' wings, and brought you to Myself. Now then, if you will indeed obey My voice and keep My covenant, then you shall be My own possession among all the peoples; and you shall be to Me a...Holy nation...And all the people answered together and said, "All that the Lord has spoken we will do!" (Ex. 19:4–8)*. Sadly, we soon learn that this commitment was fickle, insincere, *lip service* only—not from the people's heart. In just a matter of days, these same people would be melting down their gold to build a golden calf to worship as their "God."

> *And the Lord said to Moses, "Behold, I shall come to you in a thick cloud, in order that the people may hear when I speak with you. The Lord also said to Moses, "Go to the people and consecrate them today and tomorrow, and let them wash their garments; and let them be ready for the third day, for on the third day the Lord will come down on Mount Sinai in the sight of all the people...you shall set bounds for the people all around, saying, 'Beware that you do not go up on the mountain or touch the border of it; whoever breaks through (unpurified) and touches the mountain shall surely be put to death...When the ram's horn sounds a long blast, they shall come up to the mountain."*

> *So it came about on the third day, when it was morning, that there was thunder and lightning flashes and a thick cloud upon the mountain and a very loud trumpet sound, so that all the people who were in the camp trembled. And Moses brought the people out of the camp to meet God, and they stood at the foot of the mountain. Now Mount Sinai was all in smoke because the Lord descended upon it in fire; and its*

smoke ascended like the smoke of a furnace, and the whole mountain quaked violently. When the sound of the trumpet grew louder and louder, Moses spoke and God answered him with thunder. And the Lord came down on Mount Sinai, to the top of the mountain (Ex. 19:9–20, sel.).

It was at this point that God spoke to the people from atop Mt. Sinai giving them the Ten Commandments. After He had finished speaking, the Bible says: *And all the people perceived the thunder and the lightning flashes and the sound of the trumpet and the mountain smoking; and when the people saw it, they trembled and stood at a distance. Then they said to Moses, "Speak to us yourself and we will listen; but let not God speak to us lest we die"…And Moses said to the people, "Do not be afraid; for God has come in order to test you, and in order that the fear of Him may remain with you, so that you may not sin." The people stood at a distance, while Moses approached the thick cloud where God was (Ex. 20:18–21).*

Throughout this study we have been looking at the awfulness of sin and what it cost. It was sin that destroyed Adam and Eve's intimate fellowship with God; it was sin that cast them from His presence and from the beautiful paradise of Eden; it was sin that brought death into the world; it was sin that cost God the precious life of His only beloved Son. It is sin that continues to destroy our relationship with God and others precious to us, and sin that wreaks untold havoc throughout the world and affects the lives of every man, woman, and child upon the face of the earth. No wonder <u>God hates sin</u>. And so must we if we are to escape its awful consequences—death. Because God is love and God is holy, He cannot leave unpunished that which destroys. I'm so thankful for that! Otherwise there would be no future and no hope for any of us, because eventually, sin would destroy everything! That is why God must judge sin: to protect His precious children from its destruction.

Similarly, we also learned that it is good and spiritually healthy to revere God (hold in highest esteem and reverence the perfect, transcendent love and holiness of God) and not try to break through with no respect or fear in our hearts for His holy, sovereign power. The Bible says: *The fear of the Lord* [a reverential fear and worshipful respect] *is the beginning of wisdom (Prov. 1:7).* But we must be careful not to stop there lest we become like the children of Israel who said to Moses: *Speak to us yourself and we will listen; but let not God speak to us (Ex. 20:19).*

The children of Israel did not want to get too close to God. They wanted to send Moses to speak to God, and then they would listen to what God had to say—from Moses, not from God, Himself. Why? Because the children of Israel were a selfish, stubborn and stiff-necked people—like most of us! And they had a lot of idols and a lot of sins that they harbored in which they found fleshly comfort and pleasure. Perhaps the reason they had become so hardened (stubborn and rebellious) was because of all those long years they remained in captivity to the flagrantly pagan world system of the Egyptian culture. So many were born into families whose parents and grandparents had long abandoned a close and intimate walk with God. He was but a distant fragment in their own personal experience. Because of things they had heard at various gatherings most knew *about* God, but they did not *know Him* personally. And that was OK, because they had grown comfortable with Egypt's worldly idols, which were created and designed to serve their hedonistic desires for pleasure and sensuality.

But when they began to see God's mighty acts of deliverance—the plagues, the parting of the Red Sea, the destruction of the Egyptian army—they got a firsthand glimpse of who God really is in all His power and holiness and they did not want to get too close to that! They wanted God's favor and His protection but only as it came to them buffered by another human over which they could have some control and who was like them, sinful. They did not want to stand face to face with divine holiness, because they knew that if they did, their sinful way of life would be exposed and they would have to change, and they did not want to change!

And this is the judgment, that the light is come into the world, and men loved the darkness rather than the light; for their deeds were evil (John 3:19).

I was very much like those rebellious, hedonistic children of Israel when I was first saved, because I, too, had lived in the world system so long and so much of it had made its way into who I had become, my quite unholy "image." I'd worked hard to build that image. It absolutely paralyzed me in fear to even think about giving up this image, which included my plans and my desires for the future, which I was sure a holy God would destroy if I got too close. And what about all those *darling sins* [idols] (Heb.12:1) that also had taken up residence in my heart—excessive indulgences I yet craved. Because of the demonic deception along with its always accompanying paralyzing fears, I was, even after my salvation, totally convinced that I could not live without them. And how many of those there were! They, too, were a part of that self-created, self-protecting image that had become my identity. If I cast them out, what would be left? It was just too overwhelming to even think about! So at the beginning, I settled for those short, light "happy thought" devotions every morning, letting someone else besides an awesome, holy God, speak to me sweet, uplifting inspirations. A quick prayer after that and on with my day.

That seemed to work for awhile. But after a few years, I realized that I was making no lasting progress in my battle against the destructive life-dominating sins in my life. In fact, the failures were coming even more frequently than before I was saved! It was very discouraging. No, it was more than discouraging. I began to slide into a very deep and dark depression that could not be shaken. I could never describe the intensity of the battle that ensued, for I realized at this point that I had reached another of those proverbial forks in the road. As a born-again Christian, I had to choose: the way of holiness or the way of carnality (spiritual adultery with the world). Carnality means living entrenched in the world with no distinction between your life and values and those of the world system. It means being not only *in the world*, but *of the world*. It means refusing to make the commitment to *come out from the world and be separate*, living a distinctly unique, God-centered, Christ-exalting, pure and holy life. It means attempting to *serve two masters* (2 Cor. 6:17; Jer. 3:13; Matt. 6:24). If I chose to be a carnal Christian, I—erroneously, under the power of demonic deception—believed that I could avoid the flaming fires of holiness. I could join the ranks of the Sunday morning Christians, go to church on Sunday, and live my life the other six days just as I always had. I could (again under the lies of demonic deception) have one foot in the kingdom and one foot in the world, thus enabling me to enjoy the best of both worlds. This was all the more enticing as I clearly saw that this was the way the majority of the people seemed to live. And I wanted desperately to fit in, to be loved. So it seemed like continuing on as I had always done—following along with the crowd—would avoid a lot of conflict and be the wiser choice. I also knew that if I did this, my life would get a whole lot easier because so many—most!—of my really difficult problems these days were associated with dealing with sin strongholds, and if I no longer cared about that, things would go a lot more smoothly.

As I *continued* in God's Word, however, I began to see many problems with this erroneous and very dangerous deception. One stood out, giving no peace. The Bible clearly teaches that there is no such thing as a long-term, undisciplined, *carnal Christian*. That just can't happen, because if one is truly born again, the Holy Spirit dwells in that person and He will not allow him to continue on in sin and worldliness (1 John 3:4–10; Heb. 12:8). That's why the Bible exhorts us to examine ourselves to make sure we are *in the faith* as we studied in Chapter 4. As I made this examination, I could clearly see that I was truly born again, so I was only fooling myself to think that I could continue on in my state of spiritual adultery and hypocrisy, trying to keep one foot in the world and one in the kingdom of God, for indeed, just as Jesus lovingly warned, *no one can serve two masters (Matt. 6:24)*. It is impossible! Those who try are continually torn between the two, making life very, very miserable—for them and for those around them. I could certainly see evidence of this! Still, knowing all this, I can tell you making the choice to walk the path of true Christlike holiness was not an easy one! It was, at the beginning, fraught with spiritual warfare for which I was ill-prepared. And there were times I did want to quit! It just did not seem worth the relentless, never ending battle.

But it didn't have to be this way! I was biblically ignorant of so many things. I was not making the investment in a consistent quality quiet time—time to really study and seek to apply the Truths of God's Word—to develop spiritual maturity. I all too often settled for a quick 5-minute devotional and prayer…which never penetrated deep enough to bring true godly repentance and change. I was, rather, becoming a consistent *hearer of the Word* and *not a doer (James 1:22)*. I just wanted to remain at a safe and secure distance from that Holy Mountain. So I fell for the devil's lies and deceptions nearly every time! Another reason it was so hard and so discouraging in the beginning is because I did not have any solid biblical discipleship training, nor did I pursue this by joining a small group Bible Study, actively participating in Sunday school and other opportunities to grow my faith. I was too proud to admit that I needed this kind of outside instruction. But I see now how much I paid for that pride! So many battles lost, so much precious time squandered as I vainly attempted to *go it alone*. God never intended it to work this way. That's why Jesus' last instructions before leaving this earth were: *Go and make disciples, teaching them to observe what I have commanded you*. Because I did not avail myself to the teaching and biblical exhortation of mature disciple-making Christians, I did not know what to expect when I took that right fork in the road. I was often blindsided, overwhelmed and discouraged. And because I had no one to tell me about the awfulness of sin and its consequences, spiritual warfare, and the power of the devil's lies and deceptions, the true meaning of biblical faith and perseverance, taking it "one day at a time," and resting in God's love, faithfulness, and unfailing mercy and grace, the progress was ever so slow as I attempted to learn all these things on my own. So there were times—especially at the beginning—that I came so, so close to abandoning the Holy Highway to take to the streets of carnality once again.

Then one day, I read the story of Jesus speaking to the Jews about what it means to be a true disciple. On this occasion, and on several others just prior, Jesus had explained that following Him would mean giving up their allegiance to everything else that they loved more than Him in this world. They would also have to lay down their agenda in order to follow God's agenda—His plan—for their lives. He talked about humility and serving others and forsaking all else in order to follow Him. And this, He told them, they ought gladly to do, knowing, *It is the Spirit who gives life; the flesh profits nothing; the words that I have spoken to you are Spirit and life. . . ." (John 6:63)*. But their proud pampered flesh didn't want to hear about humility and serving others and forsaking all else to follow Jesus. They only wanted their fleshly lusts and pleasures. The Bible goes on to say: *As a result of this many withdrew, and were not walking with Him anymore. Jesus said, therefore to the twelve. "You do not want to go away also, do you?" (John 6:67)*. When I read those words, my heart was pierced. How many times I had joined the crowd and *walked away*. Hope was stirred as I read Peter's response: *Lord, to whom shall we go? You have the words of eternal life. And we have come to know that You are the Holy One of God (John 6:68)*. As these words sunk deep into my heart, I made the decision to take the risk of going to that Holy Mountain and walking the blessed *Highway of Holiness to Mount Zion (Jer. 31:6; Ps. 84:5–7; Is. 35:8)*. There, on this mountain—the mountain of God's infallible Word and holy Presence—I knew that I would hear from God directly, and my heart, mind, and will would be changed…*from glory to glory into the image of Jesus,* in whom alone is found true freedom and inexpressible joy (2 Cor. 3:17,18; 1 Pet. 1:8).

And I can tell you, I have not regretted that decision for one second—not one! I've walked with God on this righteous path long enough to know that no matter how intense the battle (conflict and attacks from the enemy) may be, God's love, faithfulness, and overcoming grace is always greater! (John 16:33). Every other path—every other path—is fraught with deception and lies that lead only to destruction.

There is a way that seemeth right, but it is the way of death...The way of the transgressor is hard (Prov. 14:12, 13:15).

When I made that first huge (for me!) step of faith in coming to that majestic, holy mountain of God's abiding presence and began to walk upon its ascending highway, I was overwhelmed with joy and thanksgiving again and again as I discovered that rather than facing the condemnation and wrath of God I so dreaded (and deserved) God met me daily with His patient and tender love, mercy, forgiveness, and grace (Jer. 31:3; Lam. 3:23; Heb. 4:16).

God is love and God is holy. And He has called us, as His ambassadors upon this earth to reflect the greatness and glory of His love and holiness to others, to shine in this perverse and dark world as lights of righteousness and Truth. My heart yearns to do this—to reflect ever more and more the Spirit filled life of *Christ in me, the hope, the power, the joy of God's magnificent love, grace and glory* (Col. 1:27; 2 Cor. 5:20; Phil. 2:15; Gal. 5:16–25; Ps. 16:11!).

It is knowing and obeying the infallible Truths of God's Word that gives us the wisdom and strength to succeed in this desire—to consistently overcome sin and keep pressing on. May God help us all to never give up, give in, turn back, run away or quit as day by day we press onward, upward, on this glorious Highway of Holiness.

Come and let us go up to the mountain of the Lord, and to the house of the God of Jacob, that He may teach us His ways and we may walk in His paths (Micah 4:2).

Bible Study Supplement

Chapter 7 — Day 5 — Come, Let Us Go Up to the Mountain of the Lord

The Bible is full of promises that are "now" and "not yet"; promises that, by faith, are present realities with future consummation. In other words, when we walk in the assurance of these promises, we experience in the present a glorious foretaste of their majestic consummation at the return of Christ or the moment we enter His Presence in glory (Luke 23:43). This is what it means to be hidden with Christ, seated at His right hand in the heavenlies (Eph. 2:5,6). We really can experience, in the here and now, a wonderful foretaste of God's future glories reserved for His faithful redeemed. God's Word is full of these wonderful promises!

1. Read Is. 35:1-10.

Note: Lebanon was a beautiful land of luxurious forests and timbers and rich in natural resources. It was oft referred to as a land flowing with milk and honey.

    a. What will all those who choose to walk the Highway of Holiness experience as they anticipate their happy future? (vs. 1,2)

    b. Because of this, what are we to do? (vs. 3,4)

    c. What will be found there in the desert, and what will it be called? (vs. 8)

    d. Who will *not* travel on it? (vs. 8b)

    e. What will the ransomed of the Lord do? (vs. 10)

2. Read Is. 60:1-3.

    a. What comes to all who enter the Highway of Holiness to Zion? (vs. 1,2b)

    b. What will happen as a result? (vs. 3)

This is a beautiful promise. As God's light shines in us and through us, "nations" and "kings"—people from various ethnic groups, some highly esteemed and respected as "kings"—will be drawn to the light of Jesus they see in us.

3. Read Is. 56:1,2,6,7.

    a. What will be the reward of all who *join themselves to the Lord*? (two things - vs. 7a)

It is so important to note here the connection between joy and spending time with God in prayer. It is there, on God's holy mountain, as we fellowship with Him in His Word and prayer, that our hearts are encouraged…in the *fullness of His presence and joy* (Ps. 16:11).

4. Read Is. 58:11.

    a. What further rewards will there be for those who walk this highway to Zion? (five things)

5. Read Ps. 84:4-7. (Please use NASB translation below).

    4. How blessed are those who dwell in Thy house! They are ever praising Thee.
    5. How blessed is the man whose strength is in Thee; in whose heart are the highways to Zion!

6. Passing through the valley of Baca, they make it a spring; The early rain also covers it with blessings.
7. They go from strength to strength, Every one of them appears before God in Zion.

Note: The valley of Baca was a dry, desolate wasteland representing times of difficulties and intense, prolonged trials.

    a. Who is blessed? (three qualities – vs. 4a,5) What do they do? (vs. 4b)

    b. What happens to all who possess these qualities when they pass through Baca? (two things) (vs. 6)

    c. Because God Himself is the supplier of all that they need along the journey, those who travel this highway will go from _____ to _____. (vs. 7a)

6. Read Ps. 125:1,2.

    a. What are those who trust in the Lord like, and what quality will they possess? (vs. 1)

    b. What does the Lord do for *His people*? (vs. 2)

7. Read Micah 4:1,2.

    a. What will people from many nations be saying in the last days? (vs. 2a)

    b. Why do they want to go to this place? (two reasons – middle of verse - vs. 2)

Do you see the beauty of this Highway of Holiness? As we walk daily upon this highway, we draw closer and closer to Zion. And the closer we get to Zion, the more of its radiant glory (the glory of God) we will behold and absorb (just as Moses did). This radiant beauty will then be reflected to others drawing them also to God's glorious light of love and redemption (Ps. 34:5; Jer. 31:12; Is. 60:5; 2 Cor.3:18).

    Come, let us go up to the mountain of the Lord...that He may teach His ways (Micah 4:2).

Write out *Ps. 125:1,2* as your Bible verse today as a beautiful reminder of your inheritance!

Based upon what you have learned today, write a prayer to God expressing the desires of your heart in applying these Truths to your life.

Chapter 7 — Day 6
Closing Thoughts and a Preview of Things to Come

> *But you, beloved, building yourselves up on your most holy faith; praying in the Holy Spirit; keep yourselves in the love of God, waiting anxiously for the mercy of our Lord Jesus Christ to eternal life…Now to Him who is able to keep you from stumbling, and to make you stand in the presence of His glory blameless with great joy, to the only God our Savior…be glory, majesty, dominion and authority, before all time and now and forever. Amen (Jude 1:20,21,24,25).*

This study was based upon Jesus' beautiful promise found in John 8:31,32,36.

Then said Jesus to those who believed in Him, If you abide (continue) in my word, then are you truly my disciples; And you shall know the Truth, and the Truth shall make you free. If the Son, therefore, shall make you free, you shall be free indeed.

A similar promise is found in Galatians:

It was for freedom that Christ set us free…therefore keep standing firm and do not be subject again to a yoke of slavery (Gal. 5:1).

The heart of the gospel is freedom. It is freedom *from*: the power, the lies, the deception, the inevitable death—of sin. Freedom from debilitating fear, worry, and anxiety. Freedom from hurtful habits, mental harassment and emotional torment. Freedom from holding on to the hurts and failures of painful pasts, bitterness and resentment. Freedom from encumbrances that weigh us down and keep us from *running with endurance the race set before us (Heb. 12:1)*. Freedom from meaninglessness, purposelessness, and futility in living. Freedom from fleshly cravings to be recognized, pampered, praised and approved. Freedom from the deadly, far reaching menace of needing to be *in control*. And most of all freedom from the corrupt, insatiable obsession with the self-life: self-gratification, self-esteem, self-centered—as opposed to God-centered—living. Thank God, Jesus delivered us from this kind of futile, destructive enslavement.

But He didn't just deliver us *from* the destructive control of sin and self. Jesus delivered us *to* something far greater: *true inner soul emancipation and freedom*. Freedom to live in the wonder, beauty and security of an intimate relationship with God through His Son Jesus Christ (John 14:23; Ps. 16:11; John 17:13,21). Freedom to have a rejoicing, thankful heart that sprinkles laughter, praise, and worship throughout the day because it has experienced the inexpressible joy of *so great a salvation (John 3:16; Ps. 51:12; Rom. 5:8; 2 Cor. 9:15)*. Freedom to live and love and learn under the protection of God and in the power and provision of His Holy Spirit *(Ps. 91:1; Gal. 5:16–25; Eph. 3:16–20; John 7:38)*. Freedom to walk daily in God's precious *peace that passeth all human understanding* even in the midst of trials and tribulations, testings, and tears *(Phil. 4:7; Ps. 104:33,34; Prov. 17:22; 1 Pet. 1:8)*. Freedom to know and do the will of God in the confidence and assurance that He has promised only good to those who *trust and obey (Prov. 3:5,6;*

Heb.10:35; Rom. 8:28; Ps. 84:11). Freedom to experience courage and strength to face without fear, difficulties, hardships, any circumstance and, by faith, *go through them* triumphantly *(Deut. 31:6–8; 2 Chron. 32:7,8, 20:15–25; Rom. 8:31–37).* Freedom to remain steadfast and faithful to the end, knowing that *in the future there is laid up for me the crown of righteousness which the Lord…will award to all those who love Him (James 1:12; Heb. 3:14; 1 Cor. 15:57,58; 2 Tim. 4:8).* Freedom to anticipate with unquenchable joy the blessed assurance of our eternal home in Heaven where *every tear shall be wiped away, and there shall no longer be any death, mourning, crying, or pain (John 14:1–3; Titus 2:13; Rev. 21:4).* Freedom to persevere, never give up, never turn back, never quit because *God is our refuge and strength, a very present help in time of trouble…in all things we overwhelmingly conquer through Him who loved us and gave Himself up for us; He will never leave us nor forsake us…greater is He that is in us than He that is in the world (Ps. 46:1; Rom. 8:37; Heb. 13:5; 1 John 4:4, cf. Heb. 10:35–39; 1 Cor.15:31; 1 Pet. 5:10; Jude 1:24).* Freedom to be all that we have been created and redeemed to be, so that one day when we stand before our Savior, we will hear Him say: *Well done, thou good and faithful servant. Enter into the joy of your Master (Matt. 25:23).*

True freedom, biblical freedom is all about faith and hope and love. It's about standing firm and persevering. It's about peace and joy and victory. Biblical freedom is about life and living and singing and celebrations. But mostly, it's about a Bridegroom and a Bride and preparations and purification and a wedding and a feast and a blessed joy, *inexpressible and full of glory…ever after"! (1 Pet. 1:8).*

May God help us to remain steadfast and faithful as we *continue in His Word,* pressing ever onward and upward on the wonderful *Highway of Holiness to Mount Zion! (John 8:31,32,36; Phil. 3:12,14; Micah 4:1,2).*

God bless you!

Oh, how I love Thy law! It is my meditation all the day. Thy commandments make me wiser than my enemies…they are ever mine. I have more insight than all my teachers…I understand more than the aged, for Thy testimonies are my meditation…I have observed Thy precepts. I have restrained my feet from every evil way, that I may keep Thy Word. I have not turned aside from Thine ordinances, for Thou Thyself hast taught me. How sweet are Thy words to my taste! Yes, sweeter than honey to my mouth! From Thy precepts I get understanding…Thy Word is a lamp to my feet, and a light to my path (Ps. 119:97–105, sel.).

Thy testimonies are wonderful; Therefore my soul observes them. The unfolding of Thy words gives light; It gives understanding to the simple (Ps. 119:129,130).

I will sing to the Lord as long as I live; I will sing praise to my God while I have my being. For Thou, Lord hast made me glad by what Thou hast done; I will sing for joy at the works of Thy hands. As for me, I shall be glad in the Lord (Ps. 104:33,34, 92:4).

Bible Study Supplement

Chapter 7 — Day 6 — Closing Thoughts and a Preview of Things to Come

How quickly the time has passed, and we have come to the end of this Bible study. You've worked hard laying a firm foundation for your strong house of faith. God has seen every diligent effort and He will *reward you accordingly* (Col. 3:23,24). But there's more, so much more yet to come.

> *By wisdom a house is built, and by understanding it is established; and by knowledge the rooms are filled with all precious and pleasant riches (Prov. 24:3).*

There's a wealth of *precious and pleasant riches* yet to be gleaned, lived out, and shared with others (Prov. 21:20). It is my prayer that God, through His Holy Spirit will enable us to follow faithfully as He continues to guide us in building our indestructible house of faith which will stand strong and firm…come what may! If we are faithful in this pursuit, we will remain confident and at peace even in the midst of life's torrential rains, rising floods, and howling winds of adversity. We will be safe and secure, resting in the assurance of the never-failing provision and protection of the One whom *even the wind and waves obey*! (Mark. 4:41).

I'm excited about all that God has already done and all that He yet will do:

> *He that has begun this good work in you will perfect it until the day of Jesus Christ…for I know whom I have believed and I am convinced that He is able to guard what I have entrusted to Him until that day (Phil. 1:6; 2 Tim. 1:12).*

In the Appendix, you will find an update to my personal testimony along with the article: A Biblical Analysis of Psychology. (Please read this article if you have not already done so). In addition, I have listed a number of ministries providing additional discipleship books, teaching CD's, DVD's, and other materials to help you as you *continue* in God' precious Word, *growing in grace and the knowledge of our Lord and Savior, Jesus Christ* (John 8:31,32; 2 Pet. 3:18).

In a number of Scripture verses throughout the Bible, we are exhorted to *remember all the way(s) the Lord has led you* (Deut 8:2). We are also instructed to *examine ourselves* (2 Cor. 13:5), to accurately assess the state of our spiritual condition and relationship with God. It is good to obey this wise exhortation. In Chapter One, Day 2 of the Bible Study Supplement, you were asked to read John 8:31,32,36, then take a few moments to ponder this promise and think about your own life and where you were at that point in your walk with the Lord.

1. Please turn back to Chapter One, Day 2, Bible Study Supplement, Question 5 a-c. Read over the answers you have written there.

Keeping your response to the questions in mind, answer the following:

   a. How have you done? Have you made progress in these areas?

   b. Where are you today in your spiritual journey? Are you yet bound by an addiction, compulsion, or other life-dominating habit that keeps you *from running with endurance the race set before you* (Heb. 12:1)? If so, list these here.

   c. Is there some unmitigated *soul pain* that haunts you and robs you of the liberty and joy of a Spirit-filled, victorious life?

d. Has your spirit been encouraged that you *will* be victorious over these encumbrances as you *continue in God's Word?*

I would like to close with a word about the two other Bible Study books planned in this series, *Rivers of Joy*.

Here are just a few of the topics covered in Books Two and Three:
- Faith: Discovering the joy of confidently walking by biblical "faith," not "feelings."
- Obedience: The key to blessing
- Discernment: Knowing the Will of God (Avoiding demonic deceptions)
- Entering In: Possessing our Possessions
- The Sweet Calm of Patience: One day at a time
- A Biblical Health and Nutrition Primer
- A True, Biblical Definition of Healing: What exactly was in the atonement?
- Bringing Down Strongholds: God's solution to addiction/compulsions
- Amazing Grace! Its magnitude and glorious, never-failing sufficiency
- You Have Need of Endurance: Fighting the good fight, finishing well
- Study to Show Yourself Approved: How to do your own independent Bible Study
- Oh Lord, My God, You are My Dwelling Place: The Believer's Rest
- Strangers and Aliens: Storing Up Treasures
- Heaven: Better by Far!

We also take an in-depth look at a triad of troublesome sins that affects us all in various ways:
- The "Roots" of all Sin:
    1. Selfishness...in its many destructive forms: lust, greed, hoarding, anger
    2. Unbelief – Stubborn Disobedience; Rebellion against God's Control
    3. Pride - Results in an inner tormenting drivenness for the approval of man (achievement, success...)

How easy it is to become entangled in the things of this world, in self-centered living as opposed to God-centered living, and in an insatiable drivenness for the approval of man. But it doesn't have to be that way. God has a solution for each of these destructive sins: a solution that will result in true and lasting freedom and contentment, as we will study in these books.

Please note: The projected release date for Book Two is June 2008. Book Three will follow, Lord willing, soon after this.

In the meantime, please prayerfully consider reading through the Bible using the Bible Pathway Program. (See Appendix for further details). Your love for God and knowledge of His Word will be greatly increased, your faith will be strengthened, and your joy will begin to flow in new refreshing, reviving streams.

Remember that special Bible verse I mentioned at the beginning of the study?

But the path of the righteous is like the light of dawn, that shines brighter and brighter until the full day (Prov. 4:18).

You have been walking on this glorious righteous path for seven weeks. And I am sure that you have experienced the light of God's wisdom and grace shining ever brighter upon your way. It's only fitting that we pause for a moment to thank God for all He has done and for His precious *life-giving* Truths and promises.

Thank You, Lord, for *all* You have taught me over the past seven weeks. Thank You for Your precious Word that is continually a *lamp unto my feet and a light unto my path.* Thank You that it illumines Your will bringing direction, wisdom, encouragement, and peace to my days.

Thank You, Father, for the privilege of living each day in the joy of Your presence, love and provision. Thank You, Jesus, for dying for my sins, for making me Your child, and for giving me eternal life. Thank You for all the wonderful blessings I already enjoy as Your child, knowing that *as many as are the promises of God, they are yes and amen in Jesus* (2 Cor. 1:20). Thank You, Holy Spirit for living in me, giving me the power and strength to fulfill all God's good plans for my life.

And now, as I come to the close of this Bible study, I ask that You help me to remain faithful in my study and application of Your Word. Keep me close to You, filled with Your Holy Spirit, thankful at all times for all the blessings and privileges You, in Your mercy and grace, bestow upon me daily. Speak clearly to my heart each day, dear Holy Spirit, so that I will know my Father's will, and give me the courage and strength to faithfully fulfill it moment by moment, step by step, so that when each day is done, I can lay my head upon my pillow and hear my Father say: "Well done, good and faithful servant." Help me to remain steadfast and faithful in the fulfilling of all Your good purposes as You conform me to the image of Your Son. Help me to be a good ambassador, always ready and eager to share Your wonderful *good news* with others as You lead, open doors and provide opportunities. By Your mercy and grace, use me, Lord, to touch many more lives for the advancement of Your Kingdom while I yet have breath and life upon this earth. Help me each day, to love You with all my heart, soul, mind and strength, that my life will be pleasing to You and a sweet fragrance of Your love and joy to others. Help me, dear Lord, to be a blessing to someone each day. May every thought, word, and deed—today, and every day—be done to the praise of Your glory. In Jesus' precious Name, Amen.

Appendix

Update on Personal Testimony

Psychology: A Biblical Analysis

Resources

Update on Personal Testimony

So much has transpired since I wrote my testimony. There just won't be time here to tell *the rest of the story* concerning the more than twenty-year battle with the strange affliction, the oft confusing pain and difficulties that accompanied it, and the matchless mercy and grace of God that overcame it. God taught me *so* much that I am longing to share. But that we will have to save for Books Two and Three. For now, I just want to mention a couple highlights and give praise to God for His faithfulness and for His precious Truths that, empowered by the Holy Spirit, fill me daily with joy, peace, and overcoming strength.

Of all that God has done in the past twenty five years since my rebirth into His glorious Kingdom, the most treasured has been the way He has transformed our marriage and my relationship with my husband. Daily, I stand in awe! A Christian home and marriage surely is God's way of giving us a little taste of Heaven right here on earth. How I thank God every day for my godly husband and for our Christian home. I realize more and more how blessed I am! Mel's gentle but strong, Christlike leadership keeps our home secure and filled with blessing and joy beyond anything for which I could have hoped or dreamed (Eph. 3:20). And as God continues His good work, perfecting me in my role as Mel's helpmeet, the joy only increases.

Another special joy has been sharing God's love and the wonderful good news of His redemption and new life in Jesus with others, then seeing again and again the power of the Word of God transforming lives, rebuilding marriages, filling hearts and homes with love and peace.

I've learned to stay *grafted into the vine (John 15:5)* through daily Bible study and prayer, and to live very close to the cross, confessing immediately sins and shortcomings, then thanking God for His forgiveness and restoration. I've learned the ever-increasing joy of discovering more and more of all that we are and all that we possess in Jesus (Eph. 1:1–23; Col. 1:27; Col. 2:9–15).

God's Word has become even more precious to me. As I grow in *the wisdom and grace of our Lord Jesus (2 Peter 3:18)*, I never cease to be amazed at the power and practicality of God's Word. As I apply its life-giving principles to every area of my life (Matt. 4:4; John 6:63), I find victory and peace that truly does *pass all human understanding (Phil. 4:7)*. I think so often of the beautiful promise in *Prov. 4:18: For the path of the righteous is like the light of dawn that grows brighter and brighter until the full day.* How unfailingly true I have found it to be. As I walk in the wonderful *light of God's Word each day (1 John 1:7; John 8:12), my path is made clear, my footsteps established and secured (Ps. 43:3; Prov. 4:26; Ps. 18:36).* I walk confidently knowing that *God holds my hand and will keep me from stumbling (Ps.18:36, 37:23,24; Prov. 3:23)*. I thank God for these and for hundreds of other precious promises that keep *a song in my heart, encouragement in my spirit, and joy in the journey (Psalm 40:3; John 15:11; Phil. 1:6)*.

The longer I walk with God, the deeper the roots of my once fledgling faith extend, and, by God's ever-abounding grace and faithfulness (John 10:10; Lam. 3:22,23), the stronger and fuller grows the fruit-bearing tree (Jer. 17:8; John 15:5–8). All of those common, early doubts regarding basic foundational, unalterable Truths have long since been settled. I know that God is real: *the heavens declare the glory of God (Ps. 19:1)*, and every Word of the Bible is true: *All Scripture is inspired by God…Holy men of God spake as they were moved by the Holy Spirit (2 Tim. 3:16; 2 Pet. 1:20,21)*. God gave us all a soul that is eternal (Eccles. 3:11). Heaven is a very real place (Matt.13:31–52) and so is hell (Matt. 13:50; Rev. 20:9,10, 14:11). One day, we will all go to one place or the other, for eternity. God leaves the choice to us (John 3:16; Josh. 24:15).

How can I ever thank Him enough that He never gave up on me through all those years of prideful, obstinate rebellion, and paralyzing fears. And how can I thank Him enough for His *unspeakable gift: salvation through the redemptive blood of Jesus shed on the cross to take away my sins and the sins of the world (John 3:16; Rom. 5:8; 1 Pet. 3:18)* or for all He has done for me since that glorious day I accepted Jesus into my heart (John 1:12; 2 Cor. 3:18). Truly, *God is good (Ps. 73:1); His compassions never fail. They are new every morning. Great is His faithfulness (Lam. 3:22,23; Ps. 84:11).* I pray that you will join me in a life-long pursuit of knowing, loving, and obeying God *with all our heart, soul, mind, and strength,* that we might fulfill all His good plans and purposes for our lives with courage, joy and sweet contentment (Matt. 22:37–39; Jer. 29:11–14; John 17:4; Luke 1:74,75; Rom. 14:17). For, as we do this, we will discover the most glorious promise of all: that nothing in all the world will ever, ever again be able to *separate us from the love of God, which is in Christ Jesus our Lord (Rom. 8: 31–39).*

To God be the glory; great things He has done!

Psychology: A Biblical Analysis
by Mel and Gloria Blowers

This article was originally published in *PsychoHeresy Awareness Newsletter*, Sept/Oct 1999

And the children of Israel did evil in the sight of the Lord...And they forsook the Lord, *and served Baal and Ashtaroth. And the anger of the* Lord *was hot against Israel, and he delivered them into the hands of spoilers that (plundered) them, and he sold them into the hands of their enemies round about, so that they could no longer stand before their enemies (Judges 2:11–14).*

God is love (I John 4:8). God is also patient, kind and compassionate (Lam. 3:22,23; Ps. 103:8). But God is, in all, through all and above all, Holy! (1 Pet. 1:15). As His children, He has called us to *be Holy as He is Holy (1 Pet. 1:15,16)*—to reflect His holiness to this *wicked and perverse generation (Phil. 2:15).* Because He is God and because He is Holy, He had no choice but to deliver His disobedient sons "into the hands of plunderers" in order to discipline them, that His Holy Name would not be further maligned.

The Church of Jesus Christ is being plundered and sold into the hands of its enemies because it has played the harlot with the god of psychology, whose unbiblical goal is to make people "feel good about themselves," rather than to *love God with all their heart, soul, mind and strength,* to *glorify Him in all things,* and to be *conformed to the image of His Son"* (Deut. 6:5, Matt. 22:37; 1 Cor. 10:31; Rom. 8:29).

Psychology is a very deceptive and dangerous theory conceived in the mind of unredeemed man in his state of rebellion against God as the answer to his problems. Psychology has been the god of the people since the late 1800's, when Freud systematized his atheistic assessments about the psyche (soul) of man. Psychological theories have replaced the clear teachings of Scripture. Christians stream to its practitioners for affirmation, comfort, and guidance, rather than to God, His Word, and the body of Christ.

Because psychology, like the god of Baal, helps people temporarily "feel better about themselves," it is deceptively appealing, and thus, revered and worshiped by many. Great energies and time are invested in obeying its precepts. But the Bible says, *Be ye not unequally yoked together with unbelievers (2 Cor. 6:14).*

Rather than coming out from the godless practice of psychology, we have embraced it, incorporated it into our beliefs, and twisted and distorted Scripture to "prove" psychological theories!

I will destroy the wisdom of the wise, and will bring to nothing the understanding of the prudent. Where is the wise? . . . hath not God made foolish the wisdom of this world? . . . God is not the author of confusion (1 Cor. 1:19,20, 14:33).

There are currently over 500 conflicting and contradicting psycho-"therapies" being taught and practiced today. That in itself shows the foolishness of the wisdom of the world (1 Cor. 1:20).

Common to all psychological teaching is a biblically defective view of the nature of man. Namely, that man is basically good and able to solve his problems (when properly "enlightened"). Nothing could be further from the Truth!

But we are all as an unclean thing...Every one of them is gone back: they are altogether become filthy; there is none that doeth good, no, not one...The heart is deceitful above all things, and desperately wicked: who can know it? (Is. 64:6; Ps. 53:3; Jer. 17:9).

The gods that psychology has created—"self"-obsession and worship, materialism, pain-free living, and a thousand other "feel good" fantasies are as ungodly and pagan as the Asherim of the Sidonians. God says we should destroy these heathen idols and cling to Him alone, seeking holiness and Christ-likeness, not preoccupation with "self."

For they will turn away thy son from following me, that they may serve other gods...But thus shall ye deal with them; ye shall destroy their altars, and break down their images, and...burn their graven images with fire. For thou art an Holy people unto the LORD thy God (Deut. 7:4–6).

Whenever we attempt to "mix" the unholy with the Holy—such as "Christian Psychology"—we profane the precious Holy Name of God (Ezek. 36:22), and we make a mockery of His sovereignty, authority and sufficiency. We imply that God is not capable of dealing with a certain class of problems—"psychological." History clearly illustrates that anytime the people of God attempted to mix the Holy with the profane it was only a matter of time before they "forsook" the Holy and were "consumed" by the profane (2 Chron. 28:22,23).

Surely, we would be wise to heed the call to purity and obedience. *Now these things were our examples, to the intent we should not lust after evil things, as they also lusted" (1 Cor. 10: 6).*

Jesus, Himself, warned against the danger and impossibility of serving two masters:

No man can serve two masters: for either he will hate the one, and love the other; or else he will hold to one, and despise the other (Matt. 6:24).

It is not that we doubt for one moment the sincerity or intelligence of many Christian "experts," who boldly promote psychological "techniques" today. Many undoubtedly are saved, sincere and extremely intelligent. But even saved, sincere, and intelligent people can be deceived. All of us are, at times, deceived by the schemes of Satan (2 Cor 2:11), as he appeals to certain presuppositions based on personal experiences, unsanctified "personality bents" (sinful weaknesses), circumstantial appearances. That is why the Bible exhorts us to *not forsake the assembling of ourselves together (Heb. 10:25);* to *teach, exhort, and admonish one another (Col. 3:16; 2 Tim. 3:16; 1 Thess. 5:18);* and to have a *teachable spirit (James 3:13–18).* That is the purpose of the body of Christ. God calls preachers and teachers to speak forth the clear teachings of Scripture, warning of waywardness (Ezek. 33:7–9). In obedience to God, faithful, godly saints today who recognize the dangers are "crying out from the wilderness" concerning the deception of psychology. But who is heeding the cry?

The first 6 books of the Bible are dedicated to establishing foundational doctrinal truths regarding the sovereignty of God:

Hear, 0 Israel: The LORD our God is one LORD... Thou shalt fear the LORD thy God, and serve him, and shalt swear by his name. Ye shall not go after other gods, or the gods of the people which are round about you...For thou art an Holy people unto the LORD thy God (Deut. 6:4,13–15, 7:6).

...His divine power has granted to us everything pertaining to life and godliness, through the true knowledge of Him...do not add to the (words) of this book nor take away from (it) (2 Pet. 1:3; Rev. 22:18,19).

Whether we recognize it or not psychology adds "enlightened" man-centered theories to Scripture. Satan is a master counterfeiter. Our fallen minds are bent towards deception. In the area of psychology, scriptural terms are carefully chosen, "biblical models" are set up as altars upon which the heathen gods of humanism and reason are erected and worshiped. "Christian Psychology" is an anomaly. Psychology refuses to acknowledge the existence of God or His involvement in man's life and problem solving. Furthermore, it is impossible to wed "Holy" with the profane. Yet, respected "Christian Psychologists" have convinced troubled, hurting people that, not only is it possible to "integrate" psychology and the Bible, it is desirable and superior!

To *prove* the "goodness" of this marriage, psychologists are quick to reference anecdotal examples (experiences) of people who have been "helped" by their techniques. All outside indication would support their arguments. But is it not more deception? God is the only one who can heal. Since the devil is the perpetrator of sin, sickness and disease—especially mental and emotional disturbances—he can quite strategically lift his heavy hand of destruction for a time to make it "appear" as if the psychological technique is actually bringing healing when in reality the "healing" is not healing at all but only a temporary reprieve. Lacking a disciplined, seasoned discernment, the already weakened, unstable person is eventually led down another path of deception and failure. A vicious cycle develops:

Therapy, a reprieve, a new crisis, more therapy, a reprieve, a new crisis, more therapy…

We are fully aware that in some instances people are genuinely helped during a period of time they are under the treatment of a "Christian Psychologist." But again, it is clear that the healing did not come from the "therapist" or the "psychological technique." The healing came from a compassionate touch of the Grace of God—usually as these people received salvation or renewed their commitment to Christ and to the study and application of His Word—obedience.

At the heart of our concern in all this is that the wrong "gods" are receiving the glory—the therapist, "Christian Psychology," psychological techniques, or the newly resurrected god of "self-esteem." The Bible clearly warns:

"I am the LORD, that is my name: and my glory will I not give to another" (Is. 42:8).

The vast majority of "psychological problems" are, in reality, spiritual problems that have never been properly dealt with according to God's Word. When we try to wed God's ways of dealing with the problem of sin (the cross, forgiveness, personal responsibility, obedience) with man's ways (blaming others, "getting in touch with our past," self-pity/victimization, and relying upon "self"), we are playing the harlot (Josh. 23:8–13).

Sin and its devastating consequences—shame, guilt, feelings of worthlessness—cannot be solved by any other means than the redemptive blood of Jesus and the sanctifying work of the Holy Spirit of God. Putting a psychological band-aid on these spiritual problems only covers an *incurable wound (Jer. 30:12)*. It is true: *With men this (difficult problem) is impossible; but with God all things are possible…Behold, the LORD's hand is not shortened, that it cannot save; neither his ear heavy, that it cannot hear (Matt. 19:26; Is. 59:1)*.

By implying that some problems are "too serious" to be dealt with through the proper application of Scripture, we not only deny the sovereignty and power of God, we begin to develop within people a dependence on psychology, a therapist, pastor, friends, instead of a dependence on God. That is why the body of Christ is so weak. We are literally sucking the life blood out of one another in a sincere attempt to be "compassionate" apart from the power of the Holy Spirit and obedience to the Word of God.

It is tragic that many have been led to believe that victory over various emotional problems can be obtained only through "professional psychological" counseling. This is not only untrue, it is a devastating witness to the already perceived impotence of the Church.

Did God leave His people "in the dark" for over 1800 years after Christ returned to the Father until Freud appeared on the scene in the late 1800's to shed his enlightenment upon the various problems of the human dilemma? Contrarily, history confirms that some of the most productive, fruitful saints lived during this very period, and people in general were much more "stable" before this new era of enlightenment than today. In truth, countless numbers of individuals through the ages have experienced complete, perfect, and lasting victory over the most severe problems through application of Biblical truths, genuine love, the power of God working through His Holy Spirit and the body of Christ.

It is time we tore down the Asherim of Psychology and returned in pure and Holy allegiance to the One who said:

Wash you, make you clean; put away the evil of your doings from before mine eyes; cease to do evil…If ye be willing and obedient, ye shall eat the good of the land: But if ye refuse and rebel, ye shall be devoured with the sword: for the mouth of the LORD hath spoken it (Is. 1:16, 19, 20).

(Scripture is KJV).

Resources

We live in an age of abundance. God has blessed us with a myriad of Study Bibles, books, teaching tapes, videos, and a host of other helpful discipleship materials from which to gain further understanding and fortify our growing faith and freedom in Christ. But we must heed the warning of Jer. 15:19 in which God's people are exhorted to be very careful to *extract the precious from the worthless.* There is a lot of precious, solid, Bible study material easily available, but, sadly there is far more that attempts to mix the Holy with the profane (worldly), something that is an abomination to God, concerning which He clearly warns and bids us not to partake because of the harm and destruction it will cause us (2 Cor. 6:14–18; 1 Cor. 1:18–29).

The following is a list of ministries where Bible Study and other discipleship resources may be obtained. If you are interested, just give them a call and ask for a catalogue.

Caveat: Though I am personally familiar with all these ministries and have found them, for the most part, to be trustworthy in their commitment to the authority and sufficiency of God's Word, I have discovered material available from some of them to be in error to *the whole counsel of God's Word*, so I urge you always to be like the Bereans: *For these were more noble-minded…for they received the word with great eagerness, examining the Scriptures daily, to see whether these things* (that were being taught) *were so (Acts 17:11).* Everything we read should always be held up to the plumb line of God's Word. If it contradicts the clear teaching and principles of Scripture, it is false doctrine and must be rejected.

Answers in Genesis (Ken Ham)
P.O. Box 510, Hebron, KY 41048
Phone 1-800-350-3232 or (859) 727-2222
www.answersradio.com

Ken Ham's "Answers in Genesis" ministry is an excellent resource for obtaining information regarding creation including a solid defense of the young earth theory, literal 24-hour creation days. He also very clearly establishes other crucial foundational doctrines of our faith.

The Berean Call (Dave Hunt, T. A. McMahon)
P.O. Box 7019, Bend, OR 97708-7019
Ph. 1-800-937-6638
www.thebereancall.org

Great resources for developing spiritual discernment. Try a sample newsletter. You'll be blessed and your faith will be strengthened.

Bible Pathway Ministries (John Hash)
P.O. Box 20123, Murfreesboro, TN 37129
Phone: 1-800-598-7884 or (615) 896-4243
www.biblepathway.org

Bible Pathway is a very special "Read Through the Bible in One Year" program. <u>Please go to end of resource list for additional information about this excellent program</u>—highly recommended!

Bold Christian Living (Jonathan Lindvall)
P.O. Box 820, Springville, CA 93265
Phone for orders: 1-800-4LINDVALL (1-800-454-6382) Other information 1-559-539-0500
www.BoldChristianLiving.com
Lindvall@BoldChristianLiving.com

Jonathan has a heart for ministry and a love for the Word of God. Though he specializes in parenting and biblical youth ministry, his tapes and videos cover subjects pertaining to all areas of spiritual growth. When I am having an especially hard day, I grab one of Jonathan's tapes for *strengthening the weak arms (Heb. 12:12)* and getting that shield of faith back into proper position. Jonathan's clear, biblical teachings are always like a breath of heaven—a real spirit booster and faith builder.

Creation Moments
P.O. Box 839, Foley, MN 56329
Phone 1-800-569-5959
www.creationmoments.com

This is an excellent resource for information on Creation Science. An extensive catalogue of books, tapes, and videos offers infallible proof supporting the biblical account of the creation of the universe and substantially refutes the unstable, unprovable theories and fallacies of evolution. This is also where you can obtain Paul Bartz's devotional books, *Let God Create Your Day*, about all the unique plants and animals God has created that defy evolutionary theories mentioned in Chapter 1, Day 3.

Creation Moments also offers an excellent two-part video series produced by Moody Institute of Science called: "Journeys to the Edge of Creation" Part 1: Our Solar System; Part 2: The Milky Way and Beyond. The is an excellent presentation of the vastness of our universe! I have watched these videos several times and stand all the more in awe of God's awesome creation every time.

NANC – National Association of Nouthetic Counselors
3600 West 96th Street, Indianapolis, IN 46268
317 337-9100
www.NANC.org

NANC (National Association of Nouthetic Counselors) is the primary educational and certifying agency for Biblical Counseling Training. Its requirements are strict and arduous. All who complete the classroom training and practicums (supervised counseling) will be well equipped to *handle accurately the Word of God (2 Tim. 2:15)*. NANC has a number of conferences, training schools and seminars through the year. These are recorded and made available electronically so that excellent teaching material can be found on every type of mental, emotional, psychological and spiritual problem. See the NANC web site for more information.

PsychoHeresy Awareness Ministries – Martin and Deidre Bobgan
4137 Primavera Road, Santa Barbara, CA 93110
Ph. 805-683-0864; Orders: 1-800-216-4796
www.psychoheresy-aware.org

The infiltration of humanistic psychology into the church is a very real and dangerous problem because it is so popular and widely accepted and the deception is so very powerful and destructive in nature. This unholy integration of man-centered, anti-God secular psychological theories and therapies with the Bible has proliferated into every aspect of church life through books, tapes, videos, seminars, youth ministry, preaching, etc. The body of Christ was in desperate need of a *watchman on the wall (Ezek. 3:17)* to cry out the warnings of this serious corruption of truth and doctrine. Martin and Deidre Bobgan heard that call and responded with careful, thorough attention to the subject from a biblical viewpoint. They share their warnings and call to biblical discernment through their many books and bi-monthly newsletter. If you have never read any of their material, it would be good to get a sample copy of their newsletter. The Bobgans do an excellent job of exposing the subtle deceptions of psychological indoctrination through thorough biblical examination.

Revive our Hearts Ministries (Nancy Leigh DeMoss)
P.O. Box 83500, Lincoln, NE 68501
Phone 1-800-569-5959
www.ReviveOurHearts.com
info@ReviveOurHearts.com

This is an excellent resource for women. Nancy is a knowledgeable, gifted Bible teacher and committed to the authority of Scripture. I have ordered dozens of tapes and am always blessed and encouraged in my walk with the Lord through them. (Pray for protection for Nancy that she remains strong and faithful to the authority and sufficiency of Scripture, as the encroachment of man-centered psychological compromise infiltrates the church).

Truths That Transform (Dr. D. James Kennedy)
P.O. Box 33, Fort Lauderdale, FL 33302
1-800-229-WORD

Dr. Kennedy wrote the excellent book, *Why I Believe . . . in the Bible, God, Creation, Heaven, Hell, etc.* It is a very helpful tool in putting together one's personal testimony and ready defense of the Bible, God, Creation, etc. It is also an excellent resource in ministering to skeptics.

"Unshackled" Radio Program
Pacific Garden Mission
646 So. State St., Chicago, IL 60605
Phone 312-922–1462
unshackled@pgm.org
www.unshackled.org

The "Unshackled" radio program airs testimonies of lives that have been transformed by the gospel. The stories are incredible true accounts of God's love reaching out to lost sinners. For many years, I listened to nearly every broadcast and still listen as often as possible. Hearing these testimonies always encourages me and reminds me of the greatness of God's mercy and amazing grace towards His wayward children. If you haven't heard this program or haven't heard it for some time, do listen and be encouraged. You can write or call for a catalogue of all the programs by main subject, i.e., addictions, depression, anger, drugs, alcohol, unhealthy striving for achievement/approval of others, etc. The programs are also available on-line, anytime.

Zion's Hope Ministries (Marv Rosenthall)
P.O. Box 121048, Clermont, FL 34712
1-888-781-9466 or (352) 241-9085

Zion's Hope is a wonderful ministry for understanding end-times, prophecy, and other core doctrines of our faith. An excellent resource for all believers is a book entitled *The Pre-Wrath Rapture* (book and workbook) by Marv Rosenthal, which makes understanding the Books of Daniel, Amos, Joel, Isaiah, Revelation (and other prophesies) much easier through clear, simplified explanations, while remaining solidly biblical. You will definitely want to get the supplemental workbook to go with the main text book. This corresponding Bible study helps so much in explaining more clearly and solidifying the Truths of Scripture on this important topic.

A Special Word About Bible Pathway

I must take a moment here to point out one resource in particular that has been of incalculable value to both my husband and me—and countless others—in our walk with the Lord. It is the Bible Pathway, "Read Through the Bible In One Year" program. I have read through the Bible a number of times since becoming a Christian. But of all the outlines/study programs I have followed, the Bible Pathway Study Series has been by far the most edifying and faith-building. God has blessed Dr. Hash (founder and writer of the Bible Pathway meditations) with an incredible Holy Spirit inspired clear and accurate understanding of the Word of God from Genesis to Revelation. In nearly every lesson, he ties the Old Testament to the New Testament showing their interrelatedness and continuity of the promises and purposes of God. He also helps the reader to understand those passages that are often difficult to discern accurately.

Every Christian should read through the Bible at least once every three to five years in order to maintain a good understanding of *the whole counsel of God's Word (Acts 20:28)*. (Even better is to read it through every year as my husband does!) I prefer to start the Bible Pathway's program at the beginning of a new year. It just seems to start the year off in a wonderful, hope-building way. Also, by planning ahead you can make sure that you have the material and are ready to begin on January 1. If, however, it is not convenient for you to start then, Bible Pathways has a comprehensive study book that you can use to begin the program at any time in the year. Whichever plan will work best for you, I strongly encourage you to set a goal to do this as soon as possible. Your love for God will grow as you come to understand more clearly His nature, goodness and faithfulness, and in so doing, your faith will be strengthened, and your joy multiplied.

Blessings!

Printed in the United States
97498LV00007B/55/A